Praise for *Contemporary India*

... a welcome addition to the vast body of literature available on the theme. The chapters ... are well conceived and structured. They provide useful insights for a better understanding of contemporary developments and trends relating to the Indian economy, polity and society.

—M. J. Vinod, Professor
Department of Political Science
Bangalore University

... an excellent collection of articles meant for undergraduate and post-graduate students, scholars, academics and journalists. It can become an excellent reference book, too.

—Muzafar H. Assadi, Professor
Department of Political Science
University of Mysore

The division of the book into the three parts ... brings out and reflects political science's disciplinary need of expanding its contours to capture the multifaceted dynamics of contemporary India. The book will go a longer way than satisfying the needs of its basic target group.

—Amartya Mukhopadhyay, Professor
Department of Political Science
University of Calcutta

The book has been written using a framework that will aid critical thinking about Indian society. A commendable effort towards creating good textbooks for university students in India.

—Virginius Xaxa, Professor
Department of Sociology, Delhi School of Economics
University of Delhi

[This book] seeks to take stock of both India's progress in establishing and refining democracy, and also the extent to which this has yielded satisfactory outcomes. The contents of the book are interdisciplinary with lucid expositions, and the outcome is refreshing.

—Ashish Saxena, Associate Professor
Department of Sociology
University of Jammu

... well written with a clear thrust on analysing in a simple, lucid manner the three most important segments of contemporary India. A striking feature of the book is its analysis of the past and the present of Indian society and politics with equal élan.... [T]his book has combined historicity with today's India in a splendid manner.

—Aneek Chatterjee, Assistant Professor
Department of Political Science, Presidency College
University of Calcutta

... a winning combination of facts and analysis on some of the most salient facets ... of contemporary India. Admirable for its clarity and readability, it is sure to be a prized collection for any serious student of India.

—Ashok Acharya, Reader
Department of Political Science
University of Delhi

... a comprehensive text catering to the demands of undergraduate students and general readers who are interested in knowing the working of the Indian economy, democracy and sociological changes that have taken place in the country.

—Poonam Kanwal, Reader
Department of Political Science
Janki Devi Memorial College, University of Delhi

This is a wide-ranging collection that addresses the tumultuous experience of Indian democracy. [T]his book will help in understanding why democracy, despite many hurdles, still works in India and how it influences Indian politics.

—Partho Datta, Reader
Department of History, Zakir Husain Evening College
University of Delhi

This volume ... is useful and has relevance not only for students, but also for the general readers who are interested in contemporary issues that influence the nation today. The merit of the chapters lies in discussing complex issues in a manner that will help in the pedagogic exercise. Written by teachers who are actively involved in the classroom teaching, the text is lucid and has an interdisciplinary approach.... The contradictions brought out in the democracy and the democratic system of India will help students to think in a critical manner.

—Ranjeeta Dutta, Lecturer
Department of History and Culture
Jamia Millia Islamia

Contemporary India

Economy, Society, Politics

Edited by
Neera Chandhoke
Praveen Priyadarshi

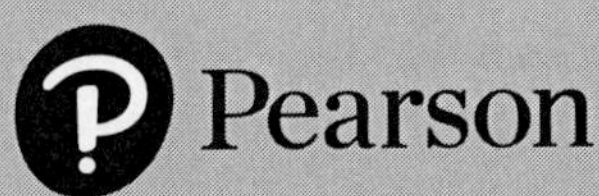

ISBN 978-81-317-1929-9

First Impression, 2009
Current Impression, 2026

Published by Pearson India Education Services Pvt. Ltd, CIN: U72200TN2005PTC057128.

Head Office: 1st Floor, Berger Tower, Plot No. C-001A/2, Sector 16B, Noida - 201 301, Uttar Pradesh, India.

Registered Office: 6th Floor, Tower A, Unit A and B, International Tech Park, CapitaLand Chennai,
200 Feet Radial Road,Zamin Pallavaram, Old Pallavaram Chennai – 600117, Tamil Nadu, India

Website: in.pearson.com; Email: companysecretary.india@pearson.com

Digitally printed in India by Trinity Academy for Corporate Training Ltd, New Delhi in the year of 2026

Contents

PART III: POLITICS

Introduction

Democracy in Contemporary India

Neera Chandhoke and Praveen Priyadarshi

This volume is the product of a joint effort by a number of scholars who carry out research and teach at the University of Delhi. Many of these scholars are fellows of the Developing Countries Research Centre of the university, where the initiative to put together a volume on contemporary India first took shape; others are fellow travellers. In view of the fact that: (*a*) a foundation course on contemporary India has been introduced at the BA level in the university; (*b*) the course straddles four disciplines of history, economics, sociology, and political science, and (*c*) there are very few original works that negotiate all the themes included in the course in one work, a group of committed scholars and teachers decided to write original and well-researched pieces on each topic of the course. The authors have written especially for students, and though the essays are the products of in-depth research, they are written in an easy, conversational style. But we hope that the volume can serve as an introduction to contemporary India for the general reading public, journalists, professionals and, of course, students, both undergraduate and postgraduate, of other universities.

The course on contemporary India covers a variety of conceptual and empirical themes ranging from the state of the economy at the time of Independence to the emergence of the new middle class. We were of the opinion that different themes should be approached from the vantage point of democracy. Democracy, in other words, provides both a perspective and a thread that ties different aspects of contemporary India together. In the following section, we chart out some of the main characteristics of democracy in the country to serve as a framework for understanding.

DEMOCRACY

'For my part,' wrote the first Prime Minister of India, Jawaharlal Nehru, 'I wish to say that, in spite of everything, I have a firm faith in India's future.... Although many of my old dreams have been shattered by recent events, yet the basic objective still holds and I see no reason to change it. That objective is to build a free India of high ideals and noble endeavours where there is equality of opportunity for all.'[1] More than five decades have passed since Pandit Nehru wrote these words and it is clear that a democratic culture has been institutionalized in the country. This culture was first introduced to the Indian society by the freedom struggle in the first half of the 20th century. The electoral and the political processes after Independence have consolidated this culture. We have a fully functional electoral system; we have one of the most politicized electorates in the world; an electorate that never fails to surprise every time a verdict is out; we have an untidy, unruly, but vibrant civil society peppered by social movements and campaigns; we have a Constitution that is arguably one of the finest in the world and is deeply respected; and even if the Parliament and the Executive let us down periodically, the Supreme Court has been highly proactive, particularly when it comes to protecting the basic rights of citizens. India's democracy is alive and kicking, and the civil society in the country, embedded as it is in a democratic culture, fiercely guards the rights of the citizens against infringements or violations.[2]

Yet, the gains of political democracy have not been accompanied by advances in social or economic democracy. If there is one lesson that we have learnt from our experience with political democracy in India, it is that though political/formal democracy ensures political and civil rights, constitutionalism, the rule of law, and a vibrant civil society, it does not by any means guarantee well-being, absence of caste discrimination, or secularism. We certainly have reason to pat ourselves on the back because India is hailed as the world's largest democracy. However, problems blight the lives of millions of citizens, largely in the rural areas, where they suffer from unimagined hardship in the form of poverty, malnutrition, illiteracy, and disease. We admittedly have reason to feel proud that we have one of the most democratic electorates in the world—the results of the 2004 general elections and of the state elections in 2006 and 2007 bear testimony to this. Yet, discrimination on the basis of caste continues to haunt the everyday lives of millions of the so-called lower castes. We can preen over the fact that civil liberties in the country are safe in the hands of a representative government, a hyperactive judiciary, and human rights groups. Yet, communal riots continue to scar the body politic, leaving wrecked lives and livelihoods in their wake. India's democratic culture has shown a remarkable capacity to tolerate economic ill-being and discrimination on the basis of ascriptive characteristics such as caste and religion, even as it zealously guards

1. Jawaharlal Nehru, 'Address to Aligarh Muslim University,' delivered on 24 January 1948, in S. Gopal (ed.), *Jawaharlal Nehru: An Anthology* (New Delhi: Oxford University Press, 1980), p. 206.
2. The state in any given democracy has to necessarily be democratic, but since states embody power, it is civil society that needs to be imbued with a democratic political culture, so that states can be pressurized through the building up of public opinion and collective action to discharge their democratic obligations.

the frontiers of political democracy. This is the paradox of democracy in our country.

But if political democracy has not led to the eradication of mind-numbing poverty, oppression, and inhuman practices which thrive on discriminating against the lower castes and religious minorities, the democratic project necessarily remains incomplete. To put the point in different words, the democratic project has neither realized its own potential nor delivered on its own promises. What are these promises? We do not have to go far in order to search for these promises. There was a time when the Cold War had frozen the distinction between formal democracy characterized by political and civil rights (liberal democracy), and substantive democracy characterized by social and economic rights (socialist democracy). The end of the Cold War, however, dissolved this distinction and, increasingly, democracy is seen not only as an institution but as a continuum, as a process that leads or at least should lead from formal to substantive democracy or from political and civil rights to social, economic, and cultural rights. In other words, democracy promises rights, justice, freedom, equality, and human dignity.

The roots of democracy are to be found in the basic axiom of our electoral democracy—universal adult franchise. Universal adult franchise promises that each citizen is free to cast his/her vote for whomsoever s/he wants; that there is no constraint whatsoever on his/her political freedom to do so. The second promise that it embeds is that of equality; each vote, and by implication each voter, counts for one and only one—no less and no more. No one is either privileged or deprived in this matter on the grounds of class, caste, gender, or religious belief. These ascriptive characteristics are morally irrelevant in our democracy.

But if political freedom is not accompanied by economic and social freedom, the democratic project remains unfinished. What is the point, a committed democrat may well ask, in granting equality to citizens on one day every five years, when people remain unequal and 'unfree' in their daily lives? In other words, though formal or political democracy is *essential* for human dignity, it is not *sufficient.* For if the vast masses of citizens remain outside the boundaries of the *demos* because they belong to, say, the beleaguered lower castes who are compelled to live life in this and not that way, or because they are religious minorities which are subjected to rank and inhuman discrimination, or because they are caught up in mind-numbing poverty, deprivation, and ill-being, the democratic project has stopped short at what is known as formal democracy. This is not the democracy that Pandit Nehru, the tallest statesman and the architect of modern India had dreamt of and articulated repeatedly in his public speeches and in his reflective writings. In his usual elegant manner, Pandit Nehru had said during the closing debate on 'The Resolution of Aims and Objects' in the Constituent Assembly. The first task of this assembly is to free India through a new constitution, to feed the starving people, and to clothe

the naked masses, and to give every Indian the fullest opportunity to develop himself according to his capacity.[3] To give each Indian the fullest opportunity to develop himself/herself according to his/her capacity means to give them equal rights and freedom in their everyday life; in other words, to extend the promises of formal democracy into the economic, social, cultural, and domestic spheres. This deepens both democracy and the democratic political culture in the country.

To phrase the point differently, a deepening of our democratic political culture can only take place when citizens carry the democratic project beyond the frontiers of political democracy into the domestic sphere, social domain, site of cultural practices, and the workplace. Citizens should believe fervently that if children die of malnutrition, people suffer from indignity caused by poverty, people are humiliated just because they belong to lower castes, and people are discriminated against or subjected to hate and hateful comments and stereotypes because they are members of a religious minority, the project of democracy has faltered; it has been short-changed. The promises of equality and freedom, which are essential for individuals to lead lives of dignity, have been violated. And democracy itself has been compromised.

Like all projects, the democratic project is not self-realizing or self-propelling. It does not follow some inexorable law that forces it towards a determined end. Democracies falter, they make sharp u-turns, and they may progress at times and regress at other times. The guiding force of the project is intentional purposive action, which continuously strives to secure these objectives. The preconditions for the realization of the project are a democratic, political culture. The building of such a culture requires not only a democratic state but a democratic civil society, which is committed to the unfolding of the project of democracy. The realization of this project requires the deepening of a democratic culture, which motivates human beings to resist oppression, exploitation, and discrimination whenever and wherever these occur. In other words, a deep, democratic, political culture is informed by the vision that democracy is negated if people suffer from economic and social unfreedom.

The democratic, political culture, which has been historically built in India through the freedom struggle, cherishes universal adult franchise as the signpost of democracy. The contributors to this volume suggest that we need to deepen this culture so that citizens who have legitimate reasons to believe that democracy can make the world less oppressive, less exploitative, less horrid, and more just, equitable, free, and favourable for human dignity, are not short-changed. In short, we wish to suggest that the culture of deep democracy must capture hearts and minds, it must govern political passions and preoccupation, and it must dominate imaginations and imaginaries if democracy has to redeem the promises implicit in the concept of universal adult franchise. People must

---

3. Constituent Assembly Debates, I, CAD II, 3 on 22 January 1947, p. 316.

feel with conviction that democracy is far better than any alternative form of governance because it embodies the kind of promises which other forms of governance do not take into account.

But the project of deepening democracy by building a democratic culture can only be realized when citizens push inexorably the empirical limits of a given democratic system towards new frontiers. The project of democracy is self-expanding, and new ends, new goals, and new purposes constantly present themselves to the public gaze, as we decide what is due to human beings simply because they are human. The path to the realization of democracy's promises is littered with obstacles. If one negotiates class inequalities, gender inequalities remain to be tackled. If gender inequalities are addressed, then caste inequalities challenge the basic norms of democracy. One addresses caste inequalities, to have on hand the oppression of forest communities, violations of child rights, dismissal of the rights of the differently abled who need special opportunities, and targeting of religious minorities. Above all, one negotiates one form of oppression, and other forms erupt to provide democracy with new goals and new challenges. But no one goal or set of goals will do; the goals of democracy revolve around the basic axiom, which is embodied in the formal avatar of democracy—the right to freedom and equality, and, thereby, the right to dignity. The values of freedom, equality, and human dignity are the reasons why democracy is a better way of arranging political, social, and economic life. This really means that at any given point of time, a particular version of democracy is a partially realized vision, which needs to be fulfilled through purposive human action such as social movement. It is to the realization of the project that a deep political culture should be committed.

THE PROBLEM OF ECONOMIC UNFREEDOM

Consider, for instance, that despite the successful institutionalization of political democracy in India, a majority of the people continue to suffer from unimaginable hardship, with the most vulnerable at tremendous risk in matters of both lives and livelihoods. The country's position has slipped from 124th to 128th according to the 2007–08 *Human Development Report*. Nearly a quarter of the world's poor live in India. The Indian case actually provides us with a supreme example of a paradox. The GDP (gross domestic product) grew by an impressive 7 per cent per annum in the years 2002–03 to 2006–07, or during the period of the Tenth Five-Year Plan. But as the Approach Paper to the Eleventh Five-Year Plan (2007–12) states clearly, though official figures for poverty in the years 1999–2000 indicated that the percentage of population in poverty had declined from 36 per cent in 1993–94 to 26 per cent in 1999–2000, revised estimates show that the pace of reduction of poverty had been overstated. The data from the sixty-first round of the National Sample Survey conducted in 2004–05, which is comparable to the data garnered in the fiftieth round of the survey conducted in 1993–94,[4] shows that the percentage of people below the poverty line in 2004–05 was above 28 per cent, which is higher than the numbers provided by official figures earlier. The reduction in poverty between 1993–94 and 2004–05 was 0.74 points per year, rather than 1.66 points per year, as implied by the earlier 1999–2000 data.[5]

In absolute terms, the number of people below the official poverty line is huge, an estimated 260 million,[6] of which 193 million live in rural areas and 67 million in urban areas. These are persons who are unable to access the minimal consumption basket. In the backward states of north India, 25–33 per cent of the people fall below the poverty line.[7] What is more disquieting are regional imbalances when it comes to poverty: in Madhya Pradesh and Orissa, the numbers of the absolutely poor went up during 1993–2000. States containing larger proportions of the poor are also marked by low human development indicators, and slower economic and higher population growth. Poverty is much higher among the landless and among marginal farmers whose small land holdings have been rendered unproductive because of environmental degradation and vagaries of the monsoon. Above all, half of India's 260 million Scheduled Castes/Tribes belong to the category of the absolute poor,[8] with no access to employment and minimum wages because they lack educational skills. Not only do nearly a quarter of the world's poor live in India, the number of illiterates, school drop-outs, persons suffering from communicable diseases, and infant, child and maternal deaths, amount to a staggering proportion of respective world totals[9]. About

---

4. The data of the 55th NSS survey conducted in 1999–2000 proved controversial, and scholars have challenged claims of poverty reduction based on this data set.
5. Planning Commission, *Towards Faster and More Inclusive Growth: An Approach to the 11th Five Year Plan* (New Delhi: Government of India, 2006), p. 58; see also Himanshu, 'Recent Trends in Poverty and Inequality: Some Preliminary Results,' *Economic and Political Weekly* 42 (6), 10–16 February 2007: 497–508.
6. *National Human Development Report 2002* (Delhi: Planning Commission, Government of India, 2002), p. 38.
7. R. Radhakrishnan and Shovan Ray, 'Poverty in India: Dimensions and Characteristics' in Kirit S. Parikh and R. Radhakrishnan (eds.), *India Development Report 2004–2005* (New Delhi: Oxford University Press, 2005), pp. 40–61, p. 41.
8. National Council of Applied Economic Research, *Human Development Profile of India: Inter-State and Inter-Group Differentials* (Delhi: NCAER, 1996).
9. The contradiction between a growth-propelled India and tremendous poverty that stalks the lives of 260 million people is glaring. The 2004 ILO report *Economic Security for a Better World* compliments India for maintaining high growth in the past two decades, but also comments adversely on the country's record of social security. India is ranked 74 out of 90 countries on the economic security index constructed by the ILO. On income security, India ranks 94 out of 96 countries, only above Congo and Sierra Leone, both of which happen to be mired in civil war. The index is constructed on seven indicators: income, work, representation, job, employment protection, labour market, and skill reproduction. It is not that the rather striking co-existence between affluence and absolute deprivation is not of concern to policy planners. The five-year plans which lay out political priorities

40 million children out of the world's 115 million children who are out of school are Indian. Infant mortality has declined significantly from 110 deaths per 1,000 live births in 1981, 66 deaths per 1,000 live births in 2004. Maternal mortality rates in the country are the highest in the world. Life expectancy has increased from 54 years in 1981 to 64.6 years in 2000,[10] but it is still low compared to 70.3 years in China. According to the 2001 census, the literacy rate for the population stands at 64.8 per cent, compared with 52.21 per cent in 1991,[11] but women constitute a high proportion of the non-literate. More than 90 per cent of polio cases in the world are found in India. Widespread malnutrition, poor infrastructure in the area of health, and high mortality rates among the poor mean that the health scene is grim. The country has a very large number of hungry people—233 million—despite the existence of huge buffer stocks of food right up to 2006. The country's record in providing services—sanitation, clean drinking water, electricity, housing, and jobs—is even bleaker. And social spending on essential basic needs has not gone up substantially over the years.

It is evident that India has not done too well when it comes to social and economic democracy, even if its gains in political democracy are impressive. This is regrettable considering that the leaders of the freedom struggle had envisaged an integrated agenda of civil, political, social, economic, and cultural rights for all in the 1928 Nehru Constitutional Draft and in the Karachi Resolution on Fundamental Rights adopted by the Indian National Congress in 1931. Members of the Constituent Assembly, however, split this integrated agenda into two autonomous units. Whereas political, civil, and cultural rights in Part III of the Constitution came to be backed by legal sanction, social and economic rights that are placed in Part IV under the Directive Principles of State Policy are *not* backed by such sanction. The cost of implementing positive rights was considered to be far too prohibitive. Consequently, the Directive Principles of State Policy are intended as general guidelines for legislatures and governments even though Dr Ambedkar, the President of the Constituent Assembly, assured members that

> ... whoever captures power will not be free to do what he likes with it. In the exercise of it, he will have to respect these Instruments of Instructions, which are called Directive Principles. He cannot ignore them. He may not have to answer for their breach in a court of law. But he will certainly have to answer for them before the electorate at election time.[12]

---

and which set the parameters of policy detail hundreds of social policy schemes, all of which are meant to alleviate poverty. However, the presence of 260 million poor does not seem to be a compelling reason for the Indian state to undertake dramatic policy measures despite rhetorical flourishes to the contrary.

10. Annual Report of the Ministry of Health and Family Welfare, 2003–04: 13.
11. http://www.censusindia.gov.in/Census_Data_2001/India_at_glance/literates1.aspx (last accessed on 17 May 2008).
12. In B. Shiva Rao, *The Framing of India's Constitution* (Delhi: Indian Institute of Public Administration, 1968), p. 329.

In pursuance of the general objectives of establishing a social order based on social and economic justice, the Directive Principles urge the state to assure the people of India a cluster of social goods that meet basic needs, on the one hand, and ensure a life of dignity for the ordinary individual, on the other. Towards this end, the Government of India has enacted several policies, which aim at: (*a*) satisfying basic needs and generating social protection, and (*b*) engendering income and employment. Whereas the first set of policies is geared towards providing *all* people with basic goods essential for leading a life of dignity, other schemes are targeted towards raising the purchasing power of the poorer sections. Yet, the definitive statement on the incapacity of the Indian state to deliver social goods effectively has been made by Drèze and Sen. They conclude that despite some notable successes, India's overall success in promoting social opportunities has been quite limited. The intensities of many basic deprivations have been considerably reduced, but there is nevertheless a long way to go in ensuring anything like acceptable living conditions for all citizens.[13]

Arguably, the ability of social policy to address deep problems of poverty is limited because it has *not* addressed the issue of redistribution. To put it sharply, in a highly iniquitous society like India, social policy can prove effective only if it addresses the structural roots of inequality. The prevalence of deep poverty in rural areas, where till today more than 60 per cent of the population lives and works, required at the very least a radical restructuring of land relations. However, the conceptualization and the administration of land reforms in India had serious shortcomings. Though intermediaries were abolished and land was transferred to the tenants through a series of legislations, not only were land reforms confined to 40 per cent of the cultivated area, but they also suffered both from flawed conceptualization, and sluggish and ineffective implementation. Administered often by recalcitrant bureaucrats, land reforms failed to transfer land to the tiller, correct imbalances in the structure of land relations, provide security to tenants, and secure implementation of land ceiling laws. More significantly, land reforms slowed down because the issue of compensation to erstwhile landowners was bogged down in massive litigation. By the 1990s, land reform was put on the backburner as the subdivision and fragmentation of land weakened the case for lowering the land ceiling. This was despite the fact that inadequate tenancy reforms had resulted in concealed tenancy, thereby denying tenants the security of tenure and rent regulation. Further, massive alienation of land from tribal communities that live off the produce of the land reduced many to penury. The decade also heralded the liberalization of land laws in sharp contrast to the post-Independence period, when considerations of equity and social justice governed land reforms. Therefore, whereas by the end of the Eighth Five-Year Plan (1992–1997), 52 lakh acres out of a ceiling surplus

13. Jean Drèze and Amartya Sen, *India: Development and Participation* (New Delhi: Oxford University Press, 2002), p. 11.

of 75 lakh acres were distributed among 5.5 million beneficiaries, the position remained unchanged at the end of the Ninth Five-Year Plan (1997–2002).[14] The net result is that in major parts of the country, the poorest of the poor, mainly belonging to the Scheduled Castes, have been unable to access land, productive assets, and skills.

This is not the democracy that Pandit Nehru had dreamt of and yearned for. In 1934, Nehru had written in *Glimpses of World History*: 'We talk of freedom for our country, but what will any freedom be worth unless it gives to the man who does the work the fruits of his toil'.[15] Twenty-three years later, when India had become free and Nehru had become its first prime minister, he continued to hold that 'political democracy by itself is not enough except that it might be used to obtain a gradually increasing measure of economic democracy. The good things of life must become available to more and more people and gross inequalities must be removed'.[16] Pandit Nehru was speaking of substantive and not only of formal democracy, because a hungry human being is not a free human being, nor is a human being who is forced to beg for his/her daily bread equal to the wealthy.

The advantage is that the grant of civil and political rights has enabled civil society groups to demand that the State undertake appropriate action to realize the objectives laid down in the Directive Principles. Ever since Independence, groups have mobilized for social and economic justice and tenaciously fought somewhat entrenched systems of domination: peasants' movements, movements for land rights, women's movements, anti-caste movements, environmental movements, movements against displacement on account of large projects, and Naxalite movements. Most of these movements have called for a radical restructuring of power relations.

Since the late 1990s, a qualitatively different series of campaigns have appeared on the political scene. Five of these campaigns—campaigns for the right to food, the right to education, the right to health, the right to work, and the right to information—are of some interest because they have catapulted issues of serious concern into the limelight. Spearheaded mainly by social activists and non-governmental organizations (NGOs), these campaigns have demanded that the provisions of Part IV of the Constitution be *upgraded* to the status of part three of the Constitution, or that social and economic rights be given the same status as political and civil rights. Some of these campaigns have fetched notable results in the form of the Right to Education Act, the Rural Employment Guarantee Act, and the Right to Information Act. The cause of these campaigns has

14. Planning Commission, *Tenth-Five Year Plan 2002–2007*, Vol. 2, *Sectoral Policies and Programmes* (Delhi: Government of India, 2002), p. 301.
15. S. Gopal (ed.), *Jawaharlal Nehru*, p. 245.
16. In *Jawaharlal Nehru's Speeches*, Vol. 3, *March 1953–August 1957*, 3rd edition (Delhi: Government of India, Publications Division, 1983), p. 138.

been immensely helped by Supreme Court interventions, particularly in the case of the right-to-food campaign.[17] In May 2002, the Supreme Court ruled that village self-government bodies shall frame employment-generation proposals in accordance with the *Sampoorna Gramin Rozgar Yojana*. Earlier in 1993, the Supreme Court in the case of *Unnikrishna J. P. vs State of Andhra Pradesh* had ruled that though right to education is not stated expressly as a Fundamental Right, it is implicit in and flows from right to life guaranteed under Article 21. The court further declared that the Directive Principles of State Policy form the fundamental feature and social conscience of the Constitution and the provisions of Parts III and IV are supplementary and complementary to each other. The court ruled that Fundamental Rights are means to ensure the goals laid down in Part IV and must be construed in light of the Directive Principles.

CONCLUSION

In sum, the realization of the democratic project and the corresponding project of building a culture of deep democracy requires two major preconditions. First, we in civil society have to understand that citizens are not merely consumers of services such as employment and education rendered by the State and by its partners, the NGOs. Citizens have an equal political stake in the collective resources of society. If resources have been concentrated in the hands of an elite, then citizens by virtue of being stakeholders have the right to demand their redistribution. Second, any democracy which is based on the core values of freedom and equality is relational in as much as no one should be poor or wealthy beyond a limit. This is not to say that each person should possess exactly the same resources as anyone else. Those who exhibit entrepreneurial skills, those who work hard, and those who are resourceful should have the right to the product of their endeavours. All that a substantive democrat argues is that everyone should have the opportunity to develop their skills and capacity. These can only be developed when each citizen possesses a 'social minimum' in the form of income, health, education, and other basic needs, which provides the opportunities to develop talents and skills. For, no matter how many jobs the government provides to its citizens, how many schools are set up, how many health services are provided, most people will continue to suffer if they do not

17. In response to the write petition filed by the PUCL in 2001, the Court issued a series of interim orders, directing the Central and State governments to ensure nutritional security. Above all, the Court ruled that the right to food directly emanates from Article 21 of the Constitution of India which protects the right to life, and from Article 47 of the Directive Principles of State Policy which *inter alia* provides that the State shall regard the raising of the level of nutrition and the standard of living of its people and the improvement of public health as among its primary duties. The Court has, in effect, accorded legal backing to the right to food.

possess a social minimum. In sum, deepening the democratic, political culture requires sustained and focused spotlight on redistribution of resources, and not only on the provision of services.

It is this perspective that informs the contributions to this volume. The volume is divided into three parts, dealing with economic, social, and political themes, respectively. Despite this thematic division, there are two reasons why they form parts of a single body of understanding. First, as discussed earlier, democracy as a system of governance, and as a value, encompasses all these three aspects of our social lives. Democracy runs as a thread, binding the economic and the social with the political. Understanding of democracy, thus, requires that an attempt is made to situate it within the social and economic conditions of its operation. Second, understanding contemporary India also requires situating it historically. Like democracy, historical and political events also begin to make sense if illuminated by the socio-economic conditions that triggered them off. For example, the long-standing tussle between the legislature and the judiciary in India cannot be understood unless we situate it historically into the right to property as a Fundamental Right granted by the Constitution and Zamindari Abolition Acts enacted by various state legislatures. Further, in order to understand the Zamindari Abolition Act, we have to not only understand the history of the zamindari system but also its social and economic implications.

We hope that the volume will serve to answer some questions that students and informed readers have or rather should have on the democracy in India, and that they will help raise new questions on and for democracy.

PART I

Economy

Basic Features of the Indian Economy in 1947

1

Samir Kumar Singh

At the time of Independence, the Indian economy was ridden with many structural constraints. The economic planners were facing a very tough task of putting the economy on the development trajectory. The problem was two-fold. First, they needed to improve the performance of the economy in generating income and fighting poverty despite the existence of various kinds of constraints and, second, these constraints had to be removed. The prime constraint that the economy was facing was acute shortage of physical capital in relation to the availability of employable persons. The industrial sector was too weak to bring about any big turnaround and the agricultural sector already had a huge surplus of unemployed or under-employed persons. Further, the agrarian economy was feudal in nature, the prime concern of which was exploitation and not the development of agriculture itself. The possibility of fast capital formation was also limited due to the low saving capacity of the poor population. Moreover, the rate of population growth was also high. Apart from this, the situation on the health, food security, infrastructure and defence fronts was quite difficult.

In order to understand the Indian economy at the time of Independence, we need to examine colonialism and the British rule during the first half of the 20th century. We also need to understand what our planners and social scientists thought regarding the problems and challenges that India faced and the possible solutions. Colonialism is the extension of a nation's sovereignty over territory beyond its borders by the establishment of either settler colonies or administrative dependencies in which indigenous populations are directly ruled or displaced. Colonizers generally dominate the resources, labour and markets of the colonial territory and may also impose socio-cultural, religious and linguistic structures on the conquered population The purposes of colonialism include economic exploitation of the colony's natural resources, creation of new markets for the colonizer, and extension of the colonizer's way of life beyond its national borders. British interests in India were of several kinds. At first, the main purpose was to achieve a monopolistic trading position. Later, it was felt that a regime of free trade would make India a major market for British goods and a source of raw materials, but British capitalists who invested in India, or who sold banking or shipping service in India, continued effectively to enjoy monopolistic privileges. India also provided interesting and lucrative employment to a sizeable portion of the British upper middle class, and the remittances they sent home made an appreciable contribution to Britain's balance of payments and capacity to save. Finally, control of India was a key element in the world power structure, in terms of geography, logistics and military manpower. The British were not averse to the Indian economic development if it increased their markets but refused to help in areas where they felt there was conflict with their own economic interests or political security. Hence, they refused to give protection to the Indian textile industry until Japan emerged as its main competitor, displacing Manchester from its privileged position, and they did almost nothing to further technical education.

So, in the following section, we start by looking at India a few decades before Independence. This section will first look at the economic growth and then move to national income, agriculture, industry and trade, respectively. The next section deals with the development debate of independent India to trace the perception of the planners and its link with the British Raj experience.

INDIA BEFORE INDEPENDENCE

The economic growth rate in colonial India was very low but the situation became far more serious during the first half of the 20th century. Colonial India was an agrarian economy. The national income heavily depended on the performance of agriculture, and the performance of agriculture was dependent on the monsoon. Thus, the performance of the economy was largely dependent on factors beyond control. The growth prospects of industry and the tertiary sector depended on the demand for their goods and services. This demand itself depended on the agriculture sector. It is important to note here that the Indian economy then was much more open than in the post-Independence era. Foreign trade, therefore, was an important source of demand for the industrial sector just as the domestic demand was the most important determinant of industrial performance. Thus, agriculture performance was the most important cause of fluctuations in the national income.

ECONOMIC GROWTH DURING BRITISH RAJ

Economic growth is defined as a sustained increase in the real per capita income. This growth depends on three crucial factors, namely, availability of resources, investment and increasing efficiency. Studies of the growth path of various countries, from being poor to becoming developed states, identify three stages through which a nation passes. In the first stage, the poor country starts with the export of resources. In the second stage, the nation graduates to the export of labour-intensive manufactured commodities and, in the last stage, as labour starts becoming scarce the nation moves towards production of capital-intensive commodities. All these stages generate growth in the national income but it is in the third stage when the nation witnesses increase in capital–labour ratio and consequently increased productivity and sustained increase in the real income. The third stage is self-enforcing. Thus, this is the most desired shift for a nation. It must be remembered, however, that the population growth rate is a very important factor that affects both the promotion to the next stage and the pace of economic growth in a particular stage. If the population is growing fast then it may take a nation a long time to increase its capital–labour ratio substantially and consequently affect the productivity and real per capita income growth adversely.

Naoroji, who made a remarkable contribution to the study of Indian national income, was also interested in comparing the per capita income in India and England, but with the particular aim of demonstrating the higher burden of taxation in India. Naoroji placed the per capita income of India at Rs 30 in 1870 compared to that of England where it was Rs 450. His estimate is of great importance in addressing both the question of the absolute level of incomes in India and the issue of establishing the poverty of India in a comparative context.[1]

Colonial India witnessed economic growth during the 19th century, which was attributable to export of labour and resource intensive goods, huge investment in irrigation and railways and slow rate of growth of population. Since the population was not growing rapidly as a result the demand for labour was greater than the supply. During the first half of the 20th century, the growth in agriculture and investments slowed down while that in industries and some of the services sectors strengthened yet agriculture maintained its major share due to which the overall income growth remained subdued. The prime reasons behinds this poor performance were low investment during the last 50 years of the British Raj and population explosion after 1921, which became a major impediment to increasing the capital–labour ratio. The low investment was due to two reasons: first, investment was a small proportion of government expenditure and it was declining and second, private investment remained low due to high risks and uncertainties. It is important to note here that the 1920s witnessed depression in the world economy and the first half of the 20th century saw two world wars.

National Income: Movement and Composition

Tables 1.1, 1.2 and 1.3 show that during the first half of the 20th century,[2] national income grew at the rate of 0.9 per cent per annum, which is lower

1. Alan Heston, 'National Income' in Dharma Kumar and Meghnad Desai (eds.), *The Cambridge Economic History of India, Vol. 2*: C. 1957–C. 1970 (Cambridge, UK: Cambridge University Press, 1983), p. 377, 379–80.
2. Ibid.

Table 1.1 Measurement of Economic Growth, 1891–1938

Real National Income	*1891*	*1921 (Base)*	*1938*
Total	70	100	126
Per capita	78	100	82
Agriculture	67	100	100
Industry	–	100	175

Source: Tirthankar Roy, *The Economic History of India 1857–1947.*

Table 1.2 National Income at 1948–49 Prices: Annual Average

Year	*National Income*	
	Total (Rs billion)	*Per capita (Rs)*
1900–05	43.4	228
1942–47	51.5	239

Source: Tirthankar Roy, *The Economic History of India 1857–1947.*

Table 1.3 National Income at 1948–49 Prices: Annual Average

Year	*Exponential Growth Rates over the Period (%)*	
	Total	*Per capita*
1900–05 to 1942–47	0.9	0.1
1942–47 to 1992–95	4.0	2.0

Source: Tirthankar Roy, *The Economic History of India 1857–1947.*

than its rate in the 19th century and so low by any standard that it would not make any significant contribution to the economic development of a nation. This 0.9 per cent rate of growth of national income means 0.1 per cent annual growth rate for per capita income. Thus, the per capita income during this time remained stagnant.

With such a low growth rate, we cannot expect any radical shift in the composition of the national income. However, some qualitative changes can be seen. During the first half of the 20th century, primary, secondary and tertiary sectors were growing at the rate of 0.4 per cent, 1.4 per cent and 1.7 per cent per annum, respectively. Thus, we find that the primary sector was really sluggish. The tertiary sector was the fastest. Due to this, the share of the primary sector in national income declined from 66 per cent at the beginning of the 20th century to 53 per cent by the time of Independence. The share of the secondary sector slightly improved and that of the tertiary sector increased from 23.5 per cent to 32.3 per cent. In the tertiary sector, the largest expansion took place in the government administration at the rate of over 2 per cent followed by commerce and transport and real estates.

AGRICULTURE

We have seen during the first half of the 20th century that the primary sector grew at the annual average growth rate of 0.4 per cent per annum and agriculture remained stagnant. So the first question that comes to our mind is: why was agriculture stagnant, even though it employed more than 70 per cent of the active population and was the single most important factor affecting growth in the national income? Second, why has the regional pattern of growth and stagnation in agriculture remained, broadly, the same before and after Independence, particularly till 1980. Even the Green Revolution that brought about a turnaround in agricultural performance was confined to those regions that witnessed better performance during the British Raj. Before we take up these two questions, a few important aspects of agriculture need to be discussed.

Agricultural Production. Due to a lack of data and comparison across time, it is difficult to make any concrete remark on the issues. Studies differ on the magnitude of performance. But it is possible to make some general observations on the issue. During the second half of the 19th century, in major regions of India, areas under cultivation were expanding. The largest beneficiary of this expansion was traded crops. There was an improvement also in agricultural productivity but the increase in production is mainly attributable to expansion in the area under cultivation. On the basis of a study by Blyn, the following findings can be noted.

The agricultural output, as can be seen in Table 1.4, was growing at the slow rate of 0.37 per cent per annum.

Table 1.4 Growth Rates of Crop Output, Acreage and Yield in British India, 1891–1946 (per cent per annum)

	Growth in Output (%)	*Growth in Acreage (%)*	*Growth in Yield per Acre (%)*	*Growth in Yield Per Acre in Selected Periods*		
				1891–1916	*1916–21*	*1921–46*
All Crops	0.37	0.40	0.01	0.47	-0.36	-0.02
Foodgrains	0.11	0.31	-0.18	0.29	-0.63	-0.44
Non-foodgrains	1.31	0.42	0.67	0.81	0.34	1.16

Source: George Blyn, *Agricultural Trends in India, 1891–1947: Output, Availability, and Productivity* (Philadelphia, PA: University of Pennsylvania Press, 1966).

In terms of growth in output, food crop growth was almost stagnant at the rate of 0.11 per cent per annum while non-food crops were registering a relatively high growth rate of 1.31 per cent per annum.

The productivity (yield per acre) growth was negative for the food crops and a low 0.67 per cent per annum for the non-food crops. It is important to keep in mind that the food crop constituted a small proportion of the agriculture output. This is why, despite the 0.67 per cent rate of growth in productivity for the non-food crop, the overall growth in productivity was virtually nil. This implies that whatever growth was visible was largely due to the expansion in the acreage under cultivation. Since the area under cultivation grew faster during the second half of the 19th century, subsequent expansion was difficult and, consequently, it was expanding at the slow rate of 0.40 per cent.

During 1891–1916, productivity was growing faster. It declined during 1961–21, largely due to the First World War (1914–19) and became negative for the food crops making agricultural growth negative. After that, the productivity for the non-food crops improved but foodgrains productivity continued to be negative making agriculture growth negative at –0.02 per cent.

A comparison of agricultural performance to population growth reveals the picture regarding the food security of the nation, which is reflected in the availability of food per person. Blyn's study shows that during the pre-war period, the rate of growth of agriculture in general and, food crops in particular, were growing at a higher rate as compared to population. During the post-war period between 1921 and 1946, the rate of growth of agriculture in general and food crops in particular was significantly lower than the population growth rate. It is to be noted here that 1921 is known as the year of the great divide in India's demographic profile. This is identified as the beginning of the population explosion. Thus, during this period, food availability started declining at an alarming rate.

Therefore, the study finds major deterioration in the agrarian economy and economy at large. Furthermore, there was a regional disparity in this performance. The rice-producing belt, in particular, was not doing well while the wheat-producing belt was doing relatively better.

Investment and Technology. During the first half of the 20th century, some improvement in investment and technology was seen. Government expenditure was the most important source of investment in agriculture. Investment was primarily in irrigation. Furthermore, improvement in investment and expansion in irrigation facilities were primarily confined to three regions, namely, British Punjab, Western UP and the Madras belt. Due to increased investment and irrigation facilities, the value of land increased and this provided an incentive for private investment in agriculture. Further, due to the research conducted by the government, improved seeds of wheat and cotton became available. This was the major reason behind the improved productivity of these crops. It is very important to remember here that these were the regions that were well endowed with irrigation facilities and brought about the green revolution in India in the late 1960s.

Market. Before the British Raj, the Indian market was highly fragmented and was largely confined to meeting local needs. The prime reason for this was the different weight system, the prevalence of the barter system and underdeveloped and risky transportation system. These constraints were eased by the British efforts. Expansion of the railway network, which was primarily meant for the transportation of troops and raw materials for export, ultimately unified the fragmented market in a big way, and provided access to the distant Indian market and world markets. Before the British Raj, Indian agriculture was subsistence agriculture. Agriculture production was meant mainly for self-consumption and sales to the local markets. But during the British Raj, commercialization of agriculture started and intensified rapidly till the First World War. Commercialization includes both long distance trade and foreign trade. During 1860–1925, Indian exports increased five times with a 70 to 80 per cent share of the non-manufactured commodities. This domestic and foreign trade was encouraged by a significant decline in rail and international shipping freight charges. During this phase, a significant gain in exports was registered by the rising prices of the primary commodities. After 1920, there was a major change in world trade. The world was becoming highly protectionist and, to the worry of the underdeveloped countries like India, the rate of growth of demand for primary products decelerated. This happened due to the emergence of many substitutes for primary products like jute, cane and sugar, and the declining use of raw material per unit of manufacturing commodities. As a result, the Indian exportable commodities started facing excess supply in the world market and, consequently, prices of primary products started declining. This affected our exports earnings quite negatively.

The adverse performance of exports after 1920 and the depression of 1929 affected the perception of the planners in independent India in a significant manner and they adopted a negative attitude to export possibilities. On the basis of the downward movement in relative price of primary products, contemporary literature claimed that any nation, which is mainly exporting primary commodities, is going to lose out in the world trade. The trade will not help them grow, rather it will retard it. A nation could benefit from international trade if and only if it largely exported manufactured commodities. At the time of Independence, India inherited a weak industrial structure, so it was not expecting to export huge amounts of manufactured commodities. The planners concluded that it was better to postpone the export issue till we acquired sufficient capabilities in the manufactured commodities. Consequently, planning in India was started with a bias against exports. This later sparked an academic debate on whether the attitude of planner towards exports was correct, and even if it was correct, if it was justified in the case of the cotton textile industry which had a huge potential in the international market.

Land Relationship. The last half-century of British rule in the United Provinces witnessed a sharp intensification of agrarian difficulties and an increasing responsiveness of the land revenue administration to political pressure. By the beginning of the century, the net cultivated area reached almost its maximum extent of some 35 to 36 million acres. But the most serious destabilizing element was prices.[3] From 1905, prices began to climb rapidly and then tilted upwards with an unprecedented severity during the inflationary period of the First World War and its aftermath. By 1926, prices had doubled over that in 1900. While rents increased correspondingly by 36 per cent and revenue demand by some 12 per cent, rural incomes started falling from 1921. The landlord class wanted to increase rent in line with the increasing price level to appropriate a significant chunk of the gain. The British administration found it politically correct to give concession to the landlord class. Though the price level took a downward direction after that due to world depression, it revealed the system's desire to protect the interests of the landlords.

The land tenure system in India during the first half of the 20th century was highly exploitative. The prime goal of the *zamindars* was to extract maximum possible rent from the land. Furthermore, there was a large chain of intermediaries between state and the actual tiller of the land. Thus, the actual tiller of the land had little incentive and resources to invest in the land. Furthermore, the caste-based control system led to not just economic exploitation of the farmers or the landless class but also social exploitation. With the acceleration in population growth since 1921, the pressure on land started increasing and the tenancy started becoming further insecure. This further added to the disincentive to invest in the land. Regions under *rayatwari* faced less exploitation. The change in property rights definitions benefited the landlord class in the **zamindari system,** which was largely prevalent in Bihar, Bengal and Orissa whereas the changes in property rights benefited the cultivators in the *rayatwari* area like Punjab and Western UP. It is again interesting to note that it is the area under *rayatwari* that helped India usher in the green revolution.

Now we come to two questions that were raised at the beginning of this section. The prime reason behind stagnancy was the exploitative land tenure system, declining investment in the irrigation facilities and slow expansion of railways primarily after the First World War and declining world demand for cash crops. Various studies find commercialization to be positively correlated with agricultural growth. The second question relates to the continuity of the regional pattern of growth before and after Independence. In order to understand this we will have to understand the green revolution policy. The green revolution technology is a highly water intensive technology; so its implementation is suitable for well-irrigated areas. Furthermore, this technology at the time of

3. Eric Stokes, 'Agrarian Relations', in *The Cambridge Economic History of India, Vol. 2.*

inception was combined with uncertainty regarding its success and its impact. This needed inputs, which were to be bought from the market unlike the traditional agriculture. Further, it required the use of a lot of chemical fertilizers and pesticides. So the cost of agricultural operation increased along with the promise of better results. Therefore, the adoption of this technology largely depended on the availability of capital with the farmers and their risk-taking capacities. The British Raj had already prepared the region and created the class that was suitable to adoption of the technology. This was primarily the well-to-do farmers from the present Haryana, Punjab and Western UP. It is important to note here that these were the regions under *rayatwari* which promoted benefit to the tillers and, thus, contributed in creating a class which was to take up the task of bringing about the green revolution.

INDUSTRY

A beginning had been made in the development of modern industry at the end of the 19th century with the setting up some textile and jute mills and development of the tea and coffee industry. But it was only in the 20th century and, more so during the inter-war period that modern industry recorded rapid growth in India. It is generally agreed that manufacturing in India had made rapid progress during the first half of the 20th century.

The history of large-scale private factory enterprise till the First World War is associated almost entirely with developments in three industries—jute, cotton, and iron and steel. It is only towards the end of the period and the inter-war period when the Indian industrial sector witnessed a diversification. The beginning of the cotton and jute industry started simultaneously in western India and Bengal respectively. The foreigners controlled the jute industry and the Indian investors dominated the cotton textile. After 1850, Indian entrepreneurs started setting up modern textile mills and, by 1875, they started to export textiles and slowly it moved to grab the domestic market once again. In 1896, the domestic mills supplied only 8 per cent of the domestic cloth demand but, by 1945, 76 per cent of the domestic demand was catered to. By 1914, India had the world's largest jute manufacturing industry, the fourth largest cotton textile industry and the third largest railway network.

The real emergence of Indian industrial houses starts with the inter-war period. Both the Indian and the foreign capitalist class made huge profits during the inter-war period. The profit was mainly coming from the sudden rise in the price of the input and from speculative activities. Quite a few people became major wealth creators during this time. Among these, G. D. Birla and Kasturbhai Lalbhai are two prominent names. The English capitalists remitted their earnings to England whereas Indians used this for creating an industrial empire after the war was over. Between 1913 and 1938, manufacturing output started rising at the rate of 5.6 per cent per annum, which was above the world average of 3.3 per cent. From 1920 onwards, the British government started providing tariff protection to Indian industry and this helped the sector diversify its product basket. The Birlas entered sugar and paper apart from jute and textiles. Hirachand entered shipping apart from the construction business and the Tatas set up an airline that later became Air India.

The significance and pattern of manufacturing changed somewhat during the inter-war period. The significance of the largest industries, cotton textile and jute, was coming down. By 1938, their share declined from just above 50 per cent to 37 per cent of total manufacturing. No new industry emerged to replace their rank. By this time iron and steel increased its share to secure the third rank in manufacturing output. The great wartime boom lasted until 1922 for the cotton textile industry. During 1922 to 1939, this industry suffered significantly due to the weak domestic demand, which was the result of poor agricultural performance during this period. On the export front, Indian mills could not withstand the Japanese challenge. The cost could not be reduced due to the inability to reduce wages for the fear of strikes and the speculative mentality of the Indian investors.

The development of the industrial sector goes along with this speculative mentality. The speculative mentality provided capital to the domestic entrepreneurs to set up an industrial empire but also proved to be a drawback when it came to facing Japanese competition in the textile industry. This led to the planners forming the view that the capitalist as a class were merely interested in the short-term gain by every possible means. This is one reason why planners were so sceptical about private capital when they started the planning process in independent India.

By the Second World War, the supremacy of British business was being challenged and Indian entrepreneurs had grown stronger. Even during the Second World War period, the diversification of the industrial structure continued. Indian entrepreneurs were in a position to buy the business of departing foreigners. At the time of Independence, the share of manufacturing increased to 7.5 per cent, which could be considered big when compared with the past performance but in absolute term this meant little. This sector provided employment to 2.5 million people only. Ultimately, at the time of Independence, we inherited a diversified but weak industrial structure. Why could the modern industrial sector not expand in India to bring about a major turnaround? The probable answer to this could be that only those industries were set up for which resources was available in abundance like cotton textile, jute and sugar. Capital was a costly and scarce factor due to which capital-intensive industrialization did not pick up. Furthermore, due to the high cost of capital output, export of manufacturing commodities were not moving fast enough to generate capital to bring about a large-scale turnaround in the industry. Thus scarcity of capital was a major constraint.

Foreign Trade

Foreign trade as a ratio of national income increased significantly since the late 19th century. During 1900–1939, exports were approximately 9 per cent of the national income. The ratio of total foreign trade (export + import) to national income, which is a representative of integration of the nation to the rest of the world, increased substantially from 10 per cent in the 1860s to nearly 20 per cent by 1914. As discussed in the agriculture section, agricultural products dominated exports. So we do not need to discuss trade separately.

The British rulers were responsible for bringing about profound changes in the Indian economy and polity during their 200 years of rule. Although the changes encompassed the entire economic and social structure, their biggest impact was in the area of the agrarian structure. The important changes brought about by the British in the agrarian structure included alteration in land settlements and right of sale and alienation of land. The British rulers worked with *zamindari* (Bihar, UP, Orissa, Bengal) and *rayatwari* or *mahalwari* in the south and in the rest of India. Vested interests created in land provided very powerful support to the British Raj. The existence of absentee ownership, occupancy tenancy, extreme inequality in land ownership and increasing indebtedness created not only large-scale impoverishment of the peasantry but acted as a formidable barrier to the improvement in productivity of agriculture. On the industrial front, little industrialization took place and that too at the beginning of the 20th century. In light of these facts, we now move to examine the development debate of independent India.

THE DEVELOPMENT DEBATE

The development debate during Independence revolved around the three approaches. These were the Bombay plan, the Gandhian approach, and Nehru's approach. The Bombay plan was a strategy of industrialization with the participation of private players. This plan was chalked out with the massive involvement of the big industrial houses of that time like the Tatas and the Birlas. This plan was not accepted as the capitalist class was seen with suspicion. There were strong economic arguments against this mind set. Since capital was identified as a scarce resource, a prudent and planned utilization was considered better. The Gandhian approach was based on voluntary limitations of wants and development of a self-sufficient village community. The idea was that the village should be developed as an economy which can produce enough to meet its demand, create employment opportunities for the villagers and, at the same time, create a better balance between man and nature. This approach was largely termed as impractical and was not given serious attention. Only the last point has received some support by recent researchers who are concerned with the ecological issues. It is Nehru's approach that enjoyed the support of the time.

Nehru's approach was based on the Lewis model. The basic idea is that an underdeveloped economy has an agriculture sector with a huge amount of surplus labour. If surplus labourers are taken away from the agriculture sector, it will not affect output in that sector. The industrial sector has positive productivity for the labourers. If this sector is promoted, it will generate profit. If this profit is invested in machines and tools, the capital per worker will increase and this, in turn, will boost profits. This profit is reinvested again and the process moves on. So, this will increase capital formation at a fast rate. Thus, the basic understanding has been that agriculture is not likely to bring about a turnaround, whereas continuous investment of profit generated by the industrial sector in industries will start a self-sustaining growth process.

Now the question was: who will do this job, the capitalist class or the government? The capitalist classes, it was felt, would generate profit but would not invest a significant proportion of it and might just increase their consumption of luxurious commodities. Nehru was emphasizing on heavy industries like iron and steel, non-ferrous metals, machinery, engineering goods, coal and cement. In the case of such investments, profits are realized after a long period. So the private players were not expected to invest in these sectors. Furthermore, private participation was expected to promote inequality by cornering a large part of the profits. Due to these reasons, it is the public sector that was entrusted with the task. It is very important to understand here that the public sector was expected to generate huge profits which could be reinvested to accelerate the process of industrialization. In reality, we have seen that multiple objectives were given to the public sector and the profit generation objective became secondary. This, in the later stages, made it difficult for the public sector to remain viable.

In this model, the production of consumer goods was left open to the private sector, with some regulation. It was considered all right to promote private players till it was possible to tax them sufficiently. For this, we created a large bureaucratic mechanism of licensing and regulation. Thus, the entire industrial sector during the Second Five-Year Plan of 1956, was divided into three main categories: industries reserved for public sectors; industries where both public and private sector were allowed; and industries left to the private players only. The last category of industries that was left open to the private players was labour intensive industries. Since heavy industrialization, which was reserved for the public sector, was highly capital intensive, this was not expected to generate huge employment. So, the government expected to generate large employment through the last category of industries, which was left to the private players.

This plan did not give due emphasis to the agriculture sector. This sector was left to the private players, that is, the farmers. As far as benefit to the masses was concerned, it was expected to happen through the 'trickle down' effect. This means industrialization will increase the income of a section of the society and, as a result, they will demand various kinds of goods and services and these will be provided by the masses. So the masses will benefit indirectly by the growth of the economy. Thus, we can see that India basically adopted a mixed economy approach. The idea was to keep the good elements of both socialism and capitalism.

CONCLUSION

It is clear that India inherited a weak and problematic economic structure. It was an agrarian economy with little industrial development and stagnating agriculture sector. Agricultural relationship and scarcity of capital were realized as the main constraints. Despite criticizing the British Raj for aggravating the agrarian relationship by protecting the vested interests in land, independent India did little to dismantle the structure. Land reform is still incomplete and has become politically infeasible. State intervention during the British Raj was low as far as the industrial sector was concerned. We started with active state control of the industrial sector. At the same time, by disallowing private capital in most of the areas, we killed private incentive and a potential for better performance. One can see some of the structural bottlenecks prevalent at the time of Independence still present today, though in a relatively weaker form. The agriculture and social sectors are still being neglected. The state in which we received India at the time of Independence reveals what wrong institutions can do. Even today we continue with many institutions, which are undermining our potential, and we need to overcome them to build a really strong India.

Suggested Readings

Chakravarty, Sukhamoy. *Development Planning: The Indian Experience*. Oxford, UK: Clarendon Press, 1987.

Roy, Tirthankar. *The Economic History of India 1857–1947. New* Delhi: Oxford University Press, 2000.

Questions

1. What were the major challenges before economic planners when India got Independence?
2. What was the composition of the national income of India at the time of Independence? Give a sector-wise analysis.
3. What were the main positions in the debate over development at the eve of Independence? Please elaborate.

The Evolution of Development Strategy Since Independence

Ambuja Kumar Tripathy

2

I

The economy of contemporary India is a great paradox. It is a strange combination of outstanding achievements as well as grave failures. Since Independence, India has achieved remarkable progress in overcoming its economic backwardness. From being a very poor country in the 1950s and a 'basket case' in the mid-1960s, it has emerged as the fourth largest economy in the world (in terms of **purchasing power parity**). Our economy has become one of the fastest growing economies in the world. Now the country is one of the leading players in the world knowledge economy with vast intellectual capital and booming software and information technology services. These factors together have made India one of the greatest destinations for foreign investment. In spite of these historic achievements, the country has pervasive poverty, malnutrition, illiteracy, and a huge unemployment problem.[1] Although we are the world's largest democracy, our country has an overwhelming majority of poor voters. While our country has joined the league of the world's top five fastest growing economies, we are in the bottom 20 among all countries in terms of the Human Development Index. While the country is celebrating its growth rate and technological wonders, it is witnessing social contradictions and the paradoxes and ironies of development. Thus, there are 'two Indias' in contemporary India. There is the India of burgeoning growth and the India of widespread want and misery. This gives rise to several questions: Where have we gone wrong? Was the development strategy adopted after Independence right? Were the economic reforms of 1991 done right? Could

1. Around 300 million people in India are poor. India has the highest number of the malnourished children in the world. We have just 180 million employed people in a population of over one billion. The effective literacy rate in India is 65.4 per cent. For more details, see Council for Social Development, *India: Social Development Report* (New Delhi: Oxford University Press, 2006). According to *The Times of India*, 6 July 2008, although India has one of the biggest education systems in the world, over 380 million people are illiterate—which is the largest number of illiterates in any one country.

the reforms have been done better? To analyse these questions, it is essential to look at the Indian economy in a historical perspective.

This essay examines India's development experience after Independence. This experience encompasses the initial socialist principles of state ownership, regulation, and control over key sectors of the economy as well as the economic reforms in 1991. For a better understanding of the evolution of these economic policies, they have been placed in the social, cultural and political settings in which they occur. This chapter is divided into three sections: the first section deals with the Nehruvian legacy (from the First Plan to the Third Plan); the second section is concerned with the period from the mid-1960s to the end of the Seventh Plan; and the last section begins with the economic reforms of 1991.

DEVELOPMENT PLANNING

Economic policies adopted in India after 1947 were conditioned by the colonial legacy and the prevailing international situation. The strategic design of these policies was tremendously influenced by the dominant ideology of the Indian national movement and the ideas of nationalist leaders, especially Nehru. At the time of Independence, India was in the stranglehold of stagnating per capita national income, static and semi-feudal agriculture, poorly developed industry and inadequate infrastructure, mass poverty, extreme unemployment and underemployment, massive illiteracy, high birth and death rates and deplorable health conditions. Independent India faced the gigantic task of undoing the damage caused by British rule. There was a need to put in huge and organized effort on a national scale to achieve substantial progress on the socio-economic front. Towards this end, planning was accepted as the key strategy of India's developmental efforts.

Planning was considered a superior way of developing the Indian economy than the market mechanism. While the market gives priority to high-profit activities, planning makes a systematic utilization of the available resources at a progressive rate to ensure quick building of the productive capacity of the country. Planning was looked upon as an instrument that could enable the state to undertake several massive development projects and unemployment and poverty alleviation programmes. Furthermore, planning was essential to deal with difficulties caused by the partition of the country in 1947, that is, huge influx of refugees from East and West Pakistan and the loss of raw material-producing areas.

Several international developments in the early decades of the 20th century revealed the limitations of market mechanism with respect to both efficiency and equity. After the 1917 revolution, the Soviet Union became the first socialist state and adopted a planned economy model. Its remarkable achievements on the socio-economic front greatly inspired the nationalist youth in India. Around the same time, the Great Depression of 1929–33 exposed the problems of a free market economy. Keynesianism, a product of the Depression, strongly advocated the case of economic management by the state through taxation and spending policies.

In fact, the economic critique of colonialism by the national movement and its explicitly articulated set of economic objectives provided the foundation to the strategy of development planning in India after Independence. While criticizing colonial underdevelopment and the dependent character of the Indian economy, Indian nationalists put forward the idea of a self-reliant independent economic development in which state planning would play the key role. In the 1930s, ideas on development planning were crystallized due to the influence of the Russian experiment, Keynesian economic ideas and the New Deal programme in the US seeking state intervention in the economic forces. The need for planning was so strongly felt that the Indian National Congress set up the National Planning Committee (NPC) in 1938 under the chairmanship of Jawaharlal Nehru. This plan was to have great implications on the post-Independence economic strategy in India. In addition to this plan, several plan documents were prepared along different ideological lines in the 1940s: the *Bombay Plan* was authored by India's eight leading capitalists, the *People's Plan* prepared by M. N. Roy took a left position, and the *Gandhian Plan* formulated by Shriman Narain pleaded for a self-sufficient village economy. However, there was a broad consensus among the Gandhians, the capitalists, the socialists and the communists on the necessity of planning as well as the nature and path of development to be followed after Independence.[2]

Jawaharlal Nehru, the chief architect of planning in India and the country's first prime minister, was greatly influenced by democratic, socialist and Gandhian values. He believed that socialism and democracy were inseparable. Hence, he described democratic socialism as the vision of independent India that would seek to make democratic social transformation an integral part of the country's economic strategy. Nehru spoke of his approach as a third way that takes the best from all existing systems—the Russian, the American and others—and seeks to create something suited to one's own history and philosophy. He thought that planning introduced in a democratic manner could become the instrument for growth and reduction of inequalities while ensuring individual freedom and avoiding the violence of revolutionary change. He hoped for a society organized on a planned basis for raising humankind to higher material and cultural levels, to cultivation of values, of cooperation and ultimately a world order. He also considered planning a positive instrument for resolving conflict in a large and heterogeneous country.

Nature and Objectives of Planning

After Independence, India adopted a democratic ideology—a representative form of government based on universal adult suffrage with rights and liberties for the

2. This consensus is emphasized by Prabhat Patnaik, 'Some Indian Debates on Planning', in T. J. Byres (ed.), *The Indian Economy: Major Debates Since Independence* (New Delhi: Oxford University Press, 1998).

masses. Democracy became central to the Indian model of development. There was unanimity among the leaders on the unique approach of India to planning within a democratic and civil-libertarian framework. It was believed that planning would create a democratic economy in the country by bringing the economy under public control. At the same time, in India's development strategy market and economic planning were regarded as complementary to each other. Development plans were to be formulated and carried out within the framework of a mixed economy that included the merits of both socialism and capitalism. A mixed economy was marked by the coexistence of private and public sectors, the latter remaining confined to infrastructure and basic and heavy industries.

The basic objectives of planning were derived from the Directive Principles of State Policy enshrined in the Constitution. These basic objectives provided the guiding principles of planning in India. These spelt out as: (i) economic growth—accelerating the growth to achieve higher level of national and per capita income;[3] (ii) modernization—implementing structural and institutional changes to make the economy progressive and independent; (iii) self-reliance—eliminating dependence on foreign aid and India's vulnerability to external pressures and disturbances; and (iv) social justice—improving the living standards of the masses, especially the underprivileged through reduction in income inequalities, removal of unemployment, elimination of poverty, land reforms and social programmes on health and education.[4] Overall, growth and social justice formed the economic and social framework of planning. With this perspective, the Planning Commission was set up in 1950 by a government resolution to formulate a plan for economic and social development and to act as an advisory body to the Union government in its behalf. The National Development Council was formed later as an adjunct to the Planning Commission to associate the states in the formulation of plans.

The Nehru–Mahalanobis Development Strategy

The era of planned development was ushered in with the launch of the First Five-Year Plan in April 1951.[5] It addressed the problems arising from massive influx of refugees, acute food shortage and mounting **inflation**. The highest

---

3. According to Jagdish Bhagwati, accelerated growth was regarded as a variable that would reduce poverty, which was the real objective of our efforts. See Bhagwati, 'The Design of Indian Development', in I. J. Ahluwalia and I. M. D. Little (eds.), *India's Economic Reforms and Development* (New Delhi: Oxford University Press, 1998).
4. Partha Chatterjee argues that it was in planning that the post-colonial state in India would claim its legitimacy as a single will and consciousness or the will of the nation, pursuing a task that was both universal and rational: the well-being of the people as a whole. See Partha Chatterjee (ed.), *State and Politics in India* (New Delhi: Oxford University Press, 2000).
5. The Harrod–Domar model with some modifications was the underlying model for the First Plan.

Table 2.1 Five-Year Plans and Plan Periods

Five-Year Plan	*Period*
First Plan	1951–56
Second Plan	1956–61
Third Plan	1961–66
Annual Plans	1966–69
Fourth Plan	1969–74
Fifth Plan	1974–79
Sixth Plan	1980–85
Seventh Plan	1985–90
Eighth Plan	1992–97
Ninth Plan	1997–2002
Tenth Plan	2002–2007

priority was given to overcoming the food crisis by raising foodgrain output, curbing inflation and the development of infrastructure (see Table 2.1).

The Second Five-Year Plan is regarded as the milestone in the trajectory of planning since it was based on the Nehru–Mahalanobis strategy of development, which guided the planning practice for more than three decades until the end of the Seventh Five-Year Plan. The draft outline of this plan was framed by P. C. Mahalanobis.[6] This development strategy was based on several assumptions regarding the causes of structural backwardness of the Indian economy. First, severe deficiency of material capital was seen as the basic constraint of development since it prevented the introduction of more productive technologies. Second, the low capacity to save was considered as the limitation on the speed of capital formation. Third, it was believed that through industrialization the surplus labour underemployed in agriculture could be productively employed in industries. Fourth, it was presumed that if the market mechanism were given primacy, this would lead to excessive consumption by higher-income groups, along with relative under-investment in the sectors essential to the accelerated development of the economy.

Given these assumptions, the basis questions before the planners were: How to increase capital stock rapidly? How to invest wisely? How to increase savings? How to regulate the market? The Nehru–Mahalanobis development strategy found the answer to these questions in rapid capital formation through the development of **capital goods industries** with direct intervention of the state in the economy. As such, it was based on the principle—higher the allocation of investments to the heavy or capital goods industries, lower will be the rate

6. The Mahalanobis model is viewed as a variant of the Soviet planning model and the Lewis model.

of growth of income in the short run, but higher will it be in the end. Thus, industrialization with preference to capital goods industries over consumer goods industries became the core of this development strategy. The basic elements of this strategy can be summed up as:

1. Raising the rate of investment since the rate of development is dependent on the rate of investment. It involved stepping up domestic and foreign savings also.
2. Rapid growth of the productive capacity of the economy by directing public investment towards development of industries, especially capital goods industries. Simultaneously, promotion of **labour-intensive** small and cottage industries for the production of consumer goods and expansion of employment opportunities.
3. **Import substitution** for self-reliance and reduction of external dependence.
4. Setting up of an elaborate system of controls and industrial licensing to allocate resources among industries as per the Plan requirements and distribute consumption goods equitably among the consumers. This was done through the Industries Development and Regulation Act (IDRA) of 1951.
5. Enhancing the scope and importance of the public sector so that this sector comes to predominate capital goods industries, and controls the commanding height of Indian economy.

In this way, the Second Five-Year Plan sought to promote a pattern of development that would ultimately lead to the establishment of a socialistic pattern of society in India. The development strategy of the Third Plan was basically the same as that of the Second Plan but the highest priority in this Plan was accorded to agriculture.

Agrarian Reconstruction

While formulating national plans and policies, the planners also tried to address the fundamental social and economic problems of the agrarian structure. The Gandhian idea of *gram swaraj* was a great influence in this regard. Two significant steps were taken in the 1950s to bring about major changes in the agrarian structure. These were the Community Development Programme and land reforms.

Community Development Programme. The Community Development Programme (CDP) was a comprehensive programme of rural upliftment that aimed at transformation of the traditional rural life by injecting forces of dynamism in the stagnant rural economy. The underlying principle of this development programme was cooperation between the government and people to improve the economic, social and cultural conditions of communities, to integrate these communities into the mainstream life of the nation, and to enable them to contribute fully to national progress. CDP was launched on a pilot project basis in 55 community project areas throughout the country on 2 October 1952. The success of CDP depended on the active participation of people. Such participation was made possible by local democratic and representative institutions introduced in 1959 under the Panchayati Raj scheme.

Land Reforms. After Independence, the need for land reforms arose owing to the exploitative nature of the land tenure system prevailing during the colonial period. The basic objectives of land reforms were: (*a*) to raise agricultural production by removing obstacles emanating from the semi-feudal agrarian structure inherited from the past; and (*b*) to deliver social justice by eliminating the exploitative features of the agrarian system and to provide equality of status and opportunity to all sections of the rural population.

Broadly, three measures were taken to achieve these objectives.[7] First, the *zamindari* system set up by the British government was abolished. By this measure, all the *zamindars*, who acted as intermediaries and collected land revenue for the state and exploited the cultivators by extracting excessive rents, were eliminated. Second, several tenancy reforms were undertaken to improve the condition of tenants working on lands owned by others. These included fixation of rents and security of tenure to protect tenants from eviction. Ownership rights were also conferred on tenants over lands they cultivated after the fulfilment of certain conditions such as payment of price for land. Third, the reforms provided for a ceiling on agricultural holdings or statutory absolute limit on the amount of land that an individual could hold. The surplus over the ceiling was to be transferred to the landless or small cultivators. Moreover, reforms had a provision for consolidation of holdings. This measure aimed at providing consolidated holdings to the farmers equal to the total of the land in different scattered plots under their possession.

ROLE OF THE STATE

The nature of the post-colonial state in India was determined by the colonial legacy and contemporary global events. The latter included the Great Depression of the 1930s, post–Second World War problems and rapid growth in the Russian economy that created a congenial atmosphere for an active role of the state in the economy. The colonial legacy was the compelling factor for direct state intervention to bring about major transformations in various spheres of the society. Before Independence, the nationalist economic perspective advocated a central role for

7. For more on land reforms, see the First and the Second Plan Documents, and the Planning Commission, *Progress of Land Reforms* (New Delhi: Government of India, 1963).

the state in the process of economic development. Even the early nationalists such as M. G. Ranade and Dadabhai Naoroji in the late 19th century favoured a crucial role for the state in India's economic development. The 1931 Karachi Resolution declared that 'the state shall own or control key industries and services, mineral resources, railways, waterways, shipping and other means of public transport'. The NPC and the Bombay Plan also recommended a comprehensive policy of direct and systematic state intervention in the economy through planning, the public sector and general control over different sectors of the economy. The unanimity among the Indian nationalists for active state intervention in the economy was found at the time of Independence also.

Given the nature of problems in India at the time of Independence, development became the core of the state's agenda. Development was 'comprehensively defined to encompass not only an industrial economy, but also simultaneously a programme of social transformation and political democratization.'[8] The state tried to achieve economic development as well as an egalitarian social order within the confines of democracy. The Constitution in 1950, having universal adult franchise and an extensive list of Fundamental Rights, officially declared India a democracy. The Directive Principles of the Constitution with the goals of social justice and preventing concentration of wealth shaped the scope and nature of state intervention.

For the attainment of economic as well as social transformation in the society, the Indian state took up the role of a developmental state. It became the central instrument in the development course through the process of planning, which involved state control over the production, distribution and exchange of goods and services. The state itself entered the fields of production and distribution to meet the developmental objectives. The Nehru–Mahalanobis strategy found the state as the most suitable agency to achieve its objectives. The state was required to intervene in the economy, promote public sector in heavy industries and guide the growth of the economy. The state launched big dams, large industrial and mining projects and institutions of higher learning as 'temples of modern India' for infrastructure development. To improve village life, the state undertook institutional reforms or land reforms. It took the primary responsibility for providing elementary education, basic healthcare, safe drinking water and employment programmes. Such a large expansion of the economic and social responsibilities of the state was consistent with the objective of the socialist pattern of society. However, this did not mean complete elimination of private enterprise. In fact, the state was pledged to maintain a mixed economy in the society based on its commitment to democracy and socialism.

8. See Niraja Gopal Jayal, *Democracy and the State* (New Delhi: Oxford University Press, 2001). Also see Zoya Hasan (ed.), *Politics and the State in India* (New Delhi: Sage, 2000). In the latter, Rajni Kothari argues that the Indian state has been made into an instrument of human freedom and social justice.

Assessment

The Nehru–Mahalanobis strategy of development faced considerable criticism from several quarters. The most important criticism came from two Mumbai economists C. N. Vakil and P. R. Brahmananda who offered an alternative at the time of formulation of the Second Plan.[9] Since it put greater emphasis on industrialization compared to agriculture, the latter suffered. The allocation of higher priority to heavy industries compared to labour-intensive industries resulted in heavy concentration of wealth and large-scale unemployment. The IDRA of 1951 did not serve its purpose fully. It created a *licence raj* in the country favouring the large industrial houses, which became an impediment to industrial development. Land reforms could not be implemented properly owing to the defects in legislations, lack of political will and bureaucratic apathy. Because of the same reasons, the CDP did not achieve considerable success.

Nevertheless, the first phase of the development effort witnessed several significant achievements. This phase created the basic physical and human infrastructure for comprehensive development in the society. The overall economic performance was far better compared to the colonial period. The rate of growth was quite impressive. Both the savings and investment rates rose substantially. Growth in agricultural production occurred because of land reforms, CDP and large investment in irrigation, power and agricultural research. Industry grew more rapidly than agriculture. The country developed a heavy industry complex with considerable diversification within the industrial structure. Furthermore, progress was made in the sphere of human capital due to the setting up of institutions of higher learning, especially in the scientific field.

II

Despite these significant achievements, India faced a **macroeconomic** crisis in the mid-1960s due to the slow growth of agriculture and exports, two successive droughts of 1965 and 1966 and the Indo-Pak War of 1965, followed by a suspension of US aid. This situation delayed the Fourth Plan and three annual plans were adopted between 1966 and 1969. The response of the state to the crisis included: (i) the adoption of restrictive **fiscal policies** by cutting down on expenditure, (ii) the **devaluation** of the rupee and (iii) the launching of the Green Revolution.

The Green Revolution

The term 'Green Revolution' is used to describe the new agricultural strategy that was put into practice for the first time in India in the *kharif* season of 1966

9. For more on this strategy see Meghnad Desai, 'Development Perspectives: Was There an Alternative to Mahalanobis?' in Ahluwalia and Little (eds.), *India's Economic Reforms and Development*.

to overcome the food problem.[10] It is also known as the High-Yielding Varieties Programme (HYVP) as the strategy was based on high-yielding varieties of seeds that had higher productivity than traditional varieties. Unlike traditional agriculture, the new strategy consisted of chemical fertilizers, pesticides and insecticides, improved varieties of seeds including hybrid seeds, agricultural machinery, extensive irrigation and use of diesel and electrical power.

Shifts from Early Development Strategy

The Nehru–Mahalanobis strategy of development came under severe attack due to the poor performance of the economy and the economic crisis of the mid-1960. Although the basic framework of the Mahalanobis strategy was retained until the end of the Seventh Plan, shifts from this strategy became visible from the Fourth Plan onwards. In the Fourth Plan, the objective of self-reliance was not discarded, but the main emphasis was shifted to rapid economic growth. Consequently, preference was given to quick-yielding projects as well as to light industry at the expense of heavy industry. The state went for an elaborate system of controls in the economy such as nationalization of banks in 1969, the Monopolies and Restrictive Trade Practices (MRTP) Act in 1969, nationalization of the insurance sector in 1972 and the coal industry in 1973, and the Foreign Exchange Regulation Act (FERA) in 1973.

A major criticism of the Mahalanobis development strategy came from the World Bank economists in the early 1970s. Challenging this growth-oriented strategy, they argued that the objective of removal of poverty could not be achieved by growth itself. Several studies undertaken by Dandekar and Rath, Pranab Bardhan and B. S. Minhas in India concluded that the benefit of growth had failed to reach the poor. Hence, the Fifth Plan allocated highest priority to the elimination of poverty and it adopted various area development programmes The Sixth Five-Year Plan adopted various redistributive measures such as the Integrated Rural Development Programme (IRDP) and the National Rural Employment Programme (NREP). The Seventh Plan adopted a new long-term development strategy focusing on growth in foodgrain production, employment opportunities and productivity.[11]

Crisis of the State

In the post-Nehru period, the country witnessed severe political instability because of decline and erosion of state institutions and political values. It was

10. For details, see C. H. Hanumantha Rao, 'Agriculture: Policy and Performance', in Bimal Jalan (ed.), *The Indian Economy: Problems and Prospects* (New Delhi: Penguin Books, 1992).
11. This plan was based on a variant of the agricultural-development-led-growth (ADLG) strategy strongly recommended to India by J. W. Miller.

manifested in the electoral blow to the Congress in 1967 and the 1969 Congress split, rampant factionalism, defections and corruption, erosion of standards of integrity in public life and growing intensity of caste, communal, ethnic and regional conflicts. In the early seventies, the process of heavy centralization of decision-making at the top combined with undue emphasis on personalities began, which culminated in the Emergency of 1975 and continued right through the 1980s. It adversely affected the effectiveness and the morale of state institutions such as the party system, parliament, judiciary, bureaucracy and law-and-order machinery. This structural crisis of the state led to a crisis of governability in the country.

The turbulence in India's democracy occurred because of political awakening and decay.[12] Political awakening refers to self-assertion and political participation of hitherto marginalized groups in society due to growing democratization in the country. These groups consisting of the lower-middle and the lower strata in villages, petty traders and workers in the organized sector emerged as strong demand groups making claims on state's scarce resources. Political decay refers to the drastic decline in the ability of state institutions to face these increasing demands.

In this situation, political leaders used populist slogans to win elections, for example, the slogan of *garibi hatao* (remove poverty) in the 1971 elections. Furthermore, policymakers resorted to several populist measures (such as tax concessions to petty traders and write-offs of rural loans), which sharply increased government expenditures or reduced government revenues. In this way, the policies of the state aggravated the deteriorating economic situation in the country.

Assessment

In spite of several domestic and external shocks, this period witnessed considerable economic achievements. Due to the Green Revolution, the post-1966 period saw substantial increase in foodgrain production, particularly wheat production, which led to food security and poverty reduction. Anti-poverty and employment programmes of the government helped tackle rural poverty and rural unemployment. The economic situation improved due to the reduction in import of food and other items increase in exports and rise in remittances made by Indian workers from West Asia. The rates of domestic savings and investment increased and the industrial growth rate started picking up. New oil discoveries at the Bombay High oil fields cut down the oil import bill. In the 1980s, the 'Hindu rate of growth' (coined by Raj Krishna) of 3 to 3.5 per cent, which India had maintained over the first three decades after Independence, was broken and the economy grew at over 5.5 per cent. At the same time, the Green Revolution and the structural

12. James Manor first used these terms in this context. See V. Joshi and I. M. D. Little, *India: Macroeconomics and Political Economy 1964–1991* (New Delhi: Oxford University Press, 1998). I have borrowed liberally from this book for this section.

weaknesses of this period caused many economic problems in the long run. Since the Green Revolution was largely wheat-based and it was implemented in a few states, it created inter-crop disparities and regional imbalances. Because of its capital-intensive nature, it could not benefit the rural poor.

III

India faced a full-scale macroeconomic crisis in the early 1990s that reached its climax in 1991. The crisis was marked by high inflation, rising food prices, large **current account** deficit, huge domestic and foreign debt, a sharp fall in **foreign exchange reserves**, a steep decline in India's credit rating, and a cut off of **commercial loans** accompanied by a net outflow of NRI (Non-Resident Indian) deposits.

The long-term constraints of the preceding decades, especially the 1980s, combined with certain immediate factors gave rise to this economic crisis. The Nehru–Mahalanobis strategy of import substitution–industrialization made the Indian industry inefficient and technologically backward due to the absence of competition. Due to the discouragement of foreign capital, India could not get the benefits of technology and excellent competition. Heavy regulation of private sector through the system of licences and permits caused a great damage to entrepreneurship and innovation. The public sector that dominated this strategy became highly inefficient and even sick due to excessive political interference. The preoccupation of the strategy with self-sufficiency caused export pessimism. This heavy industry strategy required huge imports of capital goods. Due to large imports of capital goods and foodgrain combined with little imports, the **trade deficit** increased. Instead of making necessary modifications according to the changing world situation,[13] the government itself caused fiscal deterioration in the 1980s through (i) populist policies, (ii) rapid growth of state controls over the economy, and (iii) reservation of certain areas for small-scale industries. The Gulf Crisis of 1990 came as an external shock to the Indian economy, which was in a highly vulnerable state.

Economic Reforms

In response to the internal economic crisis of 1990–91 and the changing international situation, the Narasimha Rao government decided to introduce economic reforms or the New Economic Policy (NEP). The NEP clearly reflected certain global trends, namely, the collapse of the socialist economy and growing acceptance of economic globalization across the world. Although

13. The world situation was characterized by massive flow of foreign capital and increasing role of multinational corporations due to internationalization of production.

the reforms as a part of the process of liberalization and globalization were revolutionary in nature, these were launched within the democratic framework of the country. They marked a shift from the Nehruvian consensus of the 1950s to a new consensus around reforms. While the national goals set out at Independence remained unaltered, the change came only in the strategy to achieve these goals—from Nehru–Mahalanobis development strategy to the new development strategy of liberalization and economic reforms.

The reforms programme consisted of macroeconomic stabilization and structural reforms. Macroeconomic stabilization was a short-term programme adopted to overcome the macroeconomic crisis by regulating the total demand in the economy. While structural reform was a medium- and long-term programme, it dealt with sectoral adjustments and the problems on the supply side of the economy by bringing in dynamism and competitiveness to the economy. Crisis management measures included use of gold to acquire foreign currency to meet payment obligations, devaluation of the rupee, compression of imports and seeking finances from multilateral financial institutions and bilateral donors. Structural reforms included liberalized trade and investment policies with emphasis on exports, industrial deregulation, disinvestment and public sector reforms, and reform of the capital markets and the financial sector. In this way, an attempt was made to achieve a progressive economy by removing the internal controls and further to equip it to take advantage of the opportunities provided by the worldwide globalization process. Accordingly, a new trade policy and a new industrial policy were introduced. In the face of these changes, the Eighth Plan, the Ninth Plan and the Tenth Plan were launched.

Redefining the Role of the State

The adoption of the NEP based on liberalization and privatization has given rise to a debate on the nature of the link between state and market.[14] The NEP does not imply a retreat of the state. It is based on a few propositions. First, the state and the market are not substitutes for one another but they complement each other. Second, these two actors provide mutual checks and balances in such a way that one can correct the failures of the other. Third, through proper intervention the state has to make the market people-friendly because governments are accountable to people, while markets are not. It calls for a reorientation in the role of the state that tended to take too many responsibilities in the past. It underlines a change in the nature of the state from a producer, investor and regulator to a facilitating agency. The state has to maintain general law and order and provide

14. On the theme of state–market relationship, many writings have appeared in recent times. See Paul Streeten, 'Markets and States: Against Minimalism and Dichotomy', *Political Economy Journal of India*, 3(1), 1995, and Amit Bhaduri and Deepak Nayyar, *The Intelligent Person's Guide to Liberalization* (New Delhi: Penguin Books, 1996). Except for the extreme left-or right-leaners, the balanced view has been that it is not an either/or proposition and the role of the two have to be carefully delineated in specific contexts.

an appropriate policy framework in the areas where the private sector can play a large role. The state needs to formulate policies to bring about improved transparency and greater accountability, which form the basic pillars of good governance.

The new development strategy urges the state to play an important role in creating economic and social infrastructure that is unlikely to attract private investment, such as rural infrastructure and the development of roads and railways. It also justifies state intervention in those areas where the markets either do not exist or where market activity can lead to undesirable outcomes—providing public goods such as healthcare, education and safe drinking water, and generating measures for eradication of poverty, creation of employment opportunities, empowerment of the disadvantaged and elimination of regional imbalances.

RELEVANCE OF PLANNING

Planning has been one of the basic pillars of the Indian state's approach to development since Independence. However, in the recent times the relevance of planning is much debated by the scholars. One argument is that planning has failed to achieve its goals. The second argument is that planning has become irrelevant owing to globalization and liberalization, and the consequent free movement of capital and increase in the role of the market forces in economic decision-making and investment.

However, planning based on the Mahalanobis framework was fine during the first three plans. The problems that surfaced in the economy after the Nehruvian period are not due to planning but are the product of lack of appropriate planning[15] and mismanagement by government. Planning does not become irrelevant due to internationalization of capital. Planning has to take the internationalization of capital as a fact of life, a constraint within which it has to chart out its course.[16] In a liberalized economy, the nature of planning changes corresponding to the changes in the nature of state intervention but it does not become irrelevant. Public investment will continue to have a major role in social sectors and rural economic infrastructure and the prioritization of the investment has to be property planned. The role of planning in our federal system is to coordinate the activities of all levels in the government—centre, states and local level—and that of the market and **civil society** actors. In this way, planning has to evolve a shared commitment to national goals among all the actors in the society. To make planning successful, the country has to follow a more decentralized and participatory planning. The poor are to be placed in our economic planning. To remove the regional inequalities, there is the need for regional planning, town and country planning. Further, planning in contemporary

15. Sukhamoy Chakravarty, *Development Planning: The Indian Experience* (New Delhi: Oxford University Press, 1988), p. 88.
16. Patnaik, 'Some Indian Debates on Planning', p. 186. Patnaik provides strong arguments for the relevance of planning for the internationalization of capital.

India has to be made comprehensive by including not only the conventional issues but also the emerging areas, like critical environmental issues.

Assessment

Although there is a broad consensus among all the parties (except the extreme Left and extreme Right) on the desirability of reforms, considerable debate has emerged on the contents of the reform programme, their sequencing and pace as well as their implementation and impact. The balance sheet of Indian economy in the post-reform period is mixed. The overall post-reform growth rate has been higher than the average rate achieved during the pre-reform period, largely because of the services sector. The fiscal imbalance and inflationary tendency have been controlled. India is emerging as an important player in fields such as manufacturing and medical services. Robust export growth especially software exports, and rising remittances by Indian workers abroad have created a new confidence in the Indian economy. It has led to phenomenal growth in foreign exchange reserves. The growth competitiveness and the business competitiveness of the country are increasing. India is emerging as a stable growth engine and as a Big Emerging Market (BEM) in the world due to robust economic performance supported by a vibrant democracy, increasing young population, expanding middle class and domestic market and well-developed private sector.

However, this growth is not inclusive. First, the growth is skewed within the economy. For example, there is a great divide separating industry and agriculture, and the infrastructure, especially the rural infrastructure, is in an appalling state. Second, the reforms are just confined to the economy and they are not spreading to the social sector. The social sector including healthcare, education, social security, gender equity and environmental protection has suffered a setback owing to the decline of public investment in this crucial area. Low spending by the government has led to growing inequity in education and a decline in the quality of education. Indian society is marked by four great divides: rural–urban, rich–poor, and along gender and caste lines—which pervade every aspect of life, including social services. In each category, there is the existence of a disadvantaged section that finds it extremely difficult to get access to social services and thus gets left out. Though there has been immense improvement since Independence, we do not yet have a system in place that is capable of providing equal access to public goods. As a result of liberalization, the state is increasingly transferring its constitutional responsibility of providing public goods to market forces. Hence, the state is failing to build human capability[17] and to ensure dignity of life for every citizen of the country. Since the market operates on the basis of economic power, it excludes the common

17. Jean Drèze and Amartya Sen emphasize human capability and the role of basic education in this regard. They highlight the role of public action in eliminating deprivation and expanding human freedoms in India. See Jean Drèze and Amartya Sen, *India: Economic Development and Social Opportunity* (New Delhi: Oxford University Press, 1995).

people and the marginalized sections that do not have economic power from its benefits. Free market, coupled with the lack of necessary state support in the social sector, has led to huge interpersonal and inter-regional inequalities. These inequalities have caused social instability manifested by increasing protests and farmers' suicides. Globalization as shaped by the new development paradigm has given rise to large-scale human displacement and the consequent disappearance of many communities and cultures, and massive protests.[18] The continuing paradox of India and Bharat—a fast-growing economy supported by a well-developed private sector and yet with persistent mass deprivation and no effective freedom—within the democratic framework in the country has given rise to the question of whether democracy and market are incompatible. While the market excludes common people from its outcome, democracy based on universal adult franchise includes all in economic benefits.

Nevertheless, the inherent exclusionary tendencies of the market can be limited only by the State through providing public goods and services to the marginalized and the excluded sections of the population and regions of the country. This can be done most effectively in India's highly pluralist and participative democracy with a very competitive print and electronic media, since they put pressure on governments to focus on the deprived sections of the society.[19] To foster a more inclusive growth, we need to create new employment opportunities in rural areas, improve the quality of infrastructure (both the so-called 'soft infrastructure'—political and economic policies and institutions; and hard infrastructure—roads, railways and ports) and improve human capabilities by prioritizing health and education.

Keeping these concerns in view, the government decided to introduce the second-generation reforms while continuing the beneficial measures of the first-generation reforms, or the reforms initiated in the early 1990s. The second-generation reforms focus on the predominant issues of contemporary India. These include: (*a*) extending reforms to the states; (*b*) creating infrastructure through public–private partnership; (*c*) reforming the labour market, agriculture, intellectual property rights regime and telecom sector; (*d*) improving governance through legal and political reforms; (*e*) empowering the underprivileged; (*f*) expanding primary education and improving quality of higher education; (*g*) improving human-development sector through intensive engagement with civil-society actors; and (*h*) achieving environmental sustainability. The

18. A brilliant analysis of the adverse impact of the current development strategy on land, water and trees, and on survival and livelihood, can be found in Nivedita Menon and Aditya Nigam, *Power and Contestation: India Since 1989* (London: Zed Books, 2007).
19. The SDSA Report, a result of the CSDS–Lokniti-led research collaboration of academics from India, Bangladesh, Nepal, Pakistan and Sri Lanka, based on simultaneous survey of people's attitudes to democracy, conveys the message that liberal democracy and market economy are compatible as well as complementary. See *State of Democracy in South Asia: A Report* (New Delhi: Oxford University Press, 2008).

aim of these reforms is not only to help turn India into a fast-growing economy, but also a knowledge economy by strengthening the knowledge sector; a strong democracy by building *social capital*; and finally a humane society with the highest levels of sustainable human development. In the light, of this, the government adopted policies such as the national population and health policies, and introduced programmes and missions such as the Mid-Day Meal Scheme, the *Sarva Siksha Abhiyan*, the *Bharat Nirman*, the Employment Guarantee Scheme, the National Rural Health Mission and the Knowledge Commission. This line of thinking is reflected in the Tenth Plan, the Mid-Term Appraisal of the Tenth Plan and the approach paper to the Eleventh Plan. In this light, the Planning Commission has unveiled the futuristic report titled India Vision 2020, which anticipates a resurgent and new India, achieving cent per cent literacy, eradicating unemployment and poverty, attaining a 9 per cent annual growth rate and quadrupling per capita income by 2020. If this can be achieved, India can fulfil that long-awaited promise that Jawaharlal Nehru so eloquently described as our 'tryst with destiny' at Independence.

Suggested Readings

Bardhan, Pranab. *The Political Economy of Development in India*. New Delhi: Oxford University Press, 1984.

Chakravarty, Sukhamoy. *Development Planning: The Indian Experience*. New Delhi: Oxford University Press, 1988.

Drèze, Jean and Amartya Sen, *India: Economic Development and Social Opportunity*. New Delhi: Oxford University Press, 1995.

Frankel, Francine. *India's Political Economy*. New Delhi: Oxford University Press, 2005.

Questions

1. Critically analyse the Nehru–Mahalanobis development strategy.
2. What is the New Economic Policy (NEP)? Discuss the second-generation reforms in the light of the recent Five-Year Plans.
3. Discuss the role of the state in the Indian economy before and after the adoption of the economic reforms.
4. Analyse the major reasons that led the government to adopt planning for the country's economic development after Independence. Discuss the role of planning in the era of liberalization.

Some Important Constituents of Economic Policy

3

Samir Kumar Singh

Reforms in any sector cannot be seen in isolation. There is a huge degree of complementarity among different kinds of reforms. If there is delicensing of the export of a particular item/good but production of that good remains controlled, then the benefit of the reform will be limited. Instead, if the industrial policy deregulates production of goods, then the benefit will be much greater. Similarly, external-sector reforms will reach its potential if sufficient reforms are introduced in the financial, fiscal, industrial and agricultural sectors. Although I will concentrate on the external sector in this section, the implications of reforms in the other sectors must be recognized.

India was not only exposed to free trade from a very early time, but it also maintained its competitive position in world trade. Even during the colonial period, India's competitive strength remained fairly intact. However, it lacked exposure to modern technology with well-organized markets and faced internal price repression and a deluge of non-competitive imports. In the post-Independence period, the problem of transforming an agrarian economy to an industrial one, building domestic capability in crucial sectors and addressing the immediate need and aspirations of people weighed heavily on the economy. The role of the government in economic management, therefore, grew in relative importance. India adopted a process of planning that determined how much to save, where to invest and in what forms to invest. India adopted a mixed-economy strategy with the State and the private sector competing for scarce resources. Self-reliance was the principal objective. **Import substitution** and **export pessimism** were underlying strategies/assumptions. Doubts about the effectiveness of this policy regime arose as early as the mid-1970s. After considerable thinking, a process of reorientation of the policy framework began in the late 1970s and gathered some momentum in the 1980s. The most important changes were related to reducing the domestic barriers to entry and expansion. Larger scope was also provided to enable big business groups to participate in the process of industrialization. Attempts were made to shift from direct physical controls to indirect financial incentives and disincentives. Overall, the 1980s witnessed a gradual and definite deregulation from domestic controls. Trade policy was also liberalized to some extent in the 1980s. For example, there was some liberalization in imports of capital goods in the second half of the 1980s, with emphasis on technological upgradation of the industry. Consequently, the second half of the 1980s witnessed a record growth of industrial production of 8–9 per cent per annum. The acceleration of growth during the 1980s was achieved with distinctly better productivity performance.

However, during the 1980s, the government had started to live beyond its means. Consequently, the fiscal deficit, which had remained moderate until that time, started to rise. The average fiscal deficit of the central government alone was 8.2 per cent of the GDP during 1985–86 to 1989–90. This was mainly due to the growing expenditure on subsidies, interest payments, salaries and defence. As the government borrowed internally and externally to finance the growing fiscal gaps, the economy faced serious structural problems, which posed obstacles to the sustainability of the higher growth that had been set in motion during the 1980s.

In the following section, we start with a discussion on the macroeconomic crisis of 1991 and then move on to reforms in the external sector. In the next section, the basics of fiscal policies, and the fiscal performance of the government since the 1980s are discussed to understand the reforms adopted since 1991. Next, we go on to financial and infrastructure reforms. In the final section, we summarize the discussion to assess the reforms and understand the need for future reforms.

MACROECONOMIC CRISIS

In the early 1990s, the Indian economy suffered from a very acute macroeconomic crisis, the like of which it had never faced. The foreign-currency reserves of the country had tumbled to $1 billion, just enough to pay for two weeks of imports. For the first time in its history, India was faced with the prospect of defaulting on its international payments. The inflation rate climbed to a peak of 17 per cent by August 1991. The ratio of the fiscal deficit of the central government to GDP had almost reached a double-digit level, and the current-account deficit rose to nearly 3 per cent of the GDP.

The Gulf crisis of 1990–91 may have aggravated the problem, but it cannot be regarded as the root cause of the economic crisis in the early 1990s. The crisis drew attention to the deep, structural imbalances in factor- and product-market activities, and also in the fiscal system. This, in a sense, underlined the need for a comprehensive programme of reform. The crisis was met with some decisive policy measures such as the downward adjustment of the rupee, the pledging of a part of the country's gold reserves to avert default of scheduled repayments, import-compression measures, a **tightening of monetary policy** and the timely receipt of exceptional assistance from international, **financial institutions.** A comprehensive stabilization and structural-reform programme to correct the macroeconomic imbalances followed these policy initiatives.

External-Sector Reforms

As Joshi and Little[1] argue forcefully, there were not good reasons for the level of protection that the inefficient manufacturing sector had enjoyed historically. As they also note, the really significant change on the import side was the introduction of a 'negative' list. Any item not on the list could be imported freely except for some bulk items that were still controlled by the government agencies in the mid-1990s.

The first move was the real devaluation of the exchange rate in 1991 and the switch over from a fixed-exchange-rate regime to a market-determined-exchange-rate regime under which the Reserve Bank of India (RBI) was supposed to intervene in times of crisis to maintain stability. With the changé in the exchange-rate regime and accomplishment of trade reforms, the current account is now open along with limited capital-account convertibility. The exchange-rate regime focuses on the management of volatility without a fixed-rate target and the underlying demand and supply conditions determine the exchange-rate movements in an orderly way. Furthermore, India made a gradual move towards convertibility. We have already made the currency convertible on the current account. This implies importers and exporters can acquire foreign currency at the market-determined rate as opposed to the unfavourable government-determined rate that was prevalent in the pre-reform era. On the capital account, the movement has been slow. Capital-account convertibility means allowing foreigners to buy Indian assets and Indians to borrow and invest outside. But due to volatility concerns, movement has remained quite slow on this front. Due to the policy changes regarding Foreign Direct Investment (FDI) and convertibility, the level of foreign-exchange reserves has steadily increased from US$ 5.8 billion as at end-March 1991 to US$ 113.0 billion by end-March 2004 and further to US$ 275.76 billion by end-December 2007.

The trade regime has undergone massive changes with the removal of quantitative restrictions along with rationalization of the tariff structure. India's main success in trade reform has been in the area of tariffs. In 1990–91, the unweighted average tariff was 125 per cent. That figure came down to 71 per cent in 1993–94. The peak tariff rate in 1990 was an unbelievably high 355 per cent. The peak rate in 1993–94 came down to 85 per cent. In 1995, the highest rate of tariff was further reduced to 50 per cent. Today, the average tariff rate is only 18 per cent with the peak rate below 30 per cent. On the export side,

1. Vijay Joshi and I. M. D. Little, *India's Economic Reforms, 1991–2001* (New Delhi: Oxford University Press, 1996) pp. 64–65.

quantitative export restrictions came under attack. The list of restricted items has shrunk as a result. Export-promotion schemes are also being pursued with more than usual vigour. However, many export-promotion schemes still carry large administrative costs and are quite complex in practice.

We define a policy as an export-oriented policy if it increases the profitability of selling in the external market as compared to the domestic market. Thus, increased competition due to delicensing of industries and increased competition from the external sector has resulted in a dip in the profitability of selling in the domestic market. Thus, the policy reforms started since 1991 have largely been export oriented. Therefore, in the broader policy framework, it is an attempt to encourage efficiency of the economy and help the players to do well in this competitive environment.

Countries that are highly integrated in the world economy tend to exhibit a high trade to GDP ratio. In India, this has increased over the years but not at the pace of the more dynamic, developing countries such as China. For example, the ratio of exports to GDP, which was less than 4 per cent during the 1960s and early 1970s, rose to 5 per cent in the 1980s and is now a little over 9 per cent. Exports and imports taken together today stand at about 22 per cent of India's GDP. If international transactions in services are included, the degree of openness of the Indian economy is well over 30 per cent. However, the ratio is one of lowest in the world. At the end of the 1970s, when China opened its economy to the rest of the world, external trade accounted for less than 10 per cent of its GDP. But now, it accounts for about 40 per cent of China's GDP. Another indicator for measuring a country's integration with the rest of the world is through estimation of a country's mean tariff rate. According to the World Bank, the mean tariff rate for all products in India has declined from 80 per cent in 1990 to 30 per cent in 1997. In the case of China, these rates are at about 43 and 18 per cent, respectively. This shows that while the degree of protection for Indian products has come down, it is still high compared to other developing countries.

There is evidence that countries that are integrated faster into the world economy experience not only a rapid export growth but also export diversification. The average-annual-export-volume growth for India during the period 1981–90 was 5.7 per cent. But this rate accelerated to 12 per cent during 1991–95, when there was large-scale trade liberalization. Although India's performance was better, when compared with its own past as well as that of many low-and middle-income countries, its performance did not match that of East Asia, as a whole. For example, average-annual-export-volume growth during the period 1991–95 was 17 per cent in China, about 13 per cent in Korea and Indonesia, and 18 per cent in Thailand.

The performance of our external sector looked quite encouraging before the emergence of the East Asian crisis, but after that, it has remained quite sluggish. If we take a look at the export-growth pattern in the successful countries, we find that they start with resource-intensive commodities; then specialize in labour-intensive commodities; in the third stage, move to scale-intensive commodities; in the fourth stage, to differentiated products that are skill intensive; and, finally, switch to scientific goods. While the East Asian countries have successfully graduated from the second and third stage to the fourth stage, India is still stagnating in the second and third categories. So India's inability to diversify the export basket has been the main reason behind the unsatisfactory performance of the export sector. This can be linked to the reservation policy of small-scale industries and various other institutional bottlenecks, which are obstructing such a transition. Thus, we have a huge potential for better export performance, pushing up growth and fighting poverty.

Fiscal Policy

Capital formation plays an important role in the growth rate of an economy, which needs a continuous boost. In this context, public investment is very important. The Indian economy in general and agriculture in particular have witnessed a decline in the growth rate of public investment. In the agriculture sector, an increase in the private-sector investment more than offset the decline in the public investment. But private investment is no substitute for public investment, and the latter is important for attracting private investment in the sector. In the post-liberalized era, public investment has not been increasing at the desired rate in either agriculture or infrastructure. This affects the potential growth of an economy and this is an explanation for the declining productivity in the agriculture sector during the post-liberalized era. This indicates a great need to accelerate public capital formation in the country. The main obstacle to this is the deteriorating fiscal scenario of the economy and the continuous decline in capital expenditure.

Fiscal policy deals with revenue and expenditure of the government. Some of the major objectives that fiscal policy intends to cater to are—solving redistribution issues, efficiency, macroeconomic objectives, market failure, commercial activities, provision of public goods, capital formation, etc.

Regulation of Resource Allocation. Allocation of resources by the market may not always be desirable. The reason is that the objective of private players and society may differ. So, in order to bring about harmony in their objectives, the government can use fiscal policy. For example, the government has provided subsidy to farmers to adopt the Green Revolution technology and can tax creation of pollution beyond a limit.

Solving Redistribution Issues. Various kinds of fiscal policy options are available with the government to address the problem of inequality. One of the options is transfer payments under which the government runs the poverty-alleviation programme, public distribution system, employment schemes, etc. Progressive taxation and high tax on luxuries are imposed.

Correcting Regional Disparity in Post-liberalized India. In India, private investment is the largest part of the total investment. After 1991, the government has been withdrawing from the commercial sector. So the development of industries is now dependent on the flow of private investment, which, in turn, depends on public investment.

Efficiency. An important aim of a budget is to attain its objective at the minimum cost. This means, if a particular level of revenue is to be generated, it should be done with the minimum possible disturbance in the economy, as there could be a trade off between different objectives. For example, when the government imposes taxes to generate revenue, it affects the prices of commodities in the market and, therefore, our consumption. In order to attain this, such a policy can be adopted where the elasticity of demand is inversely proportional to the rate of taxes—higher the elasticity of demand, lower would be the tax rate.

For example, higher tax should be levied on income and lower tax on food.

Macroeconomic Objectives. This policy includes the objectives of inflation control, growth promotion, employment generation, avoiding business cycle, etc. Expansionary fiscal policy in depression and strict policy in an inflationary economy can be adopted.

Market Failure. According to Amartya Sen[2], the market does two kinds of negative acts, namely, omission and commission. Commission means doing something wrong and omission means not doing something good. In the case of omission, the government needs to take active action in the area, for example, primary education and health facility in villages.

Capital Formation. A direct way of capital formation is borrowing to invest capital. An indirect way of capital formation has been deficit financing. This leads to increase in the price level due to which purchasing power of the society declines and the government gets larger resources.

Commercial Activities and Public Goods. The government invests in industries and commercial services like railways. Public goods are those that have the characteristics of non-rival consumption and non-exclusion. Here private provision is sub-optimal. So the governments take the task of production of the public goods.

2. Jean Drèze and Amartya Sen, *India: Economic Development and Social Opportunity* (New Delhi: Oxford University Press, 1995).

Government Budget. Before we get into a policy discussion, it is important to understand the classification of the government's budget and the related terms and concepts. The budget is divided into receipts and expenditures of the government. Receipts are further divided into revenue receipt and capital receipts and expenditure into revenue expenditure and capital expenditure (see Figure 3.1).

Figure 3.1: Government Budget

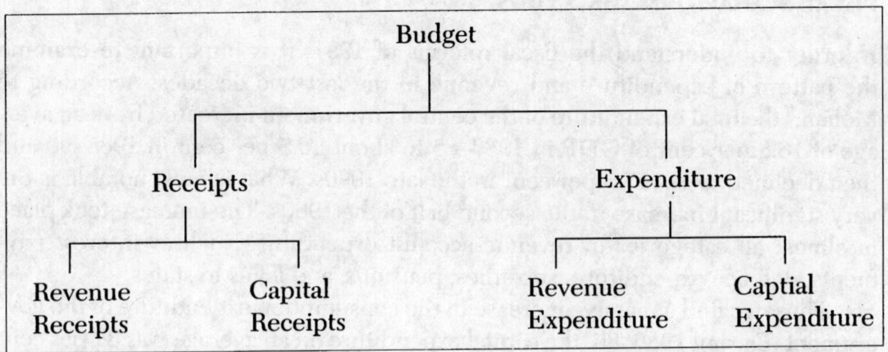

Revenue receipts include tax and non-tax revenues; and capital receipts primarily include borrowings of the government, receipts from disinvestments, and interest on loan given by the government. On the expenditure side, revenue expenditure includes the day-to-day cost of running the government. This includes interest payments, subsidy, defence expenditure, grant to states, etc. Revenue account expenditure is close to consumption expenditure and is committed in nature. This is to say one does not expect a direct return from such expenditure and, at the same time, it is very difficult to reduce such expenditure in a short span of time. The capital expenditure includes all those expenditures that add to the nation's productive capacity like infrastructure development. Thus, broadly, we can say it is a productive expenditure, while revenue account expenditure is an unproductive expenditure.

Fiscal deficit is defined as excess of total expenditure over receipts of government except borrowings. Thus, it is the amount of borrowing by the government to meet its expenditure.

- Fiscal Deficit = Total expenditure – Receipts except borrowings
- Primary Deficit = Fiscal deficit – Interest payment
- Revenue Deficit = Revenue expenditure – Revenue receipts

Primary deficit is an indicator of the fiscal behaviour of the current government as the deducted interest payment is a result of the borrowings done by the past government. The revenue account indicates the government's capacity to meet its day-to-day expenditure. Deficit implies that the government is not only entirely borrowing for the capital formation, but a part of it is also being used for current consumptions. There is nothing wrong as such with borrowing if it is utilized for larger income generation such that it is comfortably repaid. But if there is a large and sustained revenue-account deficit, it means interest obligation of the government is continuously increasing and it is becoming difficult to generate resources for developmental purposes.

Fiscal Scenario in the 1980s

In order to understand the fiscal reforms of 1991, it is important to examine the pattern of expenditure and revenue in the last two decades. According to Mohan,[3] the total expenditure of the central government increased from an average of 16.8 per cent of GDP in 1980–85 to about 20.5 per cent in 1985–90 and then declined to 16–17.5 per cent in the late 1990s. What is most notable is the very significant increase in the second half of the 1980s. The increase took place in almost all categories of revenue-account expenditure such as interest payments, defence expenditure, subsidies, pensions, and loans to states.

Thus, we find a massive increase in the consumption expenditure of the government. During 1980–85, the capital expenditure on an average was 37 per cent of the total expenditure and, by 1990, it declined to barely 17 per cent. This implies that the interest obligation of the government was bound to increase. Interest payment, which was 2.2 per cent of GDP in 1980, increased to 3.8 per cent in 1990–91. Interest payment for long has been the largest component of government expenditure. Thus, the fiscal policy in the 1980s was not sustainable and ultimately, this turned out to be an important reason for the 1991 crisis.

There are serious dangers of excessive fiscal deficits. Joshi[4] has talked about the dangers of sustainability, crowding out and flexibility of policy. A new cost that has emerged in the post-liberalization era is in terms of the capacity to control regional disparity.

Sustainability: Fiscal deficits can be financed by printing money or by borrowing from domestic and foreign sources. If carried out excessively, this can lead to a crisis. If primary deficits remain high, then it might lead a country to the debt trap. In other words, this means increasing the debt: GDP ratio leading to borrowing in order to pay the interest.

Crowds out private investment: If fiscal deficit remains high, it reflects huge expenditure from the government side. This reduces the supply of financial resources to private players and, in turn, leads to a high interest rate that implies lower investment in the private sector. In the Indian case, expenditure on infrastructure encourages private investment by increasing its profitability. So, if government expenditure is largely unproductive (revenue account), then

3. Rakesh Mohan, *Indian Economy Since Independence*, ed. by Uma Kapila (New Delhi: Academic Foundation, 2003).
4. Joshi and Little, *India's Economic Reforms*.

there will be larger displacement of private investment. Since private investment is more productive than public expenditure, rising fiscal deficit may imply reduction in overall productivity of investment and, consequently, slower growth rate of economy.

Reduces flexibility of policy: High fiscal deficit means lower financial resources in the government's hand. It, therefore, reduces the government's ability to respond to external shocks like droughts, and oil-price rise. Furthermore, as the share of revenue-account expenditure in total expenditure increases, the government capacity to invest in capital infrastructure and social sector declines. This not only constrains growth prospects in the long run, but also compromises development of the social sector. Since this deficit cannot go on forever, in a bid to control it, the government may have to resort to higher tax rates, which discourages private investment.

Special significance of fiscal health in the post-reform era: Since 1991, there has been a fundamental change in the role of the government. The government started to pull itself away from commercial activities and was expected to play the role of a facilitator rather than provider. This change in policy has made private investment the prime source of growth of different states. Since private investment is mobile and moves in the pursuit of profit, it will move to those regions where profitability is higher. This is why the 1990s witnessed an increasing regional disparity. The argument goes like this:

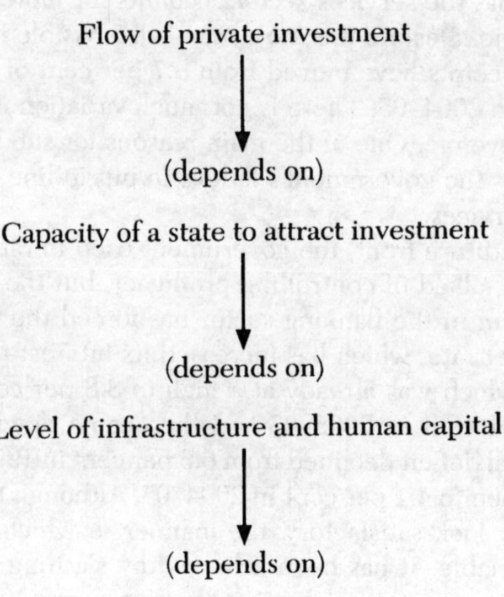

The flow of private investment is the major determinant of the growth rate of any state. It is, therefore, dependent on the state's capacity to attract it and this, in turn, depends on human capital and infrastructure, which is dependent on investment made by the central and state governments. Thus, if the government does not play an active role to address the problems of insufficient and unequal infrastructure, the disparity witnessed in the 1990s will get accentuated further. The widening gap between developed and backward states can encourage resentment and can be a big threat to further reforms. Now, the government can take up this task, if it manages to control its deficit. Since the government has to play a very active role as a facilitator, it should try to control unproductive expenditure and bring about an acceleration in collections.

The 1991 crisis and response to it: The high unsustainable fiscal policy, inefficiency of public-sector enterprises, poor management of the external sector etc., had led to the crisis of 1991. The immediate task ahead was to stabilize the economy and then do away with the structural weaknesses of the economy that made it vulnerable to external shocks. There have been policy changes aimed at raising revenues, on the one hand, and controlling expenditure, on the other.

During the initial years of reform, the government tried to restructure direct taxes. The government, in fact, reduced direct taxes to promote the growth of the economy. Direct taxes are already high in the Indian case, so the main source of tax revenue is indirect taxes and expansion of the tax base. In order to expand the base, the government has been increasing the number of services within the tax net in a phased manner. This has become very important in the light of the fact that the services sector accounts for more than 50 per cent of the national income. Despite this, no dynamism is visible in tax or non-tax revenue. Revenue receipts have moved from 9.7 per cent of GDP in 1990–91 to just 9.8 per cent in 2004–05. There is not much variation in the relative role of tax and non-tax revenue. One of the main reasons for subdued performance in non-tax revenue is the government's failure to put in line proper user charges for commercial services.

On the expenditure front, the government tried to rationalize the number of employees and talked of controlling profligacy, but the situation is far from satisfactory. Reform in the banking sector has forced the government acquire loans at the market rate, which has increased its interest-payment burden. Interest payment, which was already at a high of 3.8 per cent in 1990, reached its peak of 4.8 per cent in 2002–03 and then came down to 4.1 per cent in 2004–05. The fiscal deficit declined from 6.6 per cent in 1990–91 to 5.6 per cent in 2000–01 and then to 4.1 per cent in 2004–05. Although the movement of the deficit figure may look satisfactory, the manner in which this has been done is highly objectionable. It has been achieved by slashing the capital expenditure rather than reducing unproductive revenue-account expenditure. Capital expenditure, which was 4.4 per cent of the GDP, declined to 2.3 per cent in 2000–01. During the post-reform era, the capital expenditure of the government has significantly come down. This has continuously been lower than the interest payment. One could, thus, conclude that the situation has not substantially improved. As we talked earlier, the government is supposed to play a very active role in the various spheres of economy, but due to the poor fiscal scenario, its ability is significantly constrained.

THE FINANCIAL SECTOR

In the post-reform era, India has witnessed significant policy changes towards the financial sector. As we know, before 1991, there was primacy to centralized planning, which made it important for the state to generate resources in order to fund the developmental functions. The financial policy before 1991 was heavily based on this understanding of generating resources and that is why the government kept the banking sector in its control and kept the interest rate low for its borrowing. In the post-reform era, the role of the government changed significantly. The State was supposed to be a facilitator rather than the controller. This made it imperative to bring abut changes in the financial policy.

Since the genesis of reform, the ownership pattern of the banking sector has changed. In 1993, the RBI issued guidelines for setting up of the private-sector banks. Legislative changes were made in 1994 to enable public-sector banks to raise capital funds for the market by public issue share. Financial reforms can be reviewed under three major heads:

- Banking-sector reforms
- Stock market reforms
- Financial institutions reforms

Banking-Sector Reforms. There have been significant reforms in the banking sector in the post-liberalization era. The major policy reforms include dismantling of administered interest rate, major reduction in reserve requirements of Statutory Liquidity Ratio (SLR) and Cash Reserve Ratio (CRR), abolition of firm-specific credit controls, permission to private players in the banking sector including foreign participation and improving the supervision of the banking operation, etc. In order to understand the significance and implications of these policy changes, we need to look at the banking sector during the pre-reform era.

Ownership pattern: The banking sector in the pre-reform era was entirely under the control of the public sector. The government started with the nationalization of all the major banks in 1969. Due to the multiplicity of goals, political interference, lack of free management, accountability and incentive structure, and inherent inefficiency of the public-sector banks (PSBs), this sector became highly inefficient. It took very little changes and innovation in the banking sector to meet the changing requirements and challenges. Thus, it contributed significantly in converting India into a high-cost economy. Since the genesis of reforms, the ownership pattern of the banking sector has changed. In 1993, the RBI issued guidelines for setting up of the private-sector banks. Legislative changes were made in 1994 to enable public-sector banks to raise capital funds for the market by public issue of shares. Even now, the share of private sector in total deposits to the bank is merely 20 per cent, and 80 per cent with the PSB banks. The sector needs much more reforms to become vibrant.

Administered interest rate and credit control: During the pre-reform era, an administered interest policy was followed. This implies rate of interests were not decided by demand and supply conditions in the market but by the government. The government controlled the flow of financial resources using direct control over credit and maintaining high interest rates for the private sector. In order to encourage household savings and fulfil welfare objectives, interest rates on deposits were also kept high. At the same time, it borrowed from the banks at a low interest rate. The basic macroeconomics tells higher interest rate for loans discourage private investment. Furthermore, the government took away a significant proportion of the financial resources keeping a relatively lower amount for the private sector, that too with various kinds of control on distribution of credit.

The Reserve Bank undertook several measures to facilitate the deregulation and flexibility in interest rates. First, the Reserve Bank allowed banks the freedom to prescribe different Prime Lending Rates (PLRs) for different maturities. Banks were accorded the freedom to charge interest rates without reference to the PLR in case of certain specified loans. The RBI also allowed various kinds of financial operations like hedging products, mutual funds, etc.

Quantitative vs market-based tools: Banks are needed to keep a part of their liabilities with the RBI in the form of CRR. Furthermore, banks are required to keep a part of their liabilities in the form of cash, gold or government securities, which is called SLR. These norms are needed to safeguard the interests of the consumers. These were deliberately kept high to garner resources for carrying out huge government expenditure. But this left banks with lower resources for commercial lending. Further, lower supply of commercial lending increased the interest rates for the private sector. Thus, on the one hand, the policy restricted the capacity of banks to generate surpluses, and on the other, it killed incentives for private investments.

During the 1990s, the orientation of the banking policy was overhauled. Rather than using quantitative tools, they relied on the market-based tools. This decade witnessed significant reductions in the CRR and SLR requirements. There was a greater reliance on the open-market operations to control money supply in the economy. Open-market operation means that the government sells bonds to mop up excess supply in the economy and purchases bonds whenever it wants to increase the money supply. Due to these factors, banks' resources for commercial use increased. This increased the potential for profit generation by the banking sector, and the reduction in lending rates encouraged private investments.

Prudential norms: The Reserve Bank of India persevered with the on-going process of strengthening prudential accounting norms with the objective of improving the financial soundness of banks and to bring them at par with international standards. The Reserve Bank advised PSBs to set up Settlement Advisory Committees (SACs) for timely and speedier settlement of non-performing assets in the small-scale sector and the agricultural sector. The guidelines on SACs were aimed at reducing the stock of NPAs by encouraging the banks to go in for compromise settlements in a transparent manner. Recognizing that the high level of NPAs in the PSBs can endanger the financial-system stability, the government set up debt-recovery tribunals for speedy recovery of bad loans. An amendment in the Recovery of Debts Due to Banks and Financial Institutions Act, 1993 was effected to expedite the recovery process.

Stock-Market Reforms. The last two decades have seen the rapid development of the stock market due to deregulation and reforms. In 1980, the total market capitalization of the Indian stock markets was only 5 per cent of GDP. This increased to 13 per cent by 1990 and has already crossed 100 per cent of GDP. During the 1990s, the government phased out its control over new share issues and permitted recognized foreign-institutional investors to directly buy shares in India. Indian firms have also been allowed to raise funds abroad.

The significance of the stock market is also increasing for small investors. Earlier, deregulations have seen some scandals in the stock market, which eroded the confidence of small investors. But improved supervision and change in trading mechanisms have restored confidence in the system. The 1990s have seen the emergence of a large number of financial products, like different types of mutual funds, which meet the requirement of small investors.

Financial-Institution Reforms. In the post-liberalization era, the deregulation of the financial sector started. This made it mandatory to increase supervision of the sector. For example, it become important to ensure that banks with short-run funds do not significantly invest in long-term projects, go in for speculative investment or pose a threat to the stability of the economy. There has been a massive and active transformation in the supervisory role of the RBI. To regulate and promote the stock market, the Securities and Exchange Board of India (SEBI) had been empowered, and similarly, for the healthy development of the insurance market, the Insurance Regulatory and Development Authority (IRDA) has been set up. With the passing of the Insurance Regulatory and Development Authority (IRDA) Act, 1999, banks and Non-Banking Financial Companies (NBFCs) have been permitted to enter the insurance business. The Reserve Bank has issued guidelines in this regard. This was felt necessary in view of the fact that the insurance business does not break-even during the initial years of operation, and that the banks and NBFCs do not have adequate technical expertise in undertaking the insurance business.

Thus, the financial-sector reforms focused on improvement in prudential norms and standards, interest-rate liberalization, strengthening supervision, and increased competition in the banking sector. Banks have managed to control their non-performing assets and have met the prudential norms set by the RBI. India has made substantial progress towards improving the performance of the financial system and putting in place a new financial system with greater autonomy, transparency and accountability. But there is no room for complacency. The operational costs for the public-sector banks are still very high. There is scope for improving efficiency, bringing innovations and introducing new technology and, thus, cutting the transaction cost of the entire economy. Future reforms need to concentrate on these issues and encourage private participation with proper supervision mechanism.

Infrastructure Reforms

Sustained growth and development require a sustained and appropriate investment in the infrastructure sector. Better provision of infrastructure reduces transaction costs in the economy. This reduction could be in terms of financial resources, time or uncertainty. One of the characteristics of infrastructure is that it needs to be provided before it is needed. It, therefore, becomes important to understand the need and provide it in advance. Infrastructure investment in India is highly dominated by the public sector. Earlier, private participation was not allowed in the infrastructure sector. Even when it was opened to the private sector, investments came into a few segments only. Though the government has provided incentives in various sectors, only limited success has been registered due to many institutional problems. We will discuss briefly about two major sectors that have been opened to the private sector. These are the telecommunications sector and the power sector. Before we get into this, it is important to note that most of infrastructure sectors are natural monopolies. So just allowing private players can lead to exploitation of the consumer. In order to make the market function properly for the natural monopolies, it is very important that proper regulation is imposed to protect the interests of both consumers and producers.

The telecom sector is a successful story of India's economic reforms. Though the reform process has been generating debates on the manner in which these were being carried out and private players remained unhappy at various kinds of reforms, the telecom sector underwent a revolution in the Indian-growth story. 'The rate of growth of GDP from telecom accelerated from an average of 6.3 per cent per annum during 1980–81 to 1991–92 to 18 per cent per annum during 1992–3 to 2002–3. This was the fastest rate of growth among all sectors. In contrast to telecom, the electricity sector reforms have been the most unsuccessful so far.'[5]

5. Arvind Virmani, 'Economic Reforms: Policy and Institutions—Some Lessons from Indian Reforms', Working Paper No. 121, Indian Council for Research on International Economic Relations, January 2004.

Despite some trouble, the government managed to create a viable and competitive environment for the telecom players. In this sector, the profitability of the service providers has not been ignored. The story of the electricity sector was not encouraging. The first problem was that the pace of reforms in this sector has been very slow. Private investment in transmission was not allowed till 1998–99 and in distribution, was allowed only in 2003. Furthermore, electricity is a state subject, that is, not a central government subject. The regulatory framework for this sector has been very weak. It was not just a failure of the policy, but of the institutional set up also. The main problem imposed by the institution is lack of proper unbundling of the generation, transmission and distribution. The success with private participation heavily depends on the capability of the regulatory agency.

One of the salient features of the post-reform era is the rising share of private investment in the infrastructure sector. Apart from the above-mentioned two sectors, private participation has been encouraged in the construction of national highways. Some of the services in the railways have been given to the private players. Even in the aviation industry, the private sector has been permitted and they have started playing a very significant role. The major reforms in roadways were the imposition of a fuel cess to finance highway construction and the commissioning of the National Highway Development Project (Prime Minister's *Gram Sadak Yojana*). In the case of ports, private operators have been introduced and then the Tariff Authority of Major Ports was formed; in the civil-aviation sectors, new private airlines, new private airports and the beginning of an open skies policy are in evidence. The success of such a reform process, where the private sector is being encouraged, is largely going to depend upon the regulatory framework provided. So, the most important task that has to be taken up very seriously is the creation of different regulatory agencies, which are efficient, dynamic, accountable and professional.

CONCLUSION

There have been significant reforms in the post-1991 era and there has been some positive impact also. But the situation is far from satisfactory. In terms of Amartya Sen, a policy should be judged on the basis of its contribution to capability expansion. Here capability expansion means improving the human capital. But this is one area, which has been ignored in the successive plans and even in the post-reforms era. There is an urgent need that the government should release funds fast for the social sector. This is important not just for improving human development indicator, but also because the modern growth theory identifies the development of human capital as the driving force of the economy. Now we come to industrial-, trade-, fiscal- and financial-policy reforms. These reforms have been good but not sufficient. It needs to be realized that the benefit of reforms already taken up strongly depends on the amount and pace of future reforms. So there is a need to push up these reforms. The most important agenda of reform could be agricultural-sector reforms, power-sector and infrastructure reforms, tax reforms, reconsideration of reservation policy to small-scale industry and further simplification of the bureaucratic process. Apart from economic reforms, large reforms in the legal system and governance are also needed. These reforms are not easy to come by as many of them are state subjects and are going to be fought fiercely by the vested interests. But if we want to achieve something big, then it requires big and fundamental changes in the policy; and the reforms process should not be confined only to the economic sector, but should look beyond it.

Suggested Readings

Basu, Kaushik (ed.). *India's Emerging Economy: Performance and Prospects in the 1990s and Beyond*. New Delhi: Oxford University Press, 2005.

Drèze, Jean and Amartya Sen. *India: Economic Development and Social Opportunity*. New Delhi: Oxford University Press, 1995.

Ahluwalia, I. J. *India's Economic Reform: Essays for Manmohan Singh*. New Delhi: Oxford University Press 2005.

Krueger, Anne O. *Economic Policy Reforms and the Indian Economy*. Chicago: University of Chicago Press, 2002.

Srinivasan, T. N. and Suresh D. Tendulkar. *Reintegrating India with the World Economy*. Washington, DC: Peterson Institute, 2003.

Questions

1. Briefly explain the fiscal scenario of the 1980s. In the light of this, critically examine the post-1991 fiscal reforms.
2. Comment on the financial-sector reforms of the post-1991 era. What are the major changes in the orientation of these financial policies?
3. What are the reasons for the macroeconomic crisis of 1991? Elaborate the policy responses to the crisis.
4. Reforms were primarily targeted at the industrial, trade and financial sectors but ignored the social and agriculture sector. Do you agree with the statement? In light of this statement, assess the performance of reforms.

Regional Disparities, Poverty and Food Insecurity

4

Satyajit Puhan

What is the face of contemporary India? Is it that of the bright and shining India with its rapidly growing economy, great advancement in science and technology, an ever-expanding and upwardly mobile middle class, the sprawling city and the malls? Or, is it that of an India marked by poverty and insecurity, with millions untouched by the benefits of economic growth, without access to education and healthcare, deprived of basic needs and struggling to survive? Or may be beyond this rhetoric of poverty or progress, these sharply contrasting images do not cancel each other but coexist in the face of contemporary India.

As dealt in previous chapters, since the beginning of the 1990s, the Indian government has undertaken major macroeconomic reforms and moved towards a greater integration of the Indian economy with the global market. It is a fact that India has moved onto a higher economic growth trajectory in the last two decades in comparison to the pre-reforms period. And at an average of 7 per cent GDP growth rate annually (the present projections are even higher), India would be doubling its national income approximately every 10 years. A rapidly growing economy has led to hopes of India finally actualizing its potential as an economic superpower. What does this unprecedented growth in national income mean for the lives of the poor in India?

Does it mean that with the rising per capita income, the poor will no longer remain poor? Does it mean that there will be less hunger and destitution, less children dying because of lack of immunization or basic health care? Does it mean more employment and better wages for the landless, casual labourers in rural areas, greater access to educational opportunities, general improvement in the living conditions, more social equality and freedom of opportunity?

The Indian State periodically comes up with estimates of the level of poverty in India. The numbers suggest that poverty has been rapidly declining but still remains high with every fourth Indian still being poor in 2004–05. What does it mean? Does it mean an acknowledgement that a large section of India is still poor, but at the same time a claim that India is definitely on its way to eliminate poverty? A lot depends on what we understand by 'poverty'.

The persistence of extensive poverty in times of general prosperity raises the other troublesome question confronting democratic societies: how to ensure equality of opportunity in the face of the rising socio-economic inequality? The deprivations that characterize the lives of the poor put them at a disadvantage in terms of their capability to actualize the opportunities presented by economic growth. This means that in the absence of political and social action mediating the process of economic growth, poverty tends to reproduce itself and results in rising socio-economic inequality.

The essay begins by discussing varying notions of poverty. It distinguishes between 'poverty' as defined by the concept of the frequently referred poverty line and the much broader notion of 'poverty' as human-capability deprivation. The debate on 'poverty' in India must not be limited to lack of income or purchasing power but must include a wide array of living standard and social indicators bearing on human-capability deprivation. This essay argues that the persistence of these deprivations could be significant in determining how equitably the opportunities of economic growth are shared and what happens to socio-economic inequality in the future. It ends by appraising how contemporary India is positioned in terms of poverty and the related phenomena of food insecurity and unemployment.

The essay goes on to discuss the response of the State to poverty. It follows the shifts and changes in the orientation of the Five-Year Plans towards poverty alleviation in India. The limitations of the State policy are discussed to understand why it has remained ad hoc and narrow in focus with regard to poverty in the country.

The last section of the essay discusses the rising regional disparities and the changing perceptions of the State in the post-reforms period. It argues that this is only one aspect of the broader pattern of increasing economic inequality in this period. The essay ends by enquiring into the implications of these developments in the light of social conflicts in contemporary India.

THE NOTION OF 'ABSOLUTE POVERTY' AND MAKING OF THE 'POVERTY LINE'

Economic poverty is generally understood as the lack of means for providing material needs or comforts. Since income or wealth (representing purchasing power) is often seen as the most common means of obtaining such needs, 'poverty' is generally associated with a lack of income or wealth. When income or wealth in a society is unequally distributed, some people have more means at their command than others. The lowest segment of the population having lesser means is considered poor in comparison to the upper segments. This is poverty in a relative sense.

Among the relatively poor are those whose extreme lack of means result in deprivations that not only severely affect their well-being, but threatens their very survival. In this case, poverty is characterized by deprivation of the most basic of needs like adequate food, shelter, clothing, access to health care. Anyone suffering from such extreme deprivations is considered poor in the absolute sense. Absolute poverty also reflects what is socially considered a minimum level of resources that should be the right of every member. This threshold of minimum, socially acceptable living condition is often quantified as a minimum income level or poverty line and the absolute poor are considered to be those who live Below the Poverty Line (BPL). One of the most widely used measures of poverty has been the headcount ratio, which is nothing but the proportion of population living on a per capita income lower than the given poverty line.

The nature of absolute poverty makes it socially, morally and politically difficult to accept or overlook. The reduction of absolute poverty has been a major concern world over. The high priority attached to the task is understandable given the urgency of survival and abject suffering associated with starvation, malnutrition and vulnerability to diseases. In 2000, the United Nations adopted the millennium development goals (MDGs) as a roadmap for building a better world in the 21st century. The first of the eight goals set by the governments of the world is the eradication of extreme poverty and hunger.[1] In terms of poverty, the target is to reduce by half, between 1990 and 2015, the proportion of population living below the poverty line given by the per capita income of US $1 per day, which is one of the poverty lines used internationally.[2]

Officially Speaking, Who Is Poor?

The Indian government uses an official poverty line in terms of per capita income but calibrated to suffice for the cost of a minimum consumption basket. In 1979, the Planning Commission of India adopted a poverty line that has become common reference for poverty in India. The concept of poverty line in India is primarily based on a minimum-calorie norm or the amount of food deemed necessary for the healthy and active functioning of a human being. Using the help of nutrition experts, this calorie norm has been fixed as per capita daily calorie requirement of 2,400 kcal in rural areas and 2,100 kcal in urban areas.[3]

1. The 8 MDGs break down into 18 quantifiable targets that are measured by 48 indicators. The targets are set for the year 2015 with 1990 being the benchmark year for comparison. For the complete list of MDGs along with the list of indicators see http://www.un.org/millenniumgoals/ (last accessed on 19 May 2008).
2. The dollar value is adjusted for Purchasing Power Parity (PPP) across the countries.
3. The centrality given to food is obvious considering its primary significance for the survival of life. The differentiated per capita calorie norms for rural and urban areas is based on the perceived difference in calorie needs of rural and urban population and their respective living conditions.

The poverty line is quantified as the cost of an average consumption basket that satisfies the above calorie requirement. In other words, the per capita income that is necessary to buy the rudimentary food basket satisfying the minimum calorie norm is the poverty line dividing the poor from the non-poor in India.[4]

The concepts of 'poverty line' and 'headcount ratio' have been central to State planning towards poverty eradication in India. At the same time, both these concepts have generated considerable controversy. For instance, it has been argued that the definition of a realistic poverty line must also include the cost of provision of other basic needs apart from food.[5] Although food is one of the most fundamental human needs and is critical for survival, it is not the only component of well-being. Well-being is also dependent on many other basic material needs as significant as food such as shelter and sanitation, drinking water, medicine and health care.

The Puzzle of the 'Head Count'

The estimation of the 'headcount ratio' has been another major contentious issue. Varying methodologies and assumptions have led to varying estimates adding to the confusion. It is enough to say that there exist two official estimates of 'headcount poverty ratio' in India. The official figures for poverty in 1999–2000 indicated that 26 per cent of the population lived below the poverty line. It was hailed as a rapid decline from the official estimate of 36 per cent in 1993–94. The strict comparability of the two figures was questioned on methodological grounds by experts and many found the 1999–2000 official figures grossly underestimating the numbers of the poor.[6] The preliminary official estimates for 2004–05 show almost 28 per cent of the population living below the poverty line.[7] According to the Planning Commission, this data is fully comparable to the 1993–94 estimates but not to the 1999–2000 estimates. It simply means that the

4. It was found to be approximately Rs 49 and Rs 56 per capita per month for rural and urban areas respectively at 1973–74 prices. These figures are periodically revised and adjusted for price differentials over time and across the states. In December 2005, these figures were approximately Rs 368 per person and Rs 559 per person for rural and urban areas, respectively.
5. Mohan Guruswamy and Ronald Joseph Abraham, 'Myth of the Poverty Line', in *Redefining Poverty: A New Poverty Line for a New India* (New Delhi: Centre for Policy Alternatives, 1 April 2006). The article even argues for a revision of the minimum food basket because it only satisfies the basic calorie norm instead of meeting the requirements of a nutritious diet.
6. Angus Deaton and Jean Drèze, 'Poverty and Inequality in India: A Re-examination', *Economic and Political Weekly*, 7 September 2002: 2479–85.
7. This is the current official estimate of poverty in India based on the National Sample Survey 2004–05 results. Planning Commission, *Towards Faster and More Inclusive Growth: An Approach to the Eleventh Five-Year Plan* (New Delhi: Government of India, 2006).

Table 4.1 Official Estimates of Poverty in India*

	1977–78	*1983*	*1987–88*	*1993–94*	*1999–2000*	*2004–05*
Rural	53.07	45.65	39.09	37.27	26.8	—
Urban	45.24	40.79	38.2	32.36	24.1	—
Total	51.32	44.48	38.86	36.0	26.1	28

*Proportion of population living below the poverty line in India (%)

Source: Government of India, *Economic Survey* (various years). The estimates are based on per capita expenditure distribution data collected by National Sample Surveys and the Planning Commission on the all-India poverty line.

higher headcount ratio given by the current estimate in comparison to 1999–2000 estimates should not be misconstrued as an increase in poverty during this period (see Table 4.1 for official estimates of poverty in India).

The varying headcount estimates have been used for contradictory claims on the purported rate of decline of poverty in India in the 1990s.[8] The debate has mostly centred on the issue of the correct estimation of poverty in India with reference to the 'poverty line'. It is not clear whether the decline has been faster or slower in the 1990s in comparison to the earlier decade because of the incomparability of estimates. But there is evidence to suggest that as far as the 'headcount ratio' is concerned, poverty level in India has been consistently declining. If one takes the comparable official estimates of headcount ratio between 1993–94 and 2004–05, the figures show a decline from 36 per cent to nearly 28 per cent. India may yet achieve the target set by millennium development goals (MDGs), though the current estimates are not as reassuring as the 1999–2000 estimates were. But while acknowledging the fact that meeting the MDG target would be a significant achievement, one must also keep in mind the narrow definition of poverty that the 'headcount ratio' uses.

So what does it mean when the Planning Commission of India states that the headcount–poverty ratio was almost 28 per cent in 2004–05? It means that almost 28 per cent of the Indian population was found to subsist below the per capita income specified by the poverty line or the minimum-calorie norm; it does not say how low the income was of those below the poverty line or how acute their hunger was. The figure also means that according to the Government of India, every fourth Indian lived in absolute poverty in 2004–05; but since this absolute poverty is pegged to a bare subsistence level defined by the

8. Deaton and Drèze, 'Poverty and Inequality in India'.

'poverty line', it does not say how many of those who stayed above the line also managed to escape destitution.[9]

Poverty Beyond the 'Poverty Line'

The 'poverty line' is quite unsatisfactory when it comes to grasping the extent of poverty in India. It is not only because of its extremely narrow definition of 'who is poor' and the debatable methodology used to count the poor but also because of a more fundamental assumption underlying it. As stated earlier, it exclusively relies on the notion of poverty as insufficient income or purchasing power. One can better categorize it by calling it income poverty. If poverty is ultimately about deprivations affecting human well-being, then income poverty is only one aspect of it. Income is no doubt a vital means to the attainment of individual well-being, but it is not adequate to ensure against many other kinds of deprivation. For example, illness due to communicable diseases can seriously affect the well-being of a person in various ways ranging from depriving her of a healthy life to curtailing her income-earning abilities. It is a well-known fact that outbreak of many of the communicable diseases can be effectively prevented by the provision of safe drinking water, public sanitation and health services. Ensuring against communicable diseases and the resultant deprivations to well-being then depends on many factors like access to safe drinking water, public sanitation and health services, and social-insurance systems apart from private income. A strictly income-based approach to poverty often fails to reflect pervasive deprivations relating to many of the basic needs when the satisfaction of the need is also dependent on social provision of goods and services and not just private income and the market.[10]

It is also limiting to think of poverty essentially in terms of material deprivations relating to basic needs. One must also take into consideration sociological deprivations rooted in underlying structural inequities and inherent disadvantages. Even when resources are available, people may not be able to take full advantage of them because of pre-existing disadvantages ranging from social constraints like caste and gender to personal impediments like old age and physical disabilities. Income-based approach to poverty is again found severely wanting in taking into account these other kinds of deprivations.

9. Using a more 'realistic and holistic' poverty line by taking into account the non-food basic needs as well as an improved dietary norm, one estimate of poverty in India comes to nearly 69 per cent of the total population and nearly 85 per cent of the rural population for the given period. See Guruswamy and Abraham, 'Myth of the Poverty Line'.
10. These goods and services carry significant externalities and are often categorized as 'public goods and services' in economic literature. The rationale for the public provision of such goods and services stems from the social value attached to them and the failure of the market to adequately provide them.

Poverty as Capability Deprivation and Lack of Social Opportunity

A broader understanding of poverty needs to look beyond the income approach. One of the most influential concepts in this regard has been the notion of *human capability*. Jean Drèze and Amartya Sen write:

> Poverty of a life, in this view, lies not merely in the impoverished state in which the person actually lives, but also in the lack of real opportunity—given by social constraints as well as personal circumstances—to choose other types of living. Even the relevance of low incomes, meagre possessions, and other aspects of what are standardly seen as economic poverty relates ultimately to their role in curtailing capabilities (that is, their role in severely restricting the choices people have to lead valuable and valued lives).[11]

The freedom of opportunity available to people is influenced by their personal circumstances as well as social situations. The personal circumstances that significantly matter are not just access to 'means' like income or wealth but also the access to basic needs and amenities, like food, clothing, shelter, education and health services, safe drinking water and sanitation to list a few. Along with these material means of well-being, it is the actual states of well-being or 'outcomes' achieved by the person, like nutritional status, educational and health achievements that also impact upon the real opportunities available.

Personal circumstances are found to be embedded in social situations. Social, political and economic relations and inequalities determine how resources are distributed and what choices are available to different sections of the society. Some of the most visible examples of these are based on caste, class and gender disparities that constrain the real opportunities available to people.

Deprivations in the form of access to basic needs, actual states of well-being and social inequalities have a great role to play in the creation of economic poverty. On the other hand, economic poverty often reinforces these deprivations. And the circle is difficult to break—a unidimensional approach to poverty as essentially income poverty overlooks the other dimensions of deprivation that make inequality of opportunity persist and poverty replicate itself.

The major dimensions of poverty that persist in India relate to deprivations in nutritional, educational and health achievements, access to basic needs and amenities, quality of physical environment and various social inequalities like caste and gender disparities. In this context, some of the other targets given in the millennium development goals (MDGs), besides reduction in head-count ratio, give a sense of the challenge facing contemporary India in terms of poverty (see Table 4.2).

11. Jean Drèze and Amartya Sen, *India: Economic Development and Social Opportunity* (New Delhi: Oxford University Press, 1995), p. 11.

Table 4.2 India's Progress Towards Some Selected MDG Targets

Indicators	*Year*	*Value*	*Year*	*Value*	*MDG Target (2015)*
Proportion of population below the poverty line (as % of total population) (US $1 PPP per day)	1991	42	2003	35	21
Proportion of population below the line National Poverty Line (as % of total population)	1990–91	35.6	2004–05	28	17.8
Proportion of undernourished people (as % of total population)	1990–92	25	2001–03	20	12.5
Proportion of undernourished children under three years (%)	1990	54.8	1998	47	27.4
Ratio of girls to boys in primary education	1990	0.71	2000	0.77	1
Ratio of girls to boys in secondary education	1990	0.64	2001	0.68	1
Under-five mortality rate (per 1000 live births)	1990	123	2001	93	41
Infant mortality rate (per 1000 live births)	1990	80	2001	66	27
Maternal mortality rate (per 100,000 live births)	1991	437	1998	407	109
Population with sustainable access to an improved water source (%) rural	1990	61	2000	79	80.5
Population with access to sanitation (%) rural	1991	9.46	2001	21.91	72

Sources: Government of India, *Economic Survey*, New Delhi (various years); Registrar General of India, *Sample Registration System Bulletin*, New Delhi (various years); UNDP, *Human Development Reports*, New Delhi (various years); Indian Institute of Population Sciences, NFHS-I, (1995) and NFHS – II (2000).

India's progress has been much slower than needed to meet the targets in the reduction of incidence of mortality and morbidity among women and children, reduction of hunger and improvement in nutritional status, reduction of gender and caste-related disparities and improvement in general living conditions in terms of better access to basic amenities. India may not achieve many of these targets in spite of the likelihood of it becoming an economic superpower by 2015.

This must be qualified by the fact that social progress in India in terms of human development goals is characterized by wide inter-regional and intra-regional divergence. It means that in the absence of effective measures directed at bridging the gaps, the regions doing better in terms of human development will be better placed to seize the benefits of growth. The result can be one of growing economic inequality in India. Such a scenario cannot be considered conducive either to the process of rapid economic growth or the prospect of India becoming an economic superpower, if the growing inequalities lead to increasing regional and social conflicts within India.

A detailed discussion of the social indicators that reflect contemporary India's progress towards offering equal opportunity to its citizens is beyond the scope of this essay. This essay focuses on a few significant issues relating to poverty in India in light of the discussion so far.

Poverty, Hunger and Food Insecurity

Hunger and malnutrition are outcomes of food insecurity or the inability to access adequate food and nutrition. Hunger-related poverty remains one of the major deprivations in India. In 2001–03, every fifth Indian (20 per cent) was found to be undernourished.[12] The rate of decline in the proportion of the undernourished through the 1990s was much slower in comparison to the decline in poverty–headcount ratio. In fact, the proportion of undernourished people remained stagnant at 21 per cent in the second half of the 1990s and the number of the undernourished actually increased (see Table 4.3). It is most likely that India is going to miss the millennium development goal in this regard.

Even a greater cause of concern is the status of malnutrition among children. Malnutrition directly affects the development of the child by retarding their physical and cognitive growth and increases the risk of infection and disease. Malnutrition also affects cognitive and motor development in children, thereby influencing educational attainment, labour productivity and future income-earning ability. If lack of income means vulnerability to food insecurity and malnutrition, then the latter also reduces the lifetime-earning potential.

The deprivations relating to hunger and malnutrition, morbidity, mortality and the physical environment often reinforce each other and the general condition of economic poverty. To give an example, an illness like diarrhoea is one of the major causes of infant deaths in India, along with malaria, pneumonia and measles contributing to the high infant-mortality rates. Diarrhoea also leads to loss of absorption of nutrients, causing severe malnutrition among children. On the other hand, malnutrition has been estimated to be associated with about half of all child deaths and more than half of child deaths from

12. UNFAO, *The State of Food Security in the World: Eradicating World Hunger—Taking Stock Ten Years After World Food Summit* (Rome: Food and Agricultural Organization of United Nations, 2006).

diarrhoea (61 per cent).[13] Access to safe drinking water and basic sanitation facilities greatly reduces the incidence of diseases like diarrhoea. India's achievements in terms of proportion of population having access to either of these basic facilities is woefully low.

There is a gender dimension to hunger and malnutrition in India. Half of the country's women suffer from anaemia and the prevalence of anaemia is even higher among the pregnant women. Anaemia is one of the major causes of maternal mortality and also contributes to nearly 30 per cent of babies being born underweight.[14] The low birth weight means that there is greater risk of growth retardation, most of which occurs by the age of two and is often irreversible. In 1998–99, about 37 million children, almost one half of children below the age of three, were chronically undernourished (see Table 4.4). Approximately, 18 per cent of the children were severely underweight. Overall, two out of three children were moderately or severely malnourished.[15]

A greater prevalence of undernourishment can be seen among the children from scheduled-caste and scheduled-tribe communities. The rate of decline of undernourishment among these sections of the population was also found to be lower in comparison to the general population in the 1990s. It leads to the widening gap in terms of nutritional status among these communities and the general population. A similar observation could be made about the divergence between rural and urban areas, in the 1990s, in terms of nutritional status. The overall picture that emerges is one of growing urban–rural, inter-caste, male–female and economic class disparities in nutritional status in the 1990s.

It is the dark irony of our times that hunger and malnutrition are so pervasive in the country, while the Indian economy has achieved self-sufficiency in foodgrain production. The Indian government maintains buffer foodgrain stocks to guard against serious food shortages arising from drought and other crop failures. But in 2001, starvation deaths were reported from various parts of the country as more than 13 states were affected by drought. This happened at a time when the Food Corporation of India was finding it difficult to manage the millions of tonnes of surplus foodgrain rotting in its warehouses. Similar cases have been reported in the following years and have led to the 'Right to Food' campaign. Chronic hunger and malnutrition are not as visible and shocking as starvation deaths but they happen to be more widespread and persistent.

---

13. Michele Gragnolati et al, *India's Undernourished Children: A Call for Reform and Action* (Washington, DC: The World Bank, 2005).
14. Indian Institute of Population Sciences, *National Family and Health Survey-I: India 1992–93* (Mumbai: Indian Institute of Population Sciences, 1995).
15. Indian Institute of Population Sciences, *National Family and Health Survey-II: India 1998–99* (Mumbai: Indian Institute of Population Sciences, 2000).

Table 4.3 Status of Undernourishment in India Through the 1990s

Indicators	*1990–92*	*1995*	*1999–2001*	*2001–2003*
Number of undernourished (Millions)	214.5	194.7	213.7	212
Proportion of undernourished (as % of total population)	25	21	21	20

Source: UNFAO, *The State of Food Security in the World: Eradicating World Hunger—Taking Stock Ten Years After World Food Summit*, Rome: Food and Agricultural Organization of United Nations, 2006.

Table 4.4 Undernutrition Among Children Under 3 Years of Age

	Underweight			*Severely Underweight*		
	Prevalence 1992/93	Prevalence 1998/99	% Change	Prevalence 1992/93	Prevalence 1998/99	% Change
Total	53	47	-11	22	18	-18
Urban	44	38	-13	16	12	-27
Rural	55	50	-10	24	20	-16
Female	52	49	-6	21	19	-11
Male	53	45	-15	22	17	-24
SCs	57	53	-7	25	21	-15
STs	57	56	-2	29	26	-9
Other Castes	51	44	-14	20	16	-23

Source: Based on National Family and Health Survey I and II.

Poverty and Unemployment

Unemployment is not only a major cause of income poverty but also a deprivation of the opportunity to earn a livelihood. Poverty and unemployment are often mentioned together. In India, the linkage is a little more complex as the unemployment rate has remained much lower than what would normally be expected, given the extent of income poverty. According to official estimates, for example, 36 per cent of the population was poor in 1993–94, while the rate of unemployment was only 5.9 per cent, and the number of unemployed persons

Table 4.5 Unemployment Rates in Rural and Urban India

Year	*Number of Unemployed (In Millions)*			*Unemployment Rate (%)*		
	Rural	Urban	Total	Rural	Urban	Total
1983	16.26	5.51	21.76	7.96	9.64	8.3
1987–88	-	-	-	5.2	9.3	6.0
1993–94	14.34	5.80	20.13	5.61	7.19	5.99
1999–2000	19.50	7.11	26.58	7.21	7.65	7.32

Source: NSSO and Population Census of India. Based on National Sample Survey daily-status unemployment data, where the unemployment rate is defined as the number of days seeking (or being available for) work in the reference week as percentage of total number of days in the labour force in that period.

was 20.13 million.[16] The large gap between the incidence of poverty and the incidence of unemployment point to a phenomenon that is known as 'disguised unemployment' in economic literature: people employed in extremely low-productivity and low-income activities.

The rate of unemployment in India is seen to fluctuate over the years, but the variation has been over a narrow margin. Overall, the unemployment rate does not show any consistent trend (see Table 4.5). After a decline from 8.3 per cent in 1983 to 5.99 per cent in 1993–94, the unemployment rate has risen to 7.32 per cent in 1999–2000. Given the increase in the population and the addition to the labour force, this has meant that the absolute number of unemployed has increased considerably over the 1990s.

Looking at the figures given in Table 4.5, one could see that the bulk of the increase in the rate of unemployment comes from the rural sector. It must be remembered here that the majority of the population of India (more than 70 per cent) lived in the rural areas and more than 75 per cent of the total rural workforce was dependent on agriculture in 1999–2000.

One of the factors contributing to the rising rural unemployment in the 1990s could be found in the considerable decline in the agricultural growth during the same period. From a high of over 3 per cent in the 1980s, agricultural growth has declined to mere 1.5 per cent in the second half of the 1990s and the present decade.[17] The impact of an overall slow down of the agricultural sector would be logically more severe on the rural poor. The rural poor are primarily landless wage labourers, casual workers and marginal farmers. The casual agricultural wage labourers who constitute 35–40 per cent of rural workers also

16. Planning Commission, *Tenth Five-Year Plan 2002–2007* (New Delhi: Government of India, 2002).
17. Ministry of Finance, *Economic Survey 2004–2005* (New Delhi: Government of India, 2005).

form the bulk of those below the poverty line. They are more vulnerable to unemployment and underemployment depending on the changing demand in the agricultural sector. And, many of those who find employment are, as mentioned earlier, occupied in extremely low-income, low-productivity activities. In this context, it is relevant to note that the real agricultural wage has grown at a much slower rate in the 1990s in comparison to the earlier decade.

The depth and spread of poverty in rural India is more extensive than the official statistics suggest and the spate of suicides by farmers from different parts of India is indicative of the endemic and structural nature of the problem. These have to do with the persistence of deep socio-economic inequalities relating to caste and class, ownership of land and assets, access to education, health care, credit and social insurance. The Eleventh Five-Year Plan aims at an ambitious 4 per cent annual growth in agricultural production, which is more than double the current rate. It is possible that agricultural growth may pick up again with another Green Revolution or the non-farm sector in rural areas may really take off. But it is also a fact borne out by the earlier Green Revolution that growth does not benefit all regions and classes equally.[18] The ability to benefit from the opportunities presented by growth will depend on how the population is positioned in terms of many other basic capabilities.

A good illustration of the above point would be the extent and quality of participation of women in the labour force, which is far less in comparison to that of males. Women account for less than one-third of the total labour force. Part of this has been explained by the socio-cultural preferences relating to maternal and household responsibilities but much of it is still a matter of unequal opportunity. If one looks at the sectorial distribution of female workers, one finds it largely concentrated in the agricultural sector in the form of casual wage labourers. The disadvantage of women in terms of quality of employment could be largely ascribed to the inequality they face in educational attainment. In Table 4.2, the twin MDG targets of ratio of girls to boys in primary and secondary education reflect the persistence of gender inequality in basic education in India.

The same argument also explains the trend of labour participation of people from the SC and ST communities in the rural workforce. Though the SC and ST population together constitute only around 24.5 per cent of the total population, they accounted for nearly 43 per cent of the total poor households in rural India in 1993–94. They also constituted the majority of households involved in casual wage labour in agriculture.

18. The Green Revolution in the 1960s widened the regional gap in terms of economic growth between the north-western states, which were the major beneficiaries and relatively richer to begin with, and the poorer states in northern and eastern parts of the country.

Table 4.6 Livelihood Characteristics of the Rural Poor in 1993–94

Livelihood Category	*Scheduled-Caste Households*	*Scheduled-Tribe Households*	*Other House-holds*	*All Households*
Self-employed in agricultural households	4.76	5.62	22.49	32.87
Agricultural labour households	16.19	6.49	18.91	41.59
Self-employed in non-agriculture	2.38	0.75	7.70	10.83
Non-agricultural labour households	2.40	1.45	3.98	7.83
Other residual households	1.46	0.73	4.69	6.88
All households	27.19	15.04	57.77	100.00

Source: Government of India, *Indian Planning Experience*, New Delhi: Planning Commission of India, 2002. All figures in percentages.

Again, the great disparity in the nutritional, educational and social status of the SC and ST communities could be found to contribute to their income poverty. Social inequalities curtail the real opportunities available to people, and it is the kind of 'poverty' that economic growth on its own fails to take care of in the absence of affirmative political and social action.

State Planning and the Fight Against Poverty

After Independence, the Government of India chose the path of economic planning, and since 1951, a series of five-year plans have guided the country's economic development. Poverty alleviation has remained one of the major objectives of the succeeding plans in India.

Over the years, the orientation of the state policy to end poverty has undergone shifts and changes, which can be broadly categorized into three phases. The first three five-year plan documents, spanning the period from 1951 to 1966, show that the approach was largely 'growth centred'. Sustained high rate of economic growth was seen as the most effective means of alleviating poverty. The pursuit of the growth objective was carried out through a state-led industrialization process where the state owned and controlled key sectors of the economy. The policy thrust on industrialization was not complemented by adequate attention to the agricultural sector. Agricultural productivity stagnated, and the 1960s saw continuous food shortages.

By the mid-1960s, the achieved rate of growth for the economy as a whole was sluggish and far from the 'planned' levels. A rapidly growing population and the persistence of socio-economic inequalities in the absence of adequate institutional reforms meant that the 'growth centred' policy was hardly effective in making a significant difference to poverty in India.[19] As a result, the bulk of the population remained in abject poverty.

The food crisis of the 1960s brought into focus the need for the development and modernization of the agricultural sector. Self-sufficiency in foodgrain production became a central objective of the five-year plans. This ultimately led to the introduction of high-yielding seeds, widening of the irrigation network, improvements in the supply of fertilizer to accelerate the growth in the agricultural sector, and became known as the Green Revolution.

The 1970s saw a reappraisal of the 'growth centred' approach to poverty alleviation. The view that economic growth, though essential, cannot by itself address the needs of the poor, led to the formulation of more direct and targeted interventions by the State. This new approach to poverty alleviation found its populist expression in the '*Garibi Hatao*' slogan of Mrs Indira Gandhi and led to the launching of a series of programmes aimed as a direct attack on poverty.

The Fifth Five-Year Plan (1974–79) explicitly focused on the provision of basic minimum needs including access to such necessities as food, shelter, schooling, health services, safe drinking water and sanitation facilities and employment opportunities. The 1980s saw a host of other measures like the Integrated Rural Development Programme (IRDP), rural employment schemes, subsidized public distribution of food and other essential commodities aiming to improve the living standards of the poorer population. Interventions directly targeting the poor created the necessity for the planners to find out, 'who is poor?' and 'how many are poor?' This led to the adoption of the 'poverty line' by the Planning Commission of India in the 1970s.

The period 1967–87 showed a declining trend in poverty headcount, with the rural areas showing sharper decline in comparison to the urban areas. It has been argued that the success of the Green Revolution to raise agricultural productivity not only eased the food crisis but also had some impact on rural poverty in the 1970s and 1980s.[20] The direct interventions introduced during these years also contributed to the decline in poverty levels. But the rate of decline of income poverty in India was considerably slower and definitely less than expected levels when compared to many of its Asian neighbours.

---

19. Martin Ravallion and Gaurav Dutt, 'India's Checkered History Against Poverty: Are There Lessons for the Future?', *Economic and Political Weekly*, Special Number, September 1996: 2479–85.
20. Montek S. Ahluwalia, 'Rural Poverty and Agricultural Performance in India', *Journal of Development Studies*, 14 (3), April 1997: 298–323.

The third shift in the orientation of planning in India happened in the 1990s following the structural reforms, with rapid economic growth again assuming central significance and supplemented by the continuation of the targeted interventions for poverty alleviation.

The anti-poverty programmes of India could be broadly categorized into two groups depending on their nature of intervention: employment generation through public works and provision of subsidized food. Sometimes, the categories can overlap as in the case of food-for-work programmes where one of the major components of wage paid was in the form of foodgrain. The dominant thinking behind these interventions shows the significance attached to the notion of poverty as given by the official poverty line: insufficiency of per capita income and the failure to meet the minimum calorie consumption norm. One can question whether this definition of absolute poverty in India is not fixed too low and, thereby, excludes a large section of the population suffering from extreme deprivation and struggling for survival. There are reasons to believe that it is so when we broaden the notion of poverty to include other kinds of deprivations apart from income. The exclusive reliance on the official poverty line for the identification of eligible beneficiaries limits the scope of anti-poverty programmes. The conceptual limitation underlying the anti-poverty programmes has also meant that the fight against poverty has been essentially fragmentary in focus. They have been more about fire fighting than laying the foundations for social change; more about ensuring bare survival than building capabilities and creating equal opportunities.

The sector that accounts for the majority of the poor in India has been the predominantly agrarian rural sector. The real neglect of this sector by the State has meant that the efforts of poverty eradication have mostly remained cosmetic measures given to political expediency seen in slogans like *Garibi Hatao*.

The operational problems relating to state anti-poverty programmes can be discussed in the context of the Public Distribution System (PDS) for food and employment guarantee scheme.

Public Distribution System

Public distribution system is a programme managed by the government with the objective of ensuring access to food for all. The PDS does not provide the entire requirement of foodgrains to a household but is only supplemental. The system operates through a three-stage process. In the first stage, the Food Corporation of India procures foodgrains from farmers at a minimum support price. The procurement exercise is carried out with the purpose of providing farmers with a minimum support price and protecting them against unexpected price fluctuations in the market. The procured foodgrains are also used for the maintenance of buffer stocks in times of need and to stabilize the open-market prices. In the second stage, the procured foodgrains are allotted to the various states according to the number of poor in these states and the level of production of foodgrains in the state. This is used as a balance of availability of food between surplus and deficit states. In the third stage, the foodgrains are distributed at subsidized prices to the population in the various states through a chain of fair-price shops under PDS. The foodgrains are also used for distribution through other public programmes like food-for-work and midday-meal scheme for children in schools.

Though PDS started as a universal food distribution programme, it faced the problems of extensive leakages and the inability to reach the really vulnerable groups. In 1997, the scheme was restructured to supply the foodgrains at differential prices to households Below the Poverty Line (BPL) and those Above the Poverty Line (APL). This has been known as the Targeted Public Distribution System (TPDS). But the failure of the system was grossly highlighted when, as mentioned earlier, starvation deaths were reported in 2001, at a time when the FCI warehouses were overflowing with surplus foodgrains.

The system is found to be so corrupt and inefficient that some studies have estimated that out of every rupee spent, only 20 *paise* reaches the poor.[21] And according to the Planning Commission's programme evaluation division, in 2003–04, more than 50 per cent of the foodgrains meant for the poor did not reach them.[22] While in many states, the surveys to identify below-the-poverty-line population were not even carried out, in other states, several families did not receive the identification cards even after the surveys. And the surveys, being essentially bureaucratic exercises, have meant massive manipulation and harassment. In several cases, the administration refuses to issue cards to urban destitutes including urban homeless, migrant labourers and destitute women due to lack of proof of address. This problem is compounded by the poor quality and inadequate supply of foodgrains.

The failures of the PDS are symptomatic of what ails the government anti-poverty programmes the most. The major drawbacks have been centralized planning and lack of local-level participation leading to mismatched priorities, and bureaucratic control characterized by lack of transparency and accountability.[23]

21. K. S. Parikh, *Who Gets How Much from PDS: How Effectively Does It Reach the Poor?* (Bombay: Indira Gandhi Institute of Development Research, 1993).
22. George Cheriyan, 'Enforcing Right to Food in India: Bottlenecks in Delivering the Expected Outcomes,' Paper for Second International Workshop, ICSSR-WIDER/UNV Joint Project on Food Security (in Collaboration with UN-FAO), 2005.
23. Jean Drèze, 'Poverty in India and the IRDP Delusion', *Economic and Political Weekly,* 25 (39), 1990: 94–104.

Employment Guarantee Schemes

Public employment generation schemes have been in existence in India for long. In the 1970s, food-for-work programmes were created to provide both income and food security. Since then, a number of wage-employment programmes have been introduced like the National Rural Employment Programme (NREP) and the Rural Landless Employment Guarantee Programme (RLEGP), both later merged in 1989 into a single component—the *Jawahar Rozgar Yojana* (JRY). In many of these programmes, foodgrains have been used as a component of wage. But in spite of these interventions, widespread hunger and undernourishment has persisted in India.

In response to the public campaign for Right to Work, in November 2004, the government launched a national Food for Work programme in 150 most backward districts, for providing guaranteed employment for 100 days to BPL families. Simultaneously, a bill was drafted and in December 2004, the government introduced the National Rural Employment Guarantee (NREG) bill in Parliament. This obligates the government to provide at least 100 days of wage employment every year to every household whose adult members volunteer to do unskilled manual work. The bill was passed by Parliament and the NREG scheme was launched in 200 districts of the country in February 2006. In terms of a programme, it is significant in the sense that it can, provided the problems of implementation are overcome, supplement the income of the poor, like the casual labourers in rural areas. But this is again primarily an attempt to keep the absolutely poor from losing the battle for survival. And, while acknowledging the importance of the Right to Work, one must raise the larger question of the Right to Livelihood.

Economic Growth, Inequality of Opportunity and Regional Disparity

How does economic growth impact poverty? The relationship is not a straightforward one. To begin with, it depends on the notion of poverty used. High economic growth sustained over a long period of time eventually leads to increase in the levels of per capita income. And, if poverty is defined as a lack of income, then economic growth does lead to a general decline in *absolute* poverty defined by the 'poverty line' or minimum per capita income. This logic is sometimes called 'the trickle-down effect': the benefits of growth eventually trickling down to the poor. The rate of decline of poverty also depends on how low the level of per capita income fixed by the poverty line is; the lower the level, the higher the rate of decline.

But the above logic does not extend to relative-income poverty, which relates to the inequality in distribution of income. The impact of growth upon income inequality depends on the nature of growth and how different sections of the population stand to benefit from it. For example, in contemporary India, the high economic growth is largely driven by industry and services while the agricultural sector has shown considerable deceleration in the 1990s.[24] It means that the growth has been mostly urban centric as the majority of the rural population is still dependent on agriculture. Further, better access to quality education gives an advantage to the urban population over the rural population in terms of capability to actualize the opportunities offered in the industrial and services sectors. Evidence suggests that rural–urban disparities in per capita expenditure have significantly increased in the 1990s.[25]

The pattern of growth in the 1990s is also marked by major regional imbalances. The better-performing states in terms of growth are from the western and southern parts of the country with the exception of Andhra Pradesh.[26] These states showed high growth rates in per capita income through the 1990s, and with the exception of Rajasthan, they all had per capita incomes above the national average at the beginning of the period. On the other hand, the low-growth states forming a contiguous region in the north and east experienced marked deterioration in terms of growth of per capita income in the 1990s.[27] This is especially true of states like Assam, Orissa, Bihar, West Bengal and Uttar Pradesh, where growth has been virtually stagnant in the 1990s. All the states forming this group except West Bengal have had per capita income levels lower than the national average since the 1980s. The states that were relatively richer have done better in comparison to the poorer states. Also, the headcount–poverty ratio in the poorer states has declined at a much slower rate, and by the end of the 1990s, these states accounted for nearly 70 per cent of the below-the-poverty-line population in India. The regional disparities in terms of income have intensified in India in the 1990s.

One of the dominant perceptions of the process of economic development has been the generalization that economic progress, measured by per capita income, is initially accompanied by rising inequality, but these disparities eventually decline as the benefits of development permeate more widely.[28] Again, as in the case of the 'trickle down effect', there is an implicit assumption: the political and social structures in existence do not hinder the benefits of growth to reach all sections of the population. This is rarely the case, as inherent

24. Eight per cent growth in industries and 8.9 per cent growth in the services largely contributed to the average 7 per cent growth in GDP in the Tenth Five-Year Plan period (2002–03 to 2006–07). Agriculture grew at a mere 1.8 per cent.
25. Deaton and Drèze, 'Poverty and Inequality in India'.
26. Punjab, Rajasthan, Gujarat, Haryana, Maharashtra, Karnataka, Kerala, and Tamil Nadu.
27. Assam, West Bengal, Bihar, Uttar Pradesh, Madhya Pradesh and Orissa.
28. In development literature, it is known as the 'inverted-U hypothesis' proposed in the 1960s by the economist Simon Kuznets. The strange name of the hypothesis comes from the observed upside-down 'U' shaped trend when per capita income is plotted on one axis, and some measure of inequality on the other.

inequities in political and social structures tend to replicate with growing economic inequality, generating its own stratifications and hierarchies. There is no innate tendency for economic inequality to disappear in the long run without the mediation of affirmative political and social action for equal opportunity.

Exclusion and Social Conflict

The logic of the State intervention in poverty alleviation has been based on the twin premise of failure of the market and comparative advantages of the public agency to bring disadvantaged, marginal, bypassed social groups and regions into the mainstream process of development. The policy emphasis on market forces and economic growth does not forsake the welfarist role of the State as the provider of social goods but raises questions regarding its political commitment to social justice. Some of the ambiguities and uncertainties inherent in this situation could be seen in the light of agitations and conflicts arising out of State action.

The changes in public policy in India in the 1990s have seen the gradual withdrawal of the State from its entrepreneurial role as the prime agent of economic growth. As the Planning Commission puts it, 'the current thinking on planning in the country, in general, is that it should increasingly be of an indicative nature'. In other words, the preferred policy of the State is 'increasingly' one of least interference with the market forces in pursuit of rapid, economic growth. Gone are the days when the public sector was the biggest investor. Now, the role of the State is to promote private investment by ensuring that the freedom of the market forces is not interfered with. This trend could be seen in the post-1990s with the regional states competing with each other to attract both domestic and foreign direct investment. Some of the States have been offering various tax concessions and other special facilities to new investors on a competitive basis. The terms and conditions of the Memorandum of Understandings (MoUs) signed between the private concerns and the State have come under the scanner for allegedly giving undue advantages to the former at the cost of public interest and resources. The opening up of the mining sector in Orissa in the second half of the 1990s could be a particularly good case study. Many of these industrialization projects also require the acquisition of land and have raised the issue of displacement of population. The problem of displaced population as a result of large-scale industrialization is not new. The social cost of displacement during the earlier phase of State-led industrialization found its justification in the political rhetoric of the 'nation-building' exercise. Now that private corporations are at the helm, the State's active endorsement of displacement is seen as open partisan support of the former. The violent conflicts that have resulted in the process of what is seen as State-sponsored displacement for the benefit of private capital could be indicative of the frustration and anger at the growing economic inequality and social polarization.

The persistence of chronic poverty and deprivation in the face of economic growth poses one of the most difficult challenges for Indian democracy: to provide equality of opportunity for all. The response of contemporary India will determine whether we will have a less-divided and less-conflicting future.

Suggested Readings

Drèze, Jean and Amartya Sen. *Hunger and Public Action*. New Delhi: Oxford University Press, 1993 [1989].

Drèze, Jean and Amartya Sen. *India: Economic Development and Social Opportunity*. New Delhi: Oxford University Press, 1995.

Drèze, Jean and Amartya Sen (eds). *Indian Development: Selective Regional Perspectives*. New Delhi: Oxford University Press, 1996.

Sen, Amartya. *Development as Freedom*. New Delhi: Oxford University Press, 2000.

Questions

1. Write an essay on the politics of poverty alleviation in India.
2. Analyse the debate on the definition of poverty and poverty line. Do you think tackling 'absolute poverty' is sufficient for elimination of poverty-related problems?
3. Analyse the relationship between poverty, unemployment and food insecurity.
4. Why do certain regions perform better economically while others do not? Explain the problem of regional imbalance in India.
5. What is the relationship between economic growth and poverty? Elaborate.

Human Development: Health and Education

5

Neera Chandhoke

INTRODUCTION

What is the relationship between democracy and the **well-being** of citizens? There are two sorts of answers that we can offer in response to this question. First, people are not themselves responsible for poverty, illiteracy, or ill health that afflicts them. The causes of ill-being lie outside the control of the victims. For example, due to the distorted pattern of resource distribution, some people have more land, some have no land, and some have command over their incomes such as wages or rents, while others have nothing except their labour power. If the social distribution of resources is responsible for the ill-being of citizens, then society, or more precisely, the democratic State, which is the political organization of that society, has the responsibility to prevent this through the enactment of social policies. To put it strongly, a democratic state has reason to exist because it is charged with securing the well-being of the citizens. After all, citizens elect representatives on the assumption that the representative will take care of the needs and interests of his or her constituent. This is the bare minimum that a democratic state can do for its citizens. This is the minimum we expect of a democracy.

Citizens should not suffer from ill-being such as illiteracy, ill health, homelessness or poverty, for another reason. Democracy is based on two main principles. The first principle is the participation of citizens in the political process. Citizens participate in the political process not only by voting in elections, but also by taking part in public debates, e.g., contributing to readers' columns in newspapers, taking part in demonstrations, campaigns, and social movements, or simply by being informed and aware of the crucial issues that confront the polity, so that they can vote for the best person when the next election comes around. The second principle of democracy is that of State accountability to the citizens. Both these principles can only be realized when the citizens are informed and aware of the basic issues that confront society.

But citizens can only be informed and aware when they are provided with education, healthcare, shelter and when they have an income; in short, when they do not suffer from any serious harm. Any citizen who has been deprived of education, or suffers from malnourishment, will neither be able to participate in the political process, nor be able to hold State officials accountable. This is not to say that non-literate persons cannot be democratic. The issue is deeper; that the realization of full democracy demands an educated, informed, and politically aware citizenry, and that ill-health and non-literacy can impede the democratic process. In other words, **basic needs** for education and health have to be met before people can do anything else. Unless these needs are met, human beings will not be able to do anything else—take up a satisfying job, form enriching friendships, engage in leisure activities or, indeed, participate in an activity that the Greeks called politics.[1]

Basic needs can be met in two ways. For that section of the population that can afford to buy services such as education and health, the provisioning of basic needs can be routed through the market. But the market is indifferent to the needs of those who cannot buy goods offered in the market. For the poorer sections of the people, therefore, democratic governments are *obliged* to provide basic needs *irrespective* of the ability of the poor to pay for these goods. To phrase it starkly, the goods that satisfy basic needs—education and health—are of such *overriding importance* that they have to be placed outside the realm of market transactions for those who cannot pay for them, through the enactment of a social policy. Social policy subsidizes food, housing, education and health, so that the poor can afford these goods.

There are, therefore, two main reasons why a democratic State should secure the well-being for its citizens through the fulfilment of basic needs. First, it is not the victim of ill-being who is responsible for her or his State, but society which, through the unjust distribution of resources, renders some people harm. A democratic State, which is responsible for its citizens, has to remedy this harm through the provision of goods to meet basic needs on non-market principles. Second, the realization of democracy demands an informed, educated, politically aware, and healthy citizenry so that citizens can participate in the making of political decisions, and can ensure accountability of the State officials. If people are poor, without shelter, sick, or non-literate, the concept of democracy is left unrealized.

However, the relationship between democracy and well-being is not a causal or a straightforward one; political democracy need not always lead to social and economic democracy. On the other hand, political democracy can coexist quite happily with extreme poverty, illiteracy and ill health. Consider the case of India. The country has held regular, and free and fair elections,[2] institutionalized a competitive party system, established a functioning rule of

1. The classic formulation on this is found in John Rawls, *A Theory of Justice* (Oxford, UK: Oxford University Press, 1971).
2. This is except for the period between June 1975 and January 1977, when Prime Minister Indira Gandhi's Government had imposed an internal emergency on the country, and had, thereby, suspended democratic life.

law, granted legal sanction to political and civil rights, and established a free press, all of which have led to a vibrant and active civil society. India, without any reservation, can be called a political democracy. A majority of the people, however, continue to suffer from harm, with the most vulnerable among them—the poor among the Scheduled Castes and Tribes, hill people, forest dwellers, tribals, and women, particularly the girl child—at tremendous risk in matters of both lives and livelihoods.

It is true that we have seen an improvement in the basic parameters of human development. According to the approach paper to the Eleventh Five-Year Plan, the literacy rate for the population above the age of seven is 75.3 per cent for males, and 53.7 per cent for women. In 1990, the corresponding figures were 64.1 per cent for males and 39.3 per cent for females. The infant-mortality rate per thousand live births is 60 according to 2003 figures, compared with 80 around 1990.[3] Yet, this progress is unevenly spread across the population—across income groups, castes and religious minorities, and gender and regions. This has led to large disparities in health, nutrition, education, and skills. Kerala, for instance, has a literacy rate of 92 per cent, which is comparable to that of Vietnam; but Bihar continues to have a literacy rate of only 47.5 per cent. Also striking are urban–rural disparities, whereas the literacy rate in urban areas is 80.30 per cent, the corresponding literacy rate for rural areas is only 59.40 per cent. 'The most important challenge', states the approach paper, 'is how to provide essential public services such as education and health to large parts of our population who are denied these services at present. Education is the critical factor that will empower the poor to participate in the growth process'.[4]

The coexistence of political and civil freedom alongside social and economic unfreedom is cause for some regret. For the leaders of the freedom movement, the task of attaining political freedom had to be accompanied by social and economic freedom, and vice versa. The leadership had, for that reason, conceptualized an integrated agenda of political, civil, social, cultural, and economic rights in the 1928 Nehru Constitutional Draft[5] and in the Karachi Resolution on Fundamental Rights adopted by the Indian National Congress in 1931. This integrated agenda was, however, split into its two constituent units in the Constituent Assembly. Whereas political, civil, and cultural rights in Chapter Three of the Constitution are backed by legal sanction; social and economic rights, which are placed in Chapter Four of the Constitution under the title of Directive Principles of State Policy, are not backed by such sanction.

3. Planning Commission, *Towards Faster and More Inclusive Growth: An Approach to the 11th Five-Year Plan* (New Delhi: Government of India, 2006), p. 4.

4. Ibid., p. 4.

5. At its forty-third annual session in 1927, the Indian National Congress resolved that a working committee be empowered to draft a *Swaraj* Constitution of India on the basis of a declaration of rights.

The opening clause of the report of the sub-committee on fundamental rights clearly stated that '[w]hile these principles shall not be cognizable by any court, they are nevertheless fundamental in the governance of the country and their application in the making of laws shall be the duty of the State'.[6] Dr Ambedkar, the president of the Constituent Assembly, assured members that though the principles were not legally binding:

> whoever captures power will not be free to do what he likes with it. In the exercise of it, he will have to respect these instruments of instructions, which are called Directive Principles. He cannot ignore them. He may not have to answer for their breach in a court of law. But he will certainly have to answer for them before the electorate at election time.[7]

The legal historian Granville Austin argues that though Directive Principles of State Policy are not justiciable, 'they have become the yardstick for the measurement of government's successes and failures in social policy'.[8] However, the downgrading of social and economic rights to the status of mere objectives, and what one member of the Constituent Assembly was to term 'pious wishes' has had expected consequences. Whereas political and civil rights have functioned in some cases fairly effectively as a constraint on State power, social and economic rights have just not been treated with the seriousness that these deserve. Drèze and Sen point out that even though 'the expansion of social opportunities was very much the central theme in the vision that the leaders of the Indian Independence movement had presented to the country at the time the British left, rather little attempt has, in fact, been made to turn that vision into any kind of reality'.[9]

It is not as if policies have not been designed to implement these objectives, and it is not as if programmes have not been initiated for provision of social goods to the needy section of the people. But when it comes to the implementation of these policies, the necessary political will vanishes, perhaps because no one can take the government to court for a violation of the Directive Principles. Either social policies have not been accompanied by necessary financial outlays, or both have been provided for and the policy itself not implemented. Even if policies have been implemented, the process is attended by massive instances of corruption and mismanagement. Moreover, though the provision of social goods falls more or less within the provenance of state governments, the Planning Commission through the five-year plans determines strategy, priority, and

6. B. Shiva Rao, *Constitution of India, Select Documents*, Vol. 2 (Delhi: Indian Institute of Public Administration, 1967), p. 168.
7. B. Shiva Rao, *The Framing of India's Constitution* (Delhi: Indian Institute of Public Administration, 1968), p. 329.
8. Granville Austin, *Working a Democratic Constitution: The Indian Experience* (New Delhi: Oxford University Press, 1999), p. 8.
9. Jean Drèze and Amartya Sen, *India: Development and Participation* (New Delhi: Oxford University Press, 2002), p. xiv.

allocation of resources. However, the conceptualization of planning, as Prabhu and Sudarshan argue, is not embedded within a 'redistributive ethos'. Therefore, 'the distribution of benefits of economic growth has not been egalitarian. Social-sector policy, which could have acted as a redistributive measure, did not don this mantle. Further, the very approach of the State towards social sectors has been ambivalent. They have been considered either as constituting welfare, or as a means of enhancing human capital'.[10]

In sum, social policy in India has proved far too inadequate when it comes to addressing the challenges confronting the nation. Though Chapter Four of the Constitution lays down directives for social policy, successive central and state governments just do not seem to have taken this charge seriously enough. For instance, according to one of the main Directive Principles, the State is obliged to ensure that health care is provided to all, that maternity relief is available to women, that levels of nutrition are raised, and that free and compulsory education is provided to all children till the age of 14. Yet, as the discussion below shows, the record of the government in these two areas, which are crucial for human well-being, is not too good.

HEALTH

Between June and July 2004, 11 children in the age group of 0–5 died in the Dongiriguda *Adivasi* (forest dwellers) settlement located in the Jharigaon block of Nawrangpur district in Orissa. Other children living in the block were being treated for similar symptoms, and reports stated that the understaffed and ill-equipped Community Health Centre at Jharigaon was admitting about 40 ailing children per day. The proximate causes of death of these children were diarrhoea, acute respiratory infection and fever. The generic cause for these deaths, however, was malnutrition, which has been identified as the biggest cause of infant mortality in this district—as high as 97 deaths per 1000 live births. Since the Dongiriguda forest hamlet is a village existing within reserve forests, none of the below-poverty-line (BPL) families possesses a ration card, which would entitle them to buy rice at a subsidized rate. The only benefit that the village receives is under the **Integrated Child Development Programme**. It is not surprising that when their meagre supplies of food ran out during the monsoon, villagers were forced to survive on mango kernel, wild mushroom, tubers and leaves. Except for the fact that a health worker distributes free medicines once a month, the villagers are not entitled to any medical facilities.[11]

The tragic incident foregrounds the main problem with the public health policy adopted by the Government of India: the thrust of the policy is *curative*

10. Seetha Prabhu and R. Sudarshan (eds.), *Reforming India's Social Sector: Poverty, Nutrition, Health and Education* (Delhi: Social Science Press, 2002), pp. 4–5.
11. Prafulla Das, 'Hunger and Death', *Frontline*, 27 August 2004, pp. 49–52.

rather than *preventive*. A preventive health policy would provide nutrition, safe drinking water, sanitation, hygiene, and education as essential preconditions of health. It would also demand the institutionalization of an extensive public health system: immunization programmes, clinics and community health centres staffed by trained medical personnel and para-health workers. All this requires a great deal of public investment. Yet, according to the latest Reserve Bank report on State finances, expenditure on the social sector, and health and education in particular continues to be appallingly inadequate. The Eleventh Plan draft focuses on these sectors and has earmarked substantial increases in outlays for health. Apart from the National Rural Health Mission, government spending on health is aimed at 2 per cent of the GDP by the plan end.[12] This is a figure that is far lower than other developing countries. Cuba spends 6.2 per cent and Namibia 4.7 per cent of their respective GDPs on health. In India, health is a state subject and states are expected to contribute to a major part of the finances allotted to the sector, but the budgetary allocation of state governments has shown a consistent decline over the years.

The general neglect of preventive healthcare and the increasing push towards the involvement of the private sector in the delivery of health services highlights a dramatic lessening of public commitment to health. In 1946, on the eve of India's Independence, the report of the Bhore Committee had suggested a detailed and comprehensive plan for health security. The plan, which was intentionally biased in favour of rural areas, recommended that a uniform and comprehensive public health act be enacted, and plans made for the implementation of an Indian National Health Service. The Bhore Committee Report envisaged the establishment of a massive state-managed infrastructure for health, which would have required the State to allocate almost 10 per cent of the GDP for healthcare. Stressing that the provision of healthcare is an indispensable function of the government, and that this should be provided to all irrespective of their ability to pay, the report suggested that the focus of the health programme must be preventive rather than curative, that health services should be placed as close to the people as possible to ensure maximum benefit to communities, and that the doctor should be a social physician who combines remedial and preventive measures. If it had been implemented effectively, the Bhore Committee Report would have rendered the private sector in health irrelevant, and the level of health services in the country would have reached three-fifth of that in Britain during the Second World War.

Though the health minister's conferences in the first few years of Independence ritually referred to the report, and though the First Five-Year Plan attempted to incorporate its recommendations, very soon, policy makers dropped the recommendations. From the Fourth Five-Year Plan onwards, budgetary

12. Aditi Nigam, 'Social Sector Spending by States Dips in 2007–08', *Financial Express*, 13 January 2008, www.financialexpress.com/news (last accessed on 10 February 2008).

provisions for health shrank drastically, reaching a new low in the first decade of the 21st century, though the World Health Organization (WHO) has recommended that a minimum of 5 per cent of the GDP should be allotted to healthcare. India has one of the lowest health budgets in the world. Health does not seem to be a priority area for the nation. Neither does it seem an important priority area for political parties. For instance, in the 2004 general elections, health issues were not raised by any candidate.

In fact, we can discern an odd gap between the stated objectives of health policy and the financial outlays made by the government, for the Government of India has been sensitive to the need for a sound and fully functioning health system, which can deliver efficient services particularly to the rural poor. The public health system that was laid out in the early years of the post-Independence period consists of a three-tiered layer of primary health centres, sub-centres, and community centres, providing multi-functional outpatient facilities. The number of centres is in direct proportion to the population being served, with special provisions being made for hilly and tribal areas. The government has also initiated and implemented several disease-control programmes and immunization schemes, some of which have shown remarkable success. Under the Central Government Health Scheme, healthcare is provided to government employees, pensioners, and public officials living in big cities. The global debate on health strategy, the signing of the Alma Ata declaration of 'Health for All' by 2000, and the recommendations of various specialized bodies have resulted in the enunciation of a comprehensive, integrated, approach to healthcare in the form of the National Health Policy in 1983. The 2002 National Health Policy aims at achieving basic standards of good health among the population through national public health programmes, extension of infrastructure, medical education, research, enhanced role of stakeholders such as NGOs, enforcement of quality standards in food and drugs, and women's health.

It is also not as if India has made no progress in the past several decades in the field of health. As detailed above, infant-mortality rates have dropped and life expectancy has risen. There have been no reported cases of small pox since 1985, of guinea worm disease since 1996; and of plague since 1969 with the exception of Surat (August–September 1994). Cholera epidemics and related deaths have become more infrequent. In 1950, cholera cases numbered 176,307 with 86,997 deaths; by 2001, the total reported cases of cholera were 5000.[13] The incidence of measles, polio, whooping cough, and tetanus is lower than before. The proportion of children without immunization declined from 30 to 14 per cent between 1992–93 and 1998–99.

Yet, the presence of both communicable and non-communicable diseases casts a heavy cloud over well-being. Infant mortality rates have still to be

13. N. S. Deodhar, *Health Situation in India* (Delhi: Voluntary Health Association of India, 2001), p. 8.

brought to a level under 60 per 1,000 live births, which is the expressed goal of the 1983 health policy. The mortality rate for children under the age of five years is still high, compared with 39 deaths per 1,000 live births in China. The main causes of mortality in the age group 0–5 are common diseases, which can be easily avoided, such as lower respiratory tract infection, diarrhoeal diseases, perinatal causes and vaccine-preventable diseases. Communicable diseases like viral encephalitis, meningococcal meningitis, rabies, *kala azar*, dengue fever and tuberculosis have escaped control. Epidemics of food poisoning, infectious hepatitis, typhoid fever, measles, tetanus, and pneumonia regularly appear to trouble the citizens of the country. It is estimated that about 15 million people suffer from tuberculosis, and that 2.2 million are added to this figure every year.[14] The emergence of AIDS has begun to affect national and regional epidemiological profiles and priorities, and leprosy cases constitute a major part of the world's cases of leprosy.

The picture is not even across the country; for instance, Kerala has made progress on all health indicators, whereas Bihar, Uttar Pradesh, and parts of Madhya Pradesh and Rajasthan show tremendous vulnerability on this front. Second, the rural–urban divide, when it comes to health, is very strong, with the rural sector much more vulnerable to malnourishment and disease. What is also worrying is the massive social inequity between income groups across all the regions of the country in matters of health. A study has shown that the richest 20 per cent enjoy three times their share of the public subsidy for health compared to the poorest quintile, and that 20 per cent of the population, which belongs to the poorest section of society, has more than double the mortality rates, fertility rates, levels of under-nutrition than the richest 20 per cent of the population.[15]

Ill-health is due to the interaction of a number of factors. First, the public sector in health exists without a minimum legislative framework. Second, declining public investment and expenditure in health is compounded by bureaucratization, corruption, inadequate infrastructure, and non-availability of medicines. Third, whereas the Government of India has concentrated massive resources in specific disease eradication campaigns, such as the huge campaign initiated in 1995 to eradicate poliomyelitis through a pulse polio immunization programme, this has been at the cost of other ..ogrammes, which aim at the annihilation of common ailments such as diarrhoea and dysentery. Even though dysentery and diarrhoea along with acute respiratory infections leading to pneumonia happen to be the main killers of children below the age of five, these are not even seen by the government as diseases. Fourth, universal programmes of immunization have failed to establish efficient epidemiological surveillance services for diseases that can be controlled. Fifth, health policy in

14. Rajiv Misra, Rachel Chatterjee and Sujatha Rao, *India Health Report* (New Delhi: Oxford University Press, 2003), p. 3.

15. Ibid., pp. 1–2.

India has concentrated more on curative measures rather than on preventive measures such as the provision of safe drinking water, nutrition, and sanitation. And sixth, the health infrastructure, particularly in the rural areas, is poor, inefficient, arbitrary, and corrupt.

Given all these deficiencies in the public-health system, it is not surprising that it is the private sector that has stepped in to fill the gap in a major way since 1991 and accounts for three-fourths of the healthcare system in the country. The National Health Policy of 2002, departing from existing understanding, does not even refer to universal healthcare. What it does suggest is the privatization of existing hospitals, introduction of more private hospitals, user fees in government hospitals, and the involvement of the non-governmental sector in healthcare. However, the problems of leaving healthcare to the private sector in a predominantly poor country are many, of which four can be mentioned here. First, unlike the USA the private-health sector in India is unregulated, save for some states that have laid down guidelines and regulations. Second, the private sector, which is driven by the profit motive, is unconcerned about equity. The poor are either denied access to healthcare, or compelled to resort to cheap but under-qualified or unqualified 'practitioners of medicine'. It has been estimated that the number of poor that did not seek medical treatment because of financial constraints increased from 15 to 24 per cent in the rural areas and doubled from 10 to 20 per cent in the urban areas in the 1990s. A hospitalized Indian spends more than half of his/her total annual expenditure to buy healthcare.[16] Third, if left to the private sector, the balance in healthcare will inevitably be skewed towards urban based, tertiary-level health services, and tilted against primary healthcare. Fourth, private practitioners are not inclined towards the initiation or the implementation of measures that ensure preventive healthcare.

Assurances of health, it has become clear, require certain preconditions. If Tamil Nadu has the third lowest child-mortality rate, and the second lowest maternal mortality rate in the country, this is due to easy access to healthcare; government provision for child nutrition; immunization programmes; the attendance of professionals at childbirths; social security measures such as old age pensions and social support to widows; improved status of women, balanced gender ratios; a high presence of women in the workforce; midday meals in schools—the provision of which both improves school attendance and lessens child under-nutrition; and little gender bias in school attendance. On social development indicators, Tamil Nadu ranks just below Kerala, whose success is largely due to the almost continuous presence of a Left government, which is committed to social well-being, as well as to the social movement for health launched by the Kerala Sastra Sahitya Parishad (KSSP). Emphasizing that health is a right, the KSSP has consistently argued that health has to be located within the wider social realities of poverty, lack of proper food and an unhealthy living

16. Ibid., p. 2.

environment. It has, consequently, sought to raise public awareness through the establishment of health camps, publication of documents on people's health, and stress on indigenous system of medicines. Bihar and Uttar Pradesh, on the other hand, have high infant-mortality rates, both because of the lack of social infrastructure and the lack of the requisite political will.

For these reasons, the Jan Swasthya Abhiyan or the People's Health Movement has initiated a nationwide 'Health for All' campaign. The movement suggesting that healthcare should be a fundamental right has demanded that the government enact a National Public Health Act to amend the Constitution and mandate a right to basic healthcare in accordance with article 47 of Directive Principles of State Policy, and article 12 of the International Covenant of Economic, Social, and Cultural Rights. The Act would guarantee universal healthcare to all citizens through the enactment of comprehensive preventive measures that address mortality and morbidity in the country; strengthening of the public-health system in the rural areas, involvement of the community and local self-government bodies in healthcare, raising of public investment in the field, regulation of the private-health sector, providing every patient the right to information on every aspect of her treatment, and the institutionalization of a patient-friendly, grievance-redressal system. The Act should make it obligatory for every doctor to render essential, first-aid and medical care in situations of emergency. If the public-health system fails to deliver, this should be treated as a legal offence, remedy for which can be sought in a court of law. In sum, the overall goal of the health policy should be to move towards a system where every citizen has assured access to basic healthcare along the lines of the Canadian system of universal healthcare, the National Health Service in Britain, and the Cuban system of healthcare for all citizens.[17]

Although the Common Minimum Programme of the United Progressive Alliance (UPA) government has recommended that public expenditure on healthcare be increased from 0.9 per cent of the GDP to 2 to 3 per cent, the figure is still far lower than the 5 per cent recommended by WHO. In the meanwhile, the public-health system continues to be in disorder, healthcare delivered by the private sector continues to be out of reach of the poor, and life-taking diseases continue to stalk small children and the vulnerable sections of the population.

Education

Article 45 of the Constitution stipulates that the State shall endeavour to provide within a period of 10 years free and compulsory education for children till the age of 14.[18] The National Policy of Education, 1986, which was revised

17. www.cehat.org (last accessed on 17 May 2008).
18. This had originally been conceptualized as a fundamental right, but deliberations in the Constituent Assembly reduced education to a Directive Principle of State Policy.

in 1992, provided momentum to the task and has achieved some success. The Census of India defines literacy rates as the proportion of literates to the total population above the age of seven years. By these standards, at the time of Independence, literacy stood at merely 18.3 per cent for the age group of five years and above. Literacy rose to 43.6 per cent in 1981, to 52.21 per cent in 1991, to further rise to 65.4 per cent in 2001. In a 10-year period from 1991 to 2000, illiteracy declined for the first time by 32 million in absolute terms. Significantly, in rural areas, the literacy rate increased from 36 per cent in 1981 to 59 per cent in 2001. This was achieved despite the fact that the education budget is clearly insufficient.

The goal of universalizing elementary education is sought to be achieved through the setting up of government or government-aided primary schools. By 1993, 94 per cent of the total rural population was served by primary schools; and in the period 1950–1990, the number of schools increased by more than three times. The number of upper primary schools increased 15 times in the same period. The expansion of the school system was accompanied by the provision of midday meals, free uniforms, textbooks, and scholarships in order to increase recruitment and prevent dropouts.

The elementary educational system has been strengthened from time to time by the launch of special campaigns such as Operation Blackboard to upgrade infrastructure, train teachers, and improve the environment. To cover gaps in the educational system, the Government of India launched in 2000–01 the Sarva Shiksha Abhiyan, or the movement for education to provide elementary education to children in the age group 6–14, in partnership with state governments, local governments and communities. The school system has been decentralized to enable community participation. This, as reports show, has led to improved performances, provided community-owned education, and bridged gender and social disparities to some extent. The District Elementary Education Plan, which was launched in 1994 and supported by international agencies, is based on assessments of specific needs of each habitat, particularly in the field of early childhood care.

From 1986 onwards, the Government of India initiated several schemes to bring more than half the children in the age group of 6–14 who are outside the school system, within the ambit of education, by setting up a parallel stream of non-formal education, by opening up literacy classes to children outside the school system, and through the setting up of World Bank–sponsored district, primary-education programmes. Under the programme, 21,000 new alternative schools have been established, and 10,000 clusters for Early Childhood Care and Education have been set up. However, these initiatives, which introduced parallel streams of cheap but low-quality education for poor children, have been criticized by educationists and activists. For, instead of strengthening the existing government and government-aided school system, these schemes provided for contracting often under-qualified youths at low salaries to teach children for a period of nine months. The quality of education has, thereby, been compromised.

Adults in the age group of 15–35 are provided functional literacy through the National Literacy Mission, which was set up in May 1988 and is administered in 561 districts through local communities and self-government bodies. The purpose was to achieve full literacy for 75 per cent of the population by 2007. This, it was expected, will lead to increased productivity, improvement in healthcare, and betterment of social life. However, this has been left unrealized. More importantly, 14 states and 4 union territories have passed laws making elementary education compulsory. In 2002, the union government passed the 93rd Constitutional Amendment Bill, subsequently adopted as the 86th Constitutional Amendment Act, which grants a fundamental right to free and compulsory education.

The right to education, however, makes little sense unless the school system, which is marked by low rates on enrolment (approximately only 56 per cent of children in the age group 5–9 attend school), high rates of dropouts, distance between schools and residential areas and lack of transportation, teacher absenteeism, low levels of learning, low participation, particularly of the girl child, and critical gaps in the availability of infrastructural facilities and qualitative aspects of education, including teachers' training, educational curricula, equipment, and training material, is restructured. It has been estimated that more children drop out of school for these reasons rather than those of poverty. Families would rather incur a debt and send their children to expensive private schools. Despite the fact that the first compulsory Education Act was legislated by the Parliament for Delhi in 1960 (Delhi Primary Education Act 1960), and despite the fact that other states subsequently adopted this model act, respective legislations failed to bring about major changes in the lives of children. Child labour is still rampant in the country, social biases work against educating the girl child, who is often compelled to drop out of school in order to look after her siblings while her parents go to work, and the presence of deep-rooted poverty, particularly among the Scheduled Castes and Tribes, hill and forest communities, rules out education.

The National Human Development Report 2001 concluded that 'India's educational development is a mixed bag of remarkable successes and glaring gaps. In the post-Independence period, the pace of educational development was unprecedented by any standards. At the same time, perhaps, the policy focus and public intervention in the provision of educational services was not adequately focused or, even misplaced, to the extent that even after 50 years of planned effort in the sector, nearly one-third of the population or close to 300 million people in the age group of seven years and above are illiterate'. These figures vary across regions: literacy rates have improved in Rajasthan, Orissa, and Madhya Pradesh in the 1990s. Himachal Pradesh is also a success story with 98 per cent of the children going to school in the state by the end of 1990s. However, literacy rates continue to be modest in Uttar Pradesh and Bihar. The picture on the educational front is simply not encouraging.

In the mid-1990s, a committee of education ministers recommended that the Constitution be amended to make free and compulsory education for children in the 6–14 age group a fundamental right. The committee also recommended that parents and guardians have a fundamental duty to provide opportunities to their children with respect to education. The report of the committee was mainly a response to a 1993 ruling of the Supreme Court in the case of *J. P. Unnikrishnan vs the State of Andhra Pradesh*. The Court had ruled that 'though right to education is not stated expressly as a fundamental right, it is implicit in and flows from right to life guaranteed under article 21'. The court further declared that the Directive Principles of State Policy 'form the fundamental feature and social conscience of the Constitution and the provisions of part III and IV are supplementary and complementary to each other'. Fundamental rights, ruled the court, are means to ensure the goals laid down in part IV and must be construed in the light of the Directive Principles. The State, ruled the court, should take measures to ensure free and compulsory education to all children in the age group of 6–14 years. The initiative taken by the court was enormously significant, since the goal of universal education stipulated by article 45 of the Directive Principles of State Policy, which was supposed to be achieved by 1960, is yet to be realized. The deadline kept getting postponed, and currently it stands till the end of the Tenth Five-Year Plan that is 2007.

The 93rd Constitution Amendment Bill, which was introduced in Parliament on 28 November 2001, subsequently became the Constitution 86th Amendment Act 2002. The bill had originally been introduced in 1997 in the Rajya Sabha. However, before it could be passed by the House, the government had fallen, and the bill remained in abeyance for four years, till it was resurrected by the National Democratic Alliance government led by the Bharatiya Janata Party in 2001. The new bill inserted a new sub-clause (a) after Article 21 in Chapter Three of the Constitution, which protects the right to life. The new sub-clause guarantees that the State shall provide free and compulsory education to all children of the age of 6–14 in any manner as the State, may, by law, determine. Article 45 of the Directive Principles of State Policy has been upgraded to a fundamental right. This article has been replaced by a new article, 45, which reads that the State shall endeavour to provide early-childhood care and education for all children until the age of six years. Article 51A of the Constitution has been amended by adding Clause (k) that lays down that parents and guardians should provide opportunities for education to their children or child as the case may be, in the age group of 6–14 years.

The UPA government had constituted a Central Advisory Board for Education to enforce this right. CABE finalized the draft Right to Education Bill in June 2005. However, the central government, instead of tabling this bill in Parliament, re-sent it in June 2006 as a model Right to Education Bill to the state governments, with the request that they should legislate the right to education in conformity with the model Right to Education Bill 2006. The right to education now falls within the purview of state governments, and state governments might or might not implement this bill, if necessary resources are not forthcoming. The model bill also does not give the right to approach the court, in case this right is violated. It is not mandatory for private schools to reserve 25 per cent of their seats for the marginal communities. And the bill holds parents responsible for giving their child education, even if there are no schools nearby and even if the parents lack resources.

Social activists and experts who have come together in the National Alliance for Fundamental Right to Education and Equity (NAFRE) and who have been consistently struggling to make education a right are disappointed by the government's response. The objective of the alliance is to prevent the dilution of vital rights related to free and compulsory education as defined by the Constitution and as interpreted by the Supreme Court. The alliance states that free and compulsory education is the responsibility of the State, that the State must provide quality education to all children, and that it should invest a minimum of 6 per cent of the national income in education. Experts also criticize the neglect of Early Childhood Care and Education, which is an important component of education and which influences heavily the most vital period of the development of children in the bill. Nor are the needs of children over 14 years of age taken into account. For these reasons, the right to free and compulsory education has been diluted.

CONCLUSION

Let me return to the question that was raised at the beginning of the argument—what is the relationship between democracy and well-being? Is the relationship between the two an essential one? Or is it random and contingent? There are perhaps no clear answers to these questions, because if there was ever a time when theorists assumed that democracy essentially exists for the well-being of the people, that time seems to have long passed. As our recent history has shown us, authoritarian regimes, which deny to their people civil and political rights, also find it perfectly feasible to ensure the same people a certain level of social and economic well-being. After all, inhabitants of countries run by authoritarian regimes, say Singapore, do enjoy a far better quality of life than citizens of democracies like India. This is a reality that theorists in the business of conceptualizing democracy have had to confront with some degree of discomfort.

Does it then follow that democrats should give up on democracy and opt for a regime that can efficiently deliver services/goods that meet the basic needs of people? The answer cannot but be no, because the virtue of democracy is that it recognizes, legalizes, and codifies the fundamental rights of citizens. Among these fundamental rights is the *root* right to demand rights. It is the possession of inalienable rights which allows citizens to stake a claim to the provision of social goods as a matter of right. Therefore, the first condition that serves to translate formal into substantive democracy, or political into social and economic democracy, is the existence of democratic institutions. The codification of political and civil rights in Chapter Three, and the codification of objectives of State policy in Chapter Four of the Indian Constitution have motivated and inspired collective action on pressing social issues. Certainly, collective action may not have resulted in the production of appropriate policies that address the malaise of social and economic deprivation in every case. What is significant, however, is that campaigns to enlarge the domain of rights have insistently and pressingly fore-grounded issues that are absolutely crucial for human lives in the public domain.

In India, this has been facilitated by the fact that Chapter Four of the Constitution has codified an exhaustive list of objectives of the social policy. The Directive Principles of State Policy in India have motivated a number of campaigns, which demand that the State deliver to the people what the Constitution has promised. The Supreme Court in India has played a significant role in equating fundamental rights and directive principles in a number of cases. The institutionalization of civil rights, the codification of Directive Principles of State Policy, and the presence of a hyperactive judiciary have served to create a space wherein civil society can mobilize to demand the realization of entitlements. This is the only way that political democracy can be translated into social and economic democracy, which will, in turn, deepen democracy.

Appendix: Table 5.1A

Indices	*India*	*Sri Lanka*	*China*	*Vietnam*
Infant mortality per live 1,000 births	60 (2003)	13 (2003)	30 (2003)	19 (2003)
One year olds fully immunized for measles in %	58.0 (2002–04)	99 (2003)	84 (2003)	93 (2003)
Population with sustainable access to improved sanitation in %	30 (2003)	91 (2003)	44 (2002)	41 (2002)
Births attended by skilled birth attendant in %	47.4 (2002–04)	97 (1995–2003)	97 (1995–2003)	85 (1995–2003)
Maternal mortality per 1000,000 deliveries	407 (adjusted 2000)	92 (adjusted 2000)	56 (adjusted 2000)	130 (adjusted 2000)
Under-five mortality per 1,000 births	87 (2003)	15 (2003)	37 (2003)	23 (2003)

Source: Planning Commission, *Towards Faster and More Inclusive Growth: An Approach to the 11th Five-Year Plan* (New Delhi: Government of India, 2006), p. 53.

Suggested Readings

Bardhan, Pranab. 'Sharing the Spoils, Group Equity, Development, and Democracy'. In Atul Kohli (ed.), *The Success of India's Democracy*. Cambridge, UK: Cambridge University Press, 2001, pp. 226–41.

Corbridge, Stuart and John Harriss, *Reinventing India: Liberalization, Hindu Nationalism, and Popular Democracy*, New Delhi: Oxford University Press, 2001.

Drèze, Jean and Amartya Sen. *India: Development and Participation*. New Delhi: Oxford University Press, 2002.

Dyson, Tim, Robert Cassen and Leela Visaria. *Twenty-first Century India: Population, Economy, Human Development, and the Environment*. New Delhi: Oxford University Press, 2004.

Prabhu, Seeta and R. Sudarshan (eds.). *Reforming India's Social Sector: Poverty, Nutrition, Health and Education*. New Delhi: Social Science Press, 2002.

Questions

1. How does democracy empower citizens to claim that the State should satisfy their demand for basic goods?
2. Why are health and education the most basic of goods that every human being has a right to?
3. What in your estimation is the reason for the Indian government not honouring its obligations given in the Directive Principles of State Policy?
4. Why is political democracy, particularly the right of political participation, important for the establishment of social and economic democracy?

Science and Technology Policy: IT and Social Change

6

Neha Khanna

Somebody once said to the philosopher Wittgenstein: What a bunch of no-knows we medieval Europeans must have been! Back in the days before Copernicus, to have looked up at the sky and thought that what we saw up there was the Sun going round the Earth, when, as everybody knows, the Earth goes round the Sun, and it doesn't take too many brains to understand that! Wittgenstein replied: Yes, but I wonder what it would have looked like if the Sun had been going round the Earth. The point is that it would, of course, have looked exactly the same. What he was saying was that you see what you want to see. Consider also the medieval Londoner or an 18th-century American who, when asked what he thought of the prospect that one day everybody would have his own individual form of personal transportation, laughed at the idea of the metropolis at a standstill when the streets became, as they surely would, 14 feet deep in horse manure. The concept of any other form of transportation was outside his context.[1] Human history and society have for long been shaped by the changes or rather the revolutions in the field of science, be it the ability to make fire or unravelling the mysteries of producing a crop out of seed strewn on the ground. Over the ages, various technologies have altered our lives and the social setting in a manner we can only imagine and admire.

It is, indeed, intriguing how technologies that we take to be primitive today changed the course of human civilization during the period in which they were invented. In this chapter, we shall try to look at the impact of science and technology in two sections. We begin with a general discussion on the impact of science and technology policies and their achievements and implications. In the second part, the chapter focuses on information technology policy and its impact on the economy as well as democracy.

1. James Burke, Jules Bergman and Isaac Asimov, *The Impact of Science on Society*, prepared by the Langley Research Center, NASA SP-482, http://history.nasa.gov/sp482. pdf (last accessed on 15 May 2008).

A HISTORICAL BACKGROUND

Science and technology have been an integral part of the Indian civilization and culture over the past several millennia. Few are aware that India was the fountainhead of important foundational scientific developments and approaches. These cover many great scientific discoveries and technological achievements in mathematics, astronomy, architecture, chemistry, metallurgy, medicine, natural philosophy and other areas. A great deal of this travelled outwards from India. Equally, India also assimilated scientific ideas and techniques from elsewhere, with an open mind and a rational attitude characteristic of a scientific ethos. In the half century since Independence, India has been committed to the task of promoting the spread of science. The key role of technology as an important element of national development is also well recognized. The *Scientific Policy Resolution of 1958* and the *Technology Policy Statement of 1983* enunciated the principles on which the growth of science and technology in India has been based over the past several decades. These policies have emphasized self-reliance, as also sustainable and equitable development. They embody a vision and strategy that are applicable today, and would continue to inspire us in our endeavours.[2]

The British were quick to recognize the role and importance of science, technology and medicine in empire building.[3] So the colonial state, even though it claimed to be carrying a disinterested project of civilizing mission, actually came with an ideology, a string of institutions and a set of committed people to serve its ends. Even though the indigenous education in India included instructions in science prior to the advent of the colonial rule, the debate and discussions for the system of education to be adopted concerned primarily what kind of science and technology would eventually be institutionalized in India.[4] The Indian thinking in response to this was highlighted by an attempt at cultural synthesis. For the educated Indians, then, retrieval of this seemingly lost identity became a precondition for regaining lost sovereignty. Talking about the cultural synthesis enabled them to absorb culture shock and then promised a possible opportunity to transcend the barriers imposed by colonialism.[5]

The two major religious groupings engaged with modern scientific thought from their own vantage points governed by their political, social and economic objectives, not always in isolation from the other.[6] Within the nationalist

2. Science and Technology Policy 2003, http://dst.gov.in.
3. Deepak Kumar, 'Science and Society in Colonial India: Exploring an Agenda', *Social Scientist*, 28 (5,6), May–June 2000: 24–46.
4. Zaheer Abbas, *The Science of Empire: Scientific Knowledge, Civilization and Colonial Rule in India* (New York: State University of New York Press, 1996), pp. 186–87.
5. Ibid.
6. S. Irfan Habib, 'Reconciling Science with Islam in 19th Century India', *Contributions to Indian Sociology* (n.s), 34 (1), 2000: p. 64.

movement, the debate on the reconstruction of India heavily centred on the knowledge and use of modern science and technology. While the likes of Madan Mohan Malaviya stressed how India was reindustrialized and carried on a new watchword of scientized technology (icons of which were Japan and Germany because he felt that the British model was inadequate[7]), Gandhi ridiculed the most prized possessions of the West: modernization and industrialization. He seldom used the term science and technology and conveniently replaced it with civilization and mechanization, to which he showed his deep concern. Some of the central tendencies in modern civilization such as massive industrialization, undue importance to technology and science, which altered the concept of labour, made Gandhi a critic of that civilization.

SCIENCE AND TECHNOLOGY: THE POST-INDEPENDENCE PERIOD

After Independence, the highlight of India's development strategy was the adoption of the socialist model of planned economic development, with a great emphasis on capital goods industries. Pandit Jawaharlal Nehru ordained the huge multi-purpose projects as the new temples of modern India. This period was soon followed by the first tentative steps in the field of research in science and technology with the aim of changing the economic pattern in the nation's countryside, the reference here being made to the increase in agricultural output as a result of the Green Revolution, which relied on newer varieties of seeds and fertilizers, a move towards the mechanization of the Indian agricultural sector. Howsoever slow it might have been, the result was there for all to see.

Scientific and technological activities in India are carried out under the aegis of a wide array of governmental bodies (both central and state level), private-sector participation, non-profit organizations, etc. These institutional structures with their research laboratories are the main contributors to the scientific research being carried out in the country.[8]

Agricultural Research

The huge strides that were made in the field of agricultural research and technology related to high-yielding crop varieties that have laid the foundation of the journey from a food-deficient nation to one that has excess production of cereals and other food and cash crops. However, the irony is that while the food stocks of the country are spilling over, we still have pockets of hunger, deprivation and starvation deaths. There is a need to ensure that the benefits

7. Kumar, 'Science and Society in Colonial India'.
8. Research, Reference & Training Division (ed. and comp.), *India 2006* (New Delhi: Government of India, Ministry of Information and Broadcasting, Publication Division, 2006).

of the innovations reach all conceivable corners of the country. A step in this direction are the 'e-choupals', which have to be used as tools of information dissemination. There has been talk of the need to give another push to the productive capacity of agricultural sector through a second Green Revolution.

The technology fatigue is seen as a major cause underlying the deceleration in performance of the agricultural sector. Since the Green Revolution in the 1960s there has been no major technological innovation that could give a fresh impetus to agricultural productivity. The absence of productive technology, which also reduces risks, is particularly serious for rain-fed, dry-land situations. In the longer run, growth in agricultural productivity can be sustained only through continuous technological progress. This calls for a well-considered strategy for prioritized basic research, which is now all the more urgent in view of the mounting pressure on scarce natural resources, climate change and also the shrinking availability of spillovers from international public research. We need to usher in a second Green Revolution by adopting a strategy that frees us from past mindsets. The strategy should be operationalized in the form of challenge programmes in which central institutes and the state agricultural universities work with organic integration.

The Eleventh Plan will have to energize the National Agricultural Research System and improve its capacity to develop and deliver innovative and effective technologies relevant in the current context and needs. This will require strengthening of the basic research component of its programmes through identification of strategic research pathways in an anticipatory fashion. The exercise must go hand in hand with clearer demarcation of basic research on the one hand, which may not contribute immediately to growth, and strategic research on the other, which tackles well-identified problems in a goal-directed way. The recently established fund for National Strategic Agricultural Research must be expanded in the Eleventh Plan and oriented to stimulate research that responds to a prioritized and well-defined strategy, so that the country's large, agricultural research system, which successfully launched the Green Revolution in the past, can now be called upon to address newer and more formidable challenges and provide region-specific, problem-solving capacity. A delivery-targeted operational mechanism will have to be designed for its meaningful operation. Clearly, business as usual has no place whatsoever in this framework. The agricultural system also needs to be thoroughly revamped and restructured in the light of advice rendered by high-powered committees chaired respectively by Dr M. S. Swaminathan and Dr R. A. Mashelkar.[9]

Meteorological Services

The Indian Meteorological Department (IMD) was established in 1875. It is the national meteorological service and the principal agency in all matters

9. Approach Paper to the Eleventh Five-Year Plan 2007–2011, www.planningcommission.gov.in.

related to meteorology, seismology and allied services. The IMD issued the first operational long-range forecast of seasonal south-west monsoon rainfall (June–September) of India in 1986. The Crop Yield Formulation Unit of the department has developed statistical models using correlation and regression techniques to forecast crop yields on an operational basis over a large part of India. The Meteorological Department is perhaps also burdened with the most critical form of soothsaying—that of forecasting the monsoons. These predictions have an effect on the Indian economy that belies any belief that the economy of our country is not solely dependent on agriculture and the rains that feed it.

Apart from this, the Indian plate is notoriously unstable in terms of tectonic movements and has been the cause of many devastating earthquakes. A new challenge that the forecasters were faced with was on 25 and 26 December 2004, when the giant tsunami waves erased out of the face of the earth villages, and with them, extinguished many human lives. That experience prompted the process of making India a part of the Tsunami Early Warning System that operates through a series of warning stations that are connected via satellites. Warnings are sent across to the member country in the event of any underwater tectonic movement or any other development that could trigger a tsunami. This need to use the latest in the field of weather forecasting and supervision of tectonic movement has to be coupled with the developments in the field of communications, so that the news of impending disasters get passed on to the groups that are in the gravest danger.

Atomic Energy

With the world's reserves of fossil fuels depleting faster than the replenishment rate, there is an urgent need to look for alternative sources of energy that will continue to support the bulwark of economic development in an efficient and sustainable manner. The answer to the energy problems of the future and even the present day lies in the power that remains trapped in the building blocks of nature—the atoms. The Department of Atomic Energy (DAE) was established in 1954 with this specific object in mind. Since then, the DAE has been involved in research in the field of atomic energy technology and its application in the field of agriculture, medicine, industry and even providing a credible, nuclear-weapon-based military deterrent for the nation. The research centres of DAE are engaged in basic research in relevant areas. In addition, the autonomous research institutes, supported by grant in aid by DAE, are centres of excellence in the field of research ranging from mathematics to computers, physics to astronomy and biology to cancer. India, today, not only uses atomic energy for medical and research purposes but also possesses a credible nuclear deterrent. This nuclear weapons programme is supposedly our guarantee against any harm coming to our nation from external forces, but the question that begs an answer is this: what is our safeguard against 'Chernobyl-style' accidents? We have already paid a huge price for the careless handling of dangerous chemicals in Bhopal in 1982, where more than 25,000 lost their lives and a whole generation was cursed with a life of disabilities and deprivations. Can we risk a similar accident like the one in Bhopal at any of our nuclear facilities? What is the explanation for the huge expenditure on newer and better ways of killing fellow human beings, when in large parts of the country, hunger is doing that with a far more horrendous precision. All through 2006–07, the government tried to drum up support from the rest of the world while staking India's claim to a permanent seat in the United Nations Security Council. However, efforts should first be made to provide adequate support against the dangers of hunger, starvation and penury.

The Indian Space Programme[10]

Despite being a developing country with the economic constraints that follow with it, India has effectively developed a credible space programme that has broken new ground and put it in the select group of countries that can design its own satellites and, now, can even launch satellites.

During the formative years in the early 1960s, space research was carried out with the help of sounding rockets. The Indian Space Research Organization (ISRO), the primary body for space research in India, was founded in 1969. In the history of the Indian space programme, the 1970s was the period of experiments with the launch of experimental satellite programmes like Aryabhatta, Bhaskara, Rohini, and Apple. In the 1980s and 1990s, ISRO made impressive strides in building state-of-the-art remote sensing and communication satellites, together with their applications for national development. So far 48 major satellites, have been launched, both low Earth-orbiting ones for remote sensing and geostationary ones for meteorology and communication, half of them form India's space port at Sriharikota (using its own satellite-launching vehicles). The remote sensing satellites have been extensively used for the monitoring and management of agriculture, forests, water resources, mineral wealth, ocean resources, land use practices, environmental pollution, and natural disasters, and for initiating sustainable integrated development. The geostationary INSAT satellite, likewise, have initiated a new communication revolution in the country, and are now being extensively used for nationwide broadcasting, telecommunication, education, telemedicine and health care, weather forecasting and disaster management. Recently, ISRO launched Chandrayaan-I, India's first mission to the Moon (an unmanned exploration), which is a major boost to India's space programme. India's robust launch vehicle programme has enable the country to now offer its services to the outside world. Antrix, the commercial arm of the ISRO, has been marketing India's space services globally.

10. U. R. Rao, 'Indian Space Odyssey', in Asoke N. Mitra (ed.), *India in the World of Physics: Then and Now* (Delhi: Pearson Longman and PHISPC, 2009), pp. 541–61.

What we have discussed above are the research programmes, developmental policies and cutting-edge scientific explorations that have been carried out over the years in India, while the question that we must answer now is how these endeavours bring about a change in the social fabric of the country and how they spawn a new beginning. The answer is not too difficult to find: All the above research programmes have been carried out with one common objective and that is greater good of the greatest possible number, the development in the field of meteorology has helped us in studying the rainfall patterns and its effect on crop cycles. Nuclear energy might be the source of the most horrific killing machine that man ever invented, but it is also true that it can solve all the energy problems that the country faces. Countries like Canada and France have been using nuclear energy to meet their energy requirements and the fact that the levels of pollution due to safe nuclear energy are close to nil is something that has to be considered specially in this day and age of increased awareness about global warming and the havoc that it wreaks on our weather systems. The Indian space programme has enabled us to move to an age of easier and efficient communication and made distances disappear; the huge boom that the Indian service sector has experienced is something that stands testimony to this success story that has added a new feather in its cap.

INFORMATION TECHNOLOGY AND ITS IMPLICATIONS

Honey, will you answer the television, am watching the telephone.... As a social leveller, Information Technology ranks second only to Death.

—*Sam Pitroda*

Information technology (IT) is considered to be a social leveller in the statement because it has eliminated distance as a perceptible concept from our lives. This 'death of distance',[11] a determinant of the cost of communication, will become the single most important economic force to reshape society over the next half century. The history of human civilization, the argument goes, has been governed by three major revolutions in communication. The 19th century saw the easier and faster communication of goods. The 20th century saw cheaper, easier communication and transportation of people and the 21st century is going to be governed by a faster means of communicating ideas. The equation has now shifted from labour intensive to intellectual incentive.

The following section of this chapter is an attempt at assessing this argument. (We open the question up and try to measure up the veracity of the claim.)

11. www.deathofdistance.com (last accessed on 14 May 2008).

BACKGROUND

With the advent of IT, avenues like e-commerce, e-governance, e-mails and the e-world emerged, on the one hand, and lots of other e-things made their debut in the Indian e-conomy in the late 1990s on the other, for example e-marriages, e-ducation, e-nvironment studies and e-ntertainment. Even the English language did not remain unaffected by the change with, '4m' replacing the usual 'from' in the popular SMS text language. The 'e'-dominance in our day-to-day lives has grown so much that it has become rare to spot any technology which is 95 per cent e-free.[12]

The IT industry saw daylight in India in the 1980s. It was C=DOT, the technology centre set up in 1984 by Sam Pitroda, that pioneered the ringing out of archaic phone systems country wide and that paved the way for street-corner telephone booths mushrooming in the smallest of towns. This wave of telecom revolution gave birth to 800,000 PCOs in India. In the past one-and-a-half-decade or so, gigantic changes have taken place at the global levels. Information technology is applied in most human activities, be it production or education, defence or war, distribution or production of goods all have become simplified, effective and reliable. Telecommunications not only links all industrial processes, but also allow computerization and storage of information. Information technology established a foot in India with active support and eagerness of the government. From the outset, IT focused on overseas markets such as the USA, Japan and Western Europe. Tapping the overseas market helped Indians to establish themselves first as employed professionals and then as entrepreneurs. India has gained a name for itself in the field of excellence in IT.

Nirvikar Singh defines IT as 'the digital processing, storage and communication of information of all kinds'.[13] Roli Varma and Everett Rogers expand the definition given by Singh by stating 'it is not a single technology but a combination of four technologies, viz. tools to access information, telecommunication linkages (including networks), information-processing hardware and software storage media'.[14] The foundation of IT is the ability to represent text, data sound and visual information digitally'. IT is further woven with economy by Kalyan Raipuria who says, 'the IT economy comprises all the activities involved in value addition (i.e. GDP) adjusted for exports and imports, by way of IT services, software, systems and communication equipment such as computer companies, telecommunication utilities and related enterprise'.[15] Nasscom lists 10 categories

12. Lucy Kellaway, 'Enough! I've Had E-nough', *Financial Times*, 7 February 2000.
13. Nirvikar Singh, 'Information Technology and India's Economic Development', http://129.3.20.41/eps/dev/papers/0412/0412007.pdf (last accessed on 14 May 2008).
14. Roli Varma and Everett Rogers, 'Indian Cyber Workers in the US', *Economic and Political Weekly*, 39 (12), 25 December 2004.
15. Kalyan Raipuria, 'What Size the "New" Economy? A Conduit Approach', *Economic and Political Weekly*, 37 (11), 16 March 2002.

of IT-enabled services (ITES). The services give a broad view of the scope of the IT industry:

- Customer interaction services
- Business process outsourcing/management, back office operation
- Insurance claims processing
- Medical transcription
- Legal database
- Digital content
- Online education
- Data digitalization/GIS
- Payroll /HR services
- Web site services

The Indian IT journey to greater heights was initially chartered by private industries and IT professionals who wanted to be amongst the best in the world. A bunch of upstarts unleashed a trail of achievements, which cascaded and have created the most compelling brand—the Indian IT professional. Some of the market segments shaping the future of the IT industry are:

- IT software and services export
- IT-enabled services
- Domestic IT market
- Telecom infrastructure
- Venture capital

The niche carved out by the IT industry in our modern-day economy provides an almost perfect contrast to the Nehruvian model of development. In lieu of public-sector-led investment and growth, in this case, State policies have promoted rapid growth in the private sector through a judicious mixture of laissez faire and the hidden and visible subsidies. The new equation between the State and private enterprises that is emerging in this sector, especially in states such as Karnataka and Andhra Pradesh, suggests major shifts in the socio-economic structure of the country. Thus, it gave IT the status of a revolution. The rudimentary approach of the IT revolution is inherent in the Schumpeterian framework of creative destruction,[16] a process where a number of innovations,

16. Brishti Guha, 'IT: Deconstructing the Bust that Followed the Boom', *Economic and Political Weekly* 38 (24), 14 June 2003.

discoveries and inventions allowed the new 'sunrise industries' to dominate and displace the old 'sunset industries'. In the perspective of history, it is similar to the wave of innovations associated with the Industrial Revolution of the late 18th century, which opened up access to fossils fuels, a previously unexploited and (then) infinitely elastic source of energy, on to the railway boom, which opened up access to an elastic supply of food and natural resources from the heart of the new world. Just as these innovations opened access to an elastic supply of information, it did this by drastically lowering communication-information-processing and search costs. It is not just that the IT revolution had its origins in a phenomenon often witnessed throughout economic history.

The benefits associated with the IT revolution have, if anything, emphasized the value of traditional economic principles. It did this by increasing the importance of comparative advantage and division of labour, ushering in an era of cheap information and low transaction costs in markets with greatly reduced friction, greater competition, diminished importance of the economics of scale and arguably lower entry barriers where fixed costs were low. The income-creating effects of the IT industry led to the IT boom, which meant there was a rise in demand, and, therefore, a shift towards high-income elastic products, mainly services. These included a rise in the demand for software and computer professional—a direct consequence of IT boom. It also extended to other service professionals (medical, legal, entertainment, etc.) reflecting direct income effects and to areas like childcare and security related to the increasing complexity of life and reduced leisure.

Information Technology: The Growth Story

While information technology is the engine of the current Indian growth story, the real challenge lies in translating it to a vision in order to use it as a tool for raising the living standard of the common man and enriching their lives. Through IT, India has built up valuable brand equity in the global markets. In ITES, India has emerged as the most preferred destination for business process outsourcing (BPO), a key driver of growth for the software industry and service sector.[17] However, in order to translate this growth into social change and development, the thrust has to be on the role of IT, not only as a catalyst in accelerating the growth of India, but also on the role of the communication systems as agents of social change as well as indicators of economic development and social progress.

The significant growth of the IT sector in the past few years has been a major phenomenon. During the period 1993–2003, the revenue generated by the sector grew from about Rs 54,500 to Rs 793,370 million. The employment in this

17. Chithelen Ignatius, 'Outsourcing to India', *Economic and Political Weekly*, 39 (10), 6 March 2004.

sector has also grown significantly. According to industry sources, there were only 6,800 IT workers in India in 1986–87. This number went up to 650,000 in 2002–2003. India's most prized resource in today's knowledge economy is its readily available work. According to a Nasscom–McKinsey report, annual revenue projections for the IT industry is $17 billion for 2010. Importantly, the IT market has both domestic and internal components to it.

TELEPHONE SECTOR

The domestic component includes the telephone networks, which is one of the largest in the world. Since 1985, the communication facility has been augmented significantly from fibre-optic cable, a domestic satellite system with 254 earth stations, to mobile cellular services with urban and rural connectivity. To ensure the investment of money and technology in the telecom infrastructure, TRAI (Telecom Regulatory Authority of India) has divided the telephone sector into the following groups:

- Cellular mobile service providers, fixed service providers and cable service providers, collectively referred to as access providers
- Radio-paging-service providers
- Public-mobile-radio-trunking-service providers
- National long-distance operator
- International long-distance operator
- Other service provider
- Global mobile personal communication by satellite (GMPCS) service providers
- V-SAT-based service provider

The total number of telephone (cellular, fixed landline + WLL) crossed the 10 million mark in April 2005. Today, India is the fifth largest network in the world in terms of telephones after China, the USA, Japan and Germany.[18] India's teledensity is 9.13 per cent compared with China's 55 per cent and more then 100 per cent in the case of the USA, Japan and Germany. Telephone services cover more than 87 per cent villages. Around 5.45 million Internet connections were established in January 2005. Fixed lines increased from 17.8 million in 1998 to 58.1 million in April 2005. The total number of phones in 1998 was 18.68 million with a teledensity of 1.94 per cent. India had hoped to have 250 million telephones, 22 per cent teledensity, 18 million Internet

18. *Manorama Yearbook, 2006.*

connection and 9 million broadband connections by 2007. Cellular-phone usage increased from 1.20 million in 1999 to 41.46 million in April 2005. The impact of information technology, especially in communication, and the consequent growth of e-commerce have defined all prediction. It is uniformly being seen, especially in developing countries, as the technology that will enable these countries to leap-frog half a century of development. The above data show that we have solved the problem of communications for the have-nots with public telephones in almost every street and every village. The focus is now on the upgradation of the PCO culture to public information centres or Internet cafes.

THE INTERNET

The Internet was created in the early 1960s. It was conceived in the form of computer networking at the Massachusetts Institute of Technology in 1962. It further developed into the Advanced Research Project Agency Network (ARPANET) of the department of defence of the government of the USA. It is a two-way telecommunication application with a difference. It uses computers to receive and transmit pure, digital signals. The signals blend messaging with controls in a single, multiplied, data stream. It was in 1990 that ARPANET was converted into a public network and was thrown open to all citizens. Since 1993, the Internet has been enhanced with a new development, namely, the creation of a database that users could access without mediation coupled with a very easy-to-use, graphic-designed computer application—browsers. This has made the medium available to millions of people who do not need much more than the basic command over the written language to become adept. In fact, the growth of the Internet globally has outstripped any previous innovation. If 50 million is taken as a measure of the number of users needed to make a technology ubiquitous, then the automobile industry took some 30-odd years to reach this level and television, 20. The Internet has taken only five and is well on its way to doubling that number in less than two years. The digital and communication technology (through the Internet) by decreasing transport and information-distribution costs increased the accessibility to foreign markets. Transaction costs plummeted, so did search costs, opening up access via the Internet to new markets and supply sources, which increased competition between suppliers. A firm is no longer vulnerable to opportunistic extortion by any one supplier, undermining what used to be a precautionary motive for vertical integration. In a nutshell, the IT revolution has made it possible for an entrepreneur to set up business with little more than a PC, a telephone and a modem, benefiting many small-scale entrepreneurs.[19]

19. Manu N. Kulkarni, 'Asia's Technology Future Transforming Business or People?', *Economic and Political Weekly*, 36 (24), 16 June 2001.

E-COMMERCE: APPLYING IT TO TRADE AND COMMERCE

The Internet grew rapidly mainly because of its widespread application and it provided utility and services to the common man. The first requirement was to develop the capability of transferring files and data from one computer to another and for this purpose, a worldwide network of computers was established in such a way that any computer in the world could be connected to any of the millions and billions of computers to emerge as the World Wide Web. These three words gained an important position in further democratization of governance and market processes; thus, e-commerce and e-governance came into the picture.

India's lack of infrastructure and terrestrial telecom facilities has greatly hindered the progress of e-commerce in India. As a result, electronic commerce was still in its infancy in India till 2003. With the opening of the Internet market, however, a large number of new industries and MNCs have appeared. Given the recent apparently phenomenal growth of the IT-enabled services, the expectation of developments in e-commerce and industry prompted support for such development. With the new IT policy, there has been a lot of expectation that e-commerce will bring the global marketplace to the potentially large market in the Third World countries. The development of the country is heavily dependent on the changing price structure that makes equipment networks and services more easily and widely available.[20] E-banking with magnetic transfer of money and the popular usage of ATM cards has become an essential part of our daily lives. E-commerce is already raising other issues like e-taxation in the realm of trade and exchange. E-commerce is leading to a growth of supply capacity through capital, augmenting technological change. These, in turn, are already changing the capital and labour markets. As the volume of e-commerce grows, the significance of revenue from this mode of commerce is bound to grow and would be difficult to ignore. Thus, regulation becomes an important feature. 'Hacker lesson; wired citizens need government'.[21]

E-GOVERNANCE: APPLYING IT TO GOVERNANCE

In current literature, most of the definitions of e-governance are loaded with its advantageous or virtuous connotations. For example, e-governance is considered a system of governance that represents 'good governance'; that works better and costs less; that enhances responsiveness; that promotes civil society; and that is simple, moral, accountable, responsive and transparent—S.M.A.R.T, in short.

---

20. Editorial, 'E-Commerce: Issues for Developing Countries', *Economic and Political Weekly*, 36 (16), 21–27 April 2001.
21. Thomas L. Friedman, 'Hacker Lesson: Wired Citizens Need Government', *International Herald Tribune*, 16 February 2000.

E-governance in a layman's language means application of e-commerce techniques to government services to improve services to citizens and businesses. The USA, Australia, Singapore and Canada are leaders in e-governance. India is in the process of attaining a level where more than 25 per cent of government dealings and services will be electronically delivered.[22]

The progress of e-governance in our country is hampered because of the lack of adequate financial resources, appreciation about the benefits by all concerned including politicians and the bureaucracy. The importance of e-governance lies in the provision of information and services. The Net will not only improve transparency in governance but will also allow government officials to devote more time to the less-privileged citizens who do not have access to the Net. In 1999, the Government of India set up a National Institute of Smart Government (NISG) as a collaboration between the government, businesses and the community. However, India's teledensity is quite low and PC ownership is abysmal. The Ministry of Information Technology is trying to create a network of 100 million Internet connections and one million information kiosks (i.e. 1–2 connection per village, and its success will depend on the promotion of Indian-language usage over the Internet; re-engineering of government processes to improve governance and the launch of mass campaigns on IT awareness. Nasscom and the government together as a joint force are working towards prioritization of e-governance. A centre for developing advanced computing through Global Information System Technology (GIST), with direction from the government, initiated and commissioned the project of developing Indian-language tools with natural-language processing in evolving script and font standard.

The significant parameters of e-governance initiatives were:

- Improve government's own functioning
- Provide better service to the citizen in a transparent manner
- Potential priorities for e-governance pilot projects
- Strengthening the pressure points
- Locals 'external drivers' are to be used on a priority basis. This would mean targeting three sectors: (a) independent media (b) local NGOs and (c) public libraries, community centres, post offices and other access points, which provide information to citizens
- Priority to be given to building a data and management-information system and then moving on to the institutional links and finally to the intermediated citizens-related projects

22. C. Satapathy, 'Perspectives', *Economic and Political Weekly*, 23 September 2000.

- Projects that will be used as a demonstration site to get priority as they build knowledge
- Supportive, cross-cutting development priorities

Information Technology and the Law

With information technology being applied to trade and commerce as well as to governance, cyberspace cannot remain a government-free zone. Equally important are the issues of individual and personal privacy and other social and cultural practices. Therefore, a systematic framework of cyber laws has evolved to act as a facilitator. The framework is the following:

- Digital signatures are recognized along with the rules of encryption and secure electronic transmission
- Protection of copyright and other intellectual property rights
- Data protection and protection of privacy of individuals and corporate entities
- Consumer protection
- Prevention of cyber frauds
- Other regulatory public-morality issues (e.g., child pornography and criminality, facilitating sale of narcotic drugs, assisting terrorists, etc.)

Issues like privacy, consumer protection, intellectual-property rights, contracts and taxation are not to be self regulated for e-commerce to flourish. E-regulation is closely associated with e-governance.

Information Technology, Development and Democracy

The gigantic proportions of growth shown by the IT industry in India has not just brought about an increasing integration with the global economy but has also brought about fundamental transformation in the lives of people. Changes are visible in the relationship of labour, productivity, competitiveness, which are, in turn, responsible for changing the identities of the entrepreneurial class. The IT industry has produced a new kind of capitalist class in India. Interestingly, most of the founders of software firms have come from the middle class, building on their cultural capital of higher and technical education. Indian universities provide 13,500 engineering graduates every year. The segments that truly represent this new global class are back-office operations, remote-education departments, data search, market-research departments and customer-interaction services. This emerging class is conspicuous by its declared autonomy from the 'old Indian economy' dominated by the public sector.[23] Indians who are comfortably employed in the West, along with the ones operating as a part of the same technological circuit in India, have together formed a class— a class sharply different in its ideological orientation from the established business class. In contrast to the old business professionals, the IT business professionals emerged within the global economy and a liberalized environment, and sport a transnational outlook. This transnational IT class is an urbane concept thus, it is still relatively insignificant in terms of number, but it is significant enough to be called the representatives of resurgent India.

Information technology has increased the responsiveness of the government by providing support to democratic values of equality and liberty to its citizens on the one hand, and empowered the State by using the technology to jam, block and filter information, on the other. Vision of democracy within the scope of information technology is an important source to hasten the pace of development. With the help of scaffolding by IT, democracy is strengthened with stronger and newer forms of financial, legal and regulatory systems. To this effect, all government and most of the private Web sites are designed keeping clients ranging from students to veterans in mind. The sites give information on practically everything under the sun—services, books, employment, and advertisements. These are accessible seven days a week, 24 hours in a day and 365 days in a year to all. For instance, admission forms can be downloaded from the University of Delhi Web site, and complaints and queries can be uploaded whether on RTI or any other matter.

Though significant leaps have been taken by various state governments towards revolutionizing the process of development, Andhra Pradesh has established a landmark success under the tenure of Chandrababu Naidu. AP Online was one of the first initiatives in the country to offer multiple services at a single platform. Initiatives of this nature have completely revamped the kind of existing governance in the state. It delivers a range of services to citizens ranging from online submission of forms, applications and requests for registrations to licenses, permits, certificates and representations to any government departments along with provision to register complaints and grievances online. For effective e-governance, the state aimed this endeavour to be comprehensive in scope by making 200 informative, interactive and payment services available to all citizens.[24] The online availability of information nationwide aims to provide government to citizen services, government to business-digital-procurement processes, and development of government-to-government connectivity promises to yield significant benefits.

23. Carol Upadhyaya, 'A New Transnational Capitalist Class', *Economic and Political Weekly*, 27 November 2004.

24. http://papers.ssrn.com/so/3papers.cfm?abstract-id=994912#paper.

IT has become a part of day-to-day life and has a wide outreach. Apart from dissemination of information, it is also being used in social and political mobilizations. From election campaigns of political parties to campaigns against government policies, from building alliances and networks of civil-society organizations to promoting various causes, online campaigns are the most important tool in the hands of people. When the students of various academic and technical institutions came together to oppose the government policy of reservations in institutions of higher educations, they did not just march on the streets of the capital. Within weeks, they launched a Web site, which began to work as a virtual epicentre of the campaign. Text-message service of the mobile phone was transformed into an instrument of sloganeering. Pictures taken by mobile phones were instantly sent to the electronic media, which, in turn, asked its viewers to participate in SMS surveys and express themselves on the issue. In sum, the campaign got its character as much from the way it transformed the services of information technology into a political tool as from the political point it was making.

There are other examples in which IT, particularly the Internet, has paved the way for creative interventions. When a group of youngsters wanted to promote volunteerism by pooling together small, individual energies under the name of Bakul Foundation, opening up an office was not the first thing they did. Instead, they launched an online campaign requesting people to pledge their small resources and energies for building a children's library. Bakul Foundation announced on their official blog and on a pledge site that a library for children would be opened in Bhubaneswar, Orissa, on April 2007, if one thousand people came together to help set it up.[25] Bakul existed only on the Internet till the pledge became successful and the library was set up. However, the online campaign helped mobilize people because people gradually saw that they were not alone and that they were joining something that had acquired the contours of a movement. The pledge campaign was a transparent document of the support Bakul had been able to mobilize and as more and more people took the pledge, it became easier to mobilize further support. As the library and, indeed, Bakul Foundation came into its real existence, it was already a success story of online volunteerism. It stands testimony to the power and potency of the Internet, which is not merely a virtual world, but which can contribute to concrete changes in society.

There are problems, however, that raise questions. First, there is issue of accessibility of the IT and, as a result, the digital divide that it creates. In a country with continental proportions, providing access to IT-related facilities has been a major challenge. Second, the use of IT requires the ability to read and write and in the Indian context, with a high level of illiteracy, large sections of society are unable to have access to it. This digital divide has led to further

25. www.pledgebank.com/bakul-library.

widening of the gap between those who have access to technology and those who do not. Third, policy makers have barely been able to give concrete shape to the general directions regarding implementation of IT in the governance processes. It is quite clear that the current infrastructure in most government agencies could not support e-government at any appreciable level. The initial euphoria regarding e-commerce has been replaced by the awareness of a painstaking process that will be necessary to further exploit the coordination, control and communication potential of information technology, namely, a cumbersome process of policy change embedded in red tapism and bourgeoning hierarchies of the government and a complicated process of policy change.

Fourth, information technology has overlooked some structural problems, for instance, in rural areas, making government information accessible to anyone with a computer, a connection and an Internet service provider or else accessibility to cyber cafes. Both these options have not reached far-flung areas, thus creating a situation where technology influences choices that are already facing constraints. IT, therefore, restricts its benefits to the middle class.

CONCLUSION

After Independence, the process of nation building depended a lot on the progress in the field of science and technology. Development of technology and its applications in the fields of industry, agriculture and the daily lives of the citizens have played an important role in the development of the country over the last 60 years. The diffusion of information and communication technologies has impacted on the nature of work, creating new work cultures and ethos inside and outside the industry. However, if the aim is to expand the democratic processes with the help of information technology and science and technology in general—in terms of the new class and power relations in society— making it available to the poor sections of society should be the aim. It is not to be forgotten that technologies are a part of the social system and, thus, should serve larger social purposes. IT industry is slowly emerging from an industry with the acquired status of narrowly defined corporate objectives to one possessing social collectives and determination to cater to the needs of politics of change.

Suggested Readings

Keniston, Kenneth and Deepak Kumar (eds.). *IT Experience in India: Bridging the Digital Divide*. New Delhi: Sage Publications, 2004.

Malik, Amitav. *Indian Science and Technology*. Delhi: Observer Research Foundation, 2006.

Research, Reference & Training Division (ed. and comp.). *India 2006*. New Delhi: Government of India, Ministry of Information and Broadcasting, Publications Division, 2006.

Subbbarayappa, B. V. *Science in India—Past And Present*. Mumbai: Popular Prakashan, 2007.

Questions

1. Trace the evolution of science and technology policy in independent India. Analyse its role in nation building.
2. Discuss the role of science and technology policy in industrial and agricultural development in modern India.
3. What is information technology? Analyse the role of information technology in the process of socio-economic change.

PART

II

Society

The Changing Social Structure in Contemporary India

7

N. R. Levin

We, the educated, urban, middle-class Indians, feel very uncomfortable talking about caste. Considerations of caste reflect a sectarian and narrow worldview and remind us of rural India with its caste wars. We claim indifference to the question of caste, though our lives are inextricably interlinked with the historical legacy of the caste system. In fact, it is so inextricably linked that often, we do not notice how our lives are governed by caste.

Caste once again became a burning issue in 2006 over the issue of reservations for other backward castes (OBCs). In what was dubbed by sections of the media as Mandal II, students took to the streets to protest the reservations and to press for the repeal of the Government of India order for 27 per cent reservations in the country's premium educational institutions like the IITs, IIMs and, AIIMS. There were two major aspects of the argument against the proposed reservations: (*a*) that it was merely a plaything in the hands of crooked politicians out to grab vote-banks, and (*b*) it would compromise the merit of students and the reputation and standard of these elite institutions, which have earned a repute for the country in the world. In this highly charged emotional atmosphere, caste became the focus of discussion and it was predicted that it would divide India on sectarian and narrow lines. It was also predicted that the economic growth of the country would be affected because merit is increasingly tied up with the productivity criteria of the market and the norm of efficiency.

In all the debates that raged in the media and in popular discussions, it was often not acknowledged that the focus on merit itself made caste merely invisible, though it was very much present. For instance, during these agitations and the debates around it, it was discovered that backward caste members had a marginal presence in the mainstream media (considered a bastion of meritocracy) and that there was an absence of their voices of dissent. Merit is determined objectively through entrance examinations, marks secured, etc. But it was only students who had access to a particular kind of education at elite institutions and had the benefit of coaching classes, who lay the maximum claim to that merit. It is well known among policy makers and educational experts that the majority of these winners are particularly drawn from urban, upper-caste households. What is disturbing is that a vast majority of the rural, backward-caste students are not able to acquire the merit, and remain tied up with traditional jobs or end up as informal labourers in urban areas. To replicate the success of the reservation policy in Tamil Nadu and other southern states, where more than 50 years of reservation has assured desired levels of socio-economic progress for backward groups, the Government of India decided to implement reservations extending to the country's premium educational institutions like the IITs and IIMs.

This chapter attempts to engage with the contentious issue of caste, historically, by looking at the social structure of India over a period of hundred years and the socio-economic changes the social structure has undergone under colonial and post-colonial regimes. The chapter will also engage with the thinking on the caste question in India by intellectuals and activists from Jyotiba Phule and B. R. Ambedkar in the colonial times to the post-colonial sociologists of independent India.

CASTE IN THE COLONIAL PERIOD

Caste, as an institutional practice as we know now, had been shaped largely by colonial powers. For administration and governance, the colonial powers instituted a land assessment system and later conferred ownership status on many intermediaries to extract wealth in the form of land taxes and other cash revenues. It also introduced the Census of India by a decennial system for the enumeration of the castes and tribes of India. The idea behind the caste census was that the Indian society essentially comprised castes, which are governed hierarchically by the norms of purity and pollution. This resulted in the production of census reports that had the details of all castes, according to Brahminic textual principles. This consolidated the caste system to form a grid-like structure with a top-down model of hierarchy putting the Brahmin on the top and the Sudra/untouchable at the bottom.

Many caste association leaders challenged the census of 1902. Many of them demanded Kshatriya or Vaisya status. Many petitions were submitted to the governor generals and census commissioners for 'corrections' in the census reports. It led to widespread discussion of caste in various vernacular newspapers. Many tracts and pamphlets were produced to sensitise the reading public about the consequences. Caste had entered the emerging public domain.

It was assumed that each caste was different from another by an essential and 'original' criterion, that is, occupation. This essentialist argument of caste created a primordial self of each caste. Over a period, caste reformists could invoke this primordial identity to mobilize people behind them. The early mobilizations were intended to ameliorate the untouchable castes' woes and anomalies.

In many villages, untouchables known as *panchamas* were not allowed to use public wells for drawing drinking water. Upper-caste men punished those who violated the norms by all violent means. Many lower-caste people, therefore, organized themselves along caste lines to build opinion against upper castes. The emerging institutional spaces like schools, colleges and medical facilities were restricted to the few upper-caste men. Many lower castes were forced to become scavengers in upper-caste households. Lower-caste women often had to succumb to sexual exploitation by upper-caste men. Many lower castes were made bonded labourers whereby they were forced to work for minimal pay with little hope of escaping their servitude.

The Christian missionaries along with the reformists opened their institutional spaces to the lower castes to help them get access into public offices. Jyotiba Phule and other reform-spirited men challenged these conditions of the lower-caste majority by petitioning and complaining to the British authority against the errant upper-caste men. Through all these agitations and caste-based movements, caste gradually got politicized. Phule started the Satyashodhak Samaj for lower-caste men to challenge the upper-caste dominance and the sanskritizing tendencies of fellow caste men. He argued for the universalization of education for all, including men and women. His support for widow remarriage was challenged by the orthodoxy. His movement did not last long but the ideas were taken up by the reluctant nationalists.

In Madras too, responses to census commissioners increased with the introduction of the decennial census after 1881. Castes like Palli or Vanniyan asserted a Vaisya status. In 1901, caste associations were formed to protect self interests like participation in administrative and other official bodies apart from seeking admissions in educational and medical institutions.

Western ideas of rationality, equality and scientific education were open to all sections including the untouchables. The Christian missionaries encouraged many lower castes to enter these institutions and facilitated the spirit of reform among them. Major reformists like E. V. Ramaswamy Naicker, popularly known as Periyar, actively participated in agitations and movements against caste rigidity. His Justice Party promoted self-respect of the backward-caste people in Tamil Nadu. The British government took the initiative of positive discrimination or reservation in Madras and other areas for backward castes. Consequently, the educated among the 'lower castes' began to be appointed as government officials. Many from these castes also started to join the national movement led by Gandhi and others. The national movement, thereafter, took caste as a social evil and started agitations for temple entry for all Hindus. At the invitation of 'lower caste' Congress leader T. K. Madhavan, Gandhiji started the famous *vaikam satyagraha* in 1924 to assert the right of all untouchables to enter temples. The agitation continued and later became a national issue and eventually resulted in the decree that guaranteed temple entry for all. Thereafter, the national movement led by Gandhiji assured lower castes of alleviating their problems in the emerging independent India. In one of his articles on caste, B. R. Ambedkar defines caste as the chopping off of the population into fixed and definite units, each one prevented from fusing into another through the custom of endogamy.[1] He said that any attempt to do away with caste has to take into consideration the ideals of liberty, equality and fraternity. Thus, for him, democracy is not merely a form of government. It is primarily a mode of associated living, of conjoint communicated experience. It is essentially an attitude of respect and reverence towards fellowmen.[2] Thus, caste was perceived to be a hindrance to the development of democracy in India and it could only be achieved through the annihilation of it. Mahatma Gandhi accepted this: Through a famous pact called the Poona Pact with Ambedkar, caste was taken as a social evil to be eradicated as part of the national movement. The freedom movement led to the independence of India and soon after, Nehru, along with others including Ambedkar, drafted the Constitution of India. The Constitution guaranteed equal opportunities to all and, as part of the social welfare measures, abolished untouchability and recommended the implementation of reservations in government jobs as well as educational institutions.

WHAT IS AN INDIAN SOCIAL STRUCTURE?

A social structure, according to many sociologists, is a set of social relations conditioned by the material circumstances like socio-economic conditions. We can say that caste is the institution by which the Indian social structure is identified. What makes caste a distinctive social institution of India? Is it the innate sense of inequality or the status-maintaining occupations per se of a particular caste? It is assumed that each caste has traditionally one occupation and it is hierarchically differentiated according to the rules and status, which assign to it a lower or higher rank. Thus, a Brahmin performs priestly duties, a Kshatriya is a warrior, Vaisya is connected with trade and agriculture and a Sudra provides manual labour to all three of them. It is also said that each caste is ranked by the purity and polluting nature of their respective occupations. The Brahmins traditionally occupied a higher status in society due to their priestly functions. It is status that gave power to those groups who were dominant in their respective areas. They retained social and economic clout to assert their political dominance over other social sections that were weak. This was maintained by their control over the resources and denial of access to the needy. Women and *Dalits* were supposed to bear the burden in return for the services they rendered to the dominant groups.

1. B. R. Ambedkar, 'Castes in India: Their Mechanism, Genesis and Development', in Manoranjan Mohanty (ed.), *Class, Caste, Gender* (New Delhi: Sage, 2004), pp. 131–53.
2. Ibid., p. 150.

Defining the Nature and Function of Caste

According to sociologists like Andre Beteille,[3] caste is the fundamental social institution of modern India. The English word 'caste' might mean either *varna* or *jati*. *Varna* refers to an ideal model, a plan or design of society. *Jati* refers to the actual social group with which people identify themselves and it forms the basis on which they interact with each other. There are only four *varnas*—Brahmin, Kshatriya, Vaisya and Sudra—and they were the same and were ranked in the same order among Hindus everywhere, from ancient to modern times. The very peculiar nature of the Indian caste structure is that it has a hierarchically ordered stratification in which people are segregated according to the social group they belong to. Each caste is supposed to have a traditionally defined occupation and they stick to it mostly, even though changes have been brought about in its nature and function in the last century. This has been made possible largely by the colonial influences and new economic forces. Membership in a caste is by birth, and caste is extremely important in marriage. Most Indians marry within their caste. *Jatis* are many in number and often internally segmented. They vary from one region to another. For example, Brahmins, who are usually understood to be at the top of the social order, may not have dominance over others and some other caste, which may have control over the area. Thus, in many areas, it is those intermediary groups like Bhumihars and Yadavs in rural Bihar and Jats and Rajputs in Rajasthan and Lingayats and Vokkaligas in Karnataka that wield social power in many regions. In the past, each caste was associated with a distinct traditional occupation and a caste might be divided into sub-castes in keeping with differences in occupational practices. The emergence of a large number of modern, relatively caste-free occupations has greatly weakened the specific association between caste and occupation. But there is a different kind of association in practice now. In the superior, non-manual occupations, professionals are mostly from the upper castes and those in the inferior, manual occupations are mostly from the lower castes.

The enshrined principles guaranteed in the Constitution were not implemented properly. Many of those deprived sections were left out of the purview of the welfare and development initiatives of the State. It led to many questions related to 'caste' as the fundamental sociological problem exclusively of India, which has to be the focus of any study of rural India. The discipline of sociology was in the forefront of rural studies all over the world in the early 20th century.

Rural sociology as a disciplinary form of enquiry was initially the prerogative of colonial administrators for whom the absence of a proper market economy in land relations and a village of caste-based hierarchical social order were synonymous with the image of unchanging Oriental India. This understanding

3. Andre Beteille, *Caste, Class and Power* (New Delhi: Oxford University Press, 1965).

was instrumental in the colonial legitimacy of British rule over India. Thus, under colonialism, commodification of land, rural indebtedness and the rise of a new social class happened with changes in socio-economic conditions. The challenge of most Indian sociologists like M. N. Srinivas was to have different disciplinary forms of enquiry other than that was prevalent.

According to Srinivas, the Indian social structure and cultural patterns are characterised by unity as well as cultural diversity. He goes on to add, the institution of caste may be mentioned as a typical example of the paradox that is Indian society.[4] The institution of caste that is *sui generis* of the social structure in India is typical of Hindus, but cuts across diverse religious groups such as Sikhs, Jains, Muslims and Christians. To him, the essence of caste is the arrangement of hereditary groups in a hierarchy. Generally, each caste is divided according to occupational differences, but no caste is invariably associated with a single occupation. Thus, castes living in a village or a group of neighbouring villages are bound together by economic ties. Inter-caste relations at the village level constitute vertical ties. They may be classified into economic, ritual, political and civic ties. Srinivas says it is the functioning of a village as a political and social entity that brought together members from different castes.

As in many parts of British India, the lower castes were serfs or slaves, either attached to the land and liable to be transferred along with it or attached to the land owner and liable to be sold by him. The economic forces released under British rule enabled the law abolishing slavery to be translated into reality.[5] But the agricultural hierarchy is mixed up in different ways and degrees with the caste hierarchy in several parts of India. The caste system together with the inequalities of land ownership produced a deeply stratified society, but that did not prevent the village from functioning as a community. The rural pattern of life is largely organized around land; still the most important source of wealth. Under British rule, the village became, however, incompletely a part of the national as well as international economy. In post-Independent India, the tendency of the villages to be sucked more and more into the political economy of market relations were more visible.

These changes in the socio-economic fabric of rural India were the focus of most of Srinivas's writings. In his words, to see the monster machine pull down huge trees and cut through blocks of earth was an experience, which they (rural villagers) would not easily forget. Modern technology did indeed perform miracles, and human labour appeared pitiful in contrast.[6]

This process is best illustrated by Beteille's example of Sripuram village of Thanjavur district in Tamil Nadu. This village was selected for the study as it

4. M. N. Srinivas, *India: Social Structure* (New Delhi: National Book Trust, 1969).

5. Ibid., p. 15.

6. M. N. Srinivas, *Indian Society Through Personal Writings* (New Delhi: Oxford University Press), p. 143.

had a multi-caste presence. In earlier times, one's social position in Sripuram was defined largely in terms of one's membership of a caste, sub-caste, a lineage or a household. But the situation has changed drastically by the visible forces of social change like migration to urban areas and nearby towns, remittances and investments of money back at home. All these have partially dissolved the rigid and segmented form of caste hierarchy by sometimes subverting the social codes of dominance. Many of these groups adopted the rituals and ceremonies of the dominant upper castes to identify themselves positively against the prevalent norms, positioning them stereotypically.

It is to map these social changes that Srinivas introduced concepts like Sanskritization in his influential study on social changes happening in contemporary India.[7] For Srinivas, Sanskritization is a process by which a low Hindu caste or tribal or other group changes its custom, ritual, ideology and way of life in the direction of a high and frequently twice-born caste. Sanskritization has been a major process of cultural change in Indian history and it has occurred in every part of the Indian subcontinent. Dominant castes set the model for the majority of people living in rural areas including, occasionally, Brahmins. Along with Sanskritization, Srinivas coined another term called Westernisation to denote the changes introduced by more than 200 years of British colonialism. The term subsumes changes occurring at different levels including technology, institutions, ideology and values.

But another equally important concept of Srinivas's dominant caste, aimed to represent the conditions of limited forms of social mobility happening in rural India, drew attention to the important changes that Independence had brought. Post-Independence land reforms had transferred legal ownership rights in land previously owned by absentee landlords to the erstwhile tenant castes. These castes were also the most numerous and they formed the large vote banks that helped the leaders of these castes to gain unprecedented levels of political power in many regions. In this way, the combination of the vote and land rights converted the former tenant castes into dominant castes. We have the examples of Jats and Yadavas in north India, Khammas and Reddys in Andhra Pradesh, Thevars and Vanniyars in Tamil Nadu, asserting their power in regional polities. They deny access to many lower-caste groups to have their fair share in resource allocation. This newly found clout is instrumental in rigidifying the local patriarchal relations that women are forced to remain subservient to the male members of the family.

There are different perceptions and understandings of caste and, therefore, difficulties in arriving at a possible definition. Louis Dumont, another influential sociologist, concluded that *Homo Hierarchicus*[8] is the central and

7. M. N. Srinivas, *Social Change in Modern India* (Berkeley, MA: University of California Press, 1966), p. 6.
8. Louis Dumont, *Homo Hierarchicus* (Chicago, IL: University of Chicago Press, 1970).

substantive element of the caste system, which differentiates it from other social systems particularly of the West. Thus, broadly speaking, the caste system has been governed by the concept of purity and pollution in personal interactions, in exchanges of food and in the pursuit of occupations. The principle of pure and impure structures the divisions of labour, and favours the pure occupations of Brahmin as superior to that of the occupations of scavenging caste like Valmikis and Parayas. But Dumont's view has been criticized by scholars for emphasizing the textual views of caste and theories of Karma. The prevalence of hierarchy does not imply that lower castes give legitimacy to the theory of caste that is propounded in the shastras. Had this been the case, Dalits would not have waged struggles against dominant castes to improve their social life.

Caste and Class

According to many scholars influenced by Marxism, the caste system is essentially a class system and the stratification is based on occupation and the economic position of the group. It is generally argued by most Marxists that caste is a residue of a pre-industrial class society. Marxists reckon the concept of caste will disappear with the ultimate success of class struggle. Hence, there was less focus generally on caste and more on class analysis and class struggle. But A. R. Desai and B. T. Ranadive, two of the pioneering Marxist sociologists, gave importance to the studies of caste in their respective works.

Thus, for Desai:

> Caste has further determined the pattern of the complicated religious and secular culture of the people. It has fixed the psychology of the various social groups and has evolved such minutely graded levels of social distance and superior–inferior relationships that the social structure looks like a gigantic hierarchic pyramid with mass of untouchables as its base and a small stratum of elite, the Brahmins almost equally unapproachable at its apex.[9]

The changes introduced by the British in Indian society produced changes in caste and class relations in rural India. The increase in the speed of the modern means of communication, the introduction of the British system of administration and laws, and the growth of a modern capitalist competitive economy shattered the subsistence economy of the self-sufficient village community. Thus, the functional basis of caste has been undermined partially. The transformation of self-contained, rigid castes into modern, mobile classes has taken place in a peculiar manner. Certain castes have been monopolizing the position of the privileged, upper classes of modern society. Certain castes have been losing previous status and functions and slowly getting submerged to the lower-class

9. A. R. Desai (ed.), *Rural Sociology in India* (Bombay: Popular Prakashan, 1978), p. 38.

groups of the modern society. This new development has contributed to the emergence of a peculiar social structure in Modern India that class struggles have taken the form of caste struggles.

B. T. Ranadive, a leading political leader and Marxist theorist, argued that the anti-caste struggles by the oppressed classes were manifesting itself as demand for reservation in jobs and distribution of surplus lands for the lower castes. Thus, for him, a deeper struggle should be a transformation of property and production relations sustaining both caste and class oppression.[10] His arguments were framed in the context of the Green Revolution and the 1970s' caste conflicts. (For more on these issues, see Chapter 11.)

But the complexities of class interface with caste are so intriguing that it is difficult sometimes to say which is contributing more to social conflicts. On many occasions, the economic deprivation of lower caste or class may stem from a caste conflict depending upon the context. This happened due to the impact of capitalism in India. This was originally made by the British to enhance productivity in the industrial sector by utilizing local raw materials and later by the Indian State through the expansion of agricultural production. This was done by the introduction of modern irrigation and technological inputs to create more surplus. But the bulk of the poor in rural areas were landless, agricultural labourers and 'lower castes', including women. This new development process called the Green Revolution has been highlighted as the bloodless revolution.

Among the development programmes introduced by the post-colonial Indian State, the Green Revolution is considered to be the most successful. It led to a substantial increase in agricultural output and helped solve India's food problem. It contributed significantly to the social and political changes in rural villages and, in that sense, it was called an agricultural revolution.[11] It also intensified the interplay between caste and class links and was articulated often as violent conflicts between landowners and Dalit labourers. The Green Revolution converted many of these middle castes as commodity producers of the grain-market economy. Thus, sizeable landed areas of western UP witnessed the assertion of Jats as a political pressure group through the *kisan* unity of Mahendra Singh Tikait and, in Andhra Pradesh, Khammas and Reddys became influential in deciding the future of any political outfit. The cost-intensive regime of the Green Revolution also made the way for mechanization of the production and, thereby, alienated the vulnerable labouring groups like Dalits and poor Muslims in the Telengana region.

10. B. T. Ranadive, *Caste, Class and Property Relations* (Calcutta: National Book Agency, 1982).
11. Surinder Jodhka, *Agrarian Structures and Their Transformations,* in Veena Das (ed.), *Handbook of Indian Sociology* (New Delhi: Oxford University Press, 2004), pp. 1213–42.

CASTE AND VIOLENCE

The outbreak of mass violence from the 1960s between the upper castes and lower castes were called caste war, caste feud, and caste battle and even caste genocide by academics and journalists alike. What then is a caste war? Caste violence or caste war is the committed, oppressive form of violence normally directed at the lower-caste, landless poor, initiated largely by the landholding powerful upper castes to teach them a lesson for crossing the 'limits' like demanding more wages, violating caste hierarchy and sometimes for avenging the wrongs done by the lower castes. Thus, groups that share common interests as landlords, cattle owners, tenants and labourers recruit their members for fighting by using the language of caste.

Most Indian states like Maharashtra, Gujarat, Tamil Nadu, Karnataka, Andhra Pradesh, Bihar and UP have witnessed innumerous incidents of violence against Dalits. It is against this context that extreme movements like Maoists and Naxal movements formed alliances of poor peasants and labourers to fight against 'upper caste' forces. What resulted in this attempt was the consolidation of caste members as 'caste *senas*' to protect the honour and pride. In Bihar, *senas* of Bhumihars, Rajputs and Yadavas are prominent in their fight against Dalits and other 'lower castes'. These *senas* used violence with the 'legitimate' claim that it was always for a worthy cause like correcting the enemy's wrongs by inflicting punishment. From 1970s onwards, many Dalits invoked Gandhian and other principles of social justice to pressurize the state to take action against the upper caste *senas*. In states like Andhra Pradesh, the dominant castes like Kammas and Reddys invented the language of 'burden of the civilized' to counter the legitimate and rational claims of the Dalit activists. In this claim, they argue that the Kammas and Reddys have earned their wealth and prestige by their hard work and 'cultured virtues'. This argument was used to challenge the moral mandate of the lower castes as they were yet to be 'civilized' like Kammas and Reddys. Many would argue with comparative intentions that there were more violent caste conflicts in post-Independence India than during the colonial period that had more agrarian conflicts rather than caste conflicts. What is missed in these sweeping statements are the relative absence of lower-caste dissent against upper-caste land owners in colonial times, as the lands and other resources were in the hands of colonial State and zamindars. (For more on this, see Chapter 12.)

In post-Independence India, with the emergence of consciousness related to rights and social justice, the Dalits promoted the desire for equality as a social virtue. They demanded equal distribution of land and resources between various groups and these demands were not at all considered by the State and upper castes. The State agencies have often been manipulated by the upper castes to thwart the claims of Dalits. There are no clear-cut figures about the details of various incidents and the number of people killed in caste wars. Rough estimates put it between 40,000 and 60,000. According to government figures from mid-1980s to the late 1990s, people killed in caste wars were more in number than in the six-year conflict between Kashmiri separatists and Indian security forces during the same period.[12]

Caste in the Present Context

The Indian society and the caste system have changed tremendously over the years after Independence. For many of the contemporary sociologists, these changes may be uneven both in rural and urban areas. The caste-based hierarchy is sharply defined at least among the upper castes of Ramkheri, a village selected for the study in north India. Caste endogamy is universally practised. But its meaning has changed. Ritual purity has given way to cultural difference as a marker of separation. Through a realignment of ideas about rank and equality, status has become less important. Hence, there is a continuity as well as change in the perceptions and practices of caste in contemporary times. One may find a Brahmin sharing food with a lower caste in functions like marriage and other ceremonies. Also one may find the claims from many villagers that there is no caste left. For Fuller, these claims are made largely because of the illegitimacy to defend caste in the public domain, and now it has gone into the 'private realm' of family and marriage as a form of culture and 'difference'. Instead of *jati*, they may now use *samaj* to refer to caste difference rather than caste hierarchy.[13]

Party politics in Independent India has influenced caste and it is reflected in the electoral processes too. Across the country, one finds that leaders of the powerful and large parties are successful in translating their numerical strength into political power by mobilising horizontally their members. But since the 1980s, a more polarized caste politics has emerged around the vexed issue of reservations. The explicit purpose of reservation is to promote social, economic and political equality for Dalits, tribals, women and other low castes by following positive discrimination in education and job opportunities. By this policy, the constitutional delegitimacy of caste had acquired new levels in India. In 1990, the issue of reservation took a dramatic turn when V. P. Singh introduced Mandal Commission recommendations for implementing the 27 per cent quota for other backward castes in central government services and public undertakings. The decision to implement the report provoked violent protests from the higher castes in many areas of the country. Even in 2006, the present Congress government's decision to extend reservations to country's premier institutions was challenged in the streets by higher-caste students. But elsewhere in South

12. Susan Bayly, *Caste, Society and Politics in India: From the Eighteenth Century to the Modern Age* (Delhi: Permanent Block, 2002), p. 345.
13. C. J. Fuller, 'Caste', in Veena Das (ed.), *The Oxford India Companion to Sociology and Social Anthropology* (New Delhi: Oxford University Press, 2003), pp. 477–501.

India, reservation has been in practice for the last 50 years or more, helping to create opportunities for backward castes in education and employment. But evidence to the contrary show that compensatory discrimination was unevenly spread as some backward castes have gained nothing while some powerful castes have gained a lot. The process of Mandalization, a term coined by many sociologists, swept across many north Indian states like Bihar and UP with the backward-class, lower castes gaining political power showing the disintegration of dominant high-caste groups in the political domain. It has been argued that Mandalization is also a result of the rise of a middle-class section among lower caste OBCs. It has also been observed that the OBCs' demand for reservations are largely due to the pivotal role education has in providing social mobility and status. The key to their material prosperity over the years has been the policies of the post-Independent Indian State such as progressive land reforms, implementation of various development projects and, most importantly, with the Green Revolution familiarizing them with the market economy of grain production.

The Dalit castes at the bottom of the hierarchy have hardly experienced substantial changes in their socio-economic profile over the years. Large sections remain landless and have only their labour power to sell and, therefore, do not have any access to education, health and a secure livelihood. The contradictions are sharper in rural areas where now upwardly mobile middle castes and the Dalits that work for them enter into violent conflicts. Often, this results into the brutal subjugation of Dalits and the violation of basic human rights that are guaranteed to any citizen of India. The entire structure of class and caste linkages are being reworked under these new social processes. Thus, the historical advantages of the upper castes in relation to education and professional occupations by making use of opportunities provided by the colonial regime placed many of them and their descendants in a position of advantage in comparison with lower-caste groups.

In a similar vein, many lower-caste, backward classes benefited from historical changes like the tenancy occupation of land for agriculture and the abolition of *Zamindari* or absentee landlord system. These changes were introduced at an all-India level with different degrees of land reform implementations. Some states like Jammu and Kashmir, West Bengal and Kerala have relatively successful implementations, whereas in many north Indian states, landed groups thwarted this policy. The transformations in the agrarian structure due to land reforms had a tremendous effect in the rural areas. For example, in a village of Rajasthan, there was considerable difference in the overall landownership patterns after land reforms. The Rajputs, the erstwhile landlords, possessed much less land after the land reforms than they did before. Most of the village land had moved into the hands of those who could be called the medium and small landowners mostly from the middle castes. The untouchable Dalit groups that were called the attached land labourers remained out of the purview of land reforms even though the change in the agrarian scenario had brought the backward-caste groups to dominate the rural, social structure.

Caste and Gender

The interplay between caste and gender has been an area of concern that was neglected by most social scientists. Recently many social scientists of feminist concerns have raised the complex issue of the exclusion of women from the discussions of caste and class. There has been no sustained dialogue between the two sets of scholars representing the women's studies and caste studies. Most scholars have regarded the axis of caste and gender as mutually exclusive and, therefore, having no links between the two axes of stratification. Thus, for the first time, many feminists have taken up the case of the inextricable links between caste and gender. They also coined a term 'Brahminical patriarchy' by which caste and gender could be understood in the Indian context.

Many feminist scholars have also explored the regional and caste dimensions of the functioning of Brahminical patriarchy. The major contribution of feminist scholarship has been in raising the important question of why women become complicit in systems that subordinate them. Several answers were made in response to this question. It is argued that even though women lose in relation to their own menfolk, within a patriarchal situation they derive certain benefits from the system of which they are a part. Compliance brings them gains and deviance, on the other hand, expels them from the material and symbolic resources of the family. Women are regarded as upholding the traditions by conforming to traditions. Men, on the other hand, uphold traditions by enforcing them upon women. The greatest impact of such enforcing is most visible in the arena of marriage and reproduction. Thus, it is in the field of marriages that caste continues to structure the lives of people. If we take a look at the matrimonial columns of most newspapers, we may be able to see how caste is still governing our lives. We find that it is not just reservations or caste-based electoral politics that is keeping caste alive but other factors like unequal control over property, unequal performance of labour and the endogamous marriage system binding production and reproduction together. What is to be noted here is that not all women suffer equally under patriarchal conditions. The upper-caste women may not have the same level of advantages like upper-caste men. But upper-caste women are advantageously placed over lower-caste men in relation to access to education and occupations. This is not the case with Dalit women who face oppression at multiple levels. Dalit feminists have formulated a notion of three-way oppression of Dalit women:

1. As subject to caste oppression at the hands of the upper castes
2. As labourers subject to class-based oppression
3. As women who experience patriarchal oppression at the hands of all men, including men of their caste[14]

The Dalit women's issue has been raised for the first time and their voice has been politicized enough to make an impact on social life. Thus, our public domain is becoming sensitized to the complexities of social structure by the participation of social scientists on various issues after the agitations over the Mandal Commission Report. Their views have shaped our knowledge about the social structure in which we live.

Suggested Readings

Bayly, Susan. *Caste, Society and Politics in India*. New Delhi: Cambridge University Press, 2002.

Chakravarti, Uma. *Gendering Caste*. Calcutta: Stree, 2003.

Manoranjan, Mohanty (ed.). *Class, Caste and Gender*. New Delhi: Sage, 2002.

Questions

1. What is social structure? Analyse the changes in the social structure in rural India in the post-Independence period.
2. Caste has been the basic organizing principle of social life in rural India. Do you agree with this statement? Give arguments in favour or against the statement.
3. Define caste and class. Analyse the relationship between the two concepts in the light of the Indian situation.
4. Do you agree with the view that caste has reinvented itself as a category of political mobilization in democratic India? Elaborate.

14. Uma Chakravarti, *Gendering Caste* (Calcutta: Stree, 2003), p. 1.

The Explosion of the 'Middle Class'

8

Sujit Mahapatra

Suddenly, the middle class is everywhere, whether it is the newspapers, or social commentaries or the television. The Indian midle class is a category often used by both experts and common persons. The focus on the middle class in popular discourse is partly explained by the fact that its rise is considered the most striking feature of contemporary India. Gurcharan Das, an icon of corporate India and a prominent newspaper columnist, celebrates the unleashing of this middle class in his book *India Unbound*. This new, young and dynamic middle class has, according to Das, led to 'the biggest transformation in its (India's) history' and he says that he feels the same excitement his parents had felt at the time of Independence.[1] His arguments, however, suggest that the members of this new middle class are not midnight's children but children of a new dawn.

It is being said that the Indian economy is doing so well despite the political impediments to growth (read the Left parties) because of the young and huge middle class, which shot into prominence with the economic reforms ushered in the early 1990s. That is the first time that the size of the middle class was debated, as the MNCs saw their major market in this middle class. Although there is no clearly accepted definition of the middle class, some estimates peg the Indian middle class at 300–350 million,[2] while conservative estimates put it at about 200 million.[3] Even the latter figure makes it the biggest middle class anywhere in the world (China, as our favourite middle-class benchmark, has about 130 to 170 million that can be considered middle class). This also makes the Indian middle class bigger than the entire population of most European

1. Gurcharan Das, *India Unbound: From Independence to the Global Information Age* (New Delhi: Penguin, 2002), p. 347.
2. Shashi Tharoor, citing NCAER statistics in 'Who Is this Middle Class?' *The Hindu*, 22 May 2005.
3. Vir Sanghvi, 'Two Indias', *Seminar*, 1 February 2005.

countries and almost as huge as the US population.[4] The size of the middle class has also changed our attitude towards the question of population, which is no longer seen as a liability but as an asset.

It has almost become a cliché to talk about how the middle class enjoys power disproportionate to its size. It had always been politically powerful and, from the time of Independence (as we shall discuss), has set the agenda for the nation. It has always dominated the institutions of the judiciary, the bureaucracy and the political class itself. The middle class has become even more powerful today with the spectacular growth of two institutions they dominate—mass media and large corporations that now have a major say in an India that is liberalizing. Hence, politicians who ignore the middle class are vulnerable to punishment from these middle-class institutions. For instance, Lalu Yadav earlier fought elections with slogans such as '*Vikas nahin, samman chahiye*' making it clear that his politics was about empowerment of the lower castes and not development for the middle class. After losing the elections in Bihar, the same Lalu has reincarnated himself, as he tries to appeal to middle-class values and concerns of development and efficiency in his stint with the railways.

The middle class itself has become so huge and so powerful that it is often possible to forget that there is a world that exists outside. In fact, it is possible that if someone wakes up like Rip Van Winkle after 17 years and goes through the mass media, she may not realize that the middle class does not constitute the entire India. The case of the India Shining campaign before the general elections of 2004 illustrates how it has become increasingly difficult not to confuse the concerns and feelings of the middle class with that of the entire country. Most electoral predictions went horribly wrong about an NDA victory because, as always, the respondents of the surveys predominantly belonged to the middle classes.

The other distinctive feature of the power of the middle class in contemporary India is that like never before, the middle class now sets the tone for the other classes culturally as well. According to Ashish Nandy, middle-class cultural products:

> ... are threatening to turn both the folk and the classical into second-order presences (the way the immensely successful television serials on the *Ramayana* and the *Mahabharata* now influence the frame for interpreting the epics for a large number of Indians) and today even the global mass culture enters the subcontinent filtered through the same middle-class sensitivities epitomized by commercial cinema.[5]

4. Jan Nijman, cited by Darryl D'Monte in 'Middle Class Palaces', *India Together*, 20 July 2005.
5. Ashish Nandy, *The Secret Politics of Our Desires: Innocence, Culpability and Indian Popular Cinema* (New Delhi: Oxford University Press, 1998), p. 6.

But before we ask how the middle class became so powerful, what turned it into the engine for India's growth and what its implications are, let us try and understand the 'middle class'. This is because the question of what is middle class and who constitutes the middle class elicits varied and often contradictory answers.

THE 'MIDDLE' IN THE MIDDLE CLASS

There are two popular ways in which we understand the concept of the 'middle'. It is taken to designate that member (the median) of a group or series or that part of a whole, which has the same number of members or parts on each side. Or, it can be understood as the intermediate stage or part between two other parts in relation to which it defines itself.

Neither the middle class in India nor in the West is really in the middle if one takes one of the conventional definitions of the middle class as including families whose incomes lie between 75 per cent and 125 per cent of the median.[6] In America, for instance, the middle class practically includes the entire population. In a country like India, where statistically a third of the population lives below the poverty line, where 46 per cent of the income is accounted for by the top 20 per cent of the population and the lowest one-fifth accounts for only 8 per cent of incomes, if we define the middle class in terms of the median income, we are talking of those who are actually better off than the majority.

This definition, however, does not explain why we talk of so many middle classes—the upper middle class and the lower middle class—and why we never talk of the lower upper class or the upper lower class.[7] This is probably because in our popular imagination, there are two definite classes, the rich and the poor, and all those that come in between constitute the middle class. We have a definition for the poor, however contested, and we have some understanding of the rich, but the middle class has always been a fuzzy category. It is because there is such diversity within this class that we have these further classificatory categories.

In fact, our understanding of the rich and poor necessitates a conceptual space for the middle class. The word 'rich' comes etymologically from the Latin *reich*, which like the German *reich* stands for the power of the king. The power of the king comes from the fact that the others are subjects and not the king. Later, when the word 'rich' came to be applied to the power that comes with money, for the rich to be rich, the poor required to be poor. At the same time, this means that in a social stratification, the rich and the poor cannot meet. Hence, we need the intervening middle classes between the rich and the poor.

---

6. What is 'Middle Class', in http://www.indiatogether.org/photo/2003/class.htm.
7. Although the American sociologist William Warner talks of subdivisions within the upper class and the lower class in his study of class in American society, this view is not dominant and hardly exists in the popular imagination in India.

This middle class, because it avoids the extremities, is seen as the most desirable social location. Even when one moves beyond the middle class, one is admired for retaining a middle-class lifestyle as was epitomized by Narayan Murthy continuing to drive his old Fiat even after becoming the czar of the Indian IT industry. Moreover, in all our debates and arguments about ending poverty, what we do not state is our desire to uplift the poor into the middle class. The rich, poor and the middle class are of course relative terms—if all the poor are lifted into the middle class, what would the middle class be the middle of?

THE 'CLASS' OF THE 'MIDDLE CLASS'[8]

In modern Europe, the middle class emerged as an intermediate social class between the nobility and the peasantry. While the nobility owned the countryside, and the peasantry worked the countryside, the middle class, also called the bourgeoisie (literally town-dwellers), then arose around mercantile functions in the city. This bourgeoisie allied with the kings in uprooting the feudalist system and supported the American and French revolutions, and were instrumental in the rapid expansion of commerce.

With the expansion of commerce, trade and the market economy, the bourgeoisie grew in size, influence and power, and gradually became the ruling class in industrialized nation-states in the late 19th century, which means that it owned the bulk of the means of production (land, factories, offices, capital and resources). The middle class, disassociated from the bourgeoisie now, came to describe the professional and business class in the United Kingdom. This middle class is sometimes called the petit or petty bourgeoisie. They are the white-collar workers—those who work for wages (like all workers), but do so in conditions that are comfortable and safe compared to the conditions for blue-collar workers of the 'working class'.

It must be mentioned, however, that there is little unanimity in the understanding of the 'class' denoted by the middle class from the 20th century onwards. In the United States, by the end of the 20th century, most people identified themselves as middle class. In contrast, recent surveys in the United Kingdom indicate that up to two-thirds of Britons identify themselves as working class.[9] This is probably because in the USA, the term always has a positive connotation whereas in the UK, it often has a pejorative value due to its association with matters of culture and taste. In fact, in the USA, money is the marker of social status, whereas in the UK, markers such as accent, manners, place of education, occupation and a person's family, circle of friends and acquaintances determine one's class.

8. For the definition and detailed discussion of 'class', refer to Chapter 11 in this volume.
9. 'Middle Class' in *Wikipedia,* http://en.wikipedia.org/wiki/Middle_class (last accessed on 14 May 2008).

In this contested terrain, to understand what the middle class in India stands for, we have to examine the history of growth of the middle class in India right from its origins. It is from this exploration shall we try to arrive at a definition at the end.

The Emergence of the Indian Middle Class

One way of thinking about the Indian middle class is in terms of the adjectives commonly used to describe it such as 'urban' and 'English speaking'. It follows that an urban, English-speaking person is definitely middle class in India. The strong association of these adjectives with the middle class appears to be a historical legacy.

The middle class in India came into being with the felt need by the colonial masters to create a native elite in its own image for the colonial administration of the country. Thus, the middle class did not emerge with industrialization as in England but with the need for colonial administrators. This middle class did not emerge as the manufacturing class but was, in a way, itself manufactured in the Presidency towns of Calcutta, Bombay and Madras. Lord Macaulay said in his notorious 'Minute on Indian Education' in 1835, 'We must at present do our best to form a class, who may be interpreters between us and the millions we govern; a class of persons, Indian in blood and colour, but English in taste, in opinions, in morals, and in intellect'.[10] It is worth noting here that by 'English', Macaulay referred to the upper-class English taste because only the upper class had taste in the first place.

The native elite they created were modern Indians like Raja Rammohan Roy, who maintained two houses in Calcutta, one in which he entertained his Western guests and another in which he entertained his Indian guests. It has been famously said about him that in his Western house, everything was Western except Rammohan and in his Indian house, everything was Indian except Rammohan. In other words, the native elites like Rammohan were neither with the British nor with the Indians.

Macaulay's Minute also indicated that it was a job in the colonial administration, which also implied English education, that secured the entry into the middle class. Bankim Chandra Chatterjee, the author of *Vande Mataram*, had written of the middle class in 1873 that 'like Vishnu, they will have ten incarnations, namely clerk, teacher, Brahmo, accountant, doctor, lawyer, magistrate, landlord, editor and *unemployed*'.[11] It is significant that the question of unemployment only emerges with the failure of education to secure a job contrary to its promise, or in other words, the failure of education to deliver one into the

10. Cited in Pavan K. Varma, *The Great Indian Middle Class* (New Delhi: Viking, 2000), p. 2, italics mine.
11. Ibid., pp. 4–5.

middle class. We, therefore, do not talk of the illiterate unemployed but almost always of the educated unemployed.

The social groups not dependent on education were excluded from the middle class. They included the vast majority of the agricultural poor, and the unskilled, semi-skilled and skilled manual workers, petty clerks and employees such as postmen, constables, soldiers, peons, etc. At the other end, it excluded the rich industrialists and capitalists like the Goenkas, Birlas and Tatas, the very big *zamindars* and *taluqdars*, and members of the princely families.

Education not only promised a job, but an entry into the middle class, the *bhadralok* in colonial Bengal. The *bhadralok* are the genteel, civilized people; the native equivalent of the gentlemen. This connection has strong roots and permeates our contemporary consciousness as well. For instance, in the film *Raju Ban Gaya Gentleman*, Shah Rukh Khan graduates from a slum to a middle-class life through his education. People who have not had the privilege of middle class education, often imagine education as having a transformative effect. Hence, the traffic policeman who stopped me on my bike for not wearing a helmet said, 'What is the use of all your education if you do not follow the law?' That is why we often overhear maids bemoan, 'Look, how that husband and wife fight with each other! What is the point of all that education then?' The idea of education, they still retain, promises not only a job but also the social graces and etiquette that mark civilized behaviour.

Partha Chatterjee argues that the Indian middle class in the colonial context had a paradoxical position.[12] The middle class was culturally invented through colonial English education, yet structurally limited as it lacked a basis for economic expansion in the context of colonial economic control. So, it was never a bourgeoisie as in the West. Hence, it was not a fundamental class in Chatterjee's opinion as it made no attempts at social transformation. In fact, the existing social structure mutated itself to constitute the new middle class. The requirement of English education for entry into the hallowed circle of the middle class meant that the upper-caste Indian with traditional access to education could exploit the opportunities and become the middle class. In the process, it acquired a class identity without losing its caste moorings.

Implications of an Upper Caste Becoming Middle Class

In the existing studies of the Indian middle class, hardly any attention has been given to the historical fact of an upper caste constituting the original middle class. This has been a major gap in understanding the specificities of the Indian middle class and its distinctive development in the contemporary period. For instance,

12. Partha Chatterjee, 'A Religion of Urban Domesticity: Sri Ramakrishna and the Calcutta Middle Class', in Partha Chatterjee and Gyanendra Pandey (eds.), *Subaltern Studies VII* (New Delhi: Oxford University Press, 1992), p. 24.

the middle class that emerged in the Presidency towns in the colonial period was classical in its cultural preferences, both classical Sanskritic because of its Brahminical origins, and upper-class Western because of education. It had distaste for the popular and the folk in both the Indian and the English traditions. That is how indigenous, popular, cultural forms such as the *nautanki* and *jatra* acquired pejorative values, which continues today.

More significantly, the upper-caste location of the original Indian middle class led to the retention of their traditional roles in the social hierarchies, where the upper caste engaged itself with education and disengaged itself with any form of physical labour. This has major implications for the understanding of middle-class existence even now. One defining characteristic of a middle-class lifestyle in India today is the reliance on domestic help, whether in the form of the maid, the cook, or to a lesser extent, the driver ('chauffeur' sounds too upper class). Sometimes, it may even include middle-class help such as the home tutor for children. This presence or dependence on domestic help for the menial jobs is a distinctive feature of middle-class India (it is not the case in the West, where middle-class people do most of these jobs themselves). It has, however, been largely ignored in the studies on the middle class, perhaps, because the significance of the upper-caste origins of the middle class in India has been little explored.

The failure to acknowledge this distinctiveness of the Indian middle class has been a major problem in city planning as well. The cities of India are very different from the cities of the West on which they are modelled. The cities are of course for the civilized people or, in other words, for the middle class. In fact, the word 'civilization' comes from the Latin root, *civitas*, which signifies city. In modelling our cities on the West, we, however, forget that the urban middle class in the West does not depend on the kind of domestic help the middle class in India does. The urban poor are indispensable to the urban middle class in India. Yet, the city is never planned with the slum in mind and a slum always has an illegitimate birth. In each city, therefore, there is also what the architect Jai Sen calls 'the unintended city', which the city cannot do without, and which, in cities like Bombay and Calcutta, houses the majority of the population.[13]

Political Dominance of the Middle Class

Until the first two decades after Independence, there was the political hegemony of a small, upper-caste, English-educated elite. At the same time, the rule of the middle-class elite at the national level could not be typified with the rule of the upper castes. Even if the ruling elite had their origins in the upper castes, they had

13. For a powerful critique of city planning and its concerns for the urban poor, see Jai Sen, 'The Unintended City', http://www.india-seminar.com/2001/500/500%20jai%20sen.htm (last accessed on 14 May 2008), reproduced from 'Life and Living', *Seminar*, 200, April 1976.

become detached from their traditional ritual functions. They had acquired new interests and lifestyles, which came through modern education, non-traditional occupations and a degree of Westernization in their thinking and lifestyle.

The upper castes, reconstituted as middle class, could comfortably own both the upper-caste and middle-class identity. Even though they ceased to perform their ritual functions, their traditional high status helped them access modern education and professions and also to convert, when required, their inherited wealth into new means for acquiring elite positions of power. So their castes had fused with class and had acquired a power dimension. The modernized urban section of the upper castes functioned as a power group of elites. As this process of converting traditional status into new power was restricted to the upper castes, they sought to use that power to establish their own caste-like hegemony over the rest of the society.

Even the Indian National Congress, which was set up in 1885, catered to upper-and middle-class interests. Nehru has written in his autobiography about the culture of Congress politics in the nationalist struggle. He wrote:

> My politics had been those of my class, the bourgeoisie. Indeed, all vocal politics then (and to a great extent even now) were those of the middle classes, and Moderate and Extremist alike represented them... The Moderate represented especially the handful of the upper middle class who had on the whole prospered under British rule and wanted no sudden changes, which might endanger their position and interests. They had close relations with the British Government and the big landlord class. The Extremist represented also the lower ranks of the middle class'.[14]

It is only with the political emergence of Gandhi in the 1920s that the Congress acquired a mass character for the first time. The nationalist movement involved the masses but the leadership remained with the dominant elite, the middle class.

It is perhaps because the original middle class in India became the dominant elite that we have the confusion of the middle class with the elite. There were further implications of this political dominance of the middle class. Nehru has argued that Muslim separatism, which led to the carving out of Pakistan from British India, was the work of middle-class Muslims to protect only their interests. He remarked, 'Every one of the communal demands put forward by any communal group is, in the final analysis, a demand for jobs, and these jobs could only go to a handful of the upper middle classes'.[15]

Further, the fact that knowledge of English was a common bond with the middle class throughout the country ensured that in the impasse over the selection of Hindi as the national language with its opposition from the South,

14. Jawaharlal Nehru, *An Autobiography* (New Delhi: Oxford University Press, 1980), p. 48.
15. Ibid., p. 138.

English continued its dominance in Independent India as it was the common language of the middle-class leadership across the country, though it was spoken by a very small fraction of the population.

Changes in Urban Life with the Formation of the Middle Class

We have already mentioned that with their emergence as a middle class, the upper caste lost their ritual functions. This was an indication of the progressive breakdown of the traditional caste system. This is because the nexus between hereditary ritual status and occupations constituted one of the defining features of the caste system. One chooses an occupation for its monetary and other benefits and not for its correlation with ritual purity. Hence, a Brahmin would now have no problems in selling leather in the city, though dealing with leather was traditionally confined to a lower caste. However, castes as self-conscious communities continue to survive.

Other changes have taken place in the caste system with the emergence of a middle class from within its ranks. Earlier, within a particular caste, the members were more or less equal in terms of their lifestyle. The little differences between households in terms of wealth and status were rarely expressed in terms of power. 'Today, members of a single caste are becoming increasingly differentiated among themselves in terms of their occupations, educational and income levels and life-styles'.[16] With the increasing differentiation within a caste, people are increasingly marrying outside the sub-castes and often the caste as well.

The differentiation within castes and its impact on middle-class marriages can be seen in the increasing reliance on the matrimonial columns in newspapers, which are middle-class products. Earlier, in cohesive social groups, it was possible to find a partner from within one's social circle. However, with mobility into the middle class, one not only looks for a partner from the same caste but from the same social class as well. The reliance on newspapers and other media also suggests that the middle class itself has expanded beyond a small social community.

Expansion of the Middle Class

The middle class in the colonial period and the early years of Independence was a fairly homogenous group, urban centred with English education and mostly upper caste. This English-speaking, urban middle class continued to expand with increasing prosperity in the urban centres. However, the relatively homogeneous character of the middle class began to change with its expansion and with the emergence of new groups into the middle class.

---

16. D. L. Sheth, 'Caste and Class: Social Reality and Political Representations', in Ghanshyam Shah (ed.), *Caste and Democratic Politics in India* (Delhi: Permanent Black, 2002), p. 213.

Emergence of the Rural Middle Class

The defining urban-centredness of the middle class was lost with the emergence of an agrarian middle class on the heels of the Green Revolution, introduced from around the mid-1960s. These farmers, who constituted the new middle class, were relatively well off and they owned over 60 per cent of the total land area, though they constituted only about 25 per cent of the total agrarian population. They were the numerous middle-level cultivationists, who had benefited the most from the Zamindari Abolition Act of 1955 and now benefited the most from the Green Revolution.[17]

Unlike the very rich farmers, they farmed the land themselves and took good care to ensure maximum produce. Their land holdings were large enough to generate the capital for use of new technologies such as tractors and fertilizers. Since they had the political power, they also manipulated the policies to benefit them. With favourable government policies such as subsidies in power, water, diesel and fertilizers and on taxation and easy availability of credit and price supports for agricultural produce, their surpluses increased. This led to diversification within agriculture and many farmers also went into dairy and poultry farming and into ancillary industries such as flour mills, sugar cooperatives, transport business, trading, and brick kilns—and an agrarian middle class was born.

The power of this new political class came to be seen in 1977 with the formation of non-Congress governments. Charan Singh became one of the leaders of this agrarian middle class opposed to what was perceived to be the pro-urban policies of the Congress. With increasing prosperity, the rich farmers sent their children to the cities for education as befitting a middle-class life. With the arrival of television, the culture of the urban middle class and its lifestyle came into the courtyards of agrarian homes and it acted as a spur for the consumption seen in the cities. The confidence that came with the new-found political power also brought a desire for consumer goods earlier seen as unnecessary for poor farmers.

With increasing migration both within the country and outside from the villages, there slowly emerged a rural middle class fuelled by the remittances of migrants, which added to the already formed agrarian middle class. At the same time, the agrarian middle class was dominated by the upper caste and the middling castes. There was hardly an agrarian Dalit middle class for obvious reasons. Most Dalits were either landless or precariously marginal farmers. In fact, a survey had recorded that till as late as the mid-1980s, over 90 per cent of the bonded labour in Uttar Pradesh was from the SCs. The dalits had not constituted the urban middle class as well because they did not have the means to access modern education, having been denied education in the traditional system. As a result of reservations, however, slowly a Dalit middle class emerged in the urban centres.

17. See Varma, *The Great Indian Middle Class*, pp. 93–94.

Emergence of the Dalit Middle Class

The Congress party, which dominated national politics in the early decades after Independence, focused on the middle class and the lower castes, linking middle-class rule to lower-caste support and the ideology that legitimized it was neither caste ideology nor class ideology but the ideology of 'nation-building'. The politics and programmes of the Congress party at the centre were thus projected as representing the 'national aspirations' of the Indian people, although as articulated by the homogenous middle class or the new power elite that played the leadership role at the time of Independence. The Congress-dominated politics was through the political hegemony of the upper-caste-oriented middle class with the electoral consent of the lower castes. It was a peculiar caste–class situation where the upper castes functioned in politics with the self-identity of a class and the lower castes with the consciousness of their separate caste identities.[18]

Towards the end of the 1960s, despite tardy implementation, affirmative policies (for the lower castes and tribals, which had been in operation in some form or the other since colonial times) had created a small but significant section of individuals in lower-caste groups, who, by acquiring modern education, had joined the middle class by entering the bureaucracy and other non-traditional occupations.

The Congress party–dominated politics of social consensus, presided over by the hegemony of an upper-caste, English-educated elite, began to crumble. The elite at the top could not accommodate the ever-increasing claims and pressures from different sections of the lower castes for their share of power.[19] The lower castes, therefore, started mobilizing politically. Members of each lower caste used the advantages secured through the political mobilization of the castes collectively for entry into the middle class.

The members of the lower castes then started acquiring the self-consciousness of belonging to the middle class and it is characterized by new lifestyles (modern consumption patterns) and ownership of consumer goods/economic assets. The ritual purity or impurity of statuses held by its members in the traditional system has ceased to matter as members of the middle class. Now, members of different castes and communities, who have acquired modern education, and have taken to non-traditional occupations and/or command higher income and political power, are entering the middle class.

The lower castes, however, in seeking upward mobility to the middle class are looking to acquire modern jobs, white-collar jobs, wealth and political power, not a higher ritual status. Individuals from different castes and communities, as they enter this middle class, acquire not only economic interests

18. Sheth, 'Caste and Class'.
19. Ibid.

and modern lifestyles but also a new self image and social identity as members of a middle class.

When sections of the Dalits entered the middle class, largely through policies of reservation, and continued to face discrimination and humiliation at the hands of the upper castes, they decided to fight for their respect and dignity. This political mobilization of the scheduled castes in north India, for instance, led to the formation of the Bahujan Samaj Party (BSP) in 1984.[20] The party was financed by the new Dalit middle class mostly comprising government servants and clerks and it is this new middle class that took over the leadership of the BSP. Their argument was that humiliation and not economic deprivation was the main problem of the Scheduled Castes and hence, greater political representation and not material advantage was the solution. It rallied under the slogan of '*Vote hamara, raaj tumhara nahin chalega*', which indicates the existing pattern of politics they opposed.

Meanwhile, with the split in the Congress in 1969, and with it a split in the lower-caste support for the middle-class leaders, Indira Gandhi herself increasingly patronized and promoted different political groups to stay in power. The English language media and the popular Hindi film, both addressing the middle-class audience, consequently started bemoaning the plebeianization of the political field and held the plebeian politicians responsible for the decay in political standards and ethics. I remember stating as an undergraduate that I did not want to become a bureaucrat because I did not want to take orders from an illiterate scoundrel (read politician). It little occurred to me at that time that my iconic scoundrels were all leaders from the lower castes such as Lalu Yadav and Mulayam Singh Yadav.

This middle-class disillusionment with political class comes to a head in the recent film, *Rang De Basanti*.[21] The film has been much talked about and, in fact, been credited with creating an awakening in the youth. The politics it advocates, however, is slightly disturbing. In the film, the protagonists kill the politician but not because he was himself directly responsible for the death of their friend. His killing seems to be symbolic of the decimation of the entire political class. One must, however, note that it is only the middle class that can afford to do away with the political class. For most of our grievances in the metros, we do not turn to the politicians, but to the media, the judiciary and the bureaucracy, institutions populated by members of the middle class. However, people not belonging to the middle class, cannot do away with politics. It is probably their only redressal mechanism.

---

20. See the discussion of the middle-class basis for the formation of the BSP in Ashutosh Varshney, 'Is India Becoming More Democratic?' *The Journal of Asian Studies*, 59 (1), February 2000: 3–25.

21. For a discussion of its middle-class politics, see M. K. Raghavendra, 'Globalism and Indian Nationalism', *Economic and Political Weekly*, 22 April 2006.

The political mobilization among the lower castes had other consequences as well. Thomas Hansen has argued in *The Saffron Wave* that this has been one of the major factors for the rise of Hindu nationalism, which articulated the anxieties of the Indian middle class in the wake of these developments.[22] The fact that Hindu nationalism developed within a large and expanding middle class defied political commonsense, which sees a strong middle class as a prerequisite for a stable democracy in the postcolonial world. The assumption, of course, is that a democratic culture provides greater tolerance and pluralism.

The Middle Class and Democracy

The middle class has been taken as the cornerstone of a stable democracy. Seymour Lipset had made an influential proposition in 1959 that the more economically developed the country, the more successful a democracy it is.[23] According to this theory, economic development is closely associated with increases in education, which in turn promotes political attitudes conducive to democracy (inter-personal trust and tolerance of opposition). Second, economic development alters the pyramid-shaped social stratification in which the majority of the population is poor to a diamond-shaped social stratification, in which the majority is middle class and relatively well off. This social change moderates the intensity of class struggle by reducing the proportion of the population that is susceptible to anti-democratic parties and ideologies and by increasing the proportion of population that supports moderate pro-democratic parties. Moreover, because middle-class occupations require an educated population, the middle class will hold political attitudes conducive to democracy that are acquired through formal education. Thus, the middle class emerges as the main pro-democratic force in Lipset's analysis and this class gains in size with socio-economic development.

It must also be taken into account that capitalist development helps in the rise of democracy by weakening the feudal structure and the power of the landed gentry. The weakening of the landed gentry, of course, leads to the growth and power of the middle class. The middle class is now significant enough to be organized and it becomes more difficult for the elites to ignore them politically.

Taking cue from Lipset's proposition, in a recent book that asks why democracy succeeded in India but failed in Pakistan, Aitzaz Ahsan, the Pakistani senator, argues that the answer lies in the structure of the Pakistani and Indian society at the time of Partition. India had a strong middle class and a subordinated military, while Pakistan had a strong feudal class and a weak middle class,

22. Thomas Blom Hansen, *The Saffron Wave: Democracy and Hindu Nationalism in Modern India* (New Delhi: Oxford University Press, 1999), pp. 6–7.
23. See the discussion of Lipset's influential proposition in Edward Muller, 'Economic Determinants of Democracy', *American Sociological Review*, 60 (6), December 1995, pp. 966–82.

and this feudal class was in the charge of the military.[24] Many political commentators have, however, drawn attention to the history of the Indian democracy to show that this proposition of 'no bourgeois, no democracy' does not work in the Indian case because though the vast majority of the population has not been middle class, democracy has thrived. Rather, the political mobilization of different groups such as the lower castes and the increasing heterogenization of the middle class have been seen as indicators of the triumph of Indian democracy.

The New Industrial class

The agrarian and the Dalit middle class, however, lacked the pedigree and upbringing of the traditional middle class though they shared the money and goods. Increasingly, therefore, it is this money and consumption of goods that came to define the heterogeneous middle class. This middle-class consumer then came to be portrayed in public discourse as the primary beneficiary of new opportunities in the wake of liberalization. At the same time, policies of liberalization were changing fundamentally the character of a section of the middle class into that of a transnational global class.

With liberalization, the services sector and the IT industry became the drivers of the economy. In an agrarian economy, land and labour with capital become the determining factors for increasing the surplus. In the industrial economy, capital and labour along with energy sources become the main factors pushing productivity. In the information economy, the main source of productivity lies in the accumulation of knowledge. The structural change in the information economy changes the labour market and there is a shift from manual labour to intellectual labour. In the information economy, human capital, and not physical capital, is the driver of growth unlike in the industrial economy. It was, therefore, the educated middle class in India, which is the cause and the effect of the boom in the Indian economy, indicated among other things by the irresistible rise of the Sensex.

According to a 2005 study by Nasscom and McKinsey, India now accounts for 65 per cent of the global business in offshore IT and 46 per cent of the global BPO industry. Today, these two industries employ about 700,000 people and provide indirect employment to about 2.5 million workers. The services sector dominates the Indian economy today contributing more than half of our national income. And according to a survey by *India Today*, most middle-class parents wanted their children to work in the services sector.

A distinctive feature of the IT industry is that it has flourished largely independently of the old economy, having few links to the traditional sources of

24. See Meghnad Desai and Aitzaz Ahsan, *Divided by Democracy* (New Delhi: Roli Books, 2006).

business entrepreneurship or capital in the form of the large industrial houses or business communities. Most software companies have been founded by trained engineers of middle-class origins. The middle-class origins of many of the entrepreneurs, who have drawn on the cultural capital of their higher education and social capital derived from professional experience, have lent a distinctive culture and orientation to this industry. The entry of multinationals into IT has helped the industry grow and, therefore, the IT class is the most vociferous in supporting globalization.

The software industry has produced a new transnational capitalist class. With increasing mobility, Indian IT companies service global MNCs based all across the globe, 100,000 Indian professionals leave India every year to take jobs in the USA and 25 per cent of Silicon Valley companies are founded or managed by Indians. The new middle class is constructed as a potential promise of the benefits of globalization and the benefits are associated with the particular practices of commodity consumption. Liberalization has created a sharp divide within the middle class, as segments of this group constitute the new rich in metropolitan India. The prosperous, urban, middle-class consumer is basically the young, urban professional working in MNCs and drawing handsome salaries. This new middle class working in MNCs is also a globalized middle class with consumption patterns typical of their counterparts and colleagues in the developed countries. Consumption so defines us that our transnational identity as a consumer often takes precedence over our identity as a citizen, which is territorially defined. We are as much consumers of coke and cricket as we are Indian.[25]

Popular Hindi cinema has also been focusing on this globalized middle class, feeling at home equally in the West and in India, compared with the middle class in the colonial period, represented by Raja Ram Mohan Roy, feeling at home nowhere. This easy mobility you see, for instance, in *Dil Chahta Hai*, where Preity Zinta's character is from India, but she is at home in Sydney and can play host to Aamir Khan, whose family has business interests in India and Australia. These films appeal to the Indian middle class even when they focus on NRIs because NRIs are acutely conscious of their position as 'an apotheosis of the Indian middle class' and that is why the working-class NRI is not generally depicted.

Implications of a Culture of Consumption: Middle-Class Apathy and Activism

Just as the middle class has been celebrated for its consumption patterns, it has also been held to trenchant critique for its consumerist lifestyle. It has been accused of being indifferent to society in its obsession with consumption. To some

25. D. L. Sheth, 'Democracy and Globalization in India: Post Cold War Discourse', *Annals of the American Academy of Political and Social Science*, 540 (July 1995): 36.

extent, the self-indulgence of the middle class today and the cocoons of MNC offices, swanky shopping malls and posh apartment complexes within which the middle class lives, makes it difficult to see the poverty lying around. In fact, in a way, we have succeeded in the project of *garibi hatao*. We have removed poverty from our vision. In fact, the slogan of *garibi hatao* has always been followed in that ironic sense. Hence, only a few years after Indira Gandhi rode to victory on the back of this populist slogan, her son, Sanjay Gandhi started his slum-removal programme as poverty was a polluter and an eyesore.

This is not to say that the middle class has been completely apathetic. There has been middle-class activism as we saw in Delhi with the huge outcry against the initial verdict in the Jessica Lal case. At the same time, we take up the cudgels only for middle-class victims like Jessica Lal, Priyadarshini Mattoo, Nitish Katara and Geelani. In this discussion about middle-class activism, the popularity of Gandhigiri as packaged in *Lage Raho Munnabhai* is worth mentioning. Gandhism as an ideology does not go well with the middle class as it is against consumerism, but Gandhigiri goes well with the middle classes because it is a commodity—a self-help course—with Gandhi morphing into a kind of Sri Sri Ravi Shankar or better Ramdev, preaching the Art of Solving Personal Problems.

Environmentalism has found many supporters from the middle class but middle-class values, particularly that of consumption, inflect our attitudes to the environment as well. For instance, middle-class environmentalism is often directed at the consumption of the environment. We seek to drive out tribals from national parks so that the wildlife is safe and thriving for our consumption as tourists. The National Geographic and Discovery channels have also commodified this new environmentalism and made it possible. Our environmentalism is often anti-poor. Since the respectability of our middle-class neighbourhood depends on its lack of proximity to slums, we seek to drive away the slums to maintain clean parks for our morning walks. Although we consume more environmental goods such as water, electricity and our per capita pollution is more from our use of vehicles, fridges and ACs, our green concerns seldom affect or influence our consumerist lifestyles.

CONCLUSION

Hence, it is very difficult to speak of the Indian middle class in the singular and it will be better to speak of it in plural, as the 'the Indian middle classes'. This is because there is not just the upper middle class and the lower middle class. There is the old middle class and the new middle class; the metropolitan middle class and the small-town and agrarian middle class; the national middle class and the global middle class; the Dalit middle class and the upper-caste middle class: there is also the second-generation Dalit middle class, for many of whom, the middle-class identity overrules their caste identity. Just as most references to India seem to refer only to the middle class, most references to the middle class also seem to refer only to the metropolitan middle class today. It is the new metropolitan middle class that is criticized for its apathy and its consumption patterns by the old middle class just as the traditional rich had criticized the nouveau riche in Europe.

Our understanding of the middle class in India has also changed as the character and composition of the middle class have changed. The middle class in India was understood in the colonial period and the early decades of Independence as a small, homogenous, English-speaking elite constituted largely by the members of the upper castes, who were distinguished by their middle-class taste (which was little different from upper-class taste). As this middle class became less homogenous with the entry of people from different castes and backgrounds into the middle class, this definition/understanding of the middle class had to change. It came to be defined in terms of consumption, which was the common marker in this heterogeneous middle class. It is because of these changes in the understanding of the concept and the attendant confusions that the National Council of Applied Economic Research (NCAER), whose national-level surveys are used to gauge the size of the Indian middle class, chooses to use the term 'consuming class' instead of the fuzzy 'middle class'.

The question of how much a person should consume to be considered part of the middle class also remains unresolved. The Centre for the Study of Developing Societies (CSDS), which conducted a survey in 1996 to study middle-class formation in India, looked at five separate indicators to identify middle-class positions: (*a*) education above high-school level; (*b*) occupation: white-collar jobs; (*c*) housing: living in pucca houses, i.e. houses built of brick and lime or cement; (*d*) ownership of assets: (at least three of these) 1. car/jeep/tractor 2. scooter/motorbike 3. house/flat 4. television 5. water pump; and (*e*) self identification as members of middle class.[26] The NCAER's consuming class in comparison has an average annual income between Rs 45,000 and Rs 215,000 and typically owns a TV, cassette recorder, pressure cooker, etc., two-thirds of them own a colour TV, scooter, electric iron, sewing machine and blender.[27]

The television, perhaps, remains the archetypal middle class consumable. That is why in 2007, the Tamil Nadu government gifted television sets to families below the poverty line. If we cannot lift them into the middle class, at least we can make them feel they are middle class. This is because belonging to the middle class means having a middle-class lifestyle. Accordingly, moving into the middle class also means moving into a middle-class neighbourhood. At the same time, middle-class incomes often do not guarantee a middle-class lifestyle

26. D. L. Sheth, 'Caste and Class: Social Reality and Political Representations', in Ghanshyam Shah (ed.), *Caste and Democratic Politics in India* (Delhi: Permanent Black, 2002), p. 213.
27. Gurcharan Das, *India Unbound: From Independence to the Global Information Age* (New Delhi: Penguin, 2002), p. 287.

and in America, with the middle class shrinking, it has become a common phenomenon to find families going broke over maintaining this lifestyle to retain their middle-class identity.[28] In fact, self-identification is probably the most important marker of the middle class because as most sociologists and economists affirm, there is no clear definition of the 'middle class' as it is more a state of mind than an actual economic status.

Suggested Readings

Das, Gurcharan. 'The Rise and Rise of a Middle Class'. In *India Unbound: From Independence to the Global Information Age*. New Delhi: Penguin, 2002.

Deshpande, Satish. 'The Centrality of the Middle Class'. In *Contemporary India: A Sociological View*. New Delhi: Viking, 2003.

Fernandes, Leela. 'Restructuring the New Middle Class in Liberalizing India'. *Comparative Studies of South Asia, Africa and the Middle East,* 20 (1, 2), 2000.

Frankel, Francine. 'Middle Classes and Castes in India's Politics: Prospects for Accommodation.' In Atul Kohli (ed.), *India's Democracy: An Analysis of Changing State–Society Relations*. Princeton: Princeton University Press, 1988.

Varma, Pavan K. *The Great Indian Middle Class*. New Delhi: Penguin, 1998.

Questions

1. Is the midle class a socio-economic or a cultural category? Analyse.
2. Analyse the role of the middle class in democratic stability in India.
3. Is the middle class an urban phenomenon? Or can there be a rural middle class too? Give arguments in support of your answer.
4. How do you perceive the role of the Indian middle class in the post-globalization India?

---

28. Chris Baker, 'What Is Middle Class?', *The Washington Times,* http://www.washtimes.com/specialreport/20031129-105855-7412r.htm

Catalysts of Social Change: Adult Franchise and Education

9

Ravi Nandan Singh

INTRODUCTION

In this chapter, attempts have been made to understand Indian democracy as an institution that is continually challenged and reshaped by various constituent institutions like caste, family, tribe, religion, education, bureaucracy, market and the electoral process. The individual social actor and his/her activity would, therefore, be seen with and within these institutional practices and not distinct from these institutions. One may refer to this as a socio-anthropological elaboration of democracy because the perspectives developed here use the conceptual trajectories of the discipline of social anthropology. Keeping the positive limits of the themes of this chapter in mind (universal adult franchise and universalization of education), we are not going to trace the path these institutions have taken from the past to the present; so this is not a historical overview of events. Rather, we are going to reflect on them through the description of the establishment and the changing practices of universal adult franchise and the modern educational systems. Let us briefly sum up the scheme of discussion. The chapter is divided into three, broad sections.

The three-part discussion is loosely separated, where each part purports to introduce the basic conceptual framework, followed by the analytical arguments with relevant exemplifications. Most scholars would agree that universal adult franchise by itself is a nominal or symbolic entry (that provides a kind of formal equality) in the working of a nation. It is the complex of education, social mobility and citizenship (which, if realized, leads us towards substantive equality) that signifies the extent of indifference or sincerity of the democratic governments. This is the main thread of the arguments in the chapter, which are supported by examples. Illustrating this in detail, the first section tries to show that the history of the vote is deeply entrenched with the social divisions between different groups of society.

The institution of universal adult suffrage that was put into practice revealed the schism between various communities that had existed in social ties before the ideological adoption of a democratic form of government in Europe and America. This schism is most severely exposed when one looks at the accounts of women's movements for suffrage in Europe and America. Initially, the propertied White men were given voting rights, which they were ready to extend to the educated men amongst them. However, most of them opposed the idea of conferring the same right to women. A large number of White women then rallied to claim suffrage rights. Curiously, these women were either indifferent or vehemently opposed to the idea of extending the same right to Black men and women. Soon enough, Black men and women voiced their protest against the discrimination by the White people and demanded voting rights. Thus, on the one hand, the White families were witnessing an internal revolt and, on the other, the institution of racial relations was also questioned. Both these discourses have been crucial in setting the pattern for socio-political inequalities and their negotiations in the 20th century and the times to come.

In the second section, we look at the basic concepts regarding access to education and the difficulties in realizing the ideals of democracy and substantive citizenship by an examination of the theoretical perspectives put forth by Pierre Bourdieu and Michael W. Apple. In the final section, focusing on India, we trace the women's movements for voting rights under the colonial government; and as the discussion on Europe and America indicates in the context of family, race and class, we find that in the Indian cultural sphere, the familial structure and caste relations get questioned in the process of struggle over the vote. Notwithstanding these struggles, contemporary India inherits more of a half-formed agitation between various social groups that borders on a contested exclusion and participation of marginalized groups on the lines of caste, gender, class, tribe, religion and ethnicity. Their aspirations for social mobility through education—more than any other media—calls for an empathetic understanding of the realms of opportunities that contemporary India represents and the ways in which it can be accessed through cultural, political and educational negotiations between the citizens and with the State.

Racial Relations of Gendered Families: Women's Suffrage in 20th Century Europe and America

The practice of democracy has undergone tremendous interrogation ever since its adoption by various post-revolution states in Europe and America and, indeed, it is part of the bases of democracy that it should have room for questioning—a questioning that is critical, substantial and, at times, threatens to be destabilizing too. One way to capture this conflict, which has never been without struggles between various communities, is to analyse the history of the vote or adult franchise as it has also been called. Conceptually, as an idea, the vote signifies two important features in the history of political thought and practice. One, using the tool of vote, one gives nominal or symbolic consent or dissent to a person or a party; two, this consent or dissent is used by the said party or person to represent the people or the communities that may have voted in favour or against the prevailing stances of the government. It is also important to remember that the vote is anonymous and, thus, relations between elected ones and their represented ones is speculative and, owing to this speculative relation, the political equations may change, come elections. The shifts in political relations are structurally present within the practice of democracy and it is not a negative presence either. The voter and the elected are not eternally bound to each other and they are relatively free to make use of the changing socio-political contexts of the cultures within which they operate. One may argue that this nominal, symbolic and continuous relation of the voter with the socio-political system is mainly linked with the vote for an adult—and that this link gives rise to an entire range of features that can be accommodated under what is termed citizenship. In bureaucratic terms, this relation is also legalized and chartered: ration card, voter's list, voter's identification card, passport, differential treatment with regard to entitlements over bank accounts, property holdings, political representation, professional choices, and subsidies are just some of the common ways to ascertain privilege citizenship and also to hold a citizen under obligation to the country.

It is also important to remember that just as democracy did not get defined by its mere origin, similarly citizenship did not settle as a site of new socio-political identity over few years and at one place. As the interactions of the so-called traditional and modern cultures intensified and new institutions like judiciary, international market economy, and schools and universities took firm roots, citizenship also acquired new dimensions in people's lives. Be it in negotiating migration, poverty alleviation, minority or ethnic rights, reservation or parity rights or, in the contemporary world, the consumer-oriented policies and policing, the complexity of citizenship has to be seen in relation to social currents. These may be the key markers of a mature democracy, seen retrospectively or could be the central requirements of a normative democracy, but in practice, all of these issues have been elusive at different junctures. People have had to wage bitter struggles to redefine the prevailing social customs and cultural nuances so as to be better represented or represented at all in democratic systems. The redefinition acquires greater intricacy when the struggle involves the newly emergent, contested public spheres and some previously unquestioned quarters of the private spheres of communities. In what follows below, we are going to look at the institutions of race and family through the women's movements for suffrage in Europe and America in the late 19th and early 20th century, using the feminist scholarship, which critically evaluates the socio-political milieux of that time.

The history of the vote, or what one may call suffrage movements, has been chequered. The beginnings can be traced to the 18th century democratic revolutions of the propertied White middle class, if not the residual classes of aristocracy. Political subordination was challenged by the doctrine of inalienable civil rights and this demand was first made by the White male 'subject' (subsequently a 'citizen'). This is evident for instance in 'The French Declaration of the Rights of Man and the Citizen' of 1789. The celebrated declaration saw vote and suffrage as the exclusive prerogative of the male citizen. The declaration, however, provided the inspiration for the 'second sex' to claim similar rights for themselves. The well-known French playwright and revolutionary, Olympe de Gouges, revised the declaration of the rights of man and composed 'The Declaration of the Rights of Woman and the Female Citizen'. Subsequently, one had Mary Wollstonecraft's major text *Vindication of the Rights of Women* (1792) and John Stuart Mill's *Subjection of Women* (1873). The texts may have prepared the stage for a long drawn arduous battle to obtain the political right to vote. However, it is crucial to observe that the White male citizen was thinking of himself alone and did not see women as worthy of the vote, as their social role was primarily seen as confined to the domestic and the familial spheres. In a similar vein, the White woman talked about political emancipation exclusively in terms of the rights of White, middle-class women and shared the scorn of her male compatriot for the civil rights and liberties of coloured women and men. While many early White feminists were engaged in anti-slavery campaigns, they often saw themselves as carrying the burden for emancipation of the Black slaves. An example is Angelina Grimke, a White woman active in anti-slavery campaigns, who, in 1838, publicly declared that she could not emancipate the Negro slave until she achieved her own emancipation. Paradoxically, many White women involved in the anti-slavery campaigns of the time assumed a racist posture towards Black women. The class bias and racism of the women suffrage movements was effectively voiced in articulations of the women of colour. Sojourner Truths's *Ain't I a Woman* is one of the most militant and important historical statements in this respect. A Black American woman born into slavery, she attacked the racism of the White women as well as the male supremacists. She pointed out that neither were all women White and nor did they enjoy the middle-class life of material comfort, and she became the voice for the civil and equal rights of women of colour.

Although this fragmented account does not enable one to generalize, one may still convincingly argue that the institution of democracy in its infancy displayed a yawning chasm between the ideals that it stood for and their practice. The dominant and privileged social classes arrogated to themselves the right to decide the conditions of citizenship. As the struggles intensified, they were ready to accord only limited rights to the social groups that they otherwise deemed unfit for political discretion and participation. It is perhaps a mixed boon of democratic reason and social struggle that the universal adult franchise was won by people who were denied these rights but, if one looks at the socio-political history of any of these countries, one would find that the practice of the voting rights has been cordoned off from a direct acquisition of these people into the mainstream of these nations. Even after obtaining citizenship, they stand relatively distant from institutions that facilitate social mobility and they are not so much a part of the face of those institutions that reflect successes in the society, viz. cinema, media, industries, high political offices, professorial posts and research labs. When we look at the section on India, some of the structural similarities would stand out for us to see and compare to what is mentioned above. For now, let us conceptually analyse how education is the single most important site for social mobility and how it is also one of the most competitive ones. As already suggested, democracy seeks to resolve conflicts between communities and its greatest strength is that promise, but its failures run parallel to its successes. Education reflects this relationship, in the way it is accessible to citizens, the content or curricula on which students are honed to be citizens and through the researched disclosures of higher studies that may strengthen or threaten the settled truths of a nation-state.

Theories of Education in the Context of Democratic Social Changes

Having evoked a view of the political situations in Europe and America at the time of institutionalization of democracy, we move on to outline similar societal conflicts through the theories of sociology of education. The pre-existing political modes of being, before democratic institutionalization, had one way or the other signified the 'ruler' and the 'ruled', which in democracy becomes the 'elected' and the 'represented'. Similarly, modes of educating or training the young and the newcomer have existed in all cultures. Just as the transition from the previous modes of political existence to a democratic one requires a systemic questioning of social customs and beliefs, similarly the transformation of educational means and methods requires an adoption of new values and meanings. In both cases, the transitions and transformations are at times acceptable and at other times are posed in contrast to each other in a way that the values of the old and the new get caught in a never-ending façade, giving rise to cynicism and nostalgia in the everyday world of people.

Different social thinkers envisaged similarly paradoxical roles to modern education, as they spoke about the social transitions of cultures from the so-called traditional–rural to the industrial–urban domain. Emile Durkheim[1] argued that the existence of the institution of science would be crucial in the newly-emerged '**organic solidarities**' (an organization of societies on rational thinking, with faith in the individual as a prime moral and intellectual agent) because it would be central in defining the specialized occupation people may have in the industrial societies. However, he also argued[2] that in these newly emerged societies,

1. Emile Durkheim, *The Division of Labour in Society* (New York: Free Press, 1893).
2. Emile Durkheim, *Moral Education* (New York: Free Press, 1925 [1961]).

the new specialized roles and thus new communities of labour would have to understand the rationale behind their specialization—that every community is working for the greater good of the society. And, to make the greater good of the society sacred to everyone in the first place, Durkheim argued for a moral grounding of the future citizens in schools. Thus, it follows that schools have a greater function in democratic societies than merely imparting information; according to Durkheim, they must prepare the student to accept and respect the moral fabric of society. Another theorist called Max Weber[3] argued that to a large extent, the educational processes in industrial and modern capitalistic societies would be invested in the maintenance of the rational–bureaucratic systems of democratic institutions (which means that we have to be sufficiently literate in order to participate in most of the modern, social exchanges and contracts and, second, this literacy has to keep pace with legal and constitutional changes). So, at least three things emerge from the above viewpoints: one, in the present world, education is the most basic platform through which we are made to relate with the required values of the civil world of family, bureaucracy and the ideals of the nation and their practice, through past and present, in a standardized manner. Many scholars call this part of education a 'nationalistic agenda': instilling of secular, multicultural, racially impartial, and gender-neutral values.

However, having said that, it is significant to take note that if all this is in the hands of the government agencies to a large extent, it is very likely that the government can also use education to do the opposite of what has been mentioned. It can bring in communalism, xenophobia, class, caste and gender bias. In either case, most thinkers generally agree that the educational apparatuses are inevitably influenced by agencies that are bound to affect its content now and in times to come—be those agencies of State, market, communities, political parties or that of science. Let us call this dynamic system 'mainstream education'. The second concern is: how do we keep producing specialists or professionals who continuously avow to maintain or better the economic, cultural and academic institutions of the respective socio-cultural world? This introduces the aspect of education deciding the merit or capacity of every individual and accordingly making him or her eligible for various specialized jobs.

One of the central tenets of democracy is also that we do not allocate merit to birth-based identities (ascriptive identities) like caste, race and gender but rather see everyone through the merit of their abilities to compete on common grounds (achieved identities). This, in a certain way, means that in order to keep the social status of the family, it is not enough to be born in it; one has to try and at least equal it through educational measures, most of the time. It also means that families that are stigmatized in the society can hypothetically overcome their stigma, by possibly achieving respectable jobs (this is also the

---

3. Max Weber, *Economy and Society: An Outline of Interpretive Sociology* (Berkeley, CA: University of California Press, 1968).

reason why education is always more than the sum of its parts; it is about the transformation of social identities along with the enabling of jobs and occupations). The converse is also true, a respectable family may eventually bite dust if the new generation fails to live up to expectations. In practice, most of us wish to better our own individual positions and our familial positions in society. This could be called social mobility through educational and/or other means. Social mobility is about maintaining (remember that maintenance also is about improving familial status, because the social context changes with time: parents would want their children to do better than themselves), improving (that is seen as real upward shift) or downgrading (that is considered embarrassing or disgraceful in most cases) our familial positions and that of the community to an extent as well. Needless to say that educational means are adopted and appropriated by particular classes, castes and professional families over time. In other words, mainstream education becomes more amenable to people of a certain class, caste, race, gender and ethnicity and is, thus, instrumental in promoting these people to better social statuses, at times at the cost of the ones left behind. Therefore, we can say that mainstream education is the site of failure and success of the democratic institutions themselves (which partly explains, why even the democratic governments may try and alter the content or method of the educational system to soothe certain losses, or to deflect certain injuries of the people concerned); if it is unable to incorporate and promote the left-out communities, it would reiterate the traditional hierarchies of the pre-democracy days. Talking about the Indian context, Krishna Kumar[4] argues that the colonial government started educational facilities for the upper caste, 'wards' of the propertied natives, so that this educated class becomes the facilitator (bureaucrats) of the colonial rule. However, he also says that moving beyond this commonly held view in post-colonial India, the colonial government's educational policies should be seen as an effort to introduce a culture of science and rationality, far removed from the associations of daily lives of the students as the new civil order in a country marred with conflicts of caste, religion and regions. Further, he says that if science was to offer a secular way of civil life apart from sharing the ideals of industrialization and development, Western literature was to provide a new aesthetic fabric to the newly educated. It is all together a separate story that the notions of 'scientific is secular', 'literature is English' got reasonably challenged as the struggles for Independence from the colonial rule intensified and education became less of a site that got its pedagogic concerns planted from above. Krishna Kumar owes the disavowal of the colonial ideals in the field of education most to Gandhi's interventions and not to any nationalist obscurantism. The third issue is that education is not seen to be a pleasant thing to be a part of, by everyone, partly because there seems to be a general

4. Krishna Kumar, *Political Agenda of Education: A Study of Colonialist and Nationalist Ideas* (New Delhi: Sage, 2005 [1991]).

distance between the means-end kind of mainstream education and the creative demands of human dispositions but mostly because one may come from a particular social background to a school, where very few things may be common between the two. To many people in the world, this has been a call to think of alternative education, either in opposition or in conjunction with mainstream education. It is important for us to remember that what is alternative and what is mainstream are also socially and politically informed debates and, thus, in the end, the simple question of education is never really a simple practice or a settled idea. It characterizes as an institution, the deepest of conflicts for better (or worse) social values, progress (or regression) in social and literary thought on one hand and for greater (or minimal) technical efficiency on the other, intertwined into one. Let us now discuss the abovementioned issues in greater detail using the theories of Pierre Bourdieu and Michael W. Apple. The question of social change that we will address in this discussion relates to the asymmetries of class, race and ethnicity.

Pierre Bourdieu, a French sociologist and anthropologist, the late contemporary of another prolific anthropologist Lévi-Strauss, is commonly known for his theories of 'practice' and his contribution in expanding the understanding of 'capital' beyond the Marxian descriptions. Since, it is through his description of different kinds of 'capital' that he later on arrives at a theory of '**symbolic violence**', let us try and define his categories of capital, but, first we may want to define what he meant by the word capital. He says '... capital, which, in its objectified or embodied forms takes time to accumulate and which, as a potential capacity to produce profits and to reduce itself in identical or expanded form, contains a tendency to persist in its being, is a force inscribed in the objectivity of things so that everything is not equally possible or impossible.'[5] Bourdieu asserts that the Marxist definition of capital, which conceives capital as materially accumulated wealth, that which is invested into a capitalist venture in suitable economic conditions and is made to reproduce itself and more using exploitative work conditions, may be a sufficient analytical definition for understanding capitalism but to understand other relations of dominance, we need to expand the idiom of capital. Marx's notion of capital also becomes a basis for defining social classes; loosely one can say that the class that owns machines and capital (and profit by owning and operating them) is that of the capitalists, related with the labour of the class which does not, that is of the workers. To some extent, Bourdieu also uses the ownership of capital to signify the privileged position of individuals, families and communities in society. He retains the idea of economic capital as that '... which is immediately and directly convertible into money and may be institutionalized in the form of property rights'[6]

5. Pierre Bourdieu, 'The Forms of Capital', in Stephen J. Ball (ed.), *The Routledge Falmer Reader in Sociology of Education* (New York: Routledge, 2004 [1983]).
6. Ibid.

but goes on to describe 'cultural capital' and **'social capital'** by moving beyond the definition of economic capital. Cultural capital, he says, can be primarily differentiated from economic capital by the fact that it is an embodied capital. One has to acquire it over time and it cannot be handed down at one stroke like, for example, inheritance of wealth. What immediately comes to mind is education—a slow, gradual and rigorous incorporation of skills, values and wisdom at an individual end. If we add the objective signatures to this acquisition, then it would mean what educational degrees and certificates we have, which institution we are attached to and so on. Many people have described this as academic capital. Now there are two things to consider: one, since this acquisition is dependent on personal acquisition, it also goes along with the person to a large extent and thus we cannot equate it to a material property; it cannot be handed down or inherited like wealth but since the acquisition itself is rated highly in society, it has a symbolic value and thus academic capital in practice is a symbolic capital. Two, since it cannot be inherited and largely is incorporated within an individual, we tend to think that it does not help in social mobility of a group or a community. Let us see how it does indeed help in social mobility and has a rather hidden way of doing it. Personal acquisition is first of all directly related with the families that we come from, schools and other educational institutions that we go to, that is, symbolic capital is cultivated (at times at any cost) by our predecessors. A family of doctors may first of all inculcate in its children a deep sense of respect for the profession of medicine and surgery and, second, explain to them how they got there with slow and timely investments of hard work and intelligence, even as they try and ensure that similar cues are rooted in their children's lives. Even though they may not want their children to become doctors, or the children themselves may not want to be doctors like their elders, they would have to negotiate the symbolic capital of their families. That is, something close to what a doctor in the society stands for would be acceptable and thus promoted. Thus, we can see that the individual's social and symbolic statuses are trajectories that are built with an investment of time, energy and cultural capital (valuation of art, that involves music, literature and paintings; importance to grooming, that involves the way we dress, speak, behave and eat; current affairs and general informational awareness) by families, situations and circumstances in which they are brought up, with utmost calibration. So, logically it follows that most of these families that identify with some kind of symbolic capital rather than the other would also tend to be organized on those lines. Here comes the notion of social capital. Let us examine it with an apparent and transparent definition provided by Bourdieu himself : 'social capital is the aggregate of the actual or potential resources which are linked to possession of a durable network of more or less institutionalized relationships of mutual acquaintance and recognition—or in other words, to membership in a group—which provides each of its members with the backing of the collectively owned capital, a 'credential', which entitles them to credit, in the various senses of the word' (ibid.). This institutionalization is real and is recognized by us in the ways in which we participate in our social world. Then, just as there is a conflict and hiatus between the symbolic capitals or the lack of it amongst different social groups, this conflict also at times finds a manifestation in our classrooms and the way we look at our education. The recognition and representation of this conflict is called symbolic violence by Bourdieu. He asks why is it that children of poor migrants, of ethnic communities, of colour, of non-professional classes not only fare badly in schools but are also directly confrontational, antagonistic or evasive to their education; why do they drop out, run away, take to drugs, indulge in street fights rather than play soccer in school, be abusive rather than participate in speech or elocution competitions. He considers that the answer may partly lie in the ways in which these children are treated at home, in school, in the neighbourhoods or in the mainstream culture, that is, how their communities are seen in relation to the dominant communities of the society and how they see themselves as a part of the social world. In other words, their symbolic capital is either not recognized, is made to look like a lack or is not given enough legitimacy in the formal order of things.

Michael W. Apple, a contemporary American theorist of education, has spent most of his academic career in attempts to convince us that this symbolic violence exists and it exists in more deep-seated and more manifest ways than we recognize; but what is also true is that in democracy, the power practices of different institutions also strive harder than we think they do to ensure that education carries us all—in our thick and thin and in its hard and fast rules. These practices, he argues, are practices to bring legitimation to differing social values, conflictual relations and torn histories. He contends that all this gets represented in the curriculum of our national charter of education, which keeps varying according to the social context in which we live. That is to say, our educational texts are sites of contestation for different social groups, which seek to signify through it a cultural politics. Referring again to Krishna Kumar's discussion, we follow that most of the nationalist ideas around education in the colonial times were also about allocating 'legitimation' to issues that were neglected by the colonial government. However, the nationalist politics wished to have its 'sacred' knowledge pursued uncritically and in isolation of counter disciplines by the pupils, which was criticized then by various other political streams. The post-Independence educational reforms have largely been guarded efforts by various commissions set up by successive governments to incorporate a judicious mix of cultural legitimacy, scientific temper, managerial qualities and literary and aesthetic appreciation of thoughts and ideas, not only of that which originated in the Indian state but which also came from elsewhere. So Michael W. Apple seems justified in defining culture as:

> ... the way of life of a people, the constant and complex process by which meanings are made and shared—does not grow out of the pregiven unity of

a society. Rather, in many ways, it grows out of its divisions. It has to work to construct any unity that it has. The idea of culture should not be used to celebrate an achieved or natural harmony.

Culture is instead 'a producer and reproducer of value systems and power relations'.[7] Thus, our 'curricula' is a round about of our social lives; it is a black-lettered, revolving mirror embedded in time, which shows ourselves to us and to 'others' differently at different points of historical junctures.

India: Citizenship and Education

Using the political contextualization of the first section and the exposure of the same kind of contestation in the ostensibly peaceful field of education through various theories of sociology of education in the second section, we may try and briefly discuss the trajectories of post-Independent India. It would be perhaps apparent after going through the extended discussions of the first two sections that societal conflicts are universal and democratization is about recovering lost voices, representing those who are not yet there. But to a large extent, it is also about reiterating the mainstream and considering it 'sacred', as Durkheim would have said it. India, with its colonial past, multiple linguistic, religious, ethnic identities and big and small political initiatives and their culminations is similarly an illustration of this democratizing process. In this section, we may use few anecdotal alibis to lay out the deeply entrenched asymmetries in our democracy. We may not be able to discern the scopes and extents of the gravid past of the country here, but using few basic references of late colonialism and through it of contemporary India, we would illustrate how categories of gender and caste operate vis-à-vis education and adult franchise or citizenship. The institutions of caste and gender are used as tools vis-à-vis education and adult franchise to illustrate the possibilities in which democracy inhabits our lives and vice versa. Starting with a brief discussion of the achievement of the adult franchise for women in India, the present section follows it with an analysis of a statement by Ambedkar with regard to the institution of vote, education and democracy in the late colonial period.

There is a general feeling amongst scholars that the struggle for female, universal, adult suffrage in India that started in the early part of the 20th century, decades before Independence, under and within the presence of colonial government, was less acrimonious and violent than the European and the American struggles (discussed in the first section). Before going into the reasons for the same, let us look at another feature, over which there is a similar consent amongst scholars: the struggle for electoral representation for women

---

7. Michael W. Apple, 'Cultural Politics and the Text', in Stephen J. Ball (ed.), *The Routledge Falmer Reader*.

was primarily led and mobilized by women, organized along the lines of class and race; similarly in India, the women-led struggle also had a class and caste bases, besides having the manifest gender basis but even deeper commonality between the two is that these struggles managed to open the seams of institutions like family, race (in the European and American context) or caste, class and that of the nation itself. Let us try and expand on these comments further, which would perhaps also explain why the Indian women's struggle for voting rights is more protected than the disruptive and violent one of Europe and America. If we think of our anti-colonial struggles, then it is not hard to imagine that the way families were organized, it was only gradually that women were allowed entry into the political spaces in different capacities. So, if an organized struggle for Independence can be claimed to have started some time before the 1857 revolt (that is also termed as the first war of Independence by some historians), we can come to an agreement that a mass-based women's organization in politics could have only come by the end of the 19th century or at the beginning of the 20th century.

It is easy to visualize that by the time a gradual incorporation of women into the mainstream of politics must have happened, the 'rules' to play by in the political 'field' would have been already negotiated by different sections of caste men. Therefore, the incorporation of women in mainstream politics implied a further negotiation of the already negotiated term. That entailed in the first place an acceptance of the dominant practices to participate within the political field. As the historian Sumit Sarkar argues, the reformation movements or other nationalist struggles raised by various communities were bound within conservative limits of caste, patriarchy, scriptural moralism in their practice. So it is crucial to make sense of the gradual opening and closure of these rigidities at various historical junctures, rather than maintaining any one enclave of time as thoroughly liberated and other as deeply entrenched in bondages.[8] Thus, a major section of political elite or regional elites who had influence over politics in its negotiation with the colonial administrators in the pre-Independence era belonged to the upper castes and held major shares in property (whom M. N. Srinivas later called the dominant castes), or were educated professionals. Thus, even women's mobilization to seek voting rights reflected this. Coming primarily from political or industrial families, they demanded an equal representation in society through vote. The demand for voting rights at one level equalled to becoming what Anupama Roy in her book *Gendered Citizenship* (2005) calls 'consort citizen' to the main political players, who were the upper caste middle class men. If we take Sarkar's and Roy's views together, we may conclude that in the nationalist struggle the already existent radius of familial 'values' and caste ties was reiterated by nationalist

8. Anupama Roy, *Gendered Citizenship: Historical and Conceptual Explorations* (New Delhi: Orient Longman, 2005).

politics rather than substantially challenged. Scholars argue that this probably happened because the nationalist struggle emerged in cultural negotiation with the colonial values. While we were ready to take the political structures and constitutional methods that originated in the West, we also wished to *Indianize* it by what we thought India was all about—women as keepers of home and *Sanskriti* or *Aabru* rather than participants of public sphere; caste marriages, religious purity and pollution, the dominance of the Hindu ethos rather than intercaste marriages, revised notions of merit not based on what was considered pure–impure and multi-religious ethos (a conflict that manifested itself in the form of the Partition).

The Indian National Congress in its Karachi Convention (1931) did adopt the demand for 'universal adult franchise'; it took long before it could be realized. It is the realization of this demand and the political debates for and against it that reveals the deep-seated differences between the various communities of dominant and depressed castes and middle and lower classes. It also laid the patterns for future women citizens where caste and religious identity became entrenched and that structurally shaped their public participation. Along with the pressures of caste, we must also note the sexual connotation of a woman as a 'consort-citizen'—the freedom to participate in the social world gets routed through the man. The woman can be a citizen and a participant, as a daughter, wife or mother and ironically not only is she to be governed by her family and kinship from where her empowerment comes, she also has to maintain the structures of caste, family and kinship by indulging in a proactive familial politics. While there is no denying that through women's struggle and increasing participation, the seam of family and lines of gender and caste have become more permeable at places, however, we can not take the mobility of women in the contemporary public sphere for granted. It is more likely that a professional woman is seen as a 'woman citizen'[9] who has to continuously participate in an internal strife between the divisions that she has to cross of caste, family, kinship and professional life on an everyday basis.

Now we move on to a discussion on education with the above-mentioned themes in perspective. Ambedkar in the 1920s had argued with his political contemporaries at various junctures to demand a universal right to vote in India that cut across caste and powerful landholding groups of people. He considered the right to vote not merely as a transaction but as a direct and participatory event that allowed the vote to be used as a vehicular agent of social negotiation of one's life situation. That is, the vote was not merely a simple act of consent to a party or a person; it had a transformative capacity that could invoke change, favourable to the respective community. He argued that associated life is shared by every individual and as every individual is affected by its consequences,

9. Susie Tharu, 'Citizenship and Its Discontents', in Mary E. John and Janaki Nair (eds.), *A Question of Silence: Sexual Economies of Modern India* (New Delhi: Kali for Women, 1998).

every individual must have the right to settle its terms. From the same premises it would further follow that the poorer the individual, the greater the necessity of enfranchising him.[10] While Ambedkar uses the term 'poor' over here, we must try and relocate the poor of that context in which Ambedkar is speaking and also that of which he is speaking. One obvious struggle involved over here is that Ambedkar is speaking with a mixed audience of British officials and Indian nationalist leaders who, as noted above, were mainly upper-caste people and, thus, Ambedkar's position as a Dalit leader was in sharp contrast and a marginalized one. Second, he is trying to make a case for the 'illiterates' to have voting rights and be counted as able citizens when the landholding and relatively educated, upper-caste men and women had still not been granted the same. If we dig deeper, we would know that the social class Ambedkar wants to be given voting rights to is not merely poor in the economic sense. These are the 'illiterates', who were largely from the landless castes, because the voting rights—in whatever little percentage that had been granted to the Indian men—were given on the basis of their large land holdings and the next step the government was contemplating was to extend it to minor land holders. This, the British government could do because owing cultural allegiance to the Roman law of succession, it somehow felt that property holders were naturally disposed with discretion and prudence, which otherwise comes through the instalments of education (see the first section). Thus, property was one criteria and soon educational achievements or academic capital, as Bourdieu says, became the means for getting recognition as a citizen, who could contribute to nation building through tax, agricultural produce on one hand and through running institutions like Parliament, court, industry, schools and universities on the other. Thus, what gets questioned through Ambedkar's intervention is this proprietorship, which seems to be in the offing that the nation will progress in a set order and that is—one acquires property or gets educated through the various schools and universities set by the government (which were difficult to get in, even for the upper-caste Hindus or people of any other religion) and then gets incorporated in the symbolic order of citizenship and gets the entitlement to participate in the activities of nation building. Conceptually, this intervention poses a question: should we insist on an eligibility (property and academic capital) criteria for getting voting rights or to be counted as citizens merely to please a dominant few sections of society or should we involve everyone and their political representatives and work towards mass social mobility? The answer lies in what we have as constitutional rights post Independence that citizenship and acquisition of different kinds of capital, viz. economic, cultural and social has to happen through social mobility of different communities. In agreeing to this social composition of democracy, we also know that given our social history, the

10. B. R. Ambedkar, 'Adult Franchise', in *The Essential Writings of B. R. Ambedkar*, edited by Valerian Rodrigues (New Delhi: Oxford University Press, 2002).

nation-state would have unequal communities in terms of wealth, academic and social capital and, thus, social mobility would also be scarce and elusive. There is also a radical need to bridge these gaps and realize the needs of these communities, and clearly, educational measures seem to be most suited to enable people to realize the full potential of their citizenship.

As noted in the section on theories of education, the mere presence of schools, colleges and universities does not ensure that everyone would get enrolled and come out successful. The ones who are left out (belonging to lower castes and tribes and minorities) or the ones who drop out (a vast section of students, marred by the economic background of their families; discords in families; drugs; alienation; societal pressures or a general mismatch between what one can do as a student and person and what one is made to do) or the ones who are taken out (young women for marriage) should not blame their fate because as we have maintained from the beginning of this chapter, citizenship exists in relation to the institutions of caste, religion, race, tribe, ethnicity, and language. So any one individual's success or failure is not entirely his or her own. One can trace the history of central institutions like NCERT, CBSE, UGC or one can look at the counts of schools, colleges, universities and professional institutes, including the IITs and IIMs along with FTII, NDA, NSD, etc. that appeared on the scene as per the demands of the time. The central point, however, is to understand how important education is for social mobility and how our social organization facilitates or occludes the possibilities of our participation.

If we look at school and university as systems that create successes in the society, one can observe a three-fold scheme that repeats itself. Parents or communities feel extremely motivated to send their children for primary education because they have seen the results of higher education—that is, so and so studied for this degree and now holds a post with this or that office. Most would be aware that the colonial post of 'tax collector' was seen to be so powerful that in Independent India, most families of the older generation would wish that their sons become collectors or sahibs. The paradox, however, is that between primary education, which is largely a promise, and higher education, which is the time for results, there lies a vast span of time, at times one-third of one's life. The changes that happen in an individual's life, in his familial, communitarian, and national context determine the paths that would open up for that person. This silent period of educational life is also the most turbulent one because some students find the full course of school and college education too long and demanding as means for an end that lies outside the educational domain, and, thus, choose to opt out of it. This 'silent period' also in a certain way lays the foundation for various things that education brings forth as possibilities: our vocations, interests, orientations, faiths, friendships and most importantly a cherishing feeling for education itself as an institution. Thus, education in the society is not seen and should not be seen as a skeletal vehicle to success; it also brings the charisma of newness in cultures, and apart from the material success it may bring, it provides the cultural communities of students, reasons and spaces to criticize and change their inherited worlds. However, the pragmatic act of completing one's education in itself may be the most demanding thing in a developing economy like India, a reality that characterizes contemporary India more than anything else. If one illustration is to be added to the ongoing discussion on the links of caste, family, education and the importance of social mobility, then it is worthwhile to note that most marriages happen within caste boundaries with the groom's family and individual status considerably superior than the girl's, most of the time a kinship network of relatives comes into place. The children born to a rural or a small-town couple are often sent to an urban relative and invariably it is the boy child who is sent to avail of the better educational facilities. In fact, research shows that most girl children are not even sent to primary schools because in rural areas the schools are often outside the villages and those who manage to finish their primary education are unable to pursue higher education for the same reason. Similarly, there is a migration to the metropolitan cities for education and jobs which again depends on kinship and is gendered (relatives or a person from one's own village or town may take the male student with them). However, even with its limitations, educational mobility ultimately works in favour of the communities: Xaxa notes, owing to the affirmative actions like reservation, there is a tribal middle class in the urban centres and the same uses similar enclaves of kinship and regional identities to affirm cultural and educational spaces through political advances and pragmatic associations.[11] The key difference between the Dalit middle class, the tribal middle class, the minorities—their middle classes and that of the majority upper caste and, at times, upper and middle class Hindus is what Bourdieu says: that of investment of time and density. A set of people who have managed to establish the symbolism of their cultural and social capital over a long period of time have a greater degree of legitimation compared with the new and fragile social groups and their social capitals. That's why there is a simultaneous struggle by and for these communities of women, 'lower' castes, tribes, religious minorities to be represented in the symbolic knowledge of the nation-state (textbooks, curricula, rewritten histories, etc.) and to get entries into educational institutions of excellence and use them to mobilize their individual and communitarian interests.

In conclusion, it can be simply added to the preceding discussion that as the context of globalization and consumerist capitalism intensifies, the security of having a large amount of landholding would recede. Small-time farmers and workers in any case would not be able to produce much so as to accelerate their social mobility through the education of their children. In most cases then, there will be greater and perhaps bitter struggles to acquire social capital

---

11. Virginius Xaxa, 'Tribes in India', in Veena Das (ed.), *The Oxford Companion to Sociology and Social Anthropology* (New Delhi: Oxford University Press, 2003).

that bring in economic capital. Since what earlier happened over generations are to be achieved in a few years today, there is an undeniable presence of nerve-wracking competition and dramatic successes and failures. The battle for privileges would be experienced as citizens, but played out in the modes, means and methods of education as thoughts, ideas, techniques, policies and ways of contemporary life.

Suggested Readings

Apple, Michael W. *Official Knowledge: Democratic Knowledge in a Conservative Age*. New York: Routledge, 2000.

Deshpande, Satish. *Contemporary India: A Sociological View*. New Delhi: Viking, 2003.

Faulks, Keith. *Citizenship*. London: Routledge, 2000.

Illich, Ivan. *Deschooling Society*. London: Pelican, 1971.

Questions

1. As observed in this chapter, a crucial link can be established between education and citizenship. Try and develop similar links between healthcare and citizenship, crime and citizenship, and sexuality and citizenship.
2. Sociological descriptions reduce individual social agents to mere props of social process. Comment and possibly envisage a model of society in which individuals can be said to be doing everything independent of societal influences.
3. Why is it important to evoke the categories of race, caste, age, gender and sexuality while understanding the processes of citizenship?
4. 'Right to information', 'national identity card' (NIC), and 'consumer forum' are some of the new forums through which the citizen is addressed in contemporary India. Trace the social contexts that brought about the existence of these processes (For example, right to information against corruption, NIC against terrorism, etc.).

Social Movements and the Mass Media

Bindu Menon

10

The 2004 EPICA award (Europe's Premier Creative Awards in Advertisement) was won by the advertisement agency Y&R Italia. The visual media advertisement for Telecom Italia, the Italian telecommunications company, was enthralling for various reasons. The black-and-white advertisement starts with a medium shot of the Gandhi Ashram in Wardha and cuts to a shot of Mahatma Gandhi walking in to the ashram and on to a still of Gandhi working on his charkha. The scene cuts to Gandhi moving to his typewriter. The next shot is of a powerful camera capturing the image of Gandhi, and beaming it across the world, huge crowds of men and women listening attentively to him in various European cities—London, Rome and Paris. Equally keen are statesmen who are listening to him on television, Gandhi is also on a mobile screensaver and computer screens. Among those listening are also an old Chinese man outside a market and two native Indians with a laptop. The music soundtrack fades and over the images emerges Gandhi's voice where he says 'of course I believe in One World'. The advertisement ends in a long shot of Gandhi speaking on a huge public TV screen in Moscow and thousands listening to him on the streets. The advertisement ends with a caption that says, 'If he could communicate this way in that age, imagine the world today.' Does having better means of communication and media help movements and ideas well? Would Gandhi have had a greater impact in a tangled, conflict-ridden contemporary world if there were smarter means of communication and more mass media? To answer the wishful thinking of the advertisement, we have to look into the complex debates on the relationship between mass media and social movements.

Central to this is the relationship between the media and democracy. The discussion of media's democratic role is intimately bound up with a debate about the media's organization and regulation. The principal democratic role of the media, according to the traditional liberal theory, is to act as a check on the State. The media should monitor the full range of State activity and fearlessly expose its abuses. This watchdog role is said, in traditional liberal theory, to override all other functions of the media. Many of the received ideas of the democratic role of the media derives from a frock-coated, Western European world of the 18th century where the media consisted principally of small circulation, political publications and the State was still dominated by landed elite. The result is a legacy of old maxims with very little relationship to contemporary reality. By extension, the watchdog role also places it in the free market, to be completely independent from the State. This also was interpreted widely as a role that could be performed when it operates in an environment free of State regulation. Apart from this watchdog function, media could also be seen in an expansive way in the Liberal theory, as an agency of information and debate that facilitates the functioning of democracy. At the heart of this approach is an admirable stress on the need for civic information, public participation, robust debate and active self-participation.

The media system in the United States of America developed mainly as a commercial system, whereas it developed as public service systems with varying degrees of State regulation in most countries of Western Europe. Many of the post-colonial nations in the wake of Independence emulated public-service-broadcasting model with strict State regulations. One important feature of most media systems in the globalized world is an increased move towards deregulation of the media systems, placing them squarely in a free market system. The liberal argument about its role as a watchdog and information provider proved effective in campaigns for deregulation in most parts of the world.

Traditionally, liberal theory holds that the government is the main target of media scrutiny because the State has a monopoly of legitimated violence and is, therefore, the institution to be feared most. It would argue that for this reason, there should be a distance between the governmental systems through private ownership. This fails to take into account shareholder and other forms of authority.[1]

A significant section of the world's media has been taken over by the large industrial and commercial concerns, including General Electric, Fiat, Toshiba, etc., in a development that extends from the USA to Japan. A number of media conglomerates have also grown into huge leisure conglomerates with major investments cutting across interests like television, music, films, newspapers, books and net enterprises. The concern currently is not about the media's links to big industries but media itself, which is a huge industry.[2]

The argument about vigilantism against State abuse of power, though persuasive, ignores the way in which the world has changed after the 18th century. A magnetic field of mutual advantage has already emerged between

1. James Curran, 'Mediations of Democracy', in James Curran and Michael Gurevitch (eds), *Mass Media and Society* (London: Hodder Arnold, 2005).
2. Thomas McPhail, *Global Communication: Theories, Stakeholders and Trends* (Oxford, UK: Blackwell Publishing, 2006).

media and political realms. The government's sphere of activity has developed enormously and many policy measures could directly affect the profitability of the media organizations. The media has also become more market driven and expansionist, and are, therefore, more concerned about lobbying with the government for more market-friendly policies and are prone to corruption.

A well-known case in point is Rupert Murdoch's vetoing of the Harper Collins venture to publish former Hong Kong Mayor Chris Patten's memoirs in 1998, because he wanted to seek favour with the Chinese government in order to obtain permission for expanding his broadcast operations in mainland China. In short, the market system has given rise to media moguls who adjust their critical scrutiny to suit their business interests, says Curran.

THE MEDIA IN INDIA

To start with, let us go back to Gandhi who himself was a journalist. In fact, many of the nationalist leaders including Lokmanya Tilak, who founded the Marathi newspaper *Kesari*, and Mahatma Gandhi who campaigned in papers like the *Indian Opinion* in South Africa, *Hind Swaraj, Young India* and *Harijan*, used the media as powerful tools of communication with fellow citizens and the rulers. The impact of the print media in enhancing the nationalist movement is well recorded by many historians. More generally, newspapers in almost all vernacular languages from the 1870s onwards contributed to the creation of a public sphere, an arena in which debates took place.

The term 'public sphere' is coined by the German philosopher, Jurgen Habermas, to indicate 'a domain of our social life in which such a thing as public opinion can be formed. Access to the 'public sphere' is open in principle to all citizens.[3] A portion of the public sphere is constituted in every conversation where private persons come together to form a public. Citizens act as a public when they deal with matters of general interest without being subject to coercion; thus, with the guarantee that they may assemble and unite freely and express and publicize their opinions freely. This space includes the newspapers, coffeehouses, clubs and similar places of public gathering and discussion. When the public is large, this kind of communication requires certain means of dissemination and influence. Today, newspapers, periodicals, radio, television and the Internet comprise the media, which contribute to a 'public sphere'.

In the Indian context, the historic role of the press and the journalistic efforts of those who led the struggle for national freedom meant an opposing role for the press vis-à-vis the imperial forces. The nationalist press, which was anti-imperial and a crusader of the freedom fight assumed a more supportive

---

3. Jurgen Habermas, 'The Public Sphere , in S. Seidman (ed.), *Jurgen Habermas on Society and Politics* (Boston, MA: Beacon Press 1989 [1973]).

role towards the State-building process in the wake of the Freedom struggle. Many of the norms laid down during this period came to define the nature of Indian journalism for several years to come. A break from this came only in 1975 with the imposition of the internal emergency restrictions, which revealed a more menacing face of the 'benign' State. Censorship, which was considered repulsive during the freedom struggle, was imposed. But the resistance was meek from the mainstream newspapers, barring a few and some brave, small publications.[4] The post-Emergency period also saw the emergence of social movements like the women's movement and the environmental movement. (For detailed discussion on social movements, see Chapter 12. The post-Emergency period also heralded a more vigorous, investigative style of journalism.

The structure of the Indian media also has undergone a major change from the days of Independence to the contemporary period. In the early years following Independence, there were two kinds of newspaper owners in India. The nationalist struggle against the British produced newspapers owned by patriots who ran newspapers for the cause. The second were a few families who were in the newspaper business to make a living and did not find it necessary to fight against the British: they built strong investments and did not cause any imperial disapproval. Bodies like the Registrar of Newspapers of India, Press Council of India and the Manisana Wage Board were part of the government apparatus of direction, regulation and largesse. The broadcast medium, first the radio and then television were strictly State-owned and State-regulated. In fact, in most post-colonial nations, television and radio developed as central elements in the political and cultural processes of nation-building.[5]

But in the last 15 years or so, all these countries have seen a range of developments in their media systems. These include the international diffusion of the pro-liberalization-policy prescriptions (often from official institutions like the IMF), the desire of many of these nations to benefit from the new economic policies and the emergence of new technologies of transmission that have brought a foreign wave of programming to many of these closed media systems.[6]

In the 1990s, as the Indian economy was shorn of many government controls with the new economic policy, capitalist forces in the media industry also emerged. The Indian skies were opened to private broadcasters and, consequently, to foreign broadcasts. The question of foreign investment in newspapers invited fervent opposition from many newspapers. Some feared it as a move, which will lead to a neo-colonialism, some feared losing autonomy and jeopardizing national

---

4. Ammu Joseph and Kalpana Sharma, *Whose News? Media and Women's Issues* (Delhi: Sage Publications, 1994).
5. P. Kitley (ed.), 'Introduction' in *Television, Regulation and Civil Society in Asia.* (London: Routledge Curzon, 2003).
6. Kalyani Chadha and Anandam P. Kavoori, 'Globalization and National Media Systems: Mapping Interactions in Markets, Policies and Formats', in James Curran and Michael Gurevitch (eds), *Mass Media and Society*.

interest. The new guidelines in 2002 permits foreign investment up to 26 per cent of a company but at least 51 per cent of the equity had to be held by a single Indian shareholder.[7] In the case of newspapers, all these have led to the creation of an industry that is heavily supported by advertisement revenue, which has far-reaching implications in their ethos and approach towards journalism.

Parallel to the vertical conglomerates are the emergence of national multimedia conglomerates, which have consolidated their market hold within the nation as well as expanded to cultural, linguistic markets outside it. Though the scale on which they operate are much less compared to the global giants, they are successful in generating advertising revenue. In the Indian market, Bennett & Coleman, Zee TV, the Eenadu Group, etc., own huge chunks of market share and straddle various areas of business interests like film, music, Internet service providing, cable services, print, publishing and broadcast.[8]

THE MASS MEDIA AND SOCIAL MOVEMENTS

If the contemporary mass media is such a capital-intensive system, driven by profit, how would they function in the case of reporting on social movements? Nevertheless, the mass media—newspapers, radio, television and magazines—played an important role in the origins and development of many social movements. Thus, those who are active with those movements are ambivalent about the mass media. On the one hand, they looked at the mass media as organs of public opinion through which they would be represented in the political arena, on the other hand, they felt that the media were susceptible to ideological and governmental pressure and was never independent.

Since the 1970s, studies on mass media and social movements have observed mass media as a key site of political contention in advanced capitalism. Scholars like Gaye Tuchman[9] and Tod Gitlin[10] have described:

> … news as a hegemonic system of power into which oppositional movements step in when they contest prevailing definitions and dominant cultural and political frames. Movements in great part, it is held, depend on mass media a great deal to get the message out. In doing so, they use establishment institution to fulfil non-establishment, communicating with movement followers, reaching out to potential recruits, neutralizing or combating opponents.

---

7. Robin Jeffery, *India's Newspaper Revolution: Capitalism, Politics and the Indian Language Press* (New Delhi: Oxford University Press, 2000).
8. Vanita Kohli, *Indian Media Business* (Delhi: Response Books, 2006).
9. Gaye Tuchman, 'The Symbolic Annihilation of Women by the Mass Media', in Gaye Tuchman et al. (eds), *Home and Hearth: The Images of Women in Mass Media* (London: Oxford University Press, 1978); Gaye Tuchman, *Making News* (NewYork: Free Press, 1978).
10. Tod Gitlin, *The Whole World Is Watching* (Berkeley, CA: University of California Press, 1980).

In other words, movements make strategic use of the media for various counter hegemonic purposes, which include critiquing existing social and material conditions, disruption of dominant discourses, codes and identities, and articulation of alternatives, whether in the form of new codes and identities, ways of life or change in policies. Gitlin points out that, however, there is a tension in using a hegemonic system for oppositional purposes, which poses continuing challenges for oppositional social movements.

In pursuing this sociological problem, we make use of the sensitizing framework by Gamson and Wolfsfeld,[11] who have distilled many of the strategic considerations in movements' use of media into a model of interacting systems. They claim that the movements–media relation is one of unequal dependency, the position of the media at the centre of mass communications network, gives media a spectrum of options for making news, whereas movements have very few options beyond the mass media to get their message across to the wider public. The fact that movements need the media far more than the media needs them translates itself into unequal relationships in the transaction. According to them, movements need the media for *standing*, which is a certain quantity of news about them that makes them relevant in public discourse, preferred *framing* of the issues at hand—featuring the terms, definitions and codes of the movement and *sympathy*—coverage that is likely to gather sympathy for the movement from the public. The purpose here is to understand strategic relations between media and specific movements engaged in specific forms of struggle.

Two further distinctions are especially helpful in conceptualizing media strategies as aspects of larger political projects. In the first place, we can distinguish as complimentary and simultaneous modes of political and cultural engagement what the Italian Marxist scholar Antonio Gramsci describes as *Wars of Position and Wars of Manoeuvre*. The latter characteristically involves assaults on existing institutional structures and culture entailing rapid deployment of forces in specific conjectures to gain tactical advantage, as in the case of demonstrations and direct actions, an effect of which is often a massive surge in the media that might prevent the State from pursuing certain courses. In contrast, a movement group occupies a characteristic war of position trying to create new spaces for alternative identities, moralities and ways of life within the limits of the existing social, economic and State structures, activating a longer-term process of building a counter-hegemonic force through popular education, consciousness raising, community development, etc. Both forms of engagement are important in counter-hegemonic politics that leads to transformation. Yet, specific movements will develop niche methods of counter-hegemonic politics in the life of social movements, which has consequences for their media

11. William A. Gamson and Gadi Wolfsfeld, 'Movements and Media as Interacting Systems', *Annals of the American Academy of Political and Social Sciences,* 528 (1993): 114–27.

strategies. For example, while holding that strikes are generally wars of manoeuvres involving force, Gandhi's passive resistance was a war of position but at times did become a war of manoeuvres.[12]

Our overall aim is to analyse how social-movement groups with differing commitments to cultural, social and economic justice have been represented in the media and how the movements have intervened in this process. One aspect of social movements is that they are simply not victims of media stereotypes and engage with media to advance movement goals. We will try to analyse media strategies and consequent representation of movements in an informed manner. We attempt to do these by an analysis of selected reporting of distinct social movements in such a manner that enables us to trace the connection between media strategies and their specific political projects and the representation of them by the mass media. To do so, we will undertake an analysis of some of the news coverage of the Chipko movement, Narmada Bachao Andolan and some of the campaigns by women's movements in the 1980s. We are limiting our analysis to news because other forms like films, soap operas, musicals, etc., do not engage with movements directly. Also, these forms are disparate from each other and require an understanding of their specific language and practice, which is outside the scope of this chapter.

The Chipko Movement

In many ways, the Chipko movement has and will sustain the iconic status that it had acquired for mainly two reasons. First was its grassroots approach and second, the links that it was able to establish between the local environmental concerns of the villagers with the larger environmental discourse.

Chipko, although referred to as a movement, is actually a collective of several smaller movements that took place in the early 1970s against commercial forestry. Chipko did not begin as a conservation movement but primarily as an economic struggle, the roots of which lay in rural and peasant protests against commercial forestry during the British Raj. Post Independence, a network of roads snaked into the hill areas of Uttarakhand in the name of 'development'. These roads, armies of labourers, forest officials and contractors from outside are those whose work led to the methodical denudation of the region's forest.

The unusually heavy rains of 1970 had precipitated one of the most devastating floods in the country. In the Alakananda valley, water flooded nearly 100 square kilometres of land, washed away 6 metal bridges, 10 kilometres of motor roads, 24 buses and several other vehicles. Apart from this, houses collapsed, paddy crops were destroyed. The huge loss of life and property in this flood marked a turning point in the understanding of ecology in the region. The

12. Antonio Gramsci, *Selections from the Prison Notebooks of Antonio Gramsci*, Quintin Hoare and Geoffrey Nowell-Smith (eds. and trans.) (New York: International Publishers, 1971).

relationship between deforestation, landslides and floods were being explored in the region. It was observed that some of the villages most affected by the floods were directly below forests where felling operations had taken place.

This cause was subsequently taken up by the Dashauli Gram Swarajya Sangh, a cooperative Sangh set up in Chamoli District and Chandi Prasad Bhatt, a prominent local activist. On 27 March 1973, Bhatt vowed to 'hug the trees' to stop the felling, which was followed by a huge protest gathering in April the same year at Mandal, forcing the Symonds Company contractor to beat a hasty retreat. In 1974, the State forest movement marked trees for felling at Peng-Murrenda forest near Reni Village in Joshimath. In a singular display of courage and determination, hundreds of women in Reni led by 50-year-old Gaura Devi drove out the labourers of the contractor.

Chipko was largely a series of protests in the region by different groups and villages. Its significance lay in the fact that it was the case of poor and deprived villagers fighting the might of industry as well as the government through non-violent means.[13]

The movement received good media coverage, though erratic and stereotyped. In fact, the media's coverage of the *andolan* is a sore point with the people in the region. In one of the articles on Chipko in the environmental magazine, *Down to Earth*, Shamsher Singh Bhisht, a Chipko activist is quoted as saying that the main reason for the failure of the movement is the role that the media played. Most of the reports on Chipko missed out on the real concerns and demands of the local people. The media resorted to artificial dramatization of Chipko's image. The locals were trying to point out that their lives were so intertwined with the forests that they alone should have the right to manage the forest resources and products. Bhatt's idea of hugging trees to protect them was a powerful concept and it translated into an easily identifiable icon of protest to save the earth. The actual act of hugging came to be a media-propagated myth through media-primed shots of women embracing trees. The concept and the icon were lapped up by the media, especially the international media.[14]

Globally, the concern for and the understanding of the environment was growing around the time Chipko happened. The global concern and understanding was mostly related to the idea of conservation than rights of communities. It influenced the transformation of Chipko from a struggle to control local resource use to a national movement with a conservationist and economic bearing. Concurrently, the national and international media too gave greater emphasis on to the conservationist element in Chipko and the local reality receded to the background. Further, the national media gave more importance to the conservationist strand in the movement by focusing on the conservationist

---

13. Ramachandra Guha, *The Unquiet Woods* (New Delhi: Oxford University Press, 1989).
14. Amit Mitra, 'Chipko: An Unfinished Mission', *Down to Earth,* April 1993.

Sunderlal Bahuguna and gave him a legendary status, than on the movement as such.

There were though a few journalists, like Anil Agarwal, then a science correspondent with the *Indian Express*, who went beyond the concept and icon and focused on the appalling tales of these villages and astutely introduced all the larger issues Chipko stood for—economics of environment and the nature of development in India's hill regions.

Women's Movements

The years following the Emergency witnessed the beginnings of nation-wide campaigns by women's groups who coalesced to demand changes in laws, of special concern to women, beginning with those related to dowry. Many of these campaigns received fairly prominent coverage in the press. Journalists Ammu Joseph and Kalpana Sharma have extensively written about the coverage of women's issues in media in their 1984 book, *Whose News: The Media and Women's Issues*. Concentrating mainly on the press, both English-language and vernacular, the book is a pioneering attempt to understand the representation of women's issues in media.

The study spans roughly a decade from 1979 to 1988. Rather than concentrating only on news related to women, it decided on five landmark issues. Four of these—dowry deaths, rape, sex determination tests, and sati—were partly determined by the fact that the women's media had drawn national and media attention to them. Five English-language dailies, four periodicals and two women's magazines were selected. Apart from this, the study also analysed one newspaper, one general interest magazine and one women's magazine from the regional languages of Tamil, Hindi, Bengali and Gujarati.

In relation to women's issues, most media do not follow an openly anti-women line. The constitutionally enshrined ideal of equality between sexes and the historical legacy of the press in India, a generally liberal and reform minded approach, has benefited the coverage of women's issues. According to Joseph and Sharma, the rise of women's movement and the consequent increase in public consciousness has led to the espousal of women's concerns by the main political parties, which has nevertheless enabled the women's movement to acquire political legitimacy and enabled them to fit into the mainstream notions of what constitutes news.

This was not the case in the early days of the movement. Dominant perceptions of what constitutes news are among the most important determinants of news coverage. In the received definitions, events are more important than processes, powerful people and not the powerless, are important in news. The unusual is newsworthy, whereas everyday normal activities are not. A combination of all these extends to news stories that make many marginalized sections and many women unworthy of being in the news. Most issues of women's concern do not fit into the traditional concept of what constitutes news since women are most often not in powerful positions. This absence of women in news is termed 'symbolic annihilation' by Gaye Tuchman. Symbolic annihilation is a combination of condemnation, trivialization and erasure, according to Tuchman.[15]

Many of the important issues related to women are linked to processes rather than events, and thus, runs the risk of not getting reported. Joseph and Sharma show that news related to women's work, health, position in society, etc., were not matter of news coverage and when they appeared in news, it came from traditional news sources like the government, police, parliament, courts and NGOs. Violent atrocities against women get far more priority in reporting than issues mentioned above, say Joseph and Sharma.

The women's group campaigns against dowry deaths demanding conviction in cases as well as amendment to the 1961 Dowry Prohibition Act was started by the end of the 1970s. Some of the high points of this ongoing campaign were in 1979, 1983 and 1984. The 1961 Dowry Prohibition Act was amended and passed in Parliament in 1984. Joseph and Sharma point out that the campaign was generally located in Delhi and *The Hindustan Times* had maximum coverage of stories on dowry deaths, *The Statesman* had 13 stories but three editorials on the issue and *The Indian Express* ran a four-part survey on the news pages of 15–18 August 1983.

Though the campaign was acknowledged by all major English national dailies, the reporting was observed as inconsistent. The editorials and reports didn't follow each other, or at times, there were no editorials at all from sympathetic newspapers. Overall, Joseph and Sharma noticed an improvement in the reportage by the English national dailies, which coincided with the campaign by the women's movement. At the same time, alongside sensitive articles on the issue, there were occasional swipes at women or feeble attempts at humour by using the all-encompassing phrase 'women's liberation', which again showed an inconsistency in the recognition of women's rights from the standpoint of editorial policies of the newspapers. A similar look at the reporting in the Hindi press showed a more callous approach to the issue, lack of well-researched reporting and some events were unreported or tucked away inconspicuously.

But by 1987, when the sati controversy shook the nation, the press was able to respond with a fair amount of professionalism and sophistication. Most national dailies carried features or spot stories and editorials on the issue. Though most national dailies except for *The Indian Express* (which featured a Vishwa Hindu Parishad advertisement and prominently displayed the pro-sati views of the Sankaracharya of Puri) took a strong stand against the revival of sati, there were several incongruities with the reporting. While there was more alertness on the media's part, it was more for fear of communal and political repercussions. The editorial discussion of the issue of sati was more around religion, politics

15. Gaye Tuchman, 'The Symbolic Annihilation of Women'.

and social conflicts rather than from a gender perspective. Also, as pointed out by Joseph and Sharma, there is dissonance between editorial condemnation and glowing accounts of festivals like Chunri Mahotsav as well as unquestioned and, sometimes, interchangeable use of words like 'sati' and 'self-immolation'.

The multi-pronged strategy of the women's movement and the willingness of women activists and writers to write consistently on the issue in 'mainstream' newspapers also contributed in widening and deepening media coverage of the issue, especially in terms of keeping the women's point in perspective. This long period also saw the emergence of alternative women's journals like *Manushi*, which discussed all of these campaigns from the perspective of the women's movement.

THE NARMADA BACHAO ANDOLAN

The Narmada Bachao Andolan (NBA) is a grass-root level movement that celebrated 21 years of existence in November 2006. It was formed to fight against the environmental, social and cultural damage that the Narmada Valley Developmental Project (NVDP) has caused. The NVDP proposal consists of 30 large dams, 135 medium dams, 3,000 small dams on the river Narmada and its over four tributaries and threatens the life and livelihood of the 22 million inhabitants of the Narmada basin. The Sardar Sarovar Project (SSP), the largest dam, alone will submerge 245 villages—19 in Gujarat, 33 in Maharashtra and 193 in Madhya Pradesh. According to NBA, 250,000 people will be affected by the SSP.[16]

The government sources claim that the SSP would irrigate more than 1.8 million hectares of land and solve the water crisis in the drought-prone areas of Kutch and Saurashtra. The NBA responds by saying that these are exaggerated and the actual benefits are much less than what is projected. The NBA also argued that in the whole process of the NVDP, the riparian rights of the people who live in the valley, including the tribals and peasants were not taken into consideration. Added to this are the woes of those who have been displaced by the dam construction resumed by a court order in 2000. The projected figure of 15,000 affected families in Maharashtra, though promised rehabilitation, are yet to be rehabilitated.

The NBA has taken up a lot of issues related to the riparian rights of the people. NBA's is a politics that is a complex articulation of land rights, environmental degradation, economies of large dams and also the effects of these on the local communities. The fact that the process of development right from its origin, plan and management of resources is seen as a prerogative of the State is the basic point of opposition for the movement. The movement emphasizes

16. Bradford Morse and Thomas Berger (eds.), *Sardar Sarovar: Report of the Independent Review* (Ottawa: Resource Futures International, 1992).

that the people have the right to control their own forest, land, water and other natural resources. The movement thus is a deep-rooted critique of the development paradigm. NBA is committed to non-violent means of protest and believes that non-violence is the only path for a social movement.

NBA has relied heavily on the media to popularize their struggles and issues and the mainstream national media has been an important part of their campaigns. Leaders and activists of the movement often write in various newspapers and publications. NBA also communicates through frequent press releases giving the status of the struggle from time to time. The media is also informed about the several mass agitations and other programmes and activities. For communicating with the people of the valley, the NBA depends on other forms of media like songs, leaflets, posters, audio cassettes, etc. Though the NBA and the NVDP have been discussed quite widely in national and regional newspapers and the visual media, many of the issues discussed earlier with environmental reporting are relevant here too. The media's interest in events rather than processes has seriously affected the NBA reporting in various ways. A movement like NBA, with its issues of displacement and the development paradigm that caused this, are equally important. But the media generally does not sustain its focus on long-term processes and gives space only when there are mass actions such as rallies or a dharna in the national capital. Of the 435 stories on the Sardar Sarovar Project in 2006, including those in English dailies, TV, periodicals and Internet news sites, more than 75 per cent of the stories are when devastating events like floods happen. The rest happen to be around mass actions like rallies and dharnas. The handful of well-researched writings is either specialist columns in newspapers or Internet news sites.

The media often links issues and movements to the leaders and activists who are involved in them. One reason could be that these leaders are the ones who become the most visible while bringing to the notice of the world the needs and problems affecting the struggle. The media finds a face for the movement in Medha Patkar making the NBA look like a single-handed task, whereas in reality, it is a multi-tiered movement, consisting of *adivasis*, Dalits and caste Hindu peasants and also various middle-class activists and supporters. The movement is influenced by both community and activists. The decision-making body has two main groups: the full-time activists as well as community representatives from every village. In terms of projecting the leaders, the media often makes movements seem like individual struggles. On the flip side, often protests and rallies that do not include the respective leaders are not given adequate coverage. For instance, on 17 December 2005, the police *lathi*-charged hundreds of protestors in Badhwani, Madhya Pradesh outside the collector's office. This got little coverage, none in the mainstream national media. During the satyagraha staged by NBA in April 2006, the event got covered extensively when film actor Aamir Khan visited the *pandal* to express his solidarity with the displaced people of the valley.

As it is obvious from our discussion of various social movements and media representation, the relationship between the two interacting systems has been a battle over under-representation, misrepresentation and true representation. Aggressive campaigns have earned many of these movements the credibility and sympathy from the general public and enabled them to influence a media discourse in framing many of the issues. A public inured by visual stunts and imagery will soon lead to media disavowal or at least reduced coverage, thus foreclosing the possibilities of an expanded war of positions on long-term process and their social consequences. To prevent a growing chasm between movement needs and media response, it is a tough call on movements to reinvent innovative tactical performances, yet to link them to the overall cultural change.

Going back to the Telecom Italia advertising, one can easily see that the advertisement is a confluence of the past and present in the singular image of Gandhi on a public display television monitor, an image removed far from its context. Probably, the amount of media coverage would be able to capture Gandhi vividly and extensively because Gandhi would not have been a mythical image as in the advertisement, he would have disturbed the very media systems deeply and Gandhi and his movement would have to negotiate and strategize in a world of media corporations.

Suggested Readings

Guha, Ramachandra. *The Unquiet Woods*. New Delhi: Oxford University Press, 1989.

Jeffery, Robin. *India's Newspaper Revolution: Capitalism, Politics and the Indian Language Press*. New Delhi: Oxford University Press, 2000.

Joseph, Ammu and Kalpana Sharma. *Whose News? Media and Women's Issues*. Delhi: Sage Publications, 1994.

Kohli, Vanita. *Indian Media Business*. Delhi: Response Books, 2006.

Questions

1. What do you understand by the mass media? How important are they according to you for democratic mobilization?
2. How do you view the relationship between social movements and the mass media? Give examples from the Indian experience.
3. Discuss the media explosion in India in the post-liberalization and globalization period. How, according to you, has it impacted the social movements?

11 Social Mobility and Changes in Occupational Structure

Wasudha Bhatt

> *I was not born a Hindu for the simple reason that my parents did not know that they were Hindus. My parents had only one identity and that was their caste: they were Kurumaas.*
>
> — Kancha Ilaiah, 1996: 1.

The lines above signify one of the most provocative statements from Kancha Ilaiah, who identifies himself as a Dalitbahujan, and testifies to the intense socio-economic disparities lacing the Indian society. These differences, he writes, are deeply entrenched within the Indian social hierarchy. Playing a central role in regulating an individual's journey from life to death, they have a decisive influence on one's location on the religious, economic and the political plane.

Evidently, the interplay of 'caste' and 'class' in India, its impact on social mobility, and the impression of globalization on such processes in determining occupational attainment have long been passionately contested subjects of interest. More so, the world today is marked by a far more profound belief in endorsing equality of opportunity as a way of life, disseminating fuller economic growth, and promoting greater social cohesion[1] across the socio-political divide. As a result, social mobility attains critical significance in the present times. It is in the above context that the proposed chapter seeks to examine social mobility in India and trace the pattern of change in the occupational structure as well.

The chapter is divided into five sections. The first section undertakes a conceptual analysis of 'social mobility' and 'occupational structure'. This is followed by a theoretical analysis of 'caste' and 'class', particularly as a means for distribution of power, when conceptualized within the economic, political, and cultural landscape of India. The second-last section tries to disentangle the complexities between caste and class, as they have evolved since the 19th

1. S. Aldridge, *Social Mobility: A Discussion Paper*, 2001, http://www.strategy.gov.uk/downloads/files/socialmobility.pdf (last accessed on 15 May 2008).

century, following which, the final section tries to foreground the social-mobility debates within the entire discourse on globalization. Ordaining the new global hierarchy as the emergent means for upward mobility, crosscutting lines of class, caste, and gender, it elucidates the formidable challenges it presents for the Indian social fabric.

UNDERSTANDING SOCIAL MOBILITY AND OCCUPATIONAL STRUCTURES

'Division of labour' and a 'hierarchy of prestige' constitute an integral component of every social order. Social mobility when contextualized within such a social order signifies any transition of an individual or social object or value, which has been created or modified by human activity, from one social position to another, positions, which by general consent, have been given specific hierarchical values. Thus, when we study social mobility, we analyse the movement of individuals from positions of a certain rank to positions either higher or lower in the social system, and accentuated by privileges and prerequisites accruing in proportion to its difficulty and responsibility. Consequently, all mobility is a consequence of changes in the structure and all significant changes in the structure pose questions about the locus of political power.[2]

Whereas, it is the 'occupational structure' that comprises labour-force participation and different types of economic activity comprising the economic societal set-up, which constitutes one of the most direct links between the various modes of economic production and the social structure.[3] This link is all the more visible as an economy shifts from a decentralized, subsistence production to an interdependent production of a wide range of goods and services. As a result, the human or social counterpart gives way to a series of shifts in work roles. This shift in work roles and the demand for labour determine and are further determined in return by various other factors at work. What is thus required is a multi-dimensional analysis of the whole process of social mobility, rather than trying to view it solely from a singular standpoint—as just a sorting of persons into given positions.

SOCIAL STRATIFICATION, CASTE, AND INDIA

Stratification implies a multi-layered phenomenon, much like the Earth's crust. However, social stratification occupies a special place in the study of the Indian

---

2. Ioan Davies, *Key Concepts in Political Science: Social Mobility and Political Change* (London: Macmillan, 1970).
3. Wilbert E. Moore, 'Changes in Occupational Structures', in Neil J. Smelser and Seymour Martin Lipset (eds.), *Social Structure and Mobility in Economic Development* (London: Routledge and Kegan Paul, 1964).

society. India has long been believed to be the most stratified of all known societies in human history, whether it is with regard to stratification in the social arena or the economic sphere. Added to this, the diversity of the varied linguistic groups, which make up the nation, further strengthens the belief of India being 'the most stratified society to the point of near incontrovertibility'.[4]

However, James Tod and many other historians and political scientists using European analogies, viewed the Indian State conquered by the British as a feudal society.[5] According to this view, there was the same kind of personal link based on loyalty and the reciprocal grant of fiefs or rights to the use of land between the king, his vassals and a dependent or a servile peasantry, following which, there was similar predominance of direct methods of surplus extraction without a necessary intermediation of the market. There was the same rigidly hierarchical ordering of society with little mobility between the different classes or estates.

Quite on the contrary, for another group of social scientists, any European analogy for the Indian social development was an anathema. According to them, the Indian society was hierarchical, but at the same time, was a segmented society. The logic of segmentation and hierarchy was provided by one and the same ideology and a deeply ingrained institutional structure supporting that ideology, namely the caste system, says Amita Kumar Bagchi. In fact, according to the formulation of the most famous theorist of caste system in the modern times, M. N. Srinivas, caste represented a state of mind reflected by the emergence in various situations of various orders, generally called castes.

Disparities in historical analogies apart, existing for thousands of years, the caste system derived its name about 500 years ago from the Portuguese when they landed on the Malabar Coast and began to have direct interactions with the Indian society.[6] Derived from 'casta' in Portuguese, the term caste has since been used generally to describe the *varna–jati* system in its entirety, as well as specifically to refer to its various orders and the units within an order. Nevertheless, the Portuguese discovery of caste went beyond giving a name to India's *varna–jati* system. The Portuguese were also the first among Europeans to provide detailed accounts of its functioning.

Nevertheless, it was only after the British rule was established in India that a second discovery of caste was made by the Europeans. The Western Oriental scholars, the Christian missionaries and the British administrators began, in their different ways, to make sense of this complex phenomenon. Moreover, the colonial State acquired a legitimate authority to arbitrate and fix the status

---

4. Dipankar Gupta (ed.), *Social Stratification* (New Delhi: Oxford University Press, 1991).
5. Amiya Kumar Bagchi, 'The Ambiguity of Progress: Indian Society in Transition', *Social Scientist*, 13 (3), 1985.
6. D. L. Sheth, 'Secularisation of Caste and Making of New Middle Class', *Economic and Political Weekly*, 1999: 2502.

claims made or contested by various castes about their location in the ritual hierarchy. The colonial State then assumed a dual role: of locating and relocating disputed statuses of caste in the traditional hierarchy and of a just and modern ruler who wished to recognize rights and aspirations of his weak and poor subjects. This further helped the State to protect its colonial political economy from incursions of the emerging nationalist movement. Among other things, it also induced people into organizing and representing their interest in politics in terms of caste, identities and participating in the economy on the terms and the mechanisms set by the colonial regime.

Nonetheless, contested term that it was, the caste system deflected any single unifying definitional probe. After a long deliberation, E. R. Leach settled more or less for J. H. Hutton's descriptive statement of the caste system where **endogamy**, pollution, occupational differentiation and hierarchy, with the Brahmins at the top, are the important diacritical features of the phenomenon.[7] Nonetheless, according to C. Bougle, hierarchy, repulsion and hereditary specialization are the three important characteristics of the caste system. The spirit of the caste system for him is determined in an important way by the mutual repulsion that exists between the castes. In other words, Bougle emphasized the differences that existed between the castes. Repulsion, Bougle hence argued, manifested itself in endogamy, commensal restriction, and even contact. For this reason, different castes stayed as discrete entities, atomized, opposed, and isolated, thus significantly highlighting the coexistence of hierarchy along with repulsion. Declan Quigley, however, traced the emergence of caste into a form of political structure resulting from the inability of kingship or kinship to provide political stability.[8] Caste relations were determined herein by centrality, and the ability to command services, and not by hierarchy. Overall, caste divisions were constructed not around caste-specific occupations, but around particular ritual roles connecting groups within the sacrifice, with a dominant caste.

Such contestations apart, towards the end of the colonial rule, political policies and processes alongside the larger historical forces had produced some profound and far-reaching changes in the caste system.

The most important among the changes was the formation of a new, translocal identity among lower castes, collectively as a people with the consciousness of being oppressed by the traditional system of hierarchy, following which, the discourse of rights, until then quite alien to the concepts governing ritual hierarchy, made its first appearance in the context of the caste system. New ideological categories of social justice too began to question the idea of ritual purity and impurity according to which the traditional stratification endowed entitlements and constraints to hereditary statuses. As a result, the established

---

7. Gupta, *Social Stratification*, p. 10.
8. F. Osella, 'The Interpretation of Caste', *The Journal of the Royal Anthropological Institute* 2 (2), 1996.

categories of ritual hierarchy began to be confronted with new categories like depressed castes and oppressed classes.

Second, several castes occupying more or less similar locations in different local hierarchies began to organize themselves horizontally into regional-and national-level associations and federations as it became increasingly essential to negotiate with the State and, in the process, project their larger social identity and numerical strength.

Third, movements of the lower castes for upward social mobility, which were not new in the history of the caste system, acquired a qualitatively novel dimension as they began to attack the very ideological foundations of the ritual hierarchy of castes in modern ideological terms of justice and equality. The changes further acquired a newer dimension and greater transformative edge with India establishing itself as a liberal, democratic State.

Even though the system had served India well for two millennia, yet one could witness a variety of forces bringing about significant changes in the caste-based system of production. This change was visible both at the level of the villages and of the individual, with the individual castes competing with each other for access to secular benefits.[9]

CONSTRUCTION OF CLASS AS A MEANS FOR THE DISTRIBUTION OF POWER

The word 'class' is undoubtedly a complex one indeed, both in its range of meanings and the complexities arising within that particular meaning where it describes a 'social division'. It was the Latin word *classis*, a division according to property of the people of Rome, which came into English in with plural *classes* or *classies*.[10] Nevertheless, the development of 'class' in its modern social sense, with relatively fixed names for particular classes, belongs primarily to the period between 1770 and 1840, which also signifies the period of the industrial revolution and its decisive societal reorganization.

However, the essential history of the introduction of class as a word, which would supersede older names for social divisions, relates to the rising consciousness that 'social position is made rather than merely inherited', says Raymond Williams. All the older words, with their essential metaphors of standing, stepping and arranging in rows, belong to a society in which position was determined by birth. Individual mobility herein could be seen as a movement

9. M. N. Srinivas, 'An Obituary on Caste as a System', EPW Special Article, *Economic and Political Weekly*, 2003, P. K. Bose, *Classes and Class Relations Among Tribals of Bengal* (New Delhi: Ajanta Publications, 1985).

10. Raymond Williams, *Keywords: A Vocabulary of Culture and Society* (London: Fontana Press, 1983).

from one estate, degree, order or rank to another. Nonetheless, what was changing consciousness was not only increased individual mobility, which could be largely contained within older terms, but also, a newer sense of society and social systems, which led to the creation of social divisions, including new kinds of divisions.

For Marx, one of the most popular exponents on the subject, classes were defined and structured by the relations concerning: work and labour, and ownership or possession of property and the means of production.

The significance of the economic system of society herein was elaborated in a theory, which traced the formation of the principal social groups—the classes—to the forms of ownership of means of production and the forms of labour of non-owners. The idea of social change resulting from internal conflicts then on was formulated in a theory of class struggle, which made social classes the principal, if not the only agents of political activity. And, it was this conception, which in turn led to the distinction between the ruling and oppressed classes and to the formulation of a distinctive theory of the state.

The belief that social changes display a regular pattern further led Marx to construct, in broad framework, a historical sequence of the main types of society, proceeding from the simple, undifferentiated society of primitive communism to the complex class society of modern capitalism. And he then on drew up an explanation of the great historical transformations, which annihilated all forms of society and created new ones in terms of economic changes, which he regarded as general and constant in their operation. These economic factors more completely governed social relationships in capitalism, than they did in earlier societies.

Karl Marx hence wrote:

> [Where] the particular kind of labour—i. e., its craft mastery and consequently property in the instruments of labour—equals property in the conditions of production, this admittedly excludes slavery and serfdom. However, it may lead to an analogous negative development in the form of a caste system.[11]

Max Weber, on the other hand, differed only marginally from Marx when he defined class as a category of men who

> ... have in common a specific causal component of their life chances in so far as, this component is represented exclusively by economic interests in the possession of goods and opportunities for income, and, it is represented under the conditions of the commodity or labour market.[12]

---

11. K. Marx, *Pre-capitalist Economic Formations* (London: Lawrence and Wishart, 1964 [1857]), pp. 101–02.
12. http://www2.pfeiffer.edu/~lridener/DSS/Weber/WEBERW7.HTML.

He was fairly close to Marx's view, though not necessarily to those of latter-day Marxists; when he argued that class position do not necessarily lead to class-determined economic or political action. For Weber, a class situation was a situation that was determined by the market. It instead represented an array of different life-chances that arose from the uneven distribution of material property among 'a plurality of people': it was a situation in which 'pure market conditions prevail'.[13] He further propounded that communal class action would only emerge if and when the 'connections between the causes and the consequences of the "class situation"' become transparent. The fundamental idea being, class might exist in itself, but never actually for itself: 'it is ultimately an instance of economic rather than social or political stratification'. Therefore, Weber talked less of class in itself than of a 'class situation'.[14]

However, definitional inconsistencies apart, pure class relations as between individuals and individuals are only an abstract construct in most societies, according to Dipankar Gupta. The first thing that strikes one in the Indian scene is the plurality and heterogeneity of these classes and the conflicts in their interests,[15] especially when juxtaposed with the caste hierarchy in India, which, says Gupta, need to be explored in greater detail.

DECIPHERING THE INTERLINKAGE BETWEEN CASTE AND CLASS

CASTE AND CLASS: 19TH–21ST CENTURY

When the British, after conquering Bengal and subsequently the whole of India, set out to administer the colony, they came across two phenomena with which they were unfamiliar: 'the relation of people to land for production, and the caste system of India, namely the '*jati*' stratification of society'.[16]

However, they soon realized that the '*varna*' stratification of society was not unique to India. Jolly in 1896, Senart in 1927 and others had elucidated in the late 19th and early 20th century, that the *varnas* which denoted the status system in the Hindu society, are found with different nomenclatures in other societies of the world, says Mukherjee. However, the fact that *jatis*—namely,

---

13. Max Weber, *Economy and Society: An Outline of Interpretive Sociology*, 2 volumes, edited by Guenther Roth and Claus Wittich (Berkeley, CA: University of California Press, 1978), p. 927.
14. Nicholas Gane, 'Max Weber as Social Theorist: Class, Status, Party', *European Journal of Social Theory*, 8 (2), 2005: 211–26.
15. P. Bardhan, *The Political Economy of Development in India* (New Delhi: Oxford University Press, 1984).
16. Ramakrishna Mukherjee, 'Caste in Itself, Caste and Class, or Caste in Class', EPW Perspectives, *Economic and Political Weekly*, 1999.

the smallest endogamous groups of people within each *varna*, denote the caste system of India was universally acclaimed.

The British researchers further found that in the 18th–19th centuries, though the instruments for production were held by the Indians family-wise, yet, the land for production was held by the villagers in common, be it the Indian peasants, artisans, or the traders under the village community system. This unified strength of the village community system was, however, shattered by the introduction of the 'zamindari' system, as was later acknowledged by Lord Bentinck. First introduced in 1793 in Bengal, Bihar and Orissa (the 'subah' of Bengal) as the 'Permanent Settlement of Land', this system in due course spread all over India.[17]

Ramkrishna Mukherjee, however, asserts that it was now that the falsification of the role of caste (*jati*) system in India took a distinctive turn with the beginning of researches into the caste system by the British scholars in the 18th–19th centuries, which was later followed by the Indian academia as well. The *jati* division of society was viewed in the realm of 'cultural' relations. And, an overview of the Hindu society further substantiated the correlation between the caste hierarchy and the capitalist class structures,[18] so much so, that it was ideologically imposed that the caste structure ruled the society.

With the general run of Western scholars and the great majority of Indian scholars supporting the perception that caste sans class represented 'modern' India, Louis Dumont declared the uniqueness of caste-ridden Indian people as 'Homo Hierarchicus'. **Sanskritization** and Westernization were thus proclaimed to be the forbearers of social change in modern India.[19] The social processes bearing the triumph of class structure over the caste hierarchy were all the more visible, with M. N. Srinivas mooting the notion of 'dominant caste' in the 1960s, and listing six attributes for identifying it, namely: 'sizeable amount of the arable land locally available'; 'strength of numbers'; 'high place in the local hierarchy'; 'Western education'; 'jobs in the administration' and 'urban sources of income'.

Mukherjee further propounds that the reinforced false consciousness generated by scholars and politicians alike had been so pervading in the upper political level, that even in recent times the Mandal Commission assigned caste as the

17. However, some European scholars in late 20th century have argued that the manorial system was present in India from early times in pre-British India, and that the village community system is a myth. Nonetheless, Kosambi (1955) and as later elaborated by Irfan Habib have documented that the village community system had originated at the threshold of the present millennium or some centuries earlier, and flourished up to the 11th century AD. The steady but the slow growth of indigenous capitalism in India did try to undermine the village community system, especially during the Mughal period, and ventured upon establishing the manorial system.
18. Ramakrishna Mukherjee, *The Dyanamics of Rural Society* (Berlin: Akademie Verlag, 1957), pp. 1–58.
19. M. N. Srinivas, *Social Change in Modern India* (Bombay: Allied Publishers, 1966).

criterion of backwardness in Indian society.[20] Though Desai in a noteworthy article[21] did emphasize that the criterion of 'backwardness' should be sought in the class relations in modern India, yet his voice was stifled effectively.

In the meanwhile, as a consequence of the inevitable spread of capitalism in India, the resulting alienation of land and accumulation of crops enriched some peasants and traders who were placed still lower in the caste hierarchy. Subsequently, in conformity with their improved economic status, they sought a better 'social' status, with a new alignment between caste and class now in the offing.

Consequently, due to the impact of colonial capitalism on the Indian social structure, the 'depressed classes' clamoured for equality in economic and cultural perception and behaviour with the 'high castes', in the last days of the Raj.[22] As a result, the Raj pacified them by enacting the Scheduled Castes Order in the 1930s, for further consolidating their political position in the Indian society. Even after Independence in 1947, the Indian rulers retained the nomenclature of the Scheduled Castes, and added that of the Scheduled Tribes.[23] Later, the government further categorized the 'Other Backward Classes', thus making the caste hierarchy complete.

With reality asserting itself at the grass roots level, the correlation between caste and class in colonial India was now being transformed into 'caste in class'. Deriving its nomenclature from the official classification devised by the State in course of implementing its policy of affirmative action, the new formations—the forward or the upper castes, the backward castes, the Dalits or Scheduled Castes and the tribal or the Scheduled Tribes—were ranged within the spectrum of the high, middle, and low echelons of the class system in society, as was clearly manifested in the political alliances among these categories.

De-ritualization of Caste, the Pull of Middle Classes, and the Weakening Link

However, it is widely believed that the changes that have occurred in the Indian society, especially post-Mandalization, have lead to a **de-ritualization** of caste. This can be attributed to the improvement of communication, the spread of education, a host of governmental policies favouring the weaker sections, and the political mobilization of the people, which have all greatly weakened the link between

20. Prabhat Patnaik argues that the 'Mandal phenomenon' was believed to have had far more to it than mere job reservations or the economic threats to the middle class; it signified the political and social assertion of the poor. For details, see Prabhat Patnaik, 'Democracy as a Site for Class-Struggle', *Economic and Political Weekly*, 18 March 2000.
21. I. P. Desai, 'Should Caste Be the Basis for Recognizing Backwardness?' *Economic and Political Weekly*, 19 (28), 1984: 1115.
22. Mukherjee, 'Caste in Itself'.
23. P. K. Bose, *Classes and Class Relations Among Tribals of Bengal* (New Delhi: Ajanta Publications, 1985).

jati and traditional occupations. More so, monetization and market forces have further combined to free economic relations from their traditional baggages.

In addition to the technological and institutional changes, new ideas of democracy, equality and individual self-respect have contributed immensely in altering the nature of these social relationships. This is clearly evident in the behaviour of the so-called 'lower' castes and Dalits towards the higher castes, and the concessions and benefits conferred on the former by the policy of affirmative action taken up by the central and state governments. However, these developments cannot be attributed to a sudden change, but something, which has grown over a period of time.

It was as early as the 1920s that castes have organized themselves to obtain representation in the provincial legislatures. This phenomenon acquired further roots in the 1930s, with Independence bringing the realization, that people could now also be mobilized on the basis of caste, ethnicity and religion. This has instead resulted into a 'horizontal stretch' of caste. According to Srinivas, in fact what are called castes today are more accurately described as congeries of agnate sub-castes that have come together to compete more effectively with other similar formations for better access to such scarce political resources as political power, economic opportunities, government jobs and professional education. As a result of this, resentment is greatest with Dalits and tribals since they enjoy special representation in all legislatures from the village panchayats at the local level to Parliament itself.

However, this distribution of legislative power has acquired a very dynamic character over the last two decades, with the traditional relationship between caste and power being reversed altogether. As opposed to the past, when power was concentrated in the hands of Brahmins, today the village panchayat is controlled by non-Brahmins and the traditional elite is being relegated to the background.[24]

Power has also become relatively independent of class as compared with the past, with the ownership of land no longer being the decisive factor in acquiring power. Mobility in the caste system was always a slow and gradual process, wherin the acquisition of land and upward movement in the hierarchy of class took a generation or two. Under the new set up, the shifts in the distribution of power are, by comparison, quick and radical in nature, says Beteille.

The paradox nevertheless remains that while caste as a system is dead or dying, individual castes are thriving. Srinivas, reiterating the sentiment, argues that on the positive side, the idea of hierarchy has lost legitimacy both at the all-India and at the state levels. What is more viable, particularly in the urban areas, is the idea of difference. As is also propounded by Dipankar Gupta, for

---

24. Andre Beteille, *Caste, Class and Power: Changing Patterns of Stratification in a Tanjore Village* (Bombay: University of California Press, 1966).

a true understanding of stratification, he stresses, we must conceptually isolate it from hierarchy as the latter is but 'one of the manifestations of the former'. However, it is insufficient to just internalize or intellectualize this separation and hierarchization. Thus, we can truly talk about social stratification only when hierarchy and differentiation are externalized and socially demonstrated.[25]

Nevertheless, with the articulation of differences being contextualized within questions of group identity, one can witness considerable differentiation within the economic, social, and cultural spectrums of each caste. Furthermore, according to Srinivas, with secularization making great strides in India, and consequently leading to an erosion of rituality, a large part of the support system of caste has collapsed. Caste, which is now believed as surviving in the form of a kinship-based cultural community, operates in a different system of social stratification. More so, by forming themselves into larger horizontal social groups, members of different castes now increasingly compete for entry into the middle class, which has undergone a radical change with regard to its old, pre-Independence character and composition. These days, the Indian middle class—now believed to be around 200 million people—is becoming even more unified politically and culturally, and highly diversified in terms of the social origins of its members.[26]

The situation may be summed up by saying that a variety of forces are bringing about the destruction of the caste-based system of production in the villages and at the local level. With individual castes increasingly competing with each other for access to secular benefits, the conflict is only likely to become sharper.

Changing Class Fluidity in Contemporary India

In conclusion, it would seem that social mobility in India is neither particularly fluid, as evidenced by the large class inequalities, nor showing great signs of becoming so. The labour market too in the rural areas clearly reflects near-zero **elasticity of employment**. Even if agricultural productivity witnesses a dramatic

25. Gupta, *Social Stratification*. He further argues that the differentiation is always on the basis of a criterion, or a set of criteria. However if inequality is the key feature, then the stratificatory system can be characterized as a hierarchical one. If difference is more important than various social orders, then the various social orders face each other as horizontal and equal blocs.
26. Vir Sanghvi, 'Two Indias', http://www.india-seminar.com/2005/545/545, 2005. Membership of today's middle class is signified by new lifestyles, ownership of certain economic assets, and the consciousness of belonging to the middle class. Though there are different levels within the middle class, yet, once members of any caste group reach even the lower levels, they aspire to and work for higher levels. With education, professions, and lifestyle becoming indicators of status, caste seems to have been relegated to the background. For a detailed discussion on the Indian middle class, see Chapter 8 by Sujit Mahapatra.

increase in the following decade, it will be unable to absorb much of the rural labour, considering the drastic fall in the contribution of agriculture to GDP, from '50 per cent to 25 per cent by the beginning of this decade'.[27] This has, instead, spurred an enormous rise in the streams of migrants in search of gainful employment. These migratory processes have been further accelerated as a result of the rapid population growth and the breakdown of the **jajmani system**. Consequently, migration is now accepted in rural areas as a 'fact of life', says Srinivas. Moreover, the development of infrastructure and communications and expansion of the urban frontiers have further facilitated this phenomenon, thus also considerably enlargening the social and mental space of villagers.

These migratory streams, however, also overlap with the innumerable workers who are employed in the informal economy, and constitute around 90 to 93 per cent of the working populace. Around 6 per cent of the 10 per cent of the total workers employed in the formal sector have jobs in the public sector. However, even here (*a*) the low capacity of agriculture to absorb the workforce, and (*b*) job losses in the public sector, have led to a decline in employment opportunities.[28]

Consequently, these factors have triggered significant changes in the shape of the Indian class structure, along with the contraction of agriculture and a growing room at the top. In one sense, as almost all groups alike have been affected by these changes and the new opportunities for social advancement, there have incontrovertibly been expanding opportunities in the Indian society. However, the changes in structure apart, one can witness no systematic additional weakening of the links between caste and class positions.

Herein, with the key aspect of any society being the openness of jobs at the top,[29] in the case of India, these jobs have remained relatively closed. One possible explanation for this lack of fluidity can be that the occupational destiny is intimately tied to the caste or community of the people. A study conducted by Sanjay Kumar, Anthony Heath, and Oliver Heath does bring out some signs that sons of manual workers and Dalits have improved their chances of gaining access to the salary at a greater rate than other groups. Yet, it is evident that these gains have been nullified by declines in the chances of men from agricultural backgrounds and of Muslims, says Kumar. Moreover, few of these changes are very large; the resultant: the dominant picture remains as one of continuity rather than of change.

---

27. Neera Chandhoke, 'Democracy and Well Being in India', draft working document for the UNRISD Project on Social Policy and Democratization, 2005.
28. Ibid.
29. S. Kumar, A. Heath, and O. Heath, 'Changing Patterns of Social Mobility Some Trends over Time', EPW Commentary, *Economic and Political Weekly*, 2002.

GLOBALIZATION, SOCIAL MOBILITY AND THE 'INDIA-IN-TRANSITION'

The Indian social fabric, as is widely conceived today, and is aptly brought out by Rajni Kothari in his writings, reflects an 'India-in-transition'. The India that we know now is not only in a state of 'crisis', but also is fast entering a 'terminal phase'.[30] The India one knew, he writes, is in shambles and fast disintegrating internally, whether it be the social, or the political sphere. Culturally too, even as a civilization, India is being subjected to manifold pressures, which could upset its traditional balance. In addition, exacerbating the internal turmoil are forces of consumerism and globalization, which are fast tearing apart the country's social fabric.

The discourse of globalization, when conceived, claimed to establish a new global order, which would mark an end to all sorts of demarcations—economic, cultural and political. Nonetheless, globalization, instead, further intensified and expanded these divisive forces, without offering any viable and dignified alternative. Simultaneously, it also strengthened the constituent elements of the globalized power structure—the techno-scientific, bureaucratic, military, managerial and business elites and a small consumerist class.[31]

Consequently, the market, which increasingly became the only avenue for upward mobility was also monopolized by the upper strata of caste society, using their traditional status resources. Economic globalization did, however, offer increased standards of living to those entering the market with some entitlements usually available to members of upper castes, given their resources of land, wealth, social privilege and education. Yet, for large segments of the population outside this captivating humdrum of the market circle, and disadvantageously located in the traditional structure, it meant more malnutrition, disease and destitution.

Subsequently, such anxieties have given way to a burgeoning sense of insecurity among large sections of the people, comprising the poor and the middle classes. There is also a growing feeling that those who can attain these entitlements have it, while they relegate the 'others' to oblivion. This is specially the case among the 'upwardly mobile' middle class. But even in this hitherto upwardly mobile class, there has started taking place a downward mobility, induced by unemployment, inflation, and decline of various services, consequently unsettling their long-held assumptions about the 'good life' and human well-being.

With this decline in confidence and optimism about one's life chances, the ability of the Indian State to deliver social goods to its citizenry is being

30. R. Kothari, 'Restructuring the Indian Enterprise', reproduced from 'India 1992', *Seminar* 401, 1993. The expression 'India-in-transition' is also borrowed from Rajni Kothari's paper.
31. Sheth, 'Secularisation of Caste'.

questioned and, alongside, there is a search for new identities, and formation of new relationships across existing identities, and new understandings of emerging shifts in relationships. It now seems that new configurations of caste and community identities will take shape, within the growing backwaters of the 'unorganized sector' and the gargantuan presence within the migrant communities of the backwards, the Dalits, and the socially uprooted men, women and children.

However, any transitional society is difficult to analyse. Such difficulties are experienced both at the level of the structure and the superstructure and at crucial points of singularity where 'structural and super-structural elements blend and expose and create a new amalgam of structures and superstructures'. The colonialist state apparatus in India sometimes preserved and sometimes destroyed pre-capitalist structures to suit its own needs. World capitalism itself entered a defensive yet a flourishing phase, where it tried to forge social and political structures, which not only denied individuality to individuals, but also strenuously concealed that denial. Herein, some of the members of the traditional upper classes were trying to become modern, but full modernity in the sense of a capitalist rationality, which seeks to dissolve all ties between individuals except that of self-interest, was forever denied to them. Thus, it is in this backdrop of inherent internal contradictions—within a society that has been as heavily colonized as India, after experiencing several millennia of relatively autonomous but complicated evolution, along with the emergent interface of class, caste, gender and ethnicity—that the real challenge of restructuring the Indian political and social fabric will be faced in the coming years.

Suggested Readings

Bayly, Susan. *Caste, Society and Politics in India from Eighteenth Century to the Modern Age*. Cambridge, UK: Cambridge University Press, 1999.

Bentinck, Lord William. 'The Speech on November 8'. Reproduced in A. B. Keith, *Speeches and Documents on Indian Policy*, Vol. I, 1750–1921. Cambridge, UK: Cambridge University Press, 1829.

Bose, P. K. 'Social Mobility and Caste Violence: A Study of Gujarat Riots', *Economic and Political Weekly*, (16), 1969: 713–16.

Chandi, D. R. 'How Close to Equality are Scheduled Castes?' *Economic and Political Weekly* (4), 1969: 975–79.

Dublin, L. J. 'Shifting of Occupations Among Wage Earners', *Monthly Labor Review*, 1924.

Dumont, L. *Homo Hierarchicus*. London: Wiedenfield and Nicolson, 1970.

Ilaiah, K. *Why I Am Not a Hindu: A Sudra Critique of Hindu Philosophy, Culture and Political Economy*. Calcutta: Samya, 1996.

Lipset, Seymour Martin and Bendix Reinhard. *Social Mobility in Industrial Society*. Los Angeles, CA: University of California Press, 1966.

Patnaik, P. 'Democracy as a Site for Class-Struggle', *Economic and Political Weekly*, 2000.

Payne, G. 'Social Mobility'. *The British Journal of Sociology,* 40 (3), 1989.

Sorokin, P. *Social and Cultural Mobility*. New York: The Free Press, 1959.

Questions

1. What is social mobility, and what are the different approaches to studying social mobility?
2. Elaborate on the interlinkage between caste and class in India.
3. What effect has globalization had on the shaping of caste–class relations in India?

Social Movements: Challenges and Opportunities

12

Silky Tyagi

> *We are going to enter into a life of contradictions. In politics, we shall have equality and in social and economic life, we will have inequality ... we must remove this contradiction at the earliest possible moment or else, those who suffer from inequality will blow up the structures of political democracy, which we have so laboriously built up.*[1]
>
> —Ambedkar, 1950.

INTRODUCTION

In the 1980s, voices were raised by the Narmada Bachao Andolan activists against the Sardar Sarovar dam construction on the Narmada River. This led to large-scale displacement of *adivasis* who were neither relocated to a proper area nor granted proper compensation. Besides, the dam was causing serious environmental hazards. Why did no political party take up the issue? Or, for example, in the 1980s itself, we saw women from various strata of the society raising their voices against violence perpetrated against them. Why did no political party take up the issues they raised or why did they just pay lip service to their cause?

Democracy is largely understood as popular sovereignty where people have control over the decisions made by the State. Since it is not practically possible for the people in the modern democratic societies to participate in the decision-making process of the State directly, they do so through representatives. This representation gets its institutional form in political parties and it is through political parties that the people wish to articulate and represent their demands. But when political parties become ineffective in representing the interests of the people, we see the emergence of social movements (SMs).[2]

---

1. Quoted in Gail Omvedt, *Reinventing Revolution* (Armok: N. E. Sharpe, 1993), p. xi.
2. However, this in no way means that political parties were not representing people's interest, it is just that political parties were more interested in gaining power by politicizing people's issues. Thus, we find various coalitions or even providing reservation to certain castes or groups without really doing much at the concrete level.

Context

In the 1970s, the political parties failed to adequately represent the interests of the people within a state, which was entrusted with the responsibility of nation-building, economic growth and **social justice**. What really happened? Why did we arrive at such a crisis?

When India became independent, it expressed its full faith in the State, its institution and its policies. The State, in fact, came up as a promising figure that would take care of its people. In the two decades following Independence, the Congress was considered the legitimate representative of the people by a majority; after all, it was associated with the freedom struggle. People, therefore, had high hopes that the party would deliver to all basic primary education, health services, generate jobs and incomes, remove poverty and inequality and protect the needy, poor and the vulnerable. But all these hopes were dashed as the Congress party not only failed to fulfil its promises but also became authoritative and imposed an internal emergency in 1975. The period was, therefore, marked by agitation against prevailing corruption, food scarcity, unemployment and the imposition of internal emergency by the Union government. In fact, discontent spread to major parts of the country by the late 1960s onwards.[3]

In fact, this very crisis of representation that resulted from failure of political parties to perform its duties properly led to the emergence of, in the words of Rajni Kothari and D. L. Sheth, 'non-party formations'.[4] There was growing frustration among people who found that their most basic demands as citizens of this country were not being met. As a result, many new groups emersed as a 'new social force' and launched agitations against the State to press for their demands and rights, leading to the emergence of 'new social movements' (NSMs)[5] in India. The prominent movements that came up during this time included the civil liberties movement, **Dalit** movement, *adivasi* movement, women's movement and environment movement. These movements[6] became the thrust of Gail Omvedt's work, *Reinventing Revolution*.

These new social movements that came up in the late 1970s and, more particularly, in the 1980s were different from the political parties as they did not seek State power and were largely anti-State, criticizing the policies of the State and articulating the interests of the disadvantaged sections of the society. They were different from various pressure groups because they did not function as lobbies that depended on various political parties to protect their interests.

---

3. See Neera Chandhoke, 'Revisiting the Crisis of Representation Thesis: The Indian Context', *Democratization*, 12 (3), June 2005: 308–30.
4. Ibid.
5. The term 'new social movement' first appeared in Western society, in the wake of the post–World War II scenario and the Vietnam War in the 1960s.
6. Chandhoke, 'Revisiting the Crisis'. 308–30.

NEW SOCIAL FORCES AND NEW SOCIAL MOVEMENTS

A social force in general can be defined as any entity that has the capability to enforce, bring about, inhibit, direct or extend any change in society. When social lobbies exert pressure, they create a force that leads to social movements. These social movements then bring about change in the social, economic and political environment and, thereby, become a social force themselves. Ghanshyam Shah argues that the term social movement has no precise definition and that it is seen differently by different social activists, political leaders and scholars.[7] However, there have been a few broad definitions of the term. M. S. A. Rao defined social movement as a 'sustained collective mobilization through either informal or formal organization and which is generally oriented towards bringing about change'.[8] In fact, Shah also cited a broad definition given by Paul Wilkinson who called it, a 'deliberative collective action to promote change in any direction and by any means ... which evince a minimal degree of organization, though this may range from a loose, informal or partial level of organization to the highly institutionalized ... its commitment to change and *raison d'etre* of its organization are founded upon conscious volition, normative commitment to the movement's aims or beliefs and active participation on the part of the followers or members'.[9]

Social movement, involves:

(a) collective mass mobilization

(b) collective mass support

(c) formal or informal organization

(d) a conscious commitment towards its aims and beliefs

(e) deliberative collective action towards change

In India, we have witnessed various social uprisings even in the pre-Independence era; early tribal movements like the Santhal uprising and Tebhaga movement of the peasants are cases in point.[10] But what made the movements of Dalits, OBCs, women, *adivasis* of the late 1970s and the early 1980s different from the earlier social

---

7. Ghanshyam Shah, *Social Movements in India: A Review of Literature* (New Delhi: Sage Publications, 2004), p. 18.
8. See M. S. A. Rao, 'Conceptual Problems in the Study of Social Movements', in his (ed.), Social *Movements in India—Studies in Peasant, Backward Classes, Sectarian, Tribal and Women's Movements* (New Delhi: Manohar Publications, 2000).
9. Shah, *Social Movements in India*, pp. 19–20.
10. In fact, a group of historians called 'subalterns', which included people like Ranajit Guha, Partha Chatterjee, and Shahid Amin wanted to look at the 'history from below', i.e., they were critical of the fact that history is largely viewed from the elitist perspective and that larger toiling masses were ignored. They, therefore, looked at history through the struggles of the marginalized sections of society.

movement was a change in the kinds of issues and in the language of assertion. One of the major and largely accepted differences is that the old social movements (SMs) followed the Marxist paradigm and stressed on raising its voice against class domination, while the new social movements were not just about opposing class domination but also the domination of caste, race, gender, ethnicity and community. It, therefore, brought up the issues of human rights, civil rights and issues of identity and specific interests to the forefront and expanded the realm of democracy. While the SMs were class based (subsuming other issues and groups) and mainly aimed at taking over State power, the NSMs took up various issues (social, economic, political) of distinct groups and plural in character (for example, women's movement, environment movement, etc.) and they did not seek to take over any state or class.

However, not all are in agreement with this view and do not even identify these movements as 'new'. For example, Shah in his criticism of the concept argues that we can find struggles for identity even in the pre-modern society and that the contemporary environmental movement, women's movement and the Dalit movement have an economic context as well. He asserts that even though there has been a change in the nature of classes and class relationship in the present global capitalism, the classes still carry relevance in the perception of people towards the dominant ideology and power.[11] Similarly, what Katzenstein, Kothari and Mehta find distinctive about earlier movements are their links to political parties and the electoral process while, in the (chronologically) newer movements, the identity movements have captured the space of electoral politics and the non-identity movements of the poor and underprivileged have carved out institutional spaces, depending on bureaucracy, courts, or global institutional fora.[12]

However, it can be counter-argued that when we talk of Dalits, OBCs, *adivasis* and women forming a 'new social force' leading to the emergence of 'new social movements', we neither deny the fact that there were earlier movements by these groups nor suggest that class character is removed from contemporary movements. But what makes them stand apart from the earlier movements is the fact that the contemporary movements have highlighted the autonomous issues of each of these specific groups apart from the class character that it may entail. For example, take the case of women's movement in India: during the pre-Independence era, they were connected largely through the national movement and would demand independence by supporting the ideas of liberty and equality as a part of the mass movement. After Independence, for example in the Tebhaga movement, which re-emerged in the 1960s, women were an important force, but their voices largely faded away in the

11. Shah, *Social Movements in India*, p. 23.
12. Mary Katzenstein et al. 'Social Movement Politics in India: Institutions, Interests, and Identities', in Atul Kohli (ed.), *The Success of India's Democracy* (New Delhi: Foundation Books, 2002), p. 260.

peasant's struggle. This was also true in the case of the Naxalite movement[13] in which, again, women were an active participant. But the major difference that one could encounter in the women's movement during the 1970s and more particularly in the mid-1980s is that we see women's voices were raised not for freedom for all or in relation to questions of land or class issues but specifically for women; women as an autonomous group raised issues specific to them. Thus, the women's movement during this period had participants that cut across class character and had women from elite, poor and middle-class sections. The issue that brought them together was not class but gender relations. Again, it does not mean that the class character vanished but rather it was given a new dimension, that is, women as a class was largely an economically dependent class—and that became an issue of protest.

These social movements, therefore, sought to alter the prevailing structures of power, project values of justice, equality and freedom adding new dimensions to them[14] and marked the rise of a new social force in India. In fact, Omvedt suggests that 'Marxism has been called the historical materialism of the proletariat; what is needed today is a historical materialism of not only industrial factory workers but also of peasants, women, tribals, Dalits, and low castes, and oppressed nationalities.'[15]

Box 12.1

NSMs have the following characteristics:

(a) They are SMs as they entail all its characteristics.

(b) They are a response from the civil society that largely deals with the issues of human dignity and his/her relations with nature.

(c) NSMs radically alter the Marxist paradigm of explaining conflicts and contradictions in terms of class, thereby leaving groups with issues like gender, ecology, race, ethnicity, etc. Thus, NSMs take up issues beyond class.

(d) NSMs not only abandon the industrial workers model of union organization, but also the political model of political parties.

---

13. Named after the Naxalbari region of West Bengal, a section of CPI(M) who believed that democratic revolution could only be achieved through armed struggle erupted out of the party in 1967.
14. Manoranjan Mohanty, 'Social Movements in Creative Society: Of Autonomy and Interconnection', in Manoranjan Mohanty and P. N. Mukherji with Olle Tornquist (eds.), *People's Rights: Social Movements and the State in the Third World* (New Delhi: Sage Publications, 1998), pp. 65–66. See Rajendra Singh, *Social Movements, Old and New: A Postmodernist Critique* (New Delhi: Sage Publications, 2005), pp. 99–106.
15. Omvedt, *Reinventing Revolution*, p. xvi.

Now, within the paradigm of new social movements (NSMs), Andre Gunder Frank and Marta Fuentes described new social movements as largely 'grassroot' and apolitical whose main objective is social transformation rather than State power. According to Dhanagare and John, this is a process of depoliticization of the social realm.[16] Dhanagare and John argue that Frank and Fuentes conspire to take away political consciousness from exploited classes.[17] That the anti-caste movement in India has political power as core thrust and that women's movement having women from all classes and not just grassroot sections negates the very argument of Frank and Fuentes that NSMs are apolitical and grassroot. New social movements, therefore, are not only social but can have varied dimensions like political and economic and that it may not necessarily be grassroot but can include various other sections too.

In this chapter, Part II will concentrate on the contemporary movements of Dalits, OBCs, *adivasis* and women in India and each movement will also deal with the question of representation of each of these groups in Indian polity. However, the issues of representation in relation with social justice will be taken up in Part III of this chapter. Finally, Part IV will provide a concluding remark on the role played by these new social movements, the issues raised by them, their present status and where we can look ahead from these experiences.

The Rise of New Social Forces

A Brief History of the Dalit Movement:[18] The Dalit movement in India began around the mid-19th century. It was Jyotirao Phule, a middle-caste, social revolutionary from Maharashtra, who questioned the caste system itself

16. Shah, *Social Movements in India*, p. 23.
17. Omvedt, *Reinventing Revolution*, p. xv.
18. The term 'Dalit' literally means 'ground down' or 'broken down to pieces' and it was first used by B. R. Ambedkar in 1928 in his newspaper *Bahishkrit Bharat*. See Amrita Rao, 'Representing Dalit Selfhood', *Seminar*, February 2006, p. 34. Dalits occupy the lowest rank in the Hindu caste system and are called *avarna*, i.e. those which are outside the *chaturvarna* system. Their touch and sometimes their shadows and even their voices were believed to pollute Hindus. Legally, they are no longer untouchable, though in practice many of them still bear the stigma. See Shah, *Social Movements in India*, p. 115. The term generally refers to exploited and oppressed social groups but is more particularly used for members of Scheduled Castes. The other term used synonymous to them are 'untouchables', depressed classes, 'Harijan' (children of God). But the 'Harijan' nomenclature given by Gandhi was rejected by many Dalit leaders including Ambedkar. Rather than soothing names and soft palliatives they preferred 'Untouchable' or 'Dalit', which represents a truthful reflection of the actual situation. They are also known as *perial*, *panchama*, *atishudra*, *antyaja* or *namshudra* in different parts of the country. See Ghanshyam Shah, *Social Movements in India*, p. 118 and V. Suresh, 'The Dalit Movement in India', in T. V. Sathyamurthy (ed.), *Region, Religion, Caste, Gender and Culture in Contemporary India* (New Delhi: Oxford University Press, 1996), p. 362.

and its evil practices.[19] By the end of the 19th century, there were a number of anti-caste movements in various parts of India—Phule's Satyashodhak movement, Namashudra movement,[20] the Adi-Hindu movement, the Adi Dharma movement, the Ezahava movement of Sree Narayan Dharma Paripalana (SNDP) Yogam, the Sadhu Jana Paripalana Samajam (SJPS) and the Pulaya Mahasabha.[21]

However, these movements were largely socio-religious in nature. Later, Dalit movements got politicized in the early decades of the 20th century, and especially, when the Britishers introduced the system of a separate electorate in the Minto-Morley reforms of 1909. By 1917, Dalit movements (DMs) got separtated from non-Brahmin movements (NBMs)[22] and they got a further fillip after a resolution was passed in the Indian National Congress (INC) in the same year.[23] The resolution stressed on bringing the attention towards the socio-economic conditions and with the presidency of Gandhi in 1920, this process gathered momentum.[24]

By the 1930s, Gandhi and Ambedkar had emerged as competing spokesmen and leaders of the depressed classes in India. Gandhi thought that untouchablility was a moral issue, which is internal to the Hindu religion and that there should be a peaceful and gradual abolition of untouchability. To Gandhi, there was nothing wrong in the *varna* system and that 'ati-shudras' should be included in it too as they also constitute the part of the Hindu religion. On the contrary, Ambedkar found untouchability to be a political and economic issue. He felt that abolition of the caste system was essential for abolishing untouchability. Ambedkar favoured the issue of a separate electorate of MacDonald's proposal of 1928. But, Gandhi was vehemently against it and went on a fast-unto-death. At last, Ambedakar had to give in and signed the Poona Pact that gave reservations to Dalits within the Hindu community.[25]

Nevertheless, Ambedkar formed the Indian Labour Party (ILP) in 1936 bringing in all the depressed sections of the society—Dalits, non-Brahmins, peasants and workers. However, unable to consolidate and resolve differences between Dalits and

---

19. In Maharashtra, the peasant movement and the women's movement also look upon him as a founder. In fact, he began a new discourse and a new understanding of Indian history from the view point of the *shudra–atishudra* (Dalit–Non-Brahmin) peasantry, which continues to be relevant today. Gail Omvedt, 'The Anti-Caste Movement and the Discourse of Power', in Ghanshyam Shah (ed.), *Caste and Democratic Politics in India* (Delhi: Permanent Black, 2002), pp. 416–17.
20. See Shekhar Bandopadhyay, 'Caste, Class and Politics in Colonial Bengal: A Case Study of Namashudra Movement', in K. L. Singh (ed.), *Caste and Class in India* (Jaipur and New Delhi: Rawat Publications, 1994), pp. 19–46.
21. Suresh, 'The Dalit Movement in India', p. 356.
22. Ibid., p. 357.
23. Marc Galanter, *Competing Equalities: Law and The Backward Classes in India* (New Delhi: Oxford University Press, 1984), p. 26.
24. Ibid.
25. Ibid.

non-Brahmins, he dissolved it and formed the All India Scheduled Caste Federation (AISCF) in 1942. Later, we find disintegration within the AISCF, as some of its non-Brahmin members got disillusioned and joined the Congress.[26] Finally, Ambedkar had a plan to establish the Republican Party of India (RPI), which got established posthumously in 1956. But, eventually, it too met the same fate as the earlier ones, with most of its members disintegrating and joining the Congress.

New Anti-caste Movement: The Emergence of Dalit Panthers (1970s): The first wave of the new anti-caste movement began with the emergence of the Dalit Panthers in 1972.[27] It mainly comprised ex-untouchable youth of Maharashtra. The formation of the Dalit Panthers took place against the background of continued atrocities by the upper-caste elites and 'such oppressive developments—namely, the repeated failure of the Republican party to fulfil any of the hopes of the Dalits, rising of tensions on the countryside and of the revolutionary inspiration provided by the Naxalbari insurrection, which was crushed by the State'.[28]

The movement was largely concentrated in cities like Bombay and Poona, which began with the publication of creative literature (in socialist magazines such as *Sadhna*[29]). It was militant and aimed at power in its manifesto, yet it did not really carry any political strategy.[30] However, the Dalit Panthers fought their battle on two fronts: at the symbolic level against Brahminism and at the concrete level against Hindu peasants and artisans who were directly responsible for numerous atrocities committed against 'ati-shudras'.[31]

But like many earlier Dalit movements, it too got engulfed in party politics. There was a split in the organization when Raja Dhale and Namdev Dhasal (two prominent leaders of Dalit Panthers) developed differences of opinion. Differences arose over whether Dalit Panthers should be a caste-based movement of Scheduled Castes or a class-based movement including the poor people of all classes. Here Dhale was representing the 'Ambedkarite' position and Dhasal a 'Marxist'. The Communist Party of India (CPI) wanted to bring Dalits in its fold. But, in the end, it was the 'Ambedkarite' position that easily won this battle, when in 1974, the Dhale group took control and expelled Dhasal. This was largely due to the very real fear of the Panthers 'of the control by Brahmin leftists of supportive organizations, platforms, money for campaigns, even the media. Their deep-seated suspicion was that they were now given only hypocritical support by communists. ...'[32]

26. Suresh, 'The Dalit Movement in India', p. 357.
27. Omvedt, *Reinventing Revolution*, p. 47.
28. Omvedt, 'The Anti-Caste Movement and the Discourse of Power', p. 422 .
29. Omvedt, *Reinventing Revolution*, p. 48.
30. Omvedt, 'The Anti-Caste Movement and the Discourse of Power', p. 423.
31. Ibid.
32. Omvedt, *Reinventing Revolution*, p. 54.

While the Marxist left accepted the idea that middle-caste or OBC rich farmers were the worst enemies of Dalits and 'rhetorically pose the contradiction as *savarna*/Dalit' or 'caste Hindus versus Dalits', to this they simply added the need for a working-class alliance leadership of the working class party and so forth.[33] Naxalites too, had fallen victim to this strategy of posing a dichotomy of 'caste-Hindu' versus 'Dalit' and even landholding peasants versus agricultural labourers.[34] In fact, the Marathwada rioting in 1978 asserted this contradiction when Maratha Kunbis attacked and assaulted the Dalits over the issue of renaming Marathwada University after Ambedkar.

However, many failed to realize that it was a Congress strategy to divide the Dalits and OBCs; after all, the Congress in its bid to woo the Dalit community was working well under its KHAM (Kisan, Harijan, *adivasi*, Muslim) strategy[35]. At the same time, the continued propaganda that reservations are for Dalits who are responsible for the unemployment of low-caste poor was effective.[36] However, this situation got transformed with the proposals of the Mandal Commission (appointed by Janata government in 1978), which led to violent protests by the higher caste 'including high-caste intellectuals who continued to emphasize that the backwards were the principal enemies of the Dalits'.[37]

As far as the Dalit Panthers was concerned, it was more symbolic and cultural in focus. Though militancy continued against the atrocities inflicted on Dalits, but at the broad political level, 'Panthers like earlier Dalit leadership continually fell victim to Congress blandishments and Congress progressive rhetoric: both Dhasal and Dhale supported Indira Gandhi during Emergency and even the reorganized Panthers gradually came to be a kind of political reserve army of the Congress'.[38]

Dalit Movement in the 1980s: The 1980s can be seen as a period of Dalit and OBC unity. It was prominently marked by the emergence of the Bahujan Samaj Party (BSP) as the party of Dalits, backwards and minorities. BSP emerged as a political wing of the Backward and Minority Communities Employees Federation (BAMCEF), launched by Kanshi Ram in 1978.[39] It made its

---

33. Ibid.
34. Ibid., p. 52. While both the communist mainstream and the Naxalites wanted to bring in both the class caste contradiction together into one realm or rather incorporate caste differences into class but in vain. Though Naxalites were not much of a success in Maharashtra, they were quite a success in Bihar and Andhra Pradesh. However, Dalits have been rather apprehensive of joining with the class struggle largely because of 'upper caste' dominance even in this struggle.
35. Congress in its KHAM strategy wanted to incorporate Kisans (peasants), Harijans (Dalits), *adivasis* (tribals) and Muslims in its fold to garner the vote bank.
36. Omvedt, 'The Anti-Caste Movement and the Discourse of Power', p. 424.
37. Ibid.
38. Omvedt, *Reinventing Revolution*, p. 57.
39. Suresh, 'The Dalit Movement in India', p. 368.

appearance particularly in the northern states of India, such as Uttar Pradesh (UP), Rajasthan, Bihar, Delhi, Punjab, and Madhya Pradesh (MP).[40] The primary agenda of the party was (and remains) to acquire power through the electoral process, which it did achieve considerably. But it lacks a wider social, economic or political programme of action beyond uniting the SCs, STs, OBCs, and minorities—*vote se lenge PM/CM, arakshan se SP/DM*—shows its limited nature of acquiring power.[41] Later, by the end of the 1990s, it also became a part of coalition politics and even went on to join the BJP!

However, with regard to the Dalit–shudra unity during this period, we not only see Kanshi Ram of BSP, but there were also Rajshekhar of Dalit Voice, Sharad Patil of the Satyashodhak Communist Party and Dalit Sangharsh Samiti (DSS) of Karnataka (though we find shudras as the main enemies of the Dalits at the village level).[42]

The issue of reservation for OBCs led to riots in Gujarat in 1981 and 1985 (after the Baxi and Rane Commission's report, respectively), but unlike Marathwada, here Dalits were targeted by the upper castes who blamed them for the extension of reservation. In the first riots, the OBCs remained passive but in the second one, they attacked the upper castes. And then this Dalit/OBC conflict got transformed into communal riots.

1990s and After: By the early 1990s, the debate about reservation for OBCs became more vehement with the submission of the Mandal Commission report and its strong opposition by the upper castes.

What we now see is a mere symbolic representation of caste politics, and according to Shah, the Dalit movement has just narrowed down to pressure groups. The State has, besides providing an institutional framework of incorporating identity politics, played a very critical role in bringing about any substantial change as far as the Dalits are concerned. Yet, 'within the Dalit politics, the new generation of Dalit leadership has taken into transnational alliances and networks to further the Dalit cause. As a result, Kuala Lumpur Dalit Convention (1998); the Voice of Dalits International, London (2001); the International Dalit Conference, Vancouver (2003) and the World Conference against Racism, Racial Discrimination, Xenophobia and Related Intolerance mark the high water mark of Dalit politics.[43]

40. Omvedt, 'The Anti-Caste Movement and the Discourse of Power', p. 427.
41. Ibid.
42. Ibid., p. 426.
43. Manish K. Thakur, 'Dalit Politics in Indian State: Changing Landscape, Emerging Agendas', 2006 (unpublished paper). Besides, today, we also find opening up of debates in Dalit consciousness, in both literature and sociology, which make important contributions to Dalit politics at large. See the *Seminar* edition of December 2005, and Gopal Guru, 'The Dalit Movement in Mainstream Sociology', in S. M. Michael (ed.), *Dalits in Modern India: Vision and Values* (New Delhi: Vistaar Publications, 1999), pp. 35–145.

However, the recent incident in Khairlanji (Maharashtra) in which a whole Dalit family was killed by OBCs depicts the persistence of the deep-rooted caste system and its oppression in this 21st century India. The atrocities against the Dalits are still a part of everyday life in India[44]. According to Prakash Louis,

> If one even gleans through the Annual Reports of the Commission for the SCs and STs, the volumes of atrocities unleashed on the Dalits become amply clear. Significantly, the number of atrocities committed under the categories defined under 'Prevention of Atrocities Act' is the highest.[45]

The OBC Movement

Who are the other backward castes? While it is difficult to give any precise definition of caste, it is all the more difficult to define 'backward castes'. This is because 'backward castes' are not a homogeneous category in India. Most of the scholars consider all castes other than *dwija* (the twice-born who have the right to wear the sacred thread) as backward castes. But there are several castes in the different parts of the country, which are not *dwija* (though many of them aspire to achieve *dwija* status) and yet they do not consider themselves backward castes. They enjoy control over economic resources and political power. They struggle and mobilize for power among themselves or against the Brahmins, and hence, they cannot be considered deprived groups. These include Kayasthas of Bihar, the Jats of Rajasthan and the Patidars of Gujarat.[46] But then again, all the backward castes do not enjoy a uniform socio-economic status. In his study of the backward-caste movements, M. S. A. Rao divides non-upper castes/classes into three categories: landowners, tenants and untouchables.[47]

The main debate in the Constituent Assembly was regarding the very definition of the the backward castes and who should be included in it and whether there should be class or caste as the main criteria of considering any section as backward. In fact, both Nehru and Ambedkar had a difference of opinion regarding this, while the former preferred class, the latter stressed on caste as the basic criterion.[48] As far as the Scheduled Castes and Scheduled Tribes were

---

44. Meena Kandaswamy (translated work of Thirumaavalavan), *Talisman: Extreme Emotions of Dalit Liberation* (Kolkata: Samya, 2003), pp. 9–10.
45. Prakash Louis, *The Political Sociology of Dalit Assertion* (New Delhi: Gyan Publishing House, 2003), p. 254.
46. Ghanshyam Shah (ed.), *Caste and Democratic Politics in India* (Delhi: Permanent Black, 2002), p. 137.
47. Ibid., pp. 137–38. M. S. A. Rao includes untouchables in other backward castes and Christophe Jaffrelot also clubs Dalits and 'other backward castes' together as low castes. But, here in our discussion, we will exclude Scheduled Castes from backward caste and treat them separately.
48. Christophe Jaffrelot, *India's Silent Revolution: The Rise of Low Castes in North Indian Politics* (Delhi: Permanent Black, 2003), pp. 215–21.

concerned, the situation was quite clear. However, with regard to OBCs, the Constituent Assembly reached a decision that the president [of the republic] can, by decree, nominate a commission formed by persons he considers to be competent to investigate, within the Indian territory, on the condition of classes suffering of backwardness as well in social as in education terms, and on the problems they meet, the way of proposing measures that could be taken by the central or a state government in order to eliminate difficulties and improve their condition.[49]

And this eventually became Article 340 of the Indian Constitution. Also, the adoption of preferential treatment of backward-caste people was specifically sanctioned in Articles 15(4) and 16(4).[50]

The Classification of OBC Movements: M. S. A. Rao classifies backward-caste movements into four types: 1) The non-Brahmin movements concentrated in the southern part of India, for example, the 'self-respect' movement in Madras in the late 1920s. The non-Brahmin movements in Maharashtra and Tamil Nadu raised cultural issues. 2) Movements led by low and intermediate castes such as the Ahirs and the Kurmis in Bihar, the Noniyas in Punjab, the Kolis in Gujarat, and the Malis in Maharashtra. 3) Movements by the depressed classes or untouchables against upper and other backward castes. 4) The tribal movements.[51]

Further, Rao also deals with two kinds of ideologies with regard to the backward-caste movements. First, many castes belonging to the other backward classes claimed a higher *varna* status through a reinterpretation of and recasting of appropriate mythologies of origin, such as Ahirs in many parts of north India, the Gopas in Bengal, the Gaulis in Maharashtra, the Gollas in Andhra Pradesh and Karnataka, and the Konnars in Tamil Nadu claimed dissent from the Yadu dynasty. In the second decade of the 20th century, they organized themselves into an All India Yadava Association. In parts of north India, especially Bihar, the Yadavs came into direct conflict with Bhoomihar Brahmins, when the former donned the sacred thread (symbol of twice-born) in public. (Another variation in this approach has been the search for self-determination like the Izhavas of Kerala in the SNDP movement).

The second variety of protest ideology was based on the rejection of the Brahminical Aryan religion and culture. Adherent of these views included the Dravida Kazhagam Movement in Tamil Nadu, which idealized Dravidian culture

49. Ibid., pp. 219–20.
50. Article 15 provides special privileges to SCs, STs, OBCs, i.e. those who are socially and educationally disadvantaged, while Article 16 gives special privileges to them with regard to the employment and admissions in State offices and educational institutions respectively.
51. M. S. A. Rao, 'Conceptual Problems in the Study of Social Movements', in his (ed.), *Social Movements in India*, Vol. 1 (Delhi: Manohar, 1979) pp. 191–215.

and religion and attacked Aryan culture and religion. The Mahar movement in Maharashtra was another movement that abandoned Hinduism altogether.[52]

The OBC Movement—Post-Independence Scenario: After India gained independence, the OBC movement in India concentrated on its demands for reservation and job quota. Considering Article 340, the Government of India appointed the first Backward Classes Commission in 1953 with Kaka Kalelkar as its head. The Commission reported in 1955 identifying 2,399 castes as socially and educationally backward classes. The government, however, did not accept the recommendations on the grounds that the commission had not applied any objective tests for identifying the backward classes.[53] In fact, the commission was also doubtful about identifying the backward classes. However, though the report of the first Backward Classes Commission was shelved, it created, according to Jaffrelot, a milestone for the low-caste movement in north India, as for example, we see the emergence of the AIBCF (All India Backward Classes Federation).[54]

The next step was to be accomplished by the political actors. From the late 1960s onwards, the OBCs were to advance through the socialist movements and Charan Singh's political parties. The former—especially the parties of Ram Manohar Lohia—were quick to use reservations as a means of politicizing the lower castes. While the southern pattern of the low-caste mobilization was linked to ethnicization and strategies of empowerment, 'quota politics' in the north was the key factor.[55]

Then, it was in 1978 that the Janata coalitions displaced the Congress power at the centre. With considerable support in north India from the backward caste groups, the central government again took up the issue of the preferential treatment for the backward castes by appointing the Second Backward Classes Commission (with B. P. Mandal as its chairman). The second commission explicitly recommended 'caste as criterion' and identified 3,248 castes as backward. But by the time the Commission submitted its report in December 1980, the Congress had returned to power. The Congress government neither took a decision and nor did it reject the report. But it was in August 1990 when Prime Minister V. P. Singh, the leader of the fragile government in need of solidifying his electoral base, announced a further 27 per cent reservation in addition to the 22 per cent set aside for SCs and STs.

The commission, here, recommended reservation of jobs for backward castes not as an egalitarian measure or a step towards secularism or social justice, but primarily to boost the morale of the backward castes. It argued:

---

52. Ibid., pp. 197–198.
53. Ghanshyam Shah (ed.), *Caste and Democratic Politics in India*, p. 404.
54. This strategy of empowerment had already been implemented by the non-Brahmin movement in south India during the colonial era.
55. Ibid.

> In India, government service has always been looked upon as a symbol of prestige and power. By increasing the representation of the OBCs in government services, we give them an immediate feeling of participation in the governance of this country. … Even when no tangible benefits flow to the community at large, the feeling that it has now its 'own man' in the 'corridors of power' acts as a morale booster.[56]

The centrality accorded to power was just as clear in the remarks of former Prime Minister V. P. Singh, the chief architect of the social justice platform:

> Through Mandal, I knew we were going to bring changes in the basic nature of power. I was putting my hand on the real structures of power. I knew I was not giving jobs, Mandal is not an employment scheme but I was seeking to place people in the instruments of power.[57]

This phenomenon also led to the politicization of caste[58] in India, which not only led to various coalitions, but also created various factions, for example, in the case of Janata Dal, which has around 10 splinter groups.[59] Further, as OBCs are not a coherent category, in the last decade divisions among them such as rural/urban or poor/rich have been aggravated and a new category of the most backward castes as MBCs has taken shape.[60] In recent years, a process of politicization and awareness of MBCs; of their lowly social and economic position has begun among them creating confrontation with the OBCs and Dalits who they feel have received all the benefits from the process of development.

In fact, caste conflict and competitions came into the forefront of Indian politics only after the Nehru period, particularly after the split in the Congress in 1969 and during and after the 1971 elections. The Congress led by Mrs Gandhi intensified its appeal to the disadvantaged group, under its KHAM strategy, to counter the power of the state party bases, which rested mostly on the upper and landed castes. With this began the trend of political cooptation by various political parties to bring in various factions into their

---

56. Ghanshyan Shah, *Social Movements and the State* (New Delhi: Sage, 2002), p. 400.
57. Zoya Hasan, 'Representation and Redistribution: The New Lower Caste Politics of North India', in her (ed.), *Parties and Party Politics in India* (New Delhi: Oxford University Press, 2002), p. 380.
58. Politicization of caste can be defined as something in which both the forms of caste and the forms of politics are brought nearer to each other, in the process changing both. See Rajni Kothari, *Cast in Indian Politics* (New Delhi: Orient Blackswan, 2008, orig. Rubo in 1970).
59. These include the Samajwadi Party of Mulayam Singh Yadav; Rashtriya Lok Dal of Ajit Singh; Samajwajdi Janata Party (Rashtriya) of Chandra Shekhar; Indian National Lok Dal of Om Prakash Chautala; Janata Dal (Secular) of H. D. Deve Gowda; Rashtriya Janata Dal of Laloo Prasad Yadav; Biju Janata Dal of Naveen Patnaik; Samata Party of Nitish Kumar and George Fernandes; and Lok Shakti of Ramakrishna Hegde.
60. The term MBCs refers to those castes that stand lowest in the caste hierarchy among the backwards.

fold. In north India, for example, several political parties, particularly the Samyukta Socialist Party (SSP) of Ram Manohar Lohia and Bharatiya Kranti Dal (BKD) of Charan Singh, developed strength among the backward castes and advocated policies of preferential treatment.[61]

While in south India, where the mobilization of the non-Brahmin castes took place earlier than in the north, neither in Karnataka nor in Tamil Nadu were the non-Brahmin movements seeking a radical change but rather, aiming to gain greater power in administration and in local elected bodies and state legislatures.[62]

In Karnataka, the Congress leadership in the 1950s came predominantly from Lingayats and Vokkaligas.[63] In the 1970s, Devraj Urs as permanent Congress leader in Karnataka broadened the social base of the party by appealing to the more disadvantaged backward castes and Scheduled Castes. However, after the defeat of the Congress by the Janata Dal in 1977 there were differences between Urs and the Congress which led to a split in the party. After the split, the Congress reduced its dependence upon the non-dominant backward classes and increased the representation of the dominant Lingayat and Vokkaliga communities.[64]

In Tamil Nadu, the Dravidian movement was committed to the destruction of caste system but in practice, it used caste as a means of political mobilization and ultimately increased the political importance of caste. Though the Congress initially succeeded in gaining the support of non-Brahmin elites, the DMK was ultimately able to win control of the State by transforming its anti-Brahmin ideology into an anti-northern one.[65]

Though caste lost its moral legitimacy in Independent India, but still the same middle and the lower castes sought equality with the upper castes through the process of 'Sanskritization'. However, at the same time, they proclaimed their status as backward castes and demanded greater political power.[66]

Another issue that arose after the Mandal report and during agitation against it was redefinition of 'poverty' and 'backwardness' by a section of dominant elite.[67] As a result, the Gujarat Kshatriya Sabha argued that all Kshatriyas should

---

61. Paul R. Brass, 'The Politics of India Since Independence', in Gordon Johnson and C. A. Bayly (eds.), *The New Cambridge History of India—IV.1* (Cambridge: Cambridge University Press, 1990), pp. 21–45.
62. Myron Weiner, 'The Struggle for Equality: Caste in Indian Politics', in Atul Kohli (ed.), *The Success of India's Democracy* (New Delhi: Foundation Books, 2002), p. 198.
63. Although these two communities are the dominant, land-controlling groups in Karnataka, they both received recognition as backward castes entitled to preferential treatment.
64. See James Manor, 'Blurring the Lines Between Parties and Social Bases: Gundu Rao and the Emergence of a Janata Government in Karnataka', in J. R. Wood (ed.), *State Politics in Contemporary India: Crisis or Continuity?* (London: Westview, 1984).
65. Weiner, 'The Struggle for Equality', p. 198.
66. Ibid., p. 199.
67. D. L. Sheth, 'Changing Terms of Elite Discourse: The Case of Reservation for Other Backward Classes', in T. V. Sathyamurthy (ed.), *Region, Religion, Gender and Culture in Contemporary India*, Vol. 3 (New Delhi: Oxford University Press, 1996), p. 234.

be considered as backward because they were economically backward and the various castes among the Kshatriyas share a common culture and social customs. According to Rajputs, those who were unable to compete openly should get the benefit of reservation. Similarly, the Lingayats and the Vokkaligas communities, realizing that they would not get backward status, insisted that the Chinappa Reddy Commission adopt economic criteria to identify social and educationally backward classes.[68] But again, one of the shortcomings of these reservations was that it had largely benefited the upper echelons of the social hierarchy, leaving large sections of the lower echelons with no access to knowledge and political power and with no benefits whatsoever.

The *Adivasi* Movement

The *adivasi* or tribal movements have a long history. Numerous uprisings of the tribals have taken place beginning with the one in Bihar in 1772, followed by many revolts in Andhra Pradesh, Andaman and Nicobar Islands, Arunachal Pradesh, Assam, Mizoram and Nagaland. Tribal movements in early India had their origins in religious upheavals like Buddhism and Vaishnavism, for example, Meithie in Manipur, Bhumij in West Bengal, Nokte Naga in Assam, Bathudi in Orissa, and Gonds, Kols and Bhils in Rajasthan. Then in the 19th and 20th century, the British also faced tribal movements when they stopped head hunting human sacrifice or slavery in north-eastern India.[69] There were movements against oppressive landlords, moneylenders and harassment by police and forest officials in Bihar, Bengal, Orissa and the central Indian states.[70]

The *adivasis* and their areas largely remained out of the purview of the administration in the pre-Independence period. But the 1930s saw the emergence of a new discourse on tribal development. Sections 52 and 92 of the Government of India Act, 1935 provided for tribal majority areas to be demarcated into the excluded and partially excluded areas. This meant that these tracts were to be administered by the governor outside the framework of the Constitution, and norms and procedures of governance in the Fifth and Sixth Schedule areas were to be different from the rest of the country. The assumption of this policy was that tribals have suffered a great deal during the colonial rule and that their cultural and economic rights should now be protected. The Nehruvian view

68. Shah (ed.), *Caste and Democratic Politics in India*, p. 399.
69. The important tribes involved in revolt in the 19th century were the Mizo (1810), Kol (1795 and 1831), Munda (1889), Dafla (1875), Khasi and Garo (182, Kachari (1839), Santhal (1853), Muria Gond (1886), Naga (1884 and 1879), Bhuiya (1868) and Kondh (1817). See Ram Ahuja, *Society in India: Concepts, Theories and Changing Trends* (Jaipur and New Delhi: Rawat Publications, 1999), p. 283.
70. Ibid.

essentially was that the economic life of the tribals had to be upgraded and modernized even as their culture needed protection.[71]

The Left had, in general, supported the Nehruvian position on both modern tribal development and the need for protection of tribals from the market forces. The tribal activists have also backed the idea of Nehruvian protectionism for tribals but only to the extent that it should help in the revival of traditional tribal institutions. But their ideal is significantly different from the Nehruvian dream of slowly drawing the tribals into the mainstream of bourgeois democracy. The Left position also recognizes the importance of democratization of the tribal society, but wanted to develop a different type of democracy within India, that is, the future of tribals in the Indian democracy was thus dependent not only on political freedom and self-governing institutions but also on correcting the inequities between the tribal regions and the dominant political economy.[72]

Nehru's ideas formed the basis of the tribal policy in Independent India and he argued that modern ideas should be allowed to permeate the institutions of everyday life through the education and employment of tribals. The bulk of allocations for STs (as classified in Schedule VIII of the Constitution) were as grants for education and social services.

Among the works on tribals in India, one that stands out is by Verrier Elwin.[73] He was an English anthropologist who had spent almost his entire life in the tribal areas of India. What stands out in his work is his close association and intimacy with the tribals in India.[74] As an anthropologist since the days of the British, a member of the Scheduled Caste Commission and then, later as an adviser for tribal affairs to the administration of North East Frontier Agency (NEFA), he was a symbol and standard bearer of the movement for the recognition of tribal rights. In defending tribal people, he clashed often eloquently with those Hindu puritans who were trying to reform the tribal society in their ascetic mode. Elwin found through experiences with tribes of Gonds and Baigas that they did not require a new religion but were desperately in need of moral and political support against the oppression and exploitation of the advanced communities. Elwin had also proposed a policy of 'development in isolation' to the Brirish government in 1939 and its influence could be seen in the five

71. Archana Prasad, *Environmentalism and the Left: Contemporary Debates and Future Agendas in Tribal Areas* (New Delhi: Leftword, 2004).
72. Ibid., pp. 97–98.
73. Elwin had in total about 26 books, dealing with almost all the tribes in India. His works include: *Leaves from the Jungle, The Baiga* (1939); *The Agaria, Folk Tales of Mahakoshal* (1946); *Folk Songs of Chattisgarh* (1946); *The Muria and Their Ghotul* (1947); *The Religion of Indian Tribe*, etc.
74. According to Christoph von Fürer-Haimendorf's comment in *Anthropology Today* in 1985. Though there has been work of encyclopedic series on tribes in India by J. H. Hutton, J. P. Mills and other scholarly members of Indian Civil Services but as far as the degree of intimacy and vividness of presentation is concerned they cannot compete with Elwin's first major work. See http://www.jstor.org/view/0268540x/dm992841/90237q/0?frame

principles of Nehru's tribal Panchsheel, namely to allow people to develop along their own cultural lines, to respect land rights, to train tribals for the administration of the schemes, to work through tribal social institutions, and to judge results not by statistics and expenditure, but by the quality of human character that is evolved.[75]

But then again, the very adoption of the capitalist, economic, development paradigm weighed heavily on the tribals and resulted in marginalization and land alienation for 68 million tribals who constituted about 8 per cent of India's population.

After Independence, the tribal movements may be classified into three groups: (1) movements due to exploitation of outsiders (like those of Santhals and the Mundas), (2) movements due to economic deprivation (like those of Gonds in Madhya Pradesh and the Mahars in Andhra Pradesh), and (3) movements due to separatist tendencies (like those of Nagas and Mizos).[76]

The tribal movements may also be classified on the basis of their orientation into four types: (1) movement seeking political autonomy and formation of a state (Nagas, Mizos, Jharkhand), (2) agrarian movements, (3) forest-based movements, and (4) socio-religious or socio-cultural movements (the Bhagat movement among the Bhils of Rajasthan and Madhya Pradesh, movement among the tribals of south Gujarat or Raghunath Murmu's movement among Santhals).[77]

Surajit Sinha has also referred to five types of tribal movements in India:

(a) Ethnic (tribal) rebellions during the early days of the British rule in the 18th and 19th centuries: Sardar Larai (1885) and Birsa Movement (1895–1900) among the Munda; Ganganarain Hangama (1832) among the Bhumij; Kol rebellion (1832); Santhal rebellion (1857–58); Rebellion of the Kacha Nagas (1880s) and so on.

(b) Reform movements emulating the cultural pattern of the higher Hindu castes: Bhagat movement among the Oraon; Vaishnavite reform movements emulating the cultural pattern of higher Hindu castes: Bhagat movement among the Oraon; Vaishnavite reform movement among the Bhumij; social mobility movement Bhumij for Rajput recognition; Kherwar movement among the Santal and so on.

(c) Emergence of inter-tribal political associations and movements for recognition as 'tribal' states within the Indian Union in the post-Independence period: the Jharkhand movement among the tribes of Chhota Nagpur and Orissa; hills states movement in the Assam hills; Adisthan movement among the Bhil and so on.

---

75. See Katherine Charsley, '"Children of the Forest" or "Backward Communities": The Ideology of Tribal Development', Edinburgh papers in *South Asian Studies*, 7, 1997.
76. Ahuja, *Society in India*, p. 284.
77. Ibid.

(d) Violent secessionist movements among tribes located near the international frontier: the Nagaland movement; Mizo National Front movement and so on.

(e) Pockets of violent political movements in the tribal belt linked with the general problem of agrarian unrest and communist movement: Hajng unrest (1944); Naxalbari movement (1967); Girijan rebellion at Srikakulum (1968–69); Birsa dal movement in Ranchi (1968–69).[78]

All the above-mentioned tribal movements in India were mainly launched for liberation from (i) oppression and discrimination, (ii) neglect and backwardness, and (iii) a government which was callous to the tribals' poverty, hunger, unemployment and exploitation. Here, it is also important to mention that the withdrawal of the State from the social sector and its increasing tendency to privatize common and natural resources have further jeopardized the future of displaced people. For example, the controversy over the attempts to sell land to the S. Kumar Corporation on the banks of the Maheshwar dam by the Digvijay Singh government in the early 2000s is an example of the insensitivity of the government towards the interests of the affected people. On the other hand, any attempt by the people to relieve their own stress has been hindered by the state governments.[79]

Also, the recent Supreme Court verdict allowing the construction of the Sardar Sarovar dam when thousands of families still need rehabilitation is a violation of its own judgement of October 2000 and March 2005, that unambiguously state that further construction cannot happen until rehabilitation of temporarily and permanently affected families is completed as per the Narmada Tribunal award. Despite overwhelming evidence, protests in Delhi and a 20-day hunger strike, the Supreme Court and the Government of India turned a blind eye to this grave injustice.[80]

Women's Movements

Women's movements in India can be divided into three waves or periods:[81] 'The first wave saw social reform movements that began in the 19th century and mass mobilization of women in the national movement.'

After Independence, between 1950 and 1960, we find the growing legitimacy and power of the post-colonial State and various development plans that overpowered the other aspects of society. As a result, there was a lull in the various campaigning and political activities on the part of women.

---

78. Surajit Sinha, 'Tribal Solidarity Movements in India: A Review', in Ghanshyam Shah (ed.), *Social Movements and the State (Readings in Indian Government and Politics* Vol. 4) (New Delhi: Sage Publications, 2002) pp. 251–52.
79. Prasad, *Environmentalism and the Left*, p. 92.
80. http://www.narmada.org/sardarsarovar.html.
81. Shah, *Social Movements in India*, p. 152.

The period from the late 1960s onward can be called the second wave, which saw the resurgence of political activity from women. The very futility of the economic policies by the government that led to growing unemployment and price rise in India led to mass uprising. In the 1960s, women dissatisfied with the status quo joined the struggles of the rural poor and industrial working class.[82] The activities of women during this period can be well explained in the following words of Neera Desai: 'Participation of the women in Naxalbari movement, anti-price-rise demonstrations, Navnirman Movement in Gujarat and Bihar, rural revolt in Dhule District in Maharashtra and Chipko Movement provided a backdrop for the ensuing struggles on women's issues.'[83]

But at the same time, with the splintering of the Indian left by the early 1970s, there was a questioning of the earlier analysis of the revolution.[84] The Shahada movement in the Dhulia District of Maharashtra saw an active participation of women who began to take action against physical violence associated with alcoholism.[85] The period also saw the emergence of various women's organizations which included urban middle-class women as well as working women of various strata. The Self-Employed Women's Association (SEWA) in Ahmedabad and Working Women's Forum in Madras were formed in this period.[86]

This phase of women's struggle was associated with movements which were anti-feudal, anti-capitalist and anti-State in character as well as the beginning of women's organization in the informal sectors apart from formal party lines.

The Third Wave: While '[t]his second wave saw mass participation of women in popular upsurges against the government and the power structures in general, but the third wave, which can be said to emerge in the late 1970s, had a specific feminist focus'.[87] By the mid-1970s, devaluation of life had become an everyday experience for women.[88] This point was driven home by the report on the status of women in India:

---

82. Geraldine Forbes, *The New Cambridge History of India –IV.2– Women in Modern India.* (Cambridge, UK: Cambridge University Press, 2004) p. 242.
83. Quoted in ibid.
84. Nivedita Menon, 'Introduction', in her (ed.), *Gender and Politics in India* (New Delhi: Oxford University Press, 1999), p. 19.
85. Radha Kumar, 'From Chipko to Sati: The Contemporary Indian Women's Movement', in Amrita Basu (ed.), *Women's Movement in Global Perspective* (New Delhi: Kali for Women, 1995), pp. 60–61.
86. Nivedita Menon, 'Introduction', p. 19.
87. Ibid.
88. Vina Mazumdar and Indu Agnihotri, 'The Women's Movement in India: Emergence of New Perspective', in Bharati Ray and Aparna Basu (eds.), *From Independence Towards Freedom: Indian Women Since 1947* (New Delhi: Oxford University Press, 1999), pp. 229.

> The committee's findings made it clear that the disenchantment of women with the post-Independence development scenario was not a stance dictated by exogenous political considerations. Demographic indicators such as the accelerated decline in the sex ratio, increasing gender gaps in life expectancy, mortality and economic participation, or the rising migration rate were disturbing enough. But the utter failure of the State policy to live up to its constitutional mandates in any field of national development was found to have, in fact, contributed, even accelerated these trends. The committee noted clear linkages between existing and growing social economic disparities and women's status in education, the economy, society and polity.[89]

The period, therefore, saw the growth of 'autonomous' women's groups in towns and cities without party affiliations or formal hierarchical structures, although individual members often had party connections.[90]

> The distinguishing features of the new women's groups were that they declared themselves to be 'feminist' despite the fact that most of their members were drawn from the left, which saw feminism as bourgeois and diverse; that they insisted on being autonomous even though most of their members were affiliated to other political groups, generally of the far Left; and that they rapidly built networks among one another, ideological differences notwithstanding'.[91]

The critique from women in the left parties was that these 'autonomous' groups were urban and middle class and therefore could not represent the Indian women, and the role of feminists was therefore, to raise questions within mass organizations.[92] However, feminists within autonomous groups pointed out that left parties and trade unions were as patriarchal as any other and so it was necessary to stay independent while allying on a broad platform.[93] Many groups opted for autonomy, which was defined by separate, women-only groups without any party affiliation or conventional organizational structure, for they considered this hierarchical, self-interested, and competitive'.[94]

The women's movement in the late 1970s added growing violence as a major issue.[95] The movement, in its interaction with the State and other levels of society leaned heavily on the legal, educational and political processes to redirect the change towards empowerment—for equality and participation.[96]

---

89. Ibid., pp. 229–30.
90. Menon, 'Introduction', p. 19.
91. Kumar, 'From Chipko to Sati', p. 64.
92. Menon, 'Introduction', p. 19.
93. Ibid.
94. Kumar, 'From Chipko to Sati', p. 64.
95. Mazumdar and Agnihotri, 'The Women's Movement in India', p. 230.
96. Ibid.

The women's campaign during this period, therefore, prominently focused on violence against women and included cases of dowry deaths and rape.[97] Further, the growing forces of religious fundamentalism in the 1980s also threatened women's interest. The issue of personal, or religion-based and differentiated family laws became especially controversial for feminists in 1985 in what is now referred to as the Shah Bano case.[98] Earlier, between the period of 1982 and 1983, attempts were made by Hindu rightist forces to revive sati (the practice of immolating widows on their husband's funeral pyres). The death of Roop Kanwar became the symbol of Rajput identity politics.[99] In fact, the 1980s saw the growth and spread of the politics of identity and the increasing use of violence for political ends.[100]

The late 1980s saw a period when women's autonomous groups became funded non-governmental organizations (NGOs) along with large-scale co-option of the feminist rhetoric by the State. This funding by international agencies, in addition to the danger of co-option of taking up and 'successfully' completing specific projects meant that there was hardly any thought given to what constitutes 'feminism'.[101] Thus, autonomous women's groups, which emerged as an attempt to create spaces outside the orthodoxies of party women's wings, are now far from autonomous of the compulsions of getting and retaining funding.[102]

The 1990s, on the other hand, saw the emergence of a common platform for women at the national level with women's wings of national level political parties—All India Democratic Women's Association, All India Women's Conference, National Federation of Indian Women, Mahila Dakshata Samiti—and three national level women's organizations—the YWCA, the Joint Women's Programme and Centre for Women's Development Studies—getting together on specific issues, such as the recent bill on reservations for women in Parliament[103] and the Domestic Violence Act, 2006.[104]

Thus, the contemporary Indian women's movement has turned out to be rather complex in its character and 'encompasses and links such issues as work,

---

97. In fact, domestic violence as a criminal offence was first recognized in India in 1983 and the penal code was amended to include cruelty by the husband or his family against married women as a crime. Those found guilty could be imprisoned for up to three years and fined. See FACTBOX—Some Facts about Domestic Violence in India, 26 Oct 2006 in http://www.alertnet.org/the newsdesk/DEL271185.
98. Kumar, 'From Chipko to Sati', pp. 77–83.
99. Ibid.
100. See Radha Kumar, 'Identity Politics and the Contemporary Indian Feminist Movement', in Valentine M. Moghadam (ed.), *Identity Politics and Women: Cultural Reassertions and Feminisms in International Perspective* (Oxford, UK: Westview, 1994). Also see Anand Patwardan's film, *Father, Son and the Holy War*.
101. Menon, 'Introduction', pp. 20–21.
102. Ibid., p. 21.
103. Ibid.
104. See 'Domestic Violence Act Takes Effect Today', *The Hindu*, 26 October 2006, p. 1.

wages, environment, ecology, civil rights, sex, violence, representation, caste, class, allocation of basic resources, consumer rights, health, religion, community, and individual and social relationships'.[105] However, atrocities against women seem to be on the rise, the court fights most often proved futile and for all its creativity and new thinking as well as assertion at the grassroots level, the new women's movement has been unable to build a mass power to confront the forces of patriarchy and exploitation.[106]

Representation and Social Justice

The 'new social forces' that emerged through the movements of Dalits, OBCs, *adivasis* and women came up after there was a 'crisis of representation' as far as political parties were concerned. The issue of representation as an integral part of the contemporary democratic set up is mainly identified by various political parties taking up issues of various sections including the under-privileged sections of a society. However, when the interests of these very sections were found wanting, movements came up to rescue them. The State on its part also provided certain safeguards to disadvantaged sections of the society, through what is known as affirmative actions. Through affirmative actions the State grants certain privileges to the underprivileged sections of society, which include various land reforms, redistribution of society's resources, reservations, etc., also known as protective discrimination. This is in consonance with the very aim of social justice[107] (along with economic and political) enshrined in the very preamble of our Constitution, thereby granting special safeguards in Articles 15 and 16 of the Constitution. Further, these special privileges represented various groups that were historically disprivileged and who required a level playing field to exercise their right to equality of opportunity. These included SCs, STs, OBCs and women.

---

105. Kumar, 'From Chipko to Sati'. p. 83.
106. Gail Omvedt, p. 97. For example, in 2005, 6,787 cases of dowry-related deaths were recorded. According to 2005 report by the United Nations Population Fund (UNPF), more than two-thirds of married women in India between the ages of 15 and 49 are victims of wife beating, rape or forced sex. According to National Crime Records Bureau, there were 155, 553 crimes committed against women in 2005 and according to women's groups the real figure could be ten times more as many cases go unreported with victims unwilling to speak out fearing the shame and stigma associated with being a divorced or separated women. 'FACTBOX—Some Facts About Domestic Violence in India, 26 Oct, 2006' in http://www.alertnet.org/thenewsdesk/DEL271185.htm.
107. The term social justice is a combination of two words, 'social' and 'justice, where 'social' means pertaining to society including various socio-economic relations. 'Justice', if viewed in relation with the social aspect, is an intelligent cooperation of people in producing an organically united society with every member having an equal and real opportunity to live and grow. Social justice, therefore, stands for revision of social order and a redistribution of rights and which includes remedial actions towards the disprivileged sections of society, which have been historically deprived of material resources as morally equal beings.

However, the argument that is made for their respective representation is largely understood for all the wrong reasons. It is either seen as compensation for historical deprivation (through reservation quotas in legislature, educational institutions and in employment alone), including the demand for economic criteria for reservation or as representation of various identities. But, here it is to be made clear that for economic disadvantages there are ameliorative measures like poverty alleviation programmes and as far as group representation is concerned, it should be argued that positive discrimination is not for accommodating differences but it is for doing away with unequal relations among people that place them at a disadvantage, and social justice in India is basically furthering this aim of **egalitarianism**.[108]

Social justice, therefore, invokes a substantive concept of justice and unlike **procedural justice**,[109] it also deals with background fairness. To elaborate this, we can say that all modern States are based on the belief in some sort of equality and claim to treat their citizens equally. Minimally, it implies political and civil liberties, equal rights before the law, equal protection against arbitrary arrest, and so forth. These things provide a basis of a society of equal citizens.

However, these rights and freedom cannot stand by themselves. More than a formal level of equality is required (if the minimal demands are to be met). It is a familiar point that equality before the law does not come to much if one cannot afford a good lawyer. The 'equal freedom' of which modern democratic states boast should amount to more (as Anatole France observed) than the freedom to sleep on park benches and under bridges. Every body needs the means to make use of their freedom, which otherwise would be hollow.[110]

Social justice, therefore, tries to go behind the structure of rules to determine who is in need, say of health care, educational opportunity, housing and so on. However, some economic and social theorist suggests that these problems might be overcome by a welfare policy, which guarantees the payment of 'negative income' tax to those where earning falls below a certain level.[111] A cash payment of this kind could be spent by the individual as he wished. The school of social justice argues that this cannot take into account special circumstances such as large families, or physical and mental handicap, which generates special needs. Social justice requires that structures should be adapted and influenced

---

108. Egalitarianism holds that if people are unequally situated in a given social order, then they should be treated differently. Therefore, it reconsiders that procedural fairness needs to be supplemented by measures so that those who are unequally situated can enjoy rough and ready equality.
109. Procedural justice is associated with various rights of the individuals and in narrowed sense used to morally evaluate the actions of the individuals in terms of fairness.
110. Commission on Social Justice, 'What Is Social Justice?' in Christopher Pierson and Frances G. Castles (eds.), *The Welfare State: A Reader* (Oxford: Polity Press, Blackwell, 2000), p. 54.
111. See Milton Fisk, *The State and Justice: An Essay in Political Theory* (Cambridge, UK: Cambridge University Press, 1989), pp. 185–86.

in ways that can give more people a better chance in the first place. That is why opportunities and breaking down barriers are so important.[112] Thus, inequalities that are permissible in social justice through, say, affirmative actions and positive discrimination are acceptable. This aim becomes all the more necessary with regard to the vast inequalities (both horizontal and vertical) that exist in our country.[113] Therefore, protective discrimination authorized by the Constitution is envisaged as an exceptional and temporary measure to be used only for the purpose of mitigating inequalities; it is designed to disappear along with these inequalities. Nehru believed that the aim of protective discrimination was to eliminate inequalities based on past prejudices associated with the discriminatory social structure of society.[114] The Constitution-makers did not include it as a device to consolidate and protect the separate integrity of communal groups.[115]

However, it has been observed with regard to contemporary developments in case of affirmative action programme in general, and protective discrimination in particular under the rubric of social justice is that social justice seems to be missing and is being misinterpreted—whether it has been mobilization of caste groups for garnering votes and creating factions concentrating only on getting reservation and political power, or/and stressing the economic criteria (or economic backwardness) for reservation. Social justice seems to be missing in all these cases. Amidst such trends, Hasan observes: 'Despite the steady increases in participation in elections from the lower social order, still there remains a central contradiction at the heart of Indian democracy: an inclusive polity has so far not made for a more just and equal society'.[116]

Social justice in the present context has, therefore, been reduced to reservation, which is regarded as the only criteria for social equality. However, what has been missed here is that without tough measure at the basic level (for example, education, land reforms, etc.), this soft option of reservation will prove void. Long term measures are, therefore, found wanting in the present time.

---

112. Commission on Social Justice, 'What Is Social Justice?', pp. 55–57.
113. Zoya Hasan, 'More Equal but Still Not Equal? State and Inter-Group Equality in Contemporary India', in Imtiaz Ahmed, Partha S. Ghosh and Helmut Reifield (eds.), *Pluralism and Equality: Values in Indian Society and Politics* (New Delhi: Sage Publications, 2000), pp. 80–100. According to Hasan, inequality in India is historical as well as modern, horizontal as well as vertical. Historically, horizontal inequality is marked by the pluralism of religious, regional, linguistic and ethnic communities, while vertical inequalities can be illustrated by reference to the hierarchically ordered caste system and socio-economic inequalities expressed through class structure.
114. P. Singh, *Equality, Reservation and Discrimination in India: A Constitutional Study of Scheduled Castes and Scheduled Tribes and Other Backward Classes* (Delhi: Deep and Deep, 1982), p. 99.
115. Weiner, 'The Struggle for Equality', p. 20. See *Constituent Assembly Debates*, Vol. 8, *16th May–16th June 1949* (New Delhi: Lok Sabha Secretariat, 2001), p. 311.
116. Hasan, 'Representation and Redistribution', p. 370.

Today, politicians pick and choose which identity they want to use as the basis for political mobilization and socialization. Whichever identity they emphasize, the rhetoric is invariably one of 'social justice' and equality.[117]

NSMs, which represented various group interests and could have played a key role in bringing social justice to Dalits, women, *adivasis* and OBCs, were found to be wanting in their very aim and now seem to have disappeared. The Dalit movement, which started with vigour got engulfed in party politics, the OBCs seemed happy securing power through reservation, the fights of *adivasis* end up in courts but they remain as ignored a community as they were before, and women's movements have been reduced to functioning as NGOs, or at the most end up in courts—social injustice, however, still persists.

CONCLUSION

The rise of new social movements in India marked an important phenomenon for the Indian democracy. NSMs, in fact, deepened the very notion of democracy. India with its newly found independence and its establishment of democratic structure moved ahead in its assertion of the concept of democracy with the emergence of new social movements.

Democracy no longer remained an empty concept of mainly elections and plebiscite and thereby legitimization of State power. The very emergence of these movements made it clear that democracy creates its own space and is not just a State entity. The rise of Dalits, OBCs, *adivasis* and women as new social forces enriched the democracy by invoking the very concept of a civil society.

Civil society has become the leitmotif of movements struggling to free themselves from unresponsive and often tyrannical post-colonial elites. If the first wave of liberation took place along with decolonization, the second wave comes up against those very elites who had taken over power after decolonization.[118]

The upheaval of new, social movements raises their voices against the authoritative, oppressive and exploitative institutions, including the State and its notion of development and, thereby, reviews the fact that democracy needs to be looked in its fundamental and value-based basic principles of liberty and equality. Chandhoke writes:

> I see the beginning of an authentic civil society in the voice of those who insist that the state listens, in the voice of those who have raised issues

117. Weiner, 'The Struggle for Equality', p. 208.
118. Neera Chandhoke, 'The Assertion of Civil Society Against the State: The Case of the Post-Colonial World', in Manoranjan Mohanty, Partha Nath Mukherjee with Olle Tornquist (eds.), *People's Rights: Social Movements and the State in the Third World* (New Delhi: Sage Publications, 1998), p. 30.

> outside the ambit of norms laid down by the state—ecology, gender, class—in the resistance of those who refuse to let the state site its projects wherever it places, in the voice of those who reject corrupt elites in the political passions of those whose nerves are not numbed by consumer capitalism, in the letters to the newspapers, in oral communication. These are people who do not opt out of civil society but who demand that the state deliver what it has promised in the Constitution and the law, who demand state accountability, who expand the sphere of rights to encompass those which has arisen out of the struggles of the people.[119]

The NSMs have, therefore, made an important beginning in awakening the society against the injustices that were being dished out in the immediate post-Independence period. But what needs to be seen in today's context is the fact as to whether they were able to achieve what they were making their stand for. What have been the consequences of such movements? Have they been able to assert the very principles of democracy?

Today, we see NSMs are also about class because of the very socio-economic deprivation that still persists, thereby raising issues of rights, justice and equality. Also, we find that these movements are now struggling for State power (BSP struggles for power at the State). Thus, NSMs are now not very different from social movements. What we now see is either an 'NGOization' of social movements, which are like active citizens' group but which stick to the limits because of the involvement of large national and international funds, diverting from the real cause and end up becoming lobbies or politicization of various groups by various political parties for garnering votes for state power.[120] Then, there are social movements, like the Narmada Bachao Andolan (NBA) and other women's issues, which have ended in courts rather than active role by the State and the verdict of the courts have not been that fair either. And, if there have been any issues that have come up in recent times, they have all been mere campaigns.

The present scenario finds a critical situation for NSMs and which in the words of Omvedt can be called as 'the crisis of movement'. In fact, the NSMs find themselves in completely different direction, somewhere in the politics of reservation, in the politics of power struggle, in the politics of the whole notion of development. Today, we find the atrocities against Dalits, *adivasis* and women are still persistent and social justice has lost its very essence.

So, where do we see ourselves from here? We started with great hope when the NSMs were launched. However, all of it did not go in vain. NSMs did make an initiation in breaking down the barriers of caste, class, gender and other such

---

119. Ibid., p. 41.
120. In a survey conducted to explore the crisis of representation, people were asked which agency they would generally approach to solve their problems, and it was noted that not a single person had taken the help of NGOs. See Chandhoke, 'Revisiting the Crisis of Representation Thesis', pp. 308–30.

oppressions. But it seems that somewhere down the line they lost their way. Perhaps, we need to review, relocate or, as Gail Omvedt suggests, reinvent the revolution.

Suggested Readings

Omvedt, Gail. *Reinventing Revolution*. Armok: N. E. Sharpe, 1993.

Rao, M. S. A. (ed.). *Social Movements in India: Studies in Peasant, Backward Classes, Sectarian, Tribal and Women's Movements*. New Delhi: Manohar Publications, 2000[1984].

Ray, R. and M. Katzenstein. *Social Movements in India: Poverty, Power and Politics*. Oxford, UK: Rowman and Littlefield, 2005.

Shah, Ghanshyam. *Social Movements and the State*. New Delhi: Sage Publications, 2002.

———. *Social Movements in India: A Review of Literature*. New Delhi: Sage Publications, 2004.

Questions

1. What is a social movement? What is the difference between social movements and new social movements?
2. Discuss the various stages of the women's movement in India. Do you think it has positively impacted gender relations in society?
3. Write a short essay on the Dalit movement in India.
4. How are representation and social justice related?

Politics

The Nature and Functioning of Democracy

13

Swaha Das and Hari Nair

It is often claimed that India is the world's largest democracy. This claim is based on the fact that there are more eligible voters in India than in any other country. But, if there are more eligible voters, it is largely because of the overwhelming size of the Indian population. Nonetheless, would this one statistical detail make our country effectively democratic? We shall, in the following pages, attempt to answer this question by discussing the nature of Indian democracy and its functioning. In other words, the aim of this chapter is to broadly map certain outstanding aspects of Indian democracy at the turn of the century. These issues will be discussed in detail in the following chapters of this book.

In order to engage with the broad theme of Indian democracy, we shall first try and understand what the term democracy in general implies and why it is so sought after. Then, we shall broadly sketch the origins of democracy in independent India. Afterwards, by broadly basing ourselves on the paradigm suggested by Atul Kohli in *The Success of India's Democracy*,[1] we shall deal with the functioning of Indian democracy in two part. In the first part, we shall outline how the Indian State has worked towards consolidating its democratic institutions; and then we shall look at how marginalized groups and the national **civil society** have used the democratic institutions of the Indian State to assert their rights. Before concluding this essay, we shall consider the most disturbing critiques made against Indian democracy because no overview of the subject would do justice to it otherwise. However, we must also remind ourselves that the scope of the subject of Indian democracy is so vast that any attempt to sum it up in a few pages runs many a risk.

UNDERSTANDING DEMOCRACY

An oft-quoted answer to the question, 'What is democracy?' is the phrase attributed to Abraham Lincoln from his Gettysburg address of 1863: 'it is the government

1. Atul Kohli, 'Introduction', in his (ed.), *The Success of India's Democracy* (Cambridge, UK: Cambridge University Press, 2001), pp. 3–4.

of the people, for the people and by the people.' This idea is also supported by the etymology of the word 'democracy', which means the rule (*kratos*) by many people (*demos*). It could thus be distinguished from 'aristocracy', which means the rule by the wise; from oligarchy, which means rule by strong groups like certain families; and from monarchy, which means rule by an individual. It is, however, not easy to box democracy into a definition because it is a multi-faceted concept. Nonetheless, it is identified with political equality of citizens on the basis of their equal moral status. Such a notion of equality is manifested in equal political rights for all citizens. Nevertheless, democracy has of late been formally linked to electoral aspects.

Democracy has become increasingly appealing in the modern world, especially in the second half of the 20th century. The reason for that lies in the nature and functioning of the contemporary State. The State is best understood as an institution with a monopoly over the legitimate use of force within a certain area, to maintain order within its territory as well as to secure its frontiers. Naturally, this makes the governing authorities of a State extremely powerful as they control the instruments of force. With this arises the danger of their misuse of power and it is in this context that popular control over government assumes such immense importance. It is believed that if popular sovereignty determines who should occupy positions of power and for how long, then, democratic governments could minimize the possibility of the concentration of political power in the hands of one or a few.

The Prussian philosopher, Immanuel Kant (1724–1804), believed that if more countries across the world became democratic, then there would be a greater likelihood of perpetual peace because democracies have fewer chances of fighting each other. Such a belief is based on the assumption that public opinion within democratic countries would prevent their governments from going to war.[2] Therefore, when independent India chose democratic institutions of government, she was greeted with cheer but not without doubts about her ability to consolidate and deepen the country's newly born democratic structure.

Origins of Democracy in Independent India

Indian democracy not only incorporates elements from Graeco-Roman, French, British and American traditions but also certain indigenous aspects particular to our own culture. Democracy in independent India took root in a terrain, which

---

2. However, recent international events would remind us that popular protests across the world could not deter the US-led invasion of Iraq in 2003. This shows that the historically unprecedented act of venting of public opinion by large sections of the international civil society through global mass media, which was exerting popular pressure on governments was not sufficient to avoid wars.

was considered inhospitable.[3] The pre-conditions for the establishment of democracy, such as, an industrialized developed economy, an ethnically homogenous population and a civic culture hospitable to democracy were all missing from the Indian scenario. Yet, the consolidation of democracy in the country, despite its many failures, is evidence of a remarkable achievement of the Indian people.

The makers of the Indian Constitution believed that democracy in independent India must initiate a democratic process of governance, but more importantly, it must also aid the growth of a democratic society. This broad conceptual understanding of democracy makes it the most crucial idea that is present in the Constitution of India, which is the founding document of our **republic**. Those who framed the Indian Constitution believed that democracy was necessary and inevitable for bringing about equality between its citizens in all spheres of socio-political life, and thus, ensure justice for all.

The fundamental document for a study of the nature and functioning of democracy in independent India is our Constitution, promulgated on 26 January 1950. Ideologically and otherwise, many portions of this text derive from the Government of India Act of 1935, which was the last major framework under which the British had ruled India till 1947. Many important features of the Indian polity are a continuation of the British political practice. These include, amongst others, the liberal-democratic nature of the Indian constitution, parliamentary form of government, the Indian Civil Service and the unitary character of the Indian State, whereby the emergency and residual powers lie with the central government.

However, the Indian Constitution broke away from the colonial legacy in many important aspects. First, in defending the Indian Constitution, Sarvepalli Radhakrishnan demonstrated that the republican tradition was not foreign to India, for we had had it since the beginning of our history. In saying so, he was also arguing against the European historicist tradition, most clearly manifested in the works of John Stuart Mill. The latter had declared that Indians were not as yet fit to rule themselves and that the huge illiterate population was a hindrance to the implementation of adult suffrage. Dr Radhakrishnan dismissed Mill's claim and declared that all Indians, irrespective of gender and education, were always suited for self-rule.[4]

---

3. The author of *Democracy in America*, Alexis de Tocqueville, was a Frenchman who travelled through the United States of America in the 19th century. He believed that the prevalence of democracy in the USA was the consequence of two conditions: civic culture and equality of condition. By the term equality of condition, he was referring to the process of conducting elections, the equal access of citizens for holding public office and to anti-aristocratic tendencies. By the term civic culture, he was referring to the involvement of the Americans in popular organizations and their participation in democratic organs of local self-rule, which in turn led the citizens to develop a democratic civic spirit. Thus, for Tocqueville, the foundations of democratic government had to be rooted in the 'habits and hearts' of the citizens.
4. Dipesh Chakrabarty, *Provincializing Europe: Post-colonial Thought and Historical Difference* (Princeton, NJ: Princeton University Press, 2007), pp. 9–10.

Second, the Indian Constitution made the Fundamental Rights of citizens sacred. This was designed to avoid any arm of the Indian State from trespassing on the terrain marked out for citizens' rights. Consequently, this has of late resulted in a kind of judicial activism.[5] However, the founding fathers of the Indian Constitution believed that the rights discourse alone could not ensure equality of all its citizens, which made it necessary for them to include a section called the Directive Principles of State Policy, whereby the State was directed to implement the necessary reforms to actualize the Fundamental Rights.[6] Other important features of post-colonial Indian democracy like universal adult suffrage; federalism, particularly, the administrative division of India on the basis of linguistic states; affirmative action for the depressed classes; and secularism, visible in the absence of a State religion and the protection of the rights of religious minorities were influenced and shaped by the democratic content of the Indian national movement.[7]

Towards Consolidating Indian Democracy[8]

Democratic consolidation in India involves the entrenchment of democratic values among the intellectual and social elites as well as strengthening democratic institutions of the State. Some of the more significant features of the consolidation of Indian democracy are: an inclusive civil service avoiding nepotism in the administrative structure, the acceptance of parliamentary democracy by major communist and socialist organizations from their initial ambivalent or antagonistic attitudes towards electoral democracy, the decline of the Congress party with its family/personality-centred rule, the civilian control of the military

5. By judicial activism, we are referring to the acts by various strata of the Indian judiciary in proactively harnessing the obligations of the legislative and the executive wings of the Indian State.
6. The Indian Constitution does not explicitly define a Fundamental Right.
7. Rajeev Bhargava, 'Democratic Vision of a New Republic: India, 1950', in Francine Frankel, Zoya Hasan, Rajeev Bhargava and Balveer Arora (eds.), *Transforming India: Social and Political Dynamics of Democracy* (New Delhi: Oxford University Press, 2000), pp. 26–59 and Sumit Sarkar, 'Indian Democracy: The Historical Inheritance', in Atul Kohli (ed.), *The Success of Indian Democracy* (Cambridge, UK: Cambridge University Press, 2001), pp. 23–46.
8. Democratic consolidation refers to the recognition of democracy as the only acceptable way to resolve conflicts in society. This process includes three important elements: the behavioural, the attitudinal and the constitutional aspects. First of all, the behavioural aspect refers to a situation where no significant actors try to achieve their objectives by creating a non-democratic regime or turning to violence or foreign intervention to secede from the State. The attitudinal aspect refers to a situation where most citizens believe that democratic procedures and institutions are the best means to govern their collective life. The constitutional aspect refers to a situation where the governmental and non-governmental forces become accustomed to the idea of resolution of conflicts within the specific laws, procedures and institutions sanctioned by the democratic process. See Juan J. Linz and Alfred Stepan, Problems of Democratic Transition and Consolidation: Southern Europe, South America and Post-Communist Europe (Baltimore, MD: Johns Hopkins University Press, 1996).

and the latter's non-interference in politics. In the following paragraphs, we shall take a look at some of the more outstanding phenomena of recent years in the process of democratic consolidation in India:

i) judicial activism
ii) the recent work of the Election Commission of India
iii) the new panchayati raj or the consolidation of the institutions of local governance
iv) the right to information

The Supreme Court and the high courts in the states, which comprise the higher judiciary, have played an important role in the process of democratic consolidation. From the 1980s, the higher judiciary began to entertain public interest litigations (PILs) related to a wide variety of goals and causes, but all of them were centred on the principle of acquiring the common good of Indian citizens and protecting their rights. These cases were often related to the protection of ecology, human rights of the poor and the powerless against State abuses, particularly custodial torture and rape. Such litigations filed by members of civil society laid the foundation for what is commonly referred to as judicial activism. This term refers to the proactive role played by the higher judiciary in protecting the citizens' rights and in safeguarding public goods.

The activism of the higher judiciary is founded on the Indian Constitution by virtue of its hybrid nature that conjoined the British tradition of parliamentary supremacy with the judicial review based on the American practice. The original powers of the Supreme Court of India include Article 131 and Article 32 of the Constitution. While the former grants it the exclusive jurisdictional authority over federal disputes, the latter permits the Supreme Court to issue directions, orders or writs for the enforcement of Fundamental Rights. However, in the case of India, this has sometimes led to a conflictive relationship between Parliament and the Judiciary.

A few notable instances of such conflicts led to landmark judgements in two cases, *Golaknath vs Punjab* (1967) and *Kesavananda Bharati vs State of Kerala* (1973). The judgement in the first case held that the Parliament could not amend Fundamental Rights, while in the latter, the court declared that the basic structures of the Constitution cannot be altered. Very recently, the Supreme Court has also questioned the rule of keeping certain laws and provisions outside the purview of the judiciary. Briefly put, public interest litigations form part of the attempt by the higher judiciary to protect the law against abuses by the two other arms of the State. Votaries of judicial activism claim that this phenomenon is a response to the moral corruption of other institutions of governance.

At the beginning of the decade of the 1990s, when trust of the people in the institutional arms of the Indian State was fast eroding due to the phenomenon of the criminalization of politics, the Election Commission of India rose to the occasion by attempting to fulfil its constitutional obligations by ensuring free and fair elections. The work of the Election Commission for consolidating Indian democracy is commendable for the following reasons: first, it deals with an electorate of 600 million people, of which 57 per cent vote; second, it has been found that the participation in elections is higher among the poorly educated as well as the depressed classes and castes than the 'higher' castes and classes.[9] An interesting detail is that higher numbers have been noted at local levels than in elections to the Union parliament. Does the latter point towards a popular desire for the decentralization of governance?

The sharing of power among different politico-administrative units and the decentralization of governance is an important aspect of the Indian process of democratic consolidation. Within the ambit of political studies, this subject has been discussed under the title of federalism or centre–state relations and *panchayati raj*. The former refers to the capabilities of the federal-system to accept, accommodate and even celebrate diversity in all its forms without sacrificing the stability of federal governance.[10] The latter refers to the process of incorporating village, municipal/intermediate and district-level elites and masses into the democratic process. It became a law in 1992 and is often referred to as the 73rd Constitutional Amendment. This form of governance had at least three advantages: it offered a non-violent middle path between centralized bureaucratic planning and a revolution from below, it utilized resources tied down in the country side, and crucially, strengthened a mixed economy.[11] Experts like Subrata Mitra argue that in the case of India, in general, the level of trust in local government is higher than that in state governments or the central government. Notwithstanding this, he argues that there is a severe deficit in people's trust in *panchayati raj* governance in states like Bihar, while the case is the opposite in Maharashtra and Bengal.[12]

On 15 June 2005, the president of the republic gave his assent to the Right to Information Act of India, which permits all Indian citizens to obtain information from any public authority in the country.[13] Importantly, this Act places the onus on the government to deliver information to its citizens. The promulgation of the RTI Act is based on the fundamental belief that the production and storage of information by the State actually belongs to its citizens and, therefore, the people have a right to know how it is being put to use. Administrators have often

9. Lloyd I. Rudolph and Susan H. Rudolph, 'Redoing the Constitutional Design: From an Interventionist to a Regulatory State', in Kohli (ed.), *The Success of Indian Democracy*, p. 156.
10. This subject will be dealt in much detail elsewhere in this book.
11. Subrata K. Mitra, 'Making Local Government Work…', in Kohli (ed.), *The Success of Indian Democracy*, p. 109–10.
12. Ibid.
13. As is the case with most laws, there are exceptions to this rule as well. Please refer to the particular Act.

inclined to widen the gap that separates the rulers from the ruled by hoarding information. Such tendencies have resulted in arbitrariness, unaccountability and lack of transparency in decision-making regarding matters that lie in the public domain.

The RTI Act (2005) attempts to consolidate democracy in India by strengthening the notion of equality between the governing and the governed. It also works to offset the imperialist culture of governance created by the provisions of the Indian Evidence Act (1872) and the Official Secrets Act (1923). Ever since the pioneering legislation in the field enacted by the Tamil Nadu legislature in April 1996, the movement to exercise the citizen's right to information has gained considerable momentum. However, the history and the scope of the Right to Information Act, through its newly founded institutional agencies represented by the Central and State Information Commissions, is in a state of continuous evolution to anticipate a balanced critique of its functioning.[14]

Democratic Deepening in India

Although democracy formally took root in India at the time of Independence in 1947, this was only a beginning. The prevalence of widespread economic inequality, the lack of access to primary education and medical care, the absence of respect for cultures that are not one's own, and the deprivation faced by marginalized groups are certain manifestations of the failure of both the Indian State and the national civil society. Both these actors have a long way to go before satisfactorily realizing democratic egalitarianism in a substantive sense.

The complex process of deepening democracy in India necessarily involves two kinds of actors: the State as well as non-State actors. While in the previous section, we discussed the efforts of the State at consolidating democratic institutions, we ought to realize that the role of non-State actors in deepening democracy in India is equally striking. This process has involved the use of non-electoral means, such as the expression of dissent through the mass media and through public demonstrations by marginalized groups to assert their rightful presence within the Indian **nation**. They demand that the State ought to respond satisfactorily to their claims of greater inclusion within the mainstream society and the appropriate recognition of their rights and their differences. In this section, we will look at two instances of growing mobilization among marginalized sections to demand greater democratization.

Ever since Independence, democratic deepening has been accompanied by an attack on the hierarchies of the traditional caste system. However, it is striking

14. Given the quasi-judicial, quasi-executive nature of the Information Commission, which is the appellate authority as envisioned in the Right to Information Act, 2005, it so appears that the Indian State is moving towards a more democratic and more egalitarian culture of governance.

that members of the marginalized castes have asserted their caste identity and have politically mobilized themselves to demand an equal status, on par with other castes rather than raising demands for the abolition of the caste system in toto. The marginalized castes chose the term Dalit instead of the apparently patronizing term Harijan, which was introduced by Mahatma Gandhi to denominate the marginalized castes. This struggle of symbols cannot be missed. A prominent Dalit activist from Maharashtra, Namdeo Dhasal, sought to convert the term into a rallying point in the fight for social injustice. This auto-referential term Dalit showed the importance of naming oneself through the agency of the oppressor. However, the paradox of the political struggle by the marginalized castes has only resulted in the growing political importance of caste.[15]

The presence of democratic institutions is largely responsible for the growing consciousness and political mobilization of marginalized castes in their demand for equal status and equal respect. The electoral process has not only enabled the expression of dissent but has also widened caste distinctions. At the same time, the democratic process has incorporated castes previously excluded from political power. It has provided spaces for the pursuit of self-protection, self-respect as well as for material benefits to individuals through group membership. In this context, the steady rise of the Bahujan Samaj Party founded by Kanshi Ram to represent Dalits in 1984 and claiming to be inspired by the ideas of B. R. Ambedkar is the most noteworthy case.

We could understand social movements as a collective action on the part of civil society to effect change. These movements have for long been a permanent feature of Indian social life and have explored and defined new democratic spaces in India. Such movements have highlighted the participatory nature of democracy by aiming to achieve social justice in a more substantive sense. While social movements centred on questions of identity formation have engaged with the electoral process, other issue-based movements like those concerned with ecology or women have largely remained disengaged from the electoral process. The latter kind of social movements have concerned themselves with grass-root level activism and have engaged with the judicial and bureaucratic wings of the Indian State.

In the process of consolidating and deepening democracy, social movements have opened up new spaces for the identification and critical assessment of social practices as well as government policies. Their vision of bringing about a democratic society, and not merely a democratic polity, by empowering marginalized groups has been carried out by imaginative and novel methods such as literacy campaigns, workshops, *nukkad natak*, protests, *dharna*, publications and films. These have created new, democratic spaces and have deepened consciousness on issues related to social justice. As recently as September 2007, such activism was displayed by women students of the University of Delhi, as they protested against

---

15. Myron Weiner, 'The Struggle for Equality: Caste in Indian Poltilics', in Kohli (ed.), *The Success of Indian Democracy*, pp. 193–225.

the apathy of the administration in cases of sexual harassment—a rather common phenomenon in Delhi. This particular movement has created consciousness about the sexual harassment policy of the University as well as the necessity of a gender-sensitization of the police force. It also sought to question societal and cultural prejudices against victims of sexual harassment.

The role played by the Self-Employed Women's Association (SEWA), the Narmada Bachao Andolan (NBA), the Mazdoor Kisan Shakti Sangathan (MKSS), and other similar organizations in raising political awareness about the aims and potential beneficiaries of public policy has provided unrepresented groups with the means to locate the structural causes of inequality in the development policies of the Indian State. The recent march of Janadesh (October 2007) from Gwalior to Delhi, comprising tribes, Dalits and landless tillers from villages of 15 Indian states has raised questions about the need for land reforms, the demand for rights to land and livelihood, and the creation of special economic zones that have led to widespread dispossession of land and displacement of the dispossessed. The demands include the establishment of a national land authority to provide a clear statement on land use in the country, the identification of lands available for redistribution and the regularization of landholdings of the poor and marginal groups.

Critiques of Indian Democracy

Despite the many successes attributed to Indian democracy, the State has failed in eradicating massive poverty and continuing violence against religious minorities, depressed castes, tribes and women. Lopsided planning and the semi-feudal, semi-capitalist economic structure of the country have resulted in armed struggles against the Indian State in many parts. Although the ethical nature of the means of such fights is debatable, their causes certainly are not. Huge portions of India's population struggle weakly against inhuman living conditions. Therefore, the principal cause perhaps lies in the Indian State's failure to protect the rights of the poor and the landless. History has repeatedly shown us that the use of the repressive apparatus of the State against these 'genuine' struggles for equality has only aggravated problems rather than resolving them.

To make matters worse, the subject of economic equality is in the danger of disappearing from the debates on democracy. The ever-increasing power of private capital has resulted in the decline of the relative autonomy of the Indian State. This, in turn, threatens to debilitate the progress that the country has made through affirmative action in general. And in particular, certain important economic sectors that are vital to the sovereignty and security of the nation like agriculture, health and education are under grave threats.[16]

16. Refer to the works of Sudipta Kaviraj, who has incisively intervened in the debate on inequality in the context of Indian democracy.

It is on similar grounds that the Naxalite critique of the Indian State is based. The term comes from Naxalbari, a village in West Bengal, where a section of the Communist Party of India (Marxist) (CPI-M), led by Charu Mazumdar and Kanu Sanyal, were part of an uprising of peasants against the local landlords in 1967. Today, Naxal is an umbrella term, which includes armed revolutionary movements, taking inspiration from Maoist thought, and are spread across rural central, southern and eastern India. While the violent methods used by the Naxals to draw attention to their legitimate critique of the Indian State may be condemnable, their critique indeed raises fundamental questions about the very nature of the Indian State and its beneficiaries. The Naxal movements work towards transforming agrarian relations, securing the rights of tribal peoples, and resisting neo-imperialism and globalization in realizing the wider aim of a democratic revolution and thus changing the very character of the Indian State.

Another devastating critique of Indian democracy was made by Jayaprakash Narayan when he attacked, in a rather Gandhian vein, the concept of parliamentary democracy per se for its democratic deficit. JP criticized the parliamentary system and party politics for breeding unscrupulousness and for its tendency towards centralism and dictatorships. His suspicions were proved right with the proclamation of Emergency in India for approximately 18 months during 1975–77. This phase, which witnessed restrictions on the Fundamental Rights of the citizens, has often been described as the darkest chapter in the history of independent India.

However, the ghosts of such events are still alive as Emergency-like situations prevail in many parts of northeastern India, which have been under the Armed Forces Special Powers Act (1958) for nearly 50 years. This has resulted not only in a de facto suspension of the powers of the civil administration with the presence of the military, but has also converted military rule into one of de jure, especially when the Supreme Court of India declared in 1997 that AFSPA was constitutionally legitimate.

CONCLUSION

Democracy in independent India saw the transformation of the colonial Indian 'subject' into a 'citizen' of free India, where the citizen was recognized as a morally autonomous agent. In the preceding pages, we have seen how the twin processes of consolidating and deepening democracy in India is continuing with commendable success despite shameful blemishes. Nonetheless, the true strength of a democracy lies in its ability to digest devastating criticism and in striving to better its record. Therein, lies the destiny of Indian democracy as well.

Suggested Readings

Agarwal, Bina. *A Field of One's Own: Gender and Land Rights in South Asia*. Cambridge, UK: Cambridge University Press, 1994.

Austin, Granville. *The Indian Constitution: The Cornerstone of a Nation*. Oxford, UK: Clarendon Press, 1966.

Brass, Paul. *The New Cambridge History of India*. Vol. 4, *The Politics of India Since Independence*. 2nd edition. New Delhi: Cambridge University Press, Foundation Books, 1994.

Chandra, Bipan. *In the Name of Democracy: JP Movement and the Emergency*. New Delhi: Penguin, 2003.

Chakrabarty, Dipesh. *Provincializing Europe: Post-colonial Thought and Historical Difference*. New Delhi: Oxford University Press, 2001.

Dutta, Nilanjan. 'From Subject to Citizen: Towards a History of the Indian Civil Rights Movement.' In Michael Anderson and Sumit Guha (eds.), *Changing Concepts of Rights and Justice in South Asia*. New Delhi: Oxford India Paperbacks, 2000, pp. 275–88.

Frankel, Francine, Zoya Hasan, Rajeev Bhargava and Balveer Arora (eds.), *Transforming India: Social and Political Dynamics of Democracy*. New Delhi: Oxford University Press, 2002.

Kohli, Atul (ed.). *The Success of Indian Democracy*. Cambridge, UK: Cambridge University Press, 2001.

Rao, B. Shiv. *The Framing of India's Constitution*. New Delhi: Indian Institute of Public Administration, 1968.

Questions

1. Does democracy always mean the rule of the majority? What are the dangers inherent in such a conception of democracy? How can we safeguard democracy against the dangers imposed by a majority?
2. How have the judiciary and the Election Commission consolidated democracy in India?
3. What is the significance of the right to information in a democratic polity? Discuss some of the key issues emerging from the exercise of the Right to Information Act.
4. How have democratic institutions and practices been used by marginalized groups to assert their identities and press for their demands?
5. What measures would you suggest for consolidating and deepening democracy in your home state?

The Parliamentary System: An Evaluation

14

Kumar Rahul

INTRODUCING THE PARLIAMENTARY SYSTEM: A THEORETICAL OVERVIEW

All societies have some governing institutions. Democratic societies are desirably governed by democratic institutions. Important among them are executives, legislatures, judiciaries and bureaucracies. When we refer to a system, it entails a specific type and specific pattern of constitutional relationship among a given set of institutions. There are some cardinal principles that govern these relationships. These institutions serve as an interface between the imperatives of governance and demands of the governed. Broadly, there are two types of democratic political systems: presidential and **parliamentary**. In a presidential system, the chief executive is elected independent of the legislature. The chief executive, i.e., the President, is constitutionally vested with executive powers. All three organs of the government, namely, the executive, the legislature, and the judiciary, are independent of each other. However, they observe and abide by a 'system' of checks and balances. Presidential systems are characteristically based on the doctrine of 'separation of powers'.

The parliamentary system refers to a pattern of relationship, which is characteristically based on the 'fusion of powers' between the executive and the legislature. There are two types of executive: the political executive and the permanent executive. The fusion of power takes place between the political executive and the legislature. The political executive is a part of the legislature, hence directly elected by the people. Although the constitutional head of the State is vested with de jure executive powers, the de facto executive powers remain with the 'prime minister'. What is considered endemic to the parliamentary system is the 'collective responsibility' of the government to the legislature. Judicial independence is ruled out in favour of parliamentary sovereignty .The value of 'responsibility' and 'accountability' is preferred to 'stability'. Britain is a classic example of the parliamentary system, whereas the USA has adopted the presidential system.

The pattern of India's institutional arrangements is not typical of a parliamentary system of the British type. There are important departures. On the one hand, the balance of power is tilted towards the centre to facilitate national integration, on the other, states have their own constitutionally crafted institutional structures, like the executive, the legislature, the judiciary, the bureaucracy, etc., and they share the same pattern of parliamentary relationship as the centre. In normal circumstances, states work as federal units and enjoy functional autonomy in their own spheres. There is yet another tier of government in our political structure at the local level. We know them as 'panchayati raj institutions'. Perhaps this was an important constitutional step contemplated in deference to Gandhi's idea of 'village swaraj'. Thus, our democratic political system is best characterized by the expression 'parliamentary-federal' that suitably captures most of its salient features.

We referred to some cardinal principles that govern parliamentary relations. Those principles are ethos of what we call 'parliamentary democracy'. Parliamentary democracy can be conceived of in two ways. One, as a set of principles that embodies a democratic polity in which the affairs of the state and the business of the government are conducted by the means and devices of the parliamentary system. Besides others, the main procedural connection between parliamentary democracy and the parliamentary system is that the executive's responsibility to the legislature is given priority over all other democratic principles.

In this context, the Constitution of India enjoins upon the executive two types of responsibilities: (1) individual responsibility and (2) collective responsibility. The principle of individual responsibility to the head of the State, i.e. the President of India, is embodied in Article 75(2).[1] It is to be noted that the President of India is an integral part of Parliament (Art.79). Another type of responsibility, which the Constitution enjoins upon the government, is the principle of 'collective responsibility'. This is embodied in Article 75(3) of the Constitution, which states that the 'council of ministers' shall be collectively responsible to the 'House of the People'. This means that the executive must derive legitimacy and sanctity from the legislature. The life of the government depends on the will of the legislature. The government remains in power as long as it continues to enjoy the confidence of the House (Lok Sabha).

The other way in which parliamentary democracy is conceived is very broad and captures lofty ideas and aspirations of democratic life. It is all about developing a democratic political culture in which people learn and inculcate such democratic values as belief in deliberative decision-making, repose trust in parliamentary and representative institutions, accommodate and respect divergent views including that of the opposition, embed in participatory values, and use parliamentary language in public life. Parliamentary democracy, conceived this

---

1. 'The ministers shall hold office during the pleasure of the President.'

way, acquires a moral and substantive character. Democracy promises certain fundamental freedoms and rights to people in order to equip them to make morally relevant choices in life, what we call autonomy. Moral autonomy is necessary to capacitate people to make moral judgements about life and society. Democracy is ultimately all about making decisions and judgements in social and political life. The 'parliamentary system' is just one of the ways and means to keep this constitutional promise made to the people by the framers of the Constitution.

Why India Adopted the Parliamentary System

India has a long history of representative institutions. Some observers have remarked that India was a 'civilizational polity'. Ancient institutions like 'sabha' and 'samiti' were representative in character. They correspond to our modern parliamentary chambers—Lok Sabha and Rajya Sabha. However, in current discussions, we find two clear views. According to one school, India's democracy is a legacy of British colonialism. Atul Kohli has also observed that British colonialism was helpful and formative for India's democratic evolution. India experienced an early introduction to 'proto-democratic' institutions and practices, like civil services and legislatures. India's national elites had become socialized in liberal-democratic values and attuned to parliamentary procedures. Even the people of India were also practically accustomed to the parliamentary system under the long spell of British colonialism. According to another view, India's national movement for Independence can be credited for the birth of India's democracy.

One obvious reason for making a choice in favour of the parliamentary democracy was India's social diversity. India is a multicultural society. Given the diversity and plurality in India's social and cultural life, a unitary type of system would have been a complete misfit. For, a unitary system is intrinsically and structurally conducive to a homogeneous society, having a uniform pattern of life. There would arise a problem of compatibility between the political set up and social set up in a unitary government with a plural society. Federal aspirations of the people would have been crushed under the weight of a centralized political structure. So the 'parliamentary-federal' model with multi-party system was the natural choice.

The Working of Parliamentary System in India

As stated earlier, a system strikes specific relationship among a given set of institutions. Hence, this study does not intend to analyse the working of parliamentary institutions independent of each other. Rather, the focus of our study is to analyse and examine them in their cross-connections and constitutional setting. Throughout this chapter, the terms 'parliament' and 'legislature' have been synonymously used. Although the legislature is a general term, which also includes state legislature, the latter has been left out from this study. Similarly, the terms 'judiciary' and 'court' have been used to make reference only to the Supreme Court and high courts. The lower judiciaries have been excluded. For our purpose, we divide our study into the following heads:

1. Legislature–executive relations
2. Legislature–judiciary relations
3. Judiciary–executive relations

The yardstick for our analysis will be the three cardinal principles of a systemic relationship—responsibility, accountability, and stability.

Legislature–Executive Relations

We have outlined at the onset that the working of the parliamentary system rests on the accountability of the executive to the legislature. This is the cardinal principle of the parliamentary systems. To examine the working of the Indian parliamentary system the questions we take up are: to what extent the Parliament can exercise legislative control over the political government? What are the procedural devices to ensure it and how well have they functioned? Is accountability at all an issue in India's parliamentary politics? In the following paragraphs, we will try to examine the above questions. We divide our study of legislature–executive relations under two heads: (1) role of parliamentary committees, and (2) president in legislature–executive relations. Towards the end of this chapter, we will also briefly focus on the role of the opposition in demanding accountability.

Role of Parliamentary Committees. Parliamentary committees, to some extent, are the main sites from where the legislators can exercise structural and functional control over the government by manipulating the legislative business. These committees are meant for assisting the legislature in managing the affairs of the legislation. Sometimes they are also constituted for conducting investigations of a specific nature. Members are drawn from either or both houses. Depending on the nature of function and duration, parliamentary committees are of two types: ad hoc and standing committees. Ad hoc committees, like a select committee or joint committee, are appointed for specific purposes, for example, considering and scrutinizing legislative bills. There are standing committees in each house and they are functionally specialized. The Public Accounts Committee, the Committee on Estimates, and the Committee on Public Undertakings are most important committees. There is another set of standing committees, known as the Department Related Standing Committees (DRSCs). They were created in 1989, and then expanded in 1993. DRSCs and other parliamentary committees are very significant spots from where the legislature can exercise structural constraints on the executives.

The very fact that we have been able to institutionalize and sustain these committees into our parliamentary system is a big achievement, although the Constitution of India does not make any specific reference. Some departmental committees were in existence even prior to Independence. They enjoyed advisory functions; however, Nehru dissolved them on the pretext that such committees were not suited for a system that was modelled on the British Parliament. The re-creation of these committees into our parliamentary system is a major step to ensure greater governmental accountability to the legislature. There are now 17 standing committees related to various departments, which cover the entire gamut of governmental activities.

However, there have been some misgivings. One is that parliamentary committees have very limited utility. Their autonomy is badly impaired by partisan spirit. Their composition is dependent on the majority party/combination in the legislature. Although they are parliamentary agencies, their deliberations and recommendations in shaping the legislation is influenced by the party/alliance in power. But sometimes the converse can also be true, particularly when the majority is shaky and the coalition partners have difference of opinion. For example, the recommendations of the select committee on the bill provide reservations to the OBCs (other backward classes) in admissions to educational institutions differed from that of the government. It is to be seen how parliamentary committees function with a government having majority in coalition.

There is also a serious apprehension that these committees are going to create competing centres of power. We can look at this apprehension in two ways. On one hand, empirically such apprehensions cannot be ruled out. Governments have been unstable and shaky in the coalition era. Their majorities in the House have been precarious. And, their capacities to assert have been impaired. On the other hand, theoretically, we should allay the fear that they are going to damage the parliamentary fabric of our system because of clashes regarding jurisdiction. These committees are not separate and independent centres of power. They have merely an advisory, supervisory, and supplementary role to play. They are a part of procedures meant for safeguarding the legislature from the institutional excesses of the executive.

What is a bigger cause of worry is that their roles are sometimes utterly ignored and undermined by the government. Only a few bills are referred to the select committees and often they are passed in the form they were prepared by the minister's department. For example, in the Ninth Lok Sabha, 19 bills were passed on a single day, which also included a Constitutional Amendment Bill. The select committees were not engaged at any stage of legislation.

Notwithstanding the above, parliamentary committees have great educational value in the sense that their findings and reports are brought to the public glare. It generates awareness among the legislators and the general public. At least, it exerts moral pressure on the government and causes embarrassment. It also gives an opportunity to the political parties and other voluntary agencies to discuss, debate and politicize the matter. In turn, it helps to create an informed citizenry, which is always healthy for parliamentary democracy.

President in the Legislature–Executive Relations. In the Indian parliamentary system, the office of the President is like a 'pivot' that joins the two wheels, namely the legislature and the executive, although his role is not so 'pivotal'. As stated earlier, the parliamentary system belies the doctrine of strict separation of powers. Recall that, it is based on the fusion of powers wherein the executive is a part of the legislature. The office of the President is a constitutional conjunction where the legislative and the executive organs meet. At the head of the union executive stands the President of India and by virtue of this, all executive powers are constitutionally vested in him (Article 53). On the other hand, the president of India is also an integral component of the Indian Parliament (Article 79). No bill without the assent of the president can become a law. The president has the power to summon either House of the Parliament, prorogue either House, and dissolve the lower House. In addition to these, the president also has the power to legislate while the houses are not in session. This will form the basic premise on which the legislature–executive relations will be discussed. This segment tries to make a brief historical survey of the 'constitutional conjugation' by situating the president between legislature and executive.

In our system, all governmental functions are carried in the name of the president. Article 74 of the Constitution puts on the president strict limitations on the exercise of executive powers. Prior to the 42nd amendment, 1976, there was a little bit of ambiguity contained in this Article. It was argued that the president is not bound to render conformity to the ministerial advice. It was no secret that President (Dr) Rajendra Prasad had disagreements on many issues with Prime Minister Nehru. The disagreement erupted into the public arena. Public statements made by the president amounted to veiled criticism of the government. Harnessing the ambiguity seemingly inherent to Article 74, Dr Prasad ignited a public debate and called for the legal scrutiny of the president's power.[2]

Later, it was judicially re-established by the Supreme Court[3] that the Indian president was a constitutional head of the executive. His powers were like those of the queen in Britain. The Indira Gandhi government by the 42nd amendment, 1976, made it obligatory upon the president to act upon the ministerial advice. The 44th amendment, 1978, empowered the president to revert the advice for reconsideration.

---

2. At a ceremony of the Indian Legal Institute, in 1960, he expressed that the position of the Indian president was not identical with that of the British Crown.
3. *Sanjivi vs State of Madras* 1970, *Rao vs Indira* 1971, *Shamsher Singh vs State of Punjab*, 1974. See D. D. Basu, *Introduction to the Constitution of India* (New Delhi: Prentice-Hall of India, 1990), p. 193.

Most of the presidents after Dr Rajendra Prasad were far more restrained. The main issue here is whether presidential activism is good or bad. Does it hurt parliamentary sentiments? To respond to this question, let us first appreciate the difference between 'assertiveness' and 'activism'. Presidential assertiveness can be understood in terms of active assertion of the power and obligation within the constitutional ambit, whereas activism smacks of encroachment into another's realm of action. Whether it hurts parliamentary sentiments is a normative question. We shall raise this question at some later stage. But what Fakhruddin Ali Ahmad did, when he endorsed the declaration of Emergency in 1975 at the behest of Indira Gandhi, was the height of presidential pliability. However, when viewed sympathetically, his action can be condoned. Indira Gandhi had emerged as the most powerful leader. She started a new brand of politics by relying more on her idiosyncrasy and less on the organizational strength of her party. The Congress became a populist and personalistic organ of Mrs Gandhi. She garnered terrific power around herself and reduced the party to an organization of sycophants, making the party synonymous with her name. When challenged by a strident opposition, she imposed national Emergency, bringing all democratic practices and parliamentary procedures to a halt. Paul Brass has commented that the Indian democracy was brought to the brink. Emergency would have been the fittest case for the president to have exercised 'assertiveness', if not activism, which would not have amounted to a normative depreciation of parliamentary sentiments.

N. Sanjeeva Reddy (1977–82) and Giani Zail Singh (1982–87) can be called assertive presidents. Giani Zail Singh was made president during Indira Gandhi's tenure in the hope that he would act as a constitutional puppet. The problem started when Rajiv Gandhi became prime minister with an unprecedented majority in the Parliament, after the assassination of his mother and predecessor, Indira Gandhi. A feeling crept into Zail Singh's mind that he was being ignored and treated with ignominy by Rajiv Gandhi. It was observed that Rajiv Gandhi did not even bother to meet constitutional obligations enjoined upon him by Article 78.[4] The repercussion of this tussle became imminent when Zail Singh threatened to withhold assent from a piece of legislation, the Indian Postal Bill. He started expressing exasperation in public interviews. The political atmosphere was full with speculation that he even considered dismissing the government for irresponsibility and corruption stemming from the Bofors scandal. He also claimed that Rajiv Gandhi instructed an advisor to draw up documents to impeach him.[5]

The decade beginning 1989 can be periodized as the coalition era. This phase began with the decline of the Congress hegemony and the emergence of many

---

4. To furnish such information as the president may call for.
5. James Manor, 'The Presidency, in Public Institutions in India,' in Devesh Kapur and Pratap Bhanu Mehta (eds.), *Public Institutions in India* (New Delhi: Oxford University Press, 2005), p. 111.

regional political parties to fill the political vacuum. These parties often tend to be ideologically fickle. Depending on the political opportunities available, they can swing to any side of the coalition, keeping the dynamics of coalition making always volatile. Hence, the coalition era makes governmental stability precarious. This can be gauged from the fact that four general elections were held in the 1990s producing hung parliaments. There were eight appointments of prime ministers, in which, Vajpayee served two terms during a span of 10 years. In such circumstances, the role of the president becomes 'pivotal', particularly in the appointment of prime ministers in a hung house. N. Sanjiva Reddy was the first to have used his presidential discretion in appointing a prime minister in an unstable house. A reflection on President K. R. Narayanan's tenure in office is worthwhile here. It can be said with sufficient volume of evidence that K. R. Narayanan, in his style of functioning, broke with the past in several significant ways, which signalled 'presidential activism'. When he assumed presidency in 1997, he announced that he intended to be a 'working President' and, later, his public pronouncement that 'he was not a rubber stamp' was a confirmation of the fact. He expressed the first clear sign in 1998 when he sent back a Cabinet decision to impose the President's rule in Uttar Pradesh. The Janata government headed by I. K. Gujral had to abandon the proposal altogether. Given the public disenchantment with the repeated misuse of president's rule for purely partisan purposes, the president's assertiveness earned a lot of popular accolades.

Further, in 1998, he declined to address the nation on the eve of Independence Day. Presidents conventionally make an address to the nation on the eve of Independence Day. Precedent and convention have it that a president sends the text of his speech to the government for vetting. The text of the speech is subject to alteration on ministerial advice. Instead of the presidential address, he chose to give an interview, the content of which could not be vetted by the government. In 1999, when one of the larger parties in the BJP's ruling coalition withdrew its support, the government was asked by President Narayanan to demonstrate its majority on the floor of the House. President Narayanan delivered yet another unvetted speech at a celebration on the 50th anniversary of the Constitution in 2000. Again in 2000, Narayanan departed from the text of a speech, prepared by the external affairs ministry, which he delivered in the honour of US President Bill Clinton. Purportedly, it caused intense anxiety in the external affairs ministry and invited media criticism. According to one observer, souring relation of the government with the President was one of the main reasons behind the setting up of a Constitution Review Committee in 2000. President Kalam's tenure in office can be described as prudently modest. He modestly asserted his position on various occasions. However, his endorsement of the president's rule in Bihar on highly fictitious grounds earned more acrimony than applause for being utterly submissive. The Supreme Court also expressed its displeasure and annoyance on the hurried manner in which the Bihar Assembly was dissolved.

Legislature–Judiciary Relations

The judiciary in India has emerged as one of the most crucial institutions of governance with immense moral and legal responsibilities to administer constitutional justice. As described earlier, the parliamentary system of the Westminster model belies the theory of separation of powers. In the British political system, the judiciary is not independent. Parliamentary sovereignty is the hallmark of the British political system. Here the Indian parliamentary system departs from the typical Westminster model. It partially adopts the separation of powers as far as the judicial organ of the government is concerned. The reason is that, as democracy has progressed, India has gone federal in its attitude and attribute. The State has provided space for the growth of numerous mobilized groups and has allowed them power sharing. This is visibly evident in the changing character of federalism, which has helped the judiciary in evolving its more and more independent stature. However, this journey has not been free from upheavals. It is important for us at this juncture to examine the 'legislature–judiciary' relations that have bearing on the workability of our parliamentary system. The judiciary–legislature relations can be studied under two heads:

1. The struggle between **judicial review** and parliamentary sovereignty, and
2. The judiciary as an institution of governance.

Judicial Review vs Parliamentary Sovereignty. The tussle between judicial review and parliamentary sovereignty dominated the judiciary–legislature relationship for the first 30 years since 1950, when the Supreme Court of India was established. The court has consolidated the power of judicial review by the creative interpretation of the Constitution. There has been a presumption that the judicial review in parliamentary systems happens to be weak. But just the opposite has happened in India. In India, as elsewhere, it is not simply the formal allocation of powers but an evolving constitutional jurisprudence that has enhanced the powers of judicial review.[6] The magnitude of this tussle can be gauged from the fact that out of the first 45 Constitutional Amendments, nearly half were aimed at amputating the powers of the courts. Nehru was a champion of parliamentary sovereignty. He said in a Constituent Assembly debate, 'no Supreme Court and no judiciary can stand in judgement over the supreme will of parliament representing the will of the entire community'.[7] A major worry, which agitated Nehru and his socialist colleagues, was that the courts would

---

6. Pratap Bhanu Mehta, 'India's Judiciary: The Promise of Uncertainty,' in Kapur and Mehta (eds.), *Public Institutions in India*, p. 164.
7. Lloyd Rudolph and Susanne Rudolph, *In Pursuit of Lakshmi* (New Delhi: Orient Longman, 1987), p. 106.

create obstacles to the realization of socialist goals. The left critiques have construed Indian judiciary as an agency of class domination. The issues concerning the socialist objectives became the first venue of conflict between Parliament and the judiciary. After Independence, a legislation for giving effect to abolition of feudal privileges was passed by Parliament. The court blocked it on the ground that it was violative of fundamental rights under Articles 14, 19, and 31. In response to this, the first Constitutional Amendment was passed in 1951, which immunized such legislations from judicial review.

The intensity of struggle increased manifold during the Indira Gandhi regime. In 1970, the government sought to nationalize 14 largest commercial banks, and to deprive the princes of their privileges and privy purses. The court thwarted even this move. Again the government responded with Constitutional Amendments. Prior to this, the Supreme Court questioned the amending power of Parliament of the Fundamental Right and declared Parliament incompetent to do so in its much-debated decision in the Golak Nath vs State of Punjab case (1967). The Parliament passed the 24th amendment in 1971, which overrided the effects of the Golaknath case. Fundamental rights were again made amendable and once again the parliamentary sovereignty was pronouncedly established.

The struggle continued further. Neither side was ready to submit. It manifested in what we popularly know as the *Keshavanand Bharti vs State of Kerala* case, 1973, in which the Supreme Court made formidable pronouncements of constitutional importance. It sought to bring a thaw in the ongoing strained relations between judicial review and parliamentary sovereignty. The ramifications of this landmark judgement could be easily felt. It gave a huge discouragement to the discourse of a 'committed judiciary' which the political circle was enamoured with. In the Keshavanand Bharti case, the Supreme Court enunciated the doctrine of the 'basic feature' of the Constitution. There are certain basic features implied in the Constitution. The basic features cannot be amended by the Parliament. However, any provision of the Constitution, including the Fundamental Rights, can be amended provided it does not damage the Constitution's basic features. Judicial review was declared to be a basic feature of the Constitution. By doing so, the court immunized the judicial review from legislative incursions. What is interesting to note is that the court itself, on the basis of conceptual connectedness and organic unity of the Constitution, would evolve basic features. Later, during Emergency, the legislature tried to disarm the courts of their power of judicial review by the 42nd Amendment Act, 1976; it was struck down by the Supreme Court as unconstitutional on the ground that it was repugnant and violative of the Basic Features Doctrine. Later, in 1980, it was judicially reaffirmed in the Minerva Mills case. Yet once again, in January 2007, the Supreme Court in a landmark judgement ruled that Parliament had the power to amend the Fundamental Rights only to the extent that it did not violate the basic features of the Constitution. Moreover, there could not be any blanket immunity from judicial review of laws inserted in the Ninth Schedule[8] of the Constitution. As of now, it clearly appears that the pendulum has swung to the judiciary's side and it can safely be concluded that the Indian Parliament is not as omnipotent as the British one.

The Judiciary as an Institution of Governance. Over the years, the judiciary has emerged as an institution of governance, which ideally should have been the domain of the executive. Is this development good for parliamentary democracy? This question needs to be debated on. Let us again bring in the basic feature doctrine into discussion. There are good reasons to believe that the judiciary[9] has evolved itself as an institution of governance. The Basic Features Doctrine has been perceived in two different ways. Critics of the Basic Features Doctrine conceive this development as the judicial usurpation of the executive power and parliamentary sovereignty. On the other hand, advocates of this theory appreciate this as a constitutional device to check the parliamentary majorities, which sometimes become some sort of legislative tyranny. We can find some instances in the parliamentary history of India. The passage of the 42nd Amendment Act (during Emergency), which is also described as a mini Constitution, was one such instance to reckon the rampage that a legislative tyranny can do on the democratic fabric of India. The Basic Features Doctrine has opened a range of issues that might be protected, for example, the protection of civil rights, liberties and equalities of ordinary citizens. All these have added meaning to the theory and practice of constitutionalism and good governance.

The Supreme Court has discovered the 'due process' theory in the Indian Constitution in Article 21: 'No person shall be deprived of his life or personal liberty except according to the procedures established by law'. There is a judicial history of this invention. The expression 'procedure established by law' meant that a person could be deprived of his life or liberty by a competent legislature. The right to life and liberty was at the mercy of legislative majorities. There was no legal remedy available if a competent legislature would intend to deprive a person of life and liberty. There was no scope of judicial intervention in such deprivations. This was the position of the Supreme Court in the *A. K. Gopalan vs State of Madras* case, 1950. Procedure established by law normally

8. The Ninth Schedule was introduced first of all in 1951 to keep certain laws, particularly those on land reforms, beyond the scope of judicial review. The number of laws in the Ninth Schedule has gone up now to 284. The Supreme Court, on 11 January 2007, decried the absence of any guidelines or constitutional control regulating the insertion of laws into the Ninth Schedule and held that all laws inserted into this Schedule after 24 April 1973, i.e., the date of judgement in the Keshavnand Bharti case to escape judicial scrutiny shall be subject to the same.
9. See Pratap Bhanu Mehta, 'Inner Conflict of Constitutionalism', in Zoya Hasan, E. Sridharan and R. Sudarshan (eds.), *India's Living Constitution* (New Delhi: Permanent Black, 2002).

finds expression in constitutions that embody a parliamentary system. The Supreme Court overturned its position in the *Maneka Gandhi vs Union of India* case, 1978 and invented 'due process'. It meant that the procedure prescribed by law to deprive a person of his/her liberty must not be unfair, unreasonable and arbitrary. This emphatically imposed a judicial restraint and brought the arbitrary deprivation of liberty by legislative majorities under strict scanner. This is generally found in constitutions having presidential systems.

What seems an ostensible transformation to many observers of the Indian legal system in the outlook and assertiveness of Indian judiciary is that it has exonerated itself from the charge of dispensing capitalist morality. The courts changed their stance towards the Directive Principles of State Policy and began to look at them as a progressive index of governance. The courts were proactive in exerting considerable pressure on political governments at the centre and states to effectively implement the Directives, as they were ruled to be fundamental in the governance of the country (Article 37). The court exercised 'judicial assertiveness' in extending rights, freedoms, and justice to the socially excluded and marginalized groups of the society. The court's decision in the Indira Sawhney case, popularly known as the Mandal commission case, enlarged the scope of affirmative action. The court has also laid down the guidelines on sexual harassment in the Visakha case. Despite disagreements, there seems to have emerged a common place in legal studies that Indian judiciary has not only kept its constitutional promise to hold India's governing institutions accountable, but has also emerged as an institution of governance.

THE EXECUTIVE–JUDICIARY RELATIONS

We have discussed earlier how legislatures sometimes become helpless in ensuring the government's accountability. In parliamentary systems, the government commands a majority. Sometimes the might of the majority is so tyrannical that the question of responsibility and accountability is fictitious. We have also seen how other constitutional means are puppeteered by the executive and belie the fundamental norms of parliamentary democracy. More specifically speaking, parliamentary democracy often suffers at the hands of parliamentary sovereignty. On the other hand, parliamentary relations and executive functions also suffer when the majority is precarious. Since 1989, India has necessarily entered into a coalition era. The government cobbles up a majority in a clumsy fashion by undermining all parliamentary norms. Though the coalition has started a new democratic discourse in Indian politics, it entails an inherent instability. Lack of stability affects governance. It is here that the judiciary gets an opportunity to step in. There is a third reason that warrants repeated judicial intervention. This is a chronic reason. When the executive bodies fail to discharge their constitutionally enjoined duties and belie the popular hopes and expectations, it becomes imperative for the judiciary to step in. We often refer to this phenomenon as judicial activism. For quite some time, the courts have demonstrated activism whenever governance appeared mired in malfeasance. It has contingently made public policy pronouncements, directly taken over the supervision of executive agencies, and endeavoured to hold the executive bodies accountable.

We can discern at least four sites of contention in the executive–judiciary relationship: (1) issues affecting the federal character and the federal polity, (2) appointment of judges, (3) court as an actor in politics, and (4) governance.

There can be even more sites, but we will limit our discussion within these contours.

Federal Issues in Executive–Judiciary Relationship

In the early days, Nehru tartly attacked the judiciary for having 'purloined the constitution'.[10] The Nehru government found the judiciary obstructive of pursuing the socialist goals of the Indian State. The government resorted to Constitutional Amendments as a means of circumventing the judicial interpretation of the Constitution. However, the independence of judiciary was in general respected, which is an attribute of a federal polity. Although it has been interpreted that Nehru favoured and set in pace a model of, to quote Rudolphs's phrase, 'command polity',[11] no attempt was made to dispossess the judiciary of its power of judicial review.

Indira Gandhi was also at loggerheads with the judiciary. Three important events of federal importance can be cited here in the context of soaring executive–judiciary relations:

1. In 1970, Indira Gandhi was heading a minority government. The Constitutional Amendment for the abolition of Privy Purse fell short of the required majority by one vote. The government then issued an 'executive order' in this regard, which was struck down by the court. The court was criticized for its class bias. But, from a constitutional point of view, the court's judgement was appreciated as the right recourse. This is plainly because there was a constitutional promise made to princely states whose territories had been ceded to the Union of India.

2. During Indira Gandhi's regime, the Parliament had virtually become subservient to the prime minister. The Constitutional Amendments were used as an instrument to legitimize her highly personalized regime. The Allahabad

10. Mehta, 'India's Judiciary, p. 106.
11. Rudolph and Rudolph, *In Pursuit of Lakshmi*, p. 212. In a command polity, autonomous States are sovereign. Extractive and allocative decisions reflect the preferences of the elected and appointed officials who choose and implement policies. A necessary condition for the command polity's ability to formulate goals, strategies and policies is the State's ability to free itself from the constraints of the societal demands through leadership, persuasion or coercion.

High Court had set aside Indira Gandhi's election to the Lok Sabha on grounds of corrupt electoral practices. She puppeteered the Parliament and got the 39th amendment passed. This amendment inserted Article 329A into the Constitution. It removed the jurisdiction of the Supreme Court over election disputes involving the Prime Minister, the Speaker of the Lok Sabha, the President, and the Vice President. It was a frontal attack on the independence of the judiciary, which is essential in a federal set up. Moreover, when Emergency was declared on whimsical grounds, the court endorsed its constitutionality. This is regarded as the darkest decision in Indian judicial history. It badly besmirched the reputation of the judiciary. Nothing could be more damaging for a gradually evolving federal political structure than the declaration of Emergency. Through a series of amendments, which were passed at the command of the political executive, the courts were disarmed of their power of judicial review. However, judicial review was restored and established as a basic feature of Constitution in the Keshavanand Bharti case.

3. The repeated imposition of President's rule in states, mostly on partisan than constitutional grounds, has attracted judicial attention. The President's rule is imposed on the basis of the Governor's report and endorsed by the President. This power virtually rests with the Union government. The Council of Ministers advises the President to make such an endorsement and declare 'President's rule'. The Governor's report must state that the constitutional machinery has broken down in the State and, therefore, it is no longer possible for the government to be run in accordance with the provisions of this Constitution. In the *S. R. Bommai vs Union of India* (1994) case, the Supreme Court ruled that the subjective satisfaction of the executive's reports which warrants President's rule is subject to judicial review. This landmark judgement is in the nature of tensional wariness on the part of the government in its relationship with the judiciary.

The Appointment of Judges

The appointment of judges has been an issue of fierce controversy in the relations between the executive and the judiciary. It is one of the key elements in guaranteeing the independence of the judiciary. There is a constitutional basis for the appointment of judges, laid down in our Constitution. Judges would be appointed by the president of India in consultation with such judges of the Supreme Court and of the high courts as the president may deem necessary, the Constitution says. There is no legislative involvement in this process. There have been three stages in which the judiciary has consolidated its control over the appointment of judges. They are referred to as the 'first judges', 'second judges', and the 'third judges' cases. The basic thrust of these cases has been to secure greater judicial independence.

In the 'first judges' cases, the Chief Justice had no veto power over executive appointment of judges. The 'second judges' cases reinstated the Chief Justice's veto over appointments. In the 'third judges' cases, the Supreme Court finally settled the law relating to judges' appointments in 1998. Appointment is to be made by a collegium, consisting of the four seniormost judges of the Supreme Court including the Chief Justice of India. The executive can make a request to the collegium to reconsider any of their recommendations. But the recommendations of the collegium are final and obligatory upon the president. In December 2006, the appointment of the Chief Justice of Punjab and Haryana High Court by the collegium raised some controversy. President Kalam made some observations, which were clarified by the collegium. Effectively and legally, the judiciary has gained complete control over the appointment of judges.

What impact is the appointment of judges going to have on our parliamentary system? Arguably, it will provide more legitimacy to judicial decisions. The Constitution envisaged an independent judiciary. The appointment of judges was one area in which judicial independence was prone to executive misdemeanour. Successive law commissions have decried undue executive interference in appointments. A few examples can be cited here: Justice A. N. Ray was appointed Chief Justice by superseding three senior judges, Justices Hegde, Grover, and Shilat. They were superseded supposedly because of their judgement in the Keshavanand Bharti case, which was unfavourable to the government. Again, in 1997, Justice Beg was appointed Chief Justice of India by superseding the seniormost judge, Justice H. R. Khanna. He suffered supersession due to his dissenting judgement in the *ADM vs Shukla* (1976) case, which approved the state of Emergency.

The Judiciary as an Actor in Politics

Most legal studies have focused attention on cross-examining the inter-institutional relationship of our governing institutions. They have not paid heed to the question of whether the judiciary can be construed as a powerful participant in Indian politics. A line of argument that has recently emerged is that the judiciary is a powerful actor in the political life of India. The argument seems a little inflated. However, it can be said with conviction that some issues of normative importance in Indian politics are profoundly shaped by judicial interventions and judicial interpretations. The judiciary is the custodian of constitutional values and it has well established itself as the authoritative interpreter of the Constitution. The court's interventions have been widely seen as legitimate. At the same time, representative institutions have become corrupt and corrosive in the public eye. The courts have been successful in projecting its image as an institution of accountability of the last resort. Hence, its ruling, interpretations and interventions profoundly shape issues of Indian politics and influence public opinion. For example, the Allahabad High Court verdict pronouncing Indira Gandhi guilty of electoral malpractices was a major one. In the S. R. Bommai case, the court made use of the Basic Features Doctrine to uphold the dismissal of three BJP-ruled state governments after the demolition of the Babri Masjid. The ground was that the government's actions were violative of the principles of secularism, which is an important constitutional value. The court's interpretation of Hinduism also provided some sort of political legitimacy to its advocates. At the same time, the court refused to express its views on the Babri Masjid case when the executive sought an advisory opinion on this issue under Article 143. In the past few years, the Supreme Court and high courts have been severe on corrupt politicians and have sought to monitor cases of corruption against them. All these have been instrumental in eliciting strong public opinion.

GOVERNANCE

We have already discussed how the judiciary has evolved and established itself as an institution of governance. Judicial activism is a necessary byproduct of this evolution process. A historical survey of this judicial evolution is not intended here. We will restrict our discussion to the normative consequences of this judicial initiative on the parliamentary system.

We have noted earlier that Indian legal history, for almost the first 30 years after Independence, was dominated by a tussle between judicial review and parliamentary sovereignty. This tussle can largely be attributed to the apparently tense relationship between the Fundamental Rights and the Directive Principles. The Directives are the index of governance and constitutionally fundamental in the governance of the country (Article 37). The court began contemplating judicial initiatives to realize all values concerning governance, ranging from good life and good education to good environment. Judicial activism is the most vigorous form of judicial initiative. It is an extended form of judicial assertiveness. While the attitude of the judiciary in its 'assertive' role largely remains interpretative, in judicial activism, it becomes executive. It has been conceived in two ways. The first denigrates the judiciary for its aggressive aggrandizement of the executive functions, as it jeopardizes institutional balance. The second view hails the judiciary as a new form of judicial enthusiasm to rectify the executive and also legislative misdemeanour. The performance of representative institutions is not seen as commensurate to popular expectations in delivering good to the people. On the other hand, the activism shown by the judiciary in enforcing civil liberties, human rights, and environmental protection has enraptured the public. The Supreme Court has expanded the scope of the right to life, which is the most fundamental human right. In a Hobbesian sense, the meaning of the right to life was confined to the right to self-defence. Now it means the right to livelihood, right to basic amenities of life and a safe environment. The **public interest litigation** (PIL) initiative is an attempt to give citizens direct access to the courts. The court has innovated a new judicial initiative known as 'epistolary jurisdiction' by which the court takes *suo motu* cognizance on matters related to State impropriety and lawlessness on the basis of even a post-card letter or a media report. The phrase 'epistolary jurisdiction' was coined by a noted jurist, Upendra Baxi. The Supreme Court and the high courts have started supervising the investigating agencies, like the CBI that probe into corruption and criminal cases against politicians. In a landmark judgement on 6 December 2006, the Supreme Court ruled that no prior sanction of the competent authority was required to prosecute public servants, including the present and former ministers, in corruption cases. For example, the monitoring committee of the Supreme Court supervised the sealing drive in Delhi. There are numerous instances to corroborate that judicial activism is up.

Whether this is abrasive within a parliamentary system is a normative question, and it can be given only a normative answer. The Constitution, directly or indirectly, prescribes not only the shape of governance, but also its substance. One important role of the judiciary is to disallow the dissonance between the form and substance of governance. Ideally, the representative institutions should own responsibility to ensure good governance, but as long as this does not happen adequately, the judiciary should exercise its Constitutional morality to the extent that it makes the executive organ to 'account' for its 'responsibility'.

Problems and Prospects

Let us posit two questions: (1) What ails our parliamentary system? (2) How democratic is our democracy? To search for an answer we begin with Rudolphs's observation that the parliamentary life has deteriorated in India. Truly so. For a system to survive, grow and prosper, it needs to be supported by a democratic political culture. There is an organic connectivity between a parliamentary system and parliamentary democracy. Given the current political scenario, it appears that India is yet to develop a strong parliamentary culture; the rulership and citizenship of the Indian State is yet to learn the etiquettes of parliamentary life. We are reminiscent of what Ambedkar had said that the working of the Constitution and governing institutions would largely depend on the people. Growing intolerance for competing political greed, electoral victories of political representatives with corrupt and criminal backgrounds, deteriorating standards of political rhetoric and parliamentary debates, erupting tendencies among political leaders, political parties, legislators and party cadres of political malignance often turning into political violence, ideological dissipation and fickleness on the part of political parties are symptomatic of an impoverished state of our parliamentary politics, and a simultaneous corrosion of our governing institutions. What generally happens is that in such a disappointing state of affairs, the trust of the common people in the system becomes the first casualty. The judicial conviction of a Cabinet minister and a legislator for murder, indictment of many on criminal charges, and the instance of MPs taking bribes for asking questions in the House indicate the degree of decline in the parliamentary profile of our lawmakers and law executors. What is worrisome is that all this has morally hazardous consequences for parliamentary democracy. People are left with morally corrupt choices. They have to exercise their choice between the 'bad' and the 'worse'. In the process, democracy becomes the victim and so do the common people. After all, democracy is all about making decisions in social and political life.

In this study, the yardstick of 'accountability' has persistently and predominantly been maintained. In our analysis of legislature–executive relationship, we have noted that the legislature has been far from successful as an institution of accountability. However, democratic societies have a range of procedural devices of accountability, for example, elections. Elections provide to people direct opportunities to exercise periodic control. Even they have made little difference. One reason, as we have noted, is that people are left with corrupt choices. Another reason may be that the basis of electoral politics has shifted to communal and caste politics where performance and development issues count for little. To quote Paul Brass's term, an 'institutionalized riot system' has come into existence wherein political parties and activists look for potential electoral gains by inciting communal riots, for example, the Gujarat riots. This is a display of major disdain for parliamentary democracy.

A significant difficulty in the emergence of a robust Parliamentary democracy, which could make the government accountable for all its actions, is the absence of a meaningful opposition. Before the dawn of the coalition era, there was hardly anything that could be called an opposition. All parliamentary arrangements to seek accountability from the government would have earned nothing but mockery in the face of successive tyrannical majorities of one party. We have noted that the Emergency was the worst manifestation of the mockery of the Indian parliamentary system. Although the political configurations have changed in the coalition era, those in opposition have failed to demonstrate their democratic obligation to put pressure on the government and make it accountable.

There seems to have emerged an invisible convergence and a tacit understanding among political parties across the political spectrum on issues of congruent interest. We can well discern this trend. For example, they demonstrate a vying unity when legislation for hiking their salaries and allowances is brought. They always shirk to persistently pursue issues like corruption and criminalization of politics because they all are on the same footing. The result is that corruption and criminalization have become a non-issue in India's parliamentary politics. The question of women's reservation has also met the same fate. The repeated postponement of women's reservation bill reflects the conservative social morality of all political parties. What is troubling is that it makes our representative institutions look deradicalized and completely immobilized.

It is in this context that Gandhi becomes inescapable from social and political thinking. Readers of 'Hind Swaraj' can recall Gandhi's continued critiques of Western parliamentary institutions. He advocated for even disbanding the Indian National Congress after Independence was achieved. For Gandhi, the very notion of parliamentary democracy conceived as a mechanism of distribution and management of power was undemocratic. He was fully convinced that competitive and institutionalized party politics would breed political and moral corruption and diminish the prospect of true Swaraj. Later, neo-Gandhians, like Jai Prakash Narayan (JP), built upon the idea of partyless democracy. Gandhi's proposal concerning the new Constitution of India was based on a network of self-governing institutions of 'village republics' prospecting the attainment of Swaraj. The interpretation of Swaraj as political self-determination is narrow and simplistic. Swaraj captures the idea of moral and spiritual self-determination. Instead of legal responsibility, Swaraj is an 'order of moral responsibility'. Individuals are 'self-ruled'. Hence, an individual is accountable to oneself. In his schema, a parliamentary arrangement for ensuring the executive's accountability acquires no meaning.

India's parliamentary institutions will witness a new spate of challenges. India has departed from socialist principles, enshrined clearly in the Preamble and the Directive Principles, to embrace liberalization. It is to be seen how our governing institutions, particularly the judiciary, respond to this doctrinal shift. The judiciary will be tested in its authoritative interpretations of the Constitution, specifically when they come into conflict with the bye-laws of the liberalization regime.

The problem of political instability has been arisen since we entered into the coalition era. It has been argued and postulated that political instability seriously affects governance. Political stability is considered as a prerequisite for sustained economic growth, social development, and national security. There has been a debate on the possibility of shifting from the parliamentary to the presidential system.

It has been projected that the prospects of India's parliamentary future are murky. There are good reasons to allay this fear. India posits a complete paradox. Let us again raise the question of stability. This is a constitutional mandate that the framers of our Constitution preferred 'accountability' to 'stability'. The biggest paradox that confounds many theorists of democracy is that the spell of political instability and economic reforms have dawned together. In terms of growth rate, the Indian economy has relatively prospered amidst governmental instabilities and uncertainties. It presents a peculiar case. According to one school, there are reasons to believe that growing political instabilities are indicative of setting a pace for the democratization process in India. Democratic rights and freedoms have begun to be demanded and extended to hitherto marginalized and excluded groups. Our political system and political culture is taking its time in mutual adjustment. The current spell of instability is the by-product of this process.

However, to attach more procedural stability in India's parliamentary system, the adoption of the German model can be a good prospect. This model will enable the Parliament to have its full term of five years. This system shall obligate the installation of a new government before the existing one is brought down by a 'constructive vote of no confidence.'

Notwithstanding the problems of our parliamentary system stated above, there are good reasons to harbour the hope that the prospects of parliamentary democracy in India are fair. The fact that India's democratic journey has been full of upheavals does not belie this hope. As Robert Dahl has said, 'Achieving stable democracy is not just fair-weather sailing; it also means sailing sometimes in foul and dangerous weather'.[12] What is exciting to note about India's democracy is that it has developed a self-corrective mechanism. Although we find corrosive symptoms in the working of parliamentary institutions, we continue to repose our trust in democracy and democratic institutions even when they ostensibly appear to have lost or tend to loose the democratic character and credentials. Perhaps the biggest source of relief is that India's democratic institutions have grown in resilience in dealing with both democratic and undemocratic infirmities arising from time to time. Ultimately, the working of India's parliamentary system will depend on the extent to which we internalize constitutional morality in the fabric of our political culture.

Suggested Readings

Austin, Granville. *Working a Democratic Constitution*. New Delhi: Oxford University Press, 1999.

Basu, D. D. *Introduction to the Constitution of India*. New Delhi: Prentice-Hall of India, 1995.

Dahl, Robert. *On Democracy*. New Delhi: East-West Press, 2001

Kapur, Devesh and Pratap Bhanu Mehta (eds). *Public Institutions in India*. New Delhi: Oxford University Press, 2005.

Manor, James. 'The Presidency'. In Devesh Kapur and Pratap Bhanu Mehta (eds.), *Public Institutions in India*. New Delhi: Oxford University Press, 2005.

Mehta, Pratap Bhanu. 'India's Judiciary: The Promise of Uncertainty.' In Devesh Kapur and Pratap Bhanu Mehta (eds), *Public Institutions in India*. New Delhi: Oxford University Press, 2005.

Mehta, Pratap Bhanu. 'Inner Conflict of Constitutionalism.' In Zoya Hasan, E. Sridharan and R. Sudarshan (eds). *India's Living Constitution*. New Delhi: Permanent Black, 2002.

---

12. Robert Dahl, *On Democracy* (New Delhi: East-West Press), p. 156.

Pylee, M. V. *Constitutional Government in India*. New Delhi: Asia Publishing House, 1965.

Rudolph, Lloyd and Susanne Rudolph. *In Pursuit of Lakshmi*. New Delhi: Orient Longman, 1987.

Questions

1. What are the advantages and disadvantages of the parliamentary system of government in India?
2. Account for the tension between the legislative and the judiciary in the contemporary Indian situation.
3. Write a short essay on the changing socio-economic background of the Indian parliament.
4. Identify the challenges that confront the Parliament of India.

Democracy: Social and Economic Dimensions

15

Praveen Priyadarshi

After Independence, as the political leadership began to put their minds together to thrash out a model of future India, they had many issues to resolve. However, there was no such ambiguity on the issue of democracy. It was a foregone conclusion, even before the Constituent Assembly began the business of finalizing the political structure of the new State, that it would be a democracy. More than half a century has since passed and that consensus about democracy remains. India rightly claims to be the largest democracy in the world and it takes pride from the fact that we are one of the very few post-colonial countries where it has survived successfully. However, there have been questions about the Indian democracy too. It is true that democracy has survived in India and it has guaranteed equal political rights to all, but what about social and economic inequality? What about the abject condition in which the majority of Indians live? What about the absence of basic amenities and opportunities to them? What about communal violence and caste and gender oppression? Wasn't it a part of the consensus that democracy would eliminate all this too? Moreover, what are the implications of these unresolved questions on the functioning of the Indian democracy? Is it the case that rather than democracy bringing about changes for the better on the front of socio-economic inequalities, gender suppression and communal violence, democracy itself has made adjustments and settled down in a comfortable coexistence with these problems?

These questions reflect the paradoxes of the Indian political system and society. But more importantly, they also reflect the ways in which democracy itself has been perceived and theorized. Broadly, the scholars and commentators that acclaim India as a success case of democracy look at the success in terms of sustainability of the democratic institutions and formal procedures. On the other hand, those who perceive it only partly successful, assign to it certain substantive goals that it must attain in order to be termed as a success. In other words, the question is, do we look at democracy as an end in itself and define it in terms of the presence of regular elections, representative governments and rule of law, participation and accountability? Or we go beyond and seek to evaluate it on the basis of its ability to refashion society on the democratic principles such as freedom and equality for all? In order to answer these questions, one has to consider the following:

First, setting up of democracy was a part of the larger consensus around nation-building that was to be characterized by development, welfare and secularism.[1] Second, democracy had a dual role in the process of nation-building. On the one hand, it was an important political value to be achieved as a part of nation-building and on the other, it had instrumental value as a society based on inclusion and secularism was possible only through a democratic process. Third, distinction of democracy as a form of government is that it directly and decisively links the State to its socio-economic and cultural contexts. There are two ways in which the link between the State and its socio-economic and cultural environment is established. In democracies, people as citizens become participants in the decision-making of the State. They are given equal rights on the basis of the principle of political equality in order to exercise their right to participate in State affairs with equal measure. However, problems arise when, in most of the cases, political equality provided by the State is also accompanied by the embedded social, economic and cultural inequalities. In other words, even as democratic States constitute its citizens as political equals, socio-economic and cultural inequalities instantly recast them into political actors with unequal abilities. Thus, understanding the nature and functioning of a democracy is not possible without taking into account its socio-economic environment. Finally, States also have an ideological position on the socio-economic reality they represent and also on the social change they would like to bring about. The newly constituted Indian State was no exception in this regard.

At the time of Independence, the Indian State was also envisaged as a **developmentalist State**. The socio-economic dimensions of democracy in India becomes all the more pertinent in this regard. It was a dual responsibility for the State. Its role as a developmentalist State required that it brought about social transformation in line with 'nation-building project'; it brought about industrialization; urbanization; created job opportunities; abolished social, economic and regional inequalities; and provided social, economic and cultural freedoms to its citizens. However, because it was also envisaged as a democratic State, it was expected that the processes of development will not only have the constant sanction of the people, but also ensure their active participation.

In other words, democracy turns the state–society relation into a dynamic one in which boundaries are ever-shifting and difficult to identify. Thus, democracy as a form of government is difficult to understand unless we see it in tandem with the socio-economic reality and contextualize it historically and ideologically.

---

1. Niraja Jayal, *Democracy and State: Welfare, Secularism and Development in Contemporary India* (New Delhi: Oxford University Press, 1999).

In this respect, as the Indian democracy became operational it was also the beginning of a new relationship between the Indian State and the socio-economic and cultural environment of the Indian society. In this chapter, we will try to understand this dynamic relationship in the context of contemporary India and see if it helps us answer the questions raised above.

I

HISTORICAL BACKGROUND

The 1920s can safely be termed as a watershed in the history of democratization of the Indian nationalist struggle. This is the decade that saw the advent of the Gandhian ideology and strategy to the nationalist struggle. This was also the decade when the nationalist struggle purposefully began to be inclusive in terms of the socio-economic and religious diversity of the country. Most importantly, however, there were initiatives to institutionalize the mass mobilization that was made possible by movements such as Non-cooperation and Khilafat. Most of these initiatives were in the form of fine tuning the Congress organizational structure to make it a mass organization. Provincial party organizations were reorganized into 21 units, mainly keeping linguistic boundaries in mind. Attempts were also made to decentralize the party organization further. In order to do this, party branches were formed in every district/taluka of British India. An annual membership fee of four ana was also introduced by the party. In 1921, the year Gandhi led the Non-cooperation Movement, membership in Congress climbed to 2 million people.[2]

This process of political involvement of ordinary people through mass movements led by Gandhi and organized by the Congress party had not happened suddenly. It was preceded by a long process of intellectual and ideological fermentations that had begun in the early 19th century. It was through this process that liberal values like equality and freedom began to be internalized by sections of the Indian society that came in contact with such modern ideas of Western thinkers. A wave of social reforms in the 19th century was the first articulation of such ideas as they were applied in interpreting not only social customs and traditions, but also religious practices. All social reformers of the 19th century, from Raja Rammohan Roy to Sayeed Ahmed Khan, were reinterpreting the socio-economic and cultural reality in the light of modern ideas. Towards the end of the 19th century, this process of reinterpretation reached the arena of politics. As soon as the British rule in India began to be seen in this light, it was quite clear that it does not necessarily conform to values such as

2. Francine Frankel, *India's Political Economy: 1947–2004* (New Delhi: Oxford University Press, 2005), p. 29.

freedom and equality. It is at the turn of the century that we begin to see the first murmurs of protest against the British rule.

It was in this context that social practices based on caste and gender inequality came under attack from social reformers like Raja Rammohan Roy and Jyotiba Phule. Later, when Dada Bhai Naroji could write 'Poverty and Un-British Rule in India' explaining the colonial flight of capital from India to Britain, it was as much because of his liberal awareness as because of his sound understanding of economics.

Thus, it was the exposure to modern liberal ideas that laid the first seeds of democracy in India. Later, at least two other ideological sources contributed to the consolidation of democratic values in India. The first major source was Gandhi and his ideas. Though Gandhi too had exposure to Western ideas, he was simultaneously exposed to their limits because of his experiences in South Africa. While placing human equality and human freedom at the centrestage, Gandhi did not stick to the liberal utilitarian framework to forge them together. His contribution was not limited to merely practising such ideals in the course of the nationalist struggle, but also liberating them from the utilitarian framework and expanding them to the extent that in his scheme of things, they became important on their own. Consequently, his notion of freedom for example, is defined as *swaraj* in which the material world is constructed to facilitate human freedom and not the other way round. The second major ideological source that contributed to consolidation and expansion of democratic practices in India was socialism. Around the same period when Gandhi began to transform the nationalist struggle into a mass movement, socialism also began to catch the attention of many. In the context of a fresh socialist revolution in Russia and socialism fast emerging as the ideology of the oppressed, its popularity was only natural among those in India who had access to political and intellectual trends of the outside world. However, Gandhi and his ideas remained more accessible and popular with the illiterate masses. Socialism attracted more attention in the 1930s as USSR began to experience an economic turnaround under the socialist regime. Not only did it create a young brigade of socialism-oriented nationalist leadership but for the first time, class-based organizations such as *kisan sabha* and *majdoor sabhas* came into existence. So influential was this group of socialist leaders in the 1930s that it seriously threatened to stage an ideological coup within the Congress fold.

Socialist influence contributed in two important ways to the democratic roots of the Indian polity. To begin with, socialism exposed the limits of liberal notions of equality and freedom as empty bags unless located in and accompanied by socio-economic equality and freedom. Second, it led to the creation of a new set of class-based democratic institutions in order to articulate the crucial link between socio-economic and political aspects of social life. In this respect, both Gandhism and socialism deepened the democratic character of the nationalist struggle by adding to it the challenge of refashioning of socio-economic life for political freedom to make any sense in it. At the end of the day, it was this aspect of the Indian nationalist struggle that made democracy look like a foregone conclusion for future India.

II

The dynamism introduced by democracy in the relationship between the State and the socio-economic and cultural environment it works in is best reflected in the relationship between the distributional role of the State and bases of political mobilization.

In other words, what would the democratic Indian State do to the society? It will seek to change the society in line with democratic principles and its own ideological position. In the Indian case, the post-Independence State would have liked to take steps to eliminate socio-economic inequality, eliminate caste- and religion-based boundaries, eradicate poverty; the State would do all such things because they are in line with democratic principles and the ideological position of the post-Independence State. If we turn the question around and ask, what would society do to a democratic State? The society would try to influence the State according to its own values, would want to retain its structure and would also want that its power dynamics is reflected in the State and not the other way round. Operationally, what would Indian society want to do to the Indian State? It would want, for example, that caste rather than being eliminated, is represented in the State and values associated with caste also governs the State.

Further, this dynamism of State–society relationship is reflected in the working of actors and institutions of democracy. For example, when political parties go for elections and mobilize people to garner votes, they represent the aspirations of the society. But once in power, they formulate and execute the economic and social policy to redistribute the resources at the disposal of the State. And while they do so, they have a notion of accountability, knowing that they have to go back to the same people for political support for whom, or against whom they are making the policy.

Thus, it is through the lens of the distributional role of the State and basis of political mobilization, that one can understand that socio-economic dimensions of democracy. If we take up the Indian case, the post-Independence Indian democracy can be studied in the following phases.

Structural Social Change, Class-based Mobilization

When India became Independent, the Gandhian principle of village *swaraj* and notion of trusteeship were not the most heard phrases in the political circles. It was the socialist principles of 'State ownership, regulation and control over key sectors of economy' that provided the economic vocabulary for the Indian ruling classes. The Congress party time and again reiterated its resolve to resort to the socialist principle of State ownership and regulation of the economy in its endeavor to usher in a new phase of economic redistribution, curbing economic concentration and bringing about economic equality.

It was the early days for the new democratic State in office. It was also a phase when the democratic impulse of the State was informed more by the freedom movement rather than dictated by compulsions and agendas of parliamentary elections. It was also the early days of Nehruvian vision of grand changes leading to nation building. According to this vision, once the basics of politics and economics are set right, 'smaller details' would be taken care of automatically. Based on this understanding, the State adopted the two-pronged strategy of industrialization under the aegis of the State-owned public sector, on the one hand, and redistribution of agricultural land under a radical land-reform programme, on the other.

Throughout the first decade after Independence, the issue of land reform was high on the government agenda, even though it triggered divisions within the ruling Congress party and a barrage of court cases by the zamindars against the government.

The rhetoric of implementation of land reforms grew even louder in the aftermath of the second parliamentary elections in 1957. This was the first general election when the Congress party was not merely evaluated on the basis of its role in the nationalist movement and promises it offered, but also on the basis of its performance in office since the 1952 elections. In the 1957 elections, even though the Congress showed a minor improvement in terms of percentage of votes, consolidation of opposition votes, and particularly, the rise in strength of the Communist Party sent it in the reflective mood. The dominant direction in shift in voters' sentiment was perceived as a move towards the left. The major issues raised by all economic groups were centred on economic discontent. The election review concluded. 'So evident is this lesson of democracy that even communal organizations cannot hope to win the ear of the people unless they talk the language of radicalism and socialism.'[3] Nehru echoed the same sentiments in his review of the election results and stated that if forces released by democracy and adult franchise were not mastered, they would march on leaving the Congress aside.[4]

Clearly, a section of the Congress party, including Nehru, believed that it is the issue of radical land reforms that has to be addressed if the masses have to be mobilized under the Congress party. However, it was the same radical agenda that began to create cleavages in the party organization at the local levels. The party ranks were sharply divided on the issue of land reforms as it was too

---

3. AICC Election Review, quoted in Frankel, *India's Political Economy*, p. 158.
4. Ibid.

radical to handle for the umbrella character of the party. The land reform was beneficial only to the landless, who were mostly voiceless in the party, whereas it was going to hurt the interests of farmers and erstwhile zamindars who were the most vocal sections of the party at the local level.

As activities for collectivization of agriculture, both in the party and government, began, it divided the party vertically into two camps. While the socialist and Gandhian groups in the party argued in its favour, conservative sections feverishly opposed it. The Chinese aggression and Nehru's death put an abrupt end to the whole process.

Retreat from Structural Socio-economic Change, Diminished Mobilization

The 1960s was a period of confusion when the substance of the radical agenda of land redistribution was flattened out. On the political front, the overshadowing personality of Nehru, which helped the Congress in building a consensus around the socialist path to nation building, received death blows with the Chinese aggression. After Nehru's demise, his successor Lal Bahadur Shashtri, lacked both ideological commitment as well as political capacity to carry out such an agenda. The conditions, thus changed drastically in the post-Nehru era. By 1964, the entire planning process was in jeopardy. The attempts to 'reconcile economic growth with equity through structural changes like land transfer to tenets and millions of subsistence and land cultivators as the condition of their effective participation was rapidly being abandoned.'[5] Similarly, in the wake of the Chinese aggression, question marks were put on the way the process of nation-building was envisaged during the Nehru period. Since the basis of political mobilization was the success achieved in nation building, the Congress found it difficult to cope with questions raised by its opponents from within and outside the party. As India faced another conflict in 1965 with Pakistan, national security, which was not given as much attention during Nehru's tenure in the wake of his idealist foreign-policy pursuits, suddenly acquired utmost importance.

In the wake of such confusion at the ideological and policy levels, it was not surprising that the Congress began to suffer electoral losses for the first time since Independence.[6] Apart from the Communist Party, which had already formed the first non-Congress State government in Kerala, the forces from the right—Jan Sangh and Swatantra Party—also began to gain strength. The Congress leaders of that time believed that the emergence of these parties signified the emergence of an organized rightist reactionary opposition in Indian politics; it signalled the

---

5. Frankel, *India's Political Economy:* 1947–2004 (New Delhi: Oxford University).
6. The Congress lost the Kerala Assembly elections in 1957. However, the situation was much more serious in 1967 when it lost many State governments and came back to power with a reduced number.

determination of the propertied classes to 'fight with all resources their command and resort to all means and methods without any scruples'.[7]

Thus, the emergence of these parties as electoral forces also meant that the political consensus around socialist principles that existed between the Congress and the Communist Party of India (CPI) broke down. While echoing the Congress's plank of socio-economic equality, Jan Sangha and Swatantra Party attacked the Congress for 'preparing the ground for communism in India' by introducing measures like cooperative farming.[8] Given the ideological confusion and conflict that existed at the level of the top leadership of the Congress in the post-Nehru period, the Congress's organization was not fine tuned, and the cadre not well equipped at the grassroots level, to counter the propaganda launched by these parties against the socialist measures of wealth redistribution. Moreover, the opposition to socialist principles was not only from outside the party but also from within. The opponents of Nehruvian ideas were becoming vocal day by day. Morarji Desai, as finance minister and number two in the Cabinet, was a self-proclaimed communist baiter, and had started to defy Nehru's attempts at keeping the planning process in line with the socialist principles.

Thus, the Congress was on the defensive trying to counter the attacks launched by the opposition parties from the right, not only on the issue of national security, but also on the issue of the socio-economic policy. During most of the 1960s, the nature of political mobilization can be understood in this context.

Poverty as a Slogan for Political Mobilization

The genesis of Indira Gandhi's pro-poor and anti-princely class policies can be understood in this context. Not only did she discontinue the privy purse of the former princely States but also went on to nationalize banks—a step considered quite radical at that time. If these steps went on to reinforce the state's ideological position vis-à-vis the prevailing socio-economic structure and its willingness to change it, politically it helped Mrs Gandhi tackle the Jan Sangh and the Swatantra Party, dominated by the propertied classes on the one hand, and the old guards of the Congress party on the other. Moreover, the Bangladesh war of 1971 and the perceived Indian victory in it also helped in warding off apprehensions about national security.

In the early 1970s, Indira Gandhi launched poverty eradication programmes with the objective of directly reaching out to the poor and helping them with their livelihood strategy, rather than waiting for the benefits of macroeconomic growth to reach to them. In any case, it was becoming difficult to maintain the momentum of industrial expansion, which was achieved during the initial phases. At the time when poverty alleviation programmes were announced, at

---

7. Frankel, *India's Political Economy*, p. 209.
8. Ibid., pp. 208–09.

least two-fifths of the population, around 220 million people, lived below the poverty line.[9]

Further, it was also the stage when pure economic policy, intended to bring about economic growth, was delinked from the social policy, which was intended to help the marginalized sections of the society live their lives. This meant that the issue of poverty alleviation was also delinked from the structural issue of land redistribution. This reorientation of the State's policy of redistribution, however, has to be understood in the context of the compulsions of political mobilization. After the split in the party, the government was left with no party structure to mobilize support for its radical programmes like land redistribution. Indira Gandhi, on her part, never tried to build a party organization for the purpose; her own style of functioning was more suitable for direct communication with the masses rather than approaching them through party intermediaries. But, as she wanted to approach the people for political support on the basis of her personal appeal and charisma, the State's policy had to be equally unequivocal and direct in solving their economic woes. It is not surprising, therefore, that poverty alleviation programmes launched in this period are not remembered so much as social policies as they are remembered as *garibi hatao*—the political slogan given by Mrs Gandhi to mobilize the poorer sections of society in favour of her party.

After the Emergency, the Janata government, which was formed in the wake of the Jay Prakash Narain-led movement for 'total revolution', had socialists of various strands and members of the rightist Jan Sangh. Despite the fact that this coalition was based on anti-Indira and exigencies emerging out of anti-Emergency movement, some kind of continuity can be found in the redistributive policies of the Congress rule and the Janata rule in the 1970s. It was expected from a government dominated by the socialists that they would return to the structural issues of economic redistribution and bring back the agenda of land reforms in the political arena. However, in a short tenure laden with fundamental, ideological and political contradictions arising out of the very nature of the coalition, the Janata government could never rescue social policy from being an instrument of political mobilization.

'Structural Adjustments' and Ethnic Mobilization

When the Congress came back to power in 1980, it ushered in a different phase in the economic policy. After decades of emphasis on self-reliance, the Indian economy began to be restructured in accordance with the guidelines of multilateral financial institutions. For the first time perhaps, the Indian State began to look for an external solution to the economic problems in the country. The

9. Ibid., p. 493.

logic was that a robust financial situation was essential to carry out pro-poor policies. How the financial situation was made robust was of little relevance to the poor. Thus, the emphasis was on technological enhancements and upgradations to bridge the socio-economic divides of the Indian society. Though the government and the ruling party desisted from making overt references to the policy shift at political platforms, it was this approach now that guided the economic policy of the Congress government in the 1980s.

By the 1990s, not only the pace of restructuring became faster and much more overt, many of the outcomes of this new trend were also visible. As liberalization and globalization became buzzwords in policy circles, media, and general discussions of the common people, it created a new ideological climate that was opposite to that of the Nehruvian era of the 1950s. If the Nehruvian phase had posited its faith in the ability of socialistic ideas to bring about a socio-economic turnaround, this time around the ability of the market.

Clearly, it was a major shift in the redistributive role of the State in India. From being the prime mover of the economy with the objective to bring about socio-economic equity, the State now had to work as a facilitator for the market, which by definition worked on economic principles of demand and supply and did not care much about political values like equality. Thus, the move towards globalization was a move that not only furthered the distance between economic policy and social policy but also limited the capacity of the State to regulate the economic affairs to a great extent. This shrinking capacity of the State in the economic sphere was coupled with the democratic upsurge in the country that had begun since the 1970s and that had seen the marginal sections of the society staking their claim for political and economic largesse like never before. Various non-party political movements beginning from the 1970s had exposed the limits of conventional democratic institutions like political parties and democratic processes, such as elections, in representing one and all democratically in the political arena. These movements also ensured that hitherto unrepresented sections—Dalits, women, *adivasis*—learned to put pressure on democratic, political institutions for meeting their demands.

It was in this context of the changing nature of the State's redistributive role as well as swelling expectations of the ordinary people, importantly from marginalized sections, that the advent of identity politics should be viewed. The changing role of the State in the economic sphere ensured that 'class' as a category for political mobilization was not so useful because economic equality was something that was not on the agenda of the political elite. And 'class' could only be invoked as long as there existed at least a rhetoric of structural economic equality. Further, by delinking poverty from its structural aspects, the logic of 'class' as an explanation of poverty and consequently class-based prescription of its eradication had already been given up.

A close look at the elections held in the 1980s and the early 1990s makes the point clear. If the sympathy wave following Mrs Gandhi's assassination and the clean and young image of Rajiv Gandhi saw the Congress through in the 1984 general elections, the political agenda during the rest of the 1980s was dominated either by ethno-religious issues such as Shah Bano and Ayodhya, or by the issue of probity in public life that had come under the scanner with alleged kickbacks paid to the political leadership in a high-profile defence deal. As the ruling Congress was not very sure about the response of the economic policy from the people, it tried to first appease the Muslims by overturning the Supreme Court ruling on Shah Bano through a Constitutional Amendment, and then win over the Hindu voters by unlocking the contentious Ram Janma Bhumi-Babri Masjid site. This gave the rightist BJP, which was so far marginalized after the break up in the Janata Party, an opportunity to mobilize Hindus for the construction of a Ram temple at the contentious site in Ayodhya. The rhetoric for 'liberation of Ram Janmabhumi' was also accompanied by the rhetoric of 'pro-minority character of the Congress party' and how Hindus are discriminated against in their own 'homeland'. It was only in a Hindu *rashtra* that the Hindus could get their rightful place and, thus, it was not secular nationalism, claimed the ideologues of the BJP, but cultural nationalism that should be the guiding principle for the Indian State.

Globalization and the Fragmented Nature of Political Mobilization

With the accelerated pace of globalization in the1990s that saw further limits on the State to interfere with the economic structure, we witnessed the true advent of identity as a basis of political mobilization in Indian politics. If the BJP increased the pace of its ethno-cultural nationalism and tried successfully to mobilize people on that basis till it acquired political power at the Centre, caste became an important identity for parties to garner support. Even as the governments of the day took far-reaching decisions on the economic front, the combination of religion and caste more or less overshadowed the economic concerns as issues of democratic process in the country for the better part of the 1990s. The implementation of the Mandal Commission recommendations that led to reservation of government jobs for 'backward castes' other than SCs and STs, ensured that caste becomes not only the basis of political allegiance, but also the basis of State's patronage and support for citizens. Similarly, with the BJP trumping up the issue of cultural nationalism through the Babri Masjid debate, plurality and secularism occupied the centrestage of public debate, relegating economic policies of the State to the sidelines.

The situation, however, seemed to have changed with the elections of 2004 in which the BJP's claims of how globalization had brought about positive changes in people's lives was given a massive thumbs down by the electorate. The BJP which was in coalition with various region- and caste-based political groups, was trying to return to power by shedding its religious hard line in order to retain the coalition intact. However, as they tried to portray globalization as an achievement, people reacted with utter disapproval and ousted the combine from power. The Congress, which gained power with the help of various groups, but most importantly with the help of the Left, has since been talking about 'globalization with a human face'. Operationally, it means that while globalization at the economic level is not revertible and, therefore, will go unhindered, the State through various social policies will, however, ensure that the marginal sections are not hit too hard by it. Keeping in line with this thinking, initiatives like *Bharat Nirman* and employment guarantee schemes have been introduced.

The implications of the changing nature of such a political mobilization were far too many and too far reaching. First, identity-based political mobilization led to a democratic deficit. With caste and religion becoming the basis of political support, we witnessed a spurt of caste- and family-based parties in the political arena. These parties often worked like a family business operation and bothered very little about democratic principles, either in their intra-party dealings or in their dealings in the larger political arena.

Second, the advent of identity politics has seen the reconfiguration of the Indian political arena on caste and religious lines. Earlier, political parties and actors were identified with their ideological leanings. Now it was through their caste and religious bases that the political parties and actors were identified.

Third, it also led to a very significant change in perception of people about the process called politics. People also no longer associated it with a modern interaction based on secular identities, but as a traditional process that worked on the basis of ascribed identities.

Finally, the politics based on identity has led to fragmentation rather than cohesion and confrontation rather than dialogue. It has also led to a fierce competition for State resources with various groups scrambling for them.

CONCLUSION

The changing nature of political mobilization in Indian politics can be better understood if we study it as a gradual historical continuum and in the context of the changing distributional role of the State. It is through its distributional role that the State seeks to change the socio-economic conditions of its people and society in general. People on the other hand, give their verdict on the nature of redistributions carried out by the State through the democratic processes. They approve or disapprove the policies by voting or not voting in favour of the party in power. In turn, the State's agenda for redistribution is largely influenced by what it expects people to approve and otherwise. In sum, the dynamism introduced by democracy in the relationship between the State and the socio-economic and cultural environment it works in is best reflected in the relationship between the distributional role of the State and bases of political mobilization. As is clear from the discussion above, a study of this relationship gives a very clear picture of the socio-economic dimensions of the Indian democracy. On the historical continuum, as we see that the nature of the State's redistributional role has undergone changes, so has the basis of political mobilization. When the State sought to reorganize society in lines with socialist principles, political actors sought to mobilize people primarily on the basis of class. However, as the determination to reorganize society on socialist principle diminished, **class-based mobilization** also gave way to other types of mobilization. As we witness a complete change in the State role vis-à-vis economy in the wake of globalization, it is identity that has become an important ground for political mobilization.

Suggested Readings

Frankel, Francine. *India's Political Economy: 1947–2004*. New Delhi: Oxford University Press, 2005.

Jayal, Niraja. *Democracy and State: Welfare, Secularism and Development in Contemporary India*. New Delhi: Oxford University Press, 1999.

Kapur, Devesh and Pratap Bhanu Mehta (eds). *Public Institutions in India: Performance and Design*. New Delhi: Oxford University Press, 2005.

Kaviraj, Sudipta (ed.), *Politics in India*. New Delhi: Oxford University Press, 1997.

Kothari, Rajni. *Rethinking Democracy*. Hyderabad: Orient Longman Press, 2005.

Questions

1. What were the challenges before the Indian democracy at the time of Independence? How do you assess the performance of the Indian democracy so far?
2. Elaborate the major ideological influences on democracy in India. How do you see the relationship between the nature of nationalist struggle and the Indian democracy?
3. Analyse the changing nature of political mobilization in the Indian democratic process since Independence.
4. Do you agree with the view that the processes of liberalization and globalization have changed Indian democratic politics for good? Explain.

The Changing Nature of the Party System

16

Pushpa Kumari

In modern democracies, parties are considered as indispensable vehicles of representation. They perform a wide range of functions of interlinking people and the government, harmonizing different institutional orders and different political processes. Parliamentary democracy needs political parties for articulation of people's will and for formation of the government. In a way, the political system derives its strength from the political parties. Party politics has been vital to the successful functioning of the Indian democracy. This chapter aims at introducing the basic features and exploring the functioning of the party system in India since Independence, under the light of its gradual transformation from a **one-party-dominant system** to a multi-party system.

The existence and survival of political parties depend on their victory in capturing political power against other parties or group. They rise and grow in response to the needs of the social and political system in a particular milieu.[1] Parties regulate individual and group behaviour in a society with the aim of influencing, moulding and controlling the behaviour of the voters. Political parties stand for the act of representation, with an electoral system and process of recruitment of leaders, defining goals and resolving internal system conflicts.[2] Political parties in India are an integral and essential part of our political culture.

POLITICAL PARTY AS VEHICLE OF POLITICAL REPRESENTATION

Political parties are seen as a distinctive feature of the process of political **representation**. They reflect the citizens' consent and aspiration by representing

1. Samuel J. Eldersveld, *Political Parties: A Behavioral Analysis* (Bombay: Vora and Co., 1964), p. 2.
2. Ibid., p. 1.

their wishes through the electoral process. In the modern-day large democracies, it is not possible for all citizens to directly participate in the political process and speak for themselves. In this situation, political parties form a crucial link between citizens and the State. They articulate people's needs and aspirations and try to implement it when they come in to power. Political parties, therefore, stand to represent the citizens' demands and wishes. Hanna Fenichel Pitkin States that representation makes things present that are not literally present.[3] The political representatives act as the voice of the people whom they represent after they are elected. They are entrusted with the position to make decisions that will benefit the district they represent. This makes it necessary for the representative to maintain a balance between the views of constituents, personal belief, and the common goal of both maintaining and improving the nation as a whole.[4]

Parties provide the organizational base for mobilization and participation of the people. They provide ideologies, beliefs and symbols for political identification to the people. The party system implies an elective and, therefore, a representative government.[5] It is generally agreed that democracy requires groups such as political parties to perform critical functions—to recruit leadership, formulate policy, organize decision-making, communicate upward and downward between leaders and public, promote consensus, enforce responsibility and, thus, move the society towards the effective resolution of its conflicts.[6]

Political parties are not directly mentioned in the Constitution of India. However, the Tenth Schedule that was added by the Constitution (Fifty-second Amendment) Act, 1985 refers to the functioning of the political parties. It deals with the disqualification of a person for being a member of either House of Parliament [Art. 102(2)] or the Legislative Assembly or Legislative Council of a State[Art.191(2)], on ground of defection. The responsibilities of framing and governing the rules and regulations of political parties have been assigned to the Election Commission of India, which is an independent constitutional body. It monitors the conduct of elections and accords recognition to the political parties.

DEFINITION AND TYPOLOGY

Political parties serve as a unifying force and perform the task of social and political integration. Parties have been defined in various ways. According to

3. Hanna Fenichel Pitkin, *The Concept of Representation* (Berkeley and Los Angeles: University of California Press, 1967), p. 144.
4. Ibid., p. 144.
5. R. M. MacIver, *The Modern State* (London: Oxford University Press, 1926), p. 396.
6. Eldersveld, *Political Parties*, p. 22

Giovani Sartori, a party is any political group that presents at elections and is capable of placing through elections, candidates for public office.[7] MacIver defined political party as an association organized in support of some principle or the policy, which by constitutional means, endeavours to make the determinant of the government.[8] A political party is a social group, a system of meaningful and patterned activity within the larger society. Finer maintains that parties are legally defined by the strength shown at previous elections, a minimum being laid down in terms of votes or percentage of poll.[9] Newman defined a political party as an articulate organization of societies' active political agents, those who are concerned with the control of the government and who compete for popular support with other group or groups holding diversion views. Political parties all over the world differ in term of the context of their rise and growth, orientation, mode of operation and mobilizing strategies. A political party is a fighting organization, which exists in order to win battles against other parties or groups.

Generally, the party system is classified as a single-party, two-party and multi-party system based on the numerical strength of parties in any political system. However, the party system in India does not fit into any prescribed type of Western models of party system.[10] The Indian party system has been described as the one-party-dominant system or the Congress system by Rajni Kothari, which can be seen as a model of party system in itself. Indian party politics gives the impression of the country as a pluralist society, where the interests of multiplicity of private associations and other various forces is aggregated, and they have considerable influence on policy formation.[11]

Unlike a one-party system, the Indian system is a competitive one with the constituent parts playing dissimilar roles.[12] The 'Congress system' model suggests that the Congress has been pivotal in the Indian party system as it forms the core whereas, the rest of the parties operate from the periphery in order to put pressure on the core. They operate and exert pressure from the margins. The Congress, which has been the ruling party most of the time, survived by sustaining the pressure, accommodating and assimilating various forces like several opposition groups, interest groups, and dissident groups. Yet, such forces

---

7. Giovanni Sartori, *Parties and Party System: A Framework of Analysis* (London: Cambridge University Press, 1976), p. 1.
8. Ibid., p. 396.
9. Herman Finer, *Theory and Practice of Modern Government* (New York: A. Henry Holt and Company, 1950), p. 220.
10. Political parties are accorded the status of a national or state political party in India in accordance with the review of their status, based on their performance in the elections. Important national political parties at present are the Indian National Congress, Bharatiya Janata Party, Communist Party of India, Communist Party of India (Marxist), Janata Dal and Bahujan Samaj Party.
11. Paul R. Brass, *The New Cambridge History of India: The Politics of India Since Independence* (Cambridge, UK: Cambridge University Press), p. 65.
12. Ibid, p. 40.

do not constitute any alternative to the Congress. The prime purpose of their existence is to constantly put pressure on, criticize, censure and influence the ruling political power.[13] Thus, the role of the opposition basically has been to act as a watchdog and maintain a constant vigil over the ruling Congress. Whereas this results in the latent threat[14] from the margins, the factionalism inside the ruling party provides the instrument of inbuilt correction. In case of India, the opposition is divided and fragmented due to a lack of consensus and coherence. The opposition survives on gaining where the Congress loses. The Indian party system consists of 'party of consensus and parties of pressure'.[15]

LEGACY OF THE INDIAN PARTY SYSTEM

The rise of nationalism in the 19th century India is believed to provide the backdrop for the emergence of political parties and the party system in the country. In the beginning, political parties emerged as public forums in reaction to the colonial rule. The growth of national consciousness gradually led to its galvanization into a mass movement. The Indian National Congress is revered as the oldest political party in India. It was created in 1885 through the union of presidency associations of middle-class professionals. The Indian National Congress was able to capture unexplored, political space at the national level and projected itself as an authentic repository of spirit of Indian nationalism. By presenting the Indian interest to the British Crown in a systematic and organized manner, the Indian National Congress soon became a leading voice of the Indian middle class, constantly clamouring for more jobs under the colonial government and for greater political participation.[16] From the time of 19th century nationalism till the present day, the Congress remains a persistent political party. Most of the major non-Congress parties originated from within, and not outside, the Indian National Congress; among them were the Congress Socialist Party, which became the nucleus of the Praja Socialist Party, and even the Communist Party.

There have been lots of debates about the party system in India. M. K. Gandhi, the pioneer of the Indian liberation struggle, was never comfortable with party politics. He believed that the State and all its institutions represent violence in a concentrated and organized form that poses a threat to the liberty of the individual. He prescribed a democratic system based on village self-government and called it Gram Swaraj, where political parties will have no

---

13. Rajni Kothari, 'The Congress "System" in India', in Zoya Hasan (ed.), *Parties and Party Politics in India* (New Delhi: Oxford University Press, 2002), p. 41.
14. Ibid, p. 41.
15. Ibid, p. 40.
16. Subrata K. Mitra, Mike Enskat and Clemens Spiess, 'Introduction', in their (ed.) *Political Parties in South Asia* (Praeger: Westpost, 2004), p. 8.

role. In his scheme of decentralization of power, he believed that since there was no necessity of representation, therefore, there was no place for power seeking political parties.[17] In his last piece of writing *Last Will and Testament*, Gandhi suggested the dissolution of the Congress as a political organization and its replacement by the Lok Sewak Sangh (Servant of People Association).[18] But the working committee of the Congress rejected Gandhi's proposal and decided that it wanted the organization to be a political party. Similarly, Jayaprakash Narayan advocated for a partyless democracy with emphasis on decentralization of power, village autonomy and more representative legislature.[19] He aimed to introduce democracy at the grassroots level, based on the principle of unanimity and consensus.

Indian National Congress:[20] Origin and Growth

The theory of the Congress system has been widely acknowledged as a useful framework to analyse the nature and significance of the party system in India. There has been dominance of the Congress in the Indian political system, which reconciled the diverse interests and various layers of peripheries from State and regional levels. The Congress has played a crucial role in setting the basic parameters of party politics in India. It will be interesting to trace the trajectory of performance of the Congress, which has gone through various changes and several splits.

The birth of the Indian National Congress has been seen as a milestone, which became the bedrock for the foundation of the party system in India. Mr Allan Octavian Hume facilitated its foundation. The contribution of the Indian National Congress is invaluable on several accounts. It provided a national platform to its members to represent India and address their colonizers. It inculcated a sense of solidarity and national consciousness among the Indians to oust the foreign rule eventually. After Independence, the Congress was transformed from a movement into a ruling party and shifted its attention from political mobilization to administrative consolidation except for the purpose of contending elections. However, Rajni Kothari maintains that even after Independence, the Congress retained its legacy of being a movement, as it had to carry on with the formidable task of nation building.[21]

17. J. P. Narayan, 'Gandhi and Politics of Decentralization', in Sibnarayan Ray (ed.), *Gandhi, India and the World* (Bombay: Nachiketa Publication Limited, 1970), p. 240.
18. Ibid., p. 235.
19. J. P. Narayan, *A Plea for Reconstruction of Indian Polity* (Kashi: Akhil Bharat Sarva Seva Sangh, 1959), p. 66.
20. Indian National Congress and Congress have been used synonymously.
21. Kothari, 'The Congress "System"', p. 47.

Organization: The Congress displays the character of a mass party with a well-developed organizational structure. It has an elaborate, hierarchical, organizational structure that extends from local to district to Stateto All India Congress Committee (AICC) culminating at the top in the working committee, which is the executive committee of the national party. The executive committee has an elected president as its head. The working committee and the president look after the functioning of the organization as a whole. Also, there are State and Central Parliamentary Boards, which play crucial roles in the allocation of party nominations to Congressmen to contest the election to the State legislative assemblies and to Parliament. In its earlier days, Nehru remained in complete command of policy and politics in the Congress party and also in the government. The national leadership provided by Nehru was called the high command and it included the trusted political confidants of Nehru. These political leaders performed the task of mediation and arbitration of factional conflict at the State level.[22]

Social Base of the Congress: The support base of the Congress is composed of varied sections and interest groups displaying the character of a mass organization. The leadership is also derived from a diffused social base. The Congress, by accommodating divergent socio-economic interest and ideological preferences, had projected itself as a party of broadest consensus.[23] It has been seen as an umbrella organization that provided a haven to all divergent forces belonging to different religions, castes, classes and cultures. The Congress has projected itself as the legitimate heir of nationalist historical consensus. It has internalized and assimilated political competition, consequently forming a system of factions at every level of political and governmental activity. These factions operated by tactics of pressure, mediation, conflict, bargaining, compromise and consensus.[24] The Indian party system has taken the shape of a single-party-dominant system or the Congress system or one-party-dominance system[25] in which, there has been monopoly enjoyed by the Congress and yet pluralism finds its way in intra-party factions. Across four decades since Independence, both in terms of percentage of the votes received and the seats captured in parliament, the Congress has consistently dominated its rivals and its opponents have never forged a stable challenge.[26]

In the first few decades, the Congress derived its strength from the landlords in the countryside, the urban capitalist and the expanding middle

---

22. Brass, *The New Cambridge History of India*, p. 66.
23. Ibid, p. 41.
24. Ibid, p. 42.
25. Kothari, 'The Congress"System"', p. 40.
26. Pradip K. Chhibber and John R. Petrocik, 'Social Cleavage, Elections, and Indian Party System', in Hasan (ed.), *Parties and Party Politics in India*, p. 62.

class. However, the decade of 1980 marked a clear shift in the support base of the Congress due to the new challenges put by the emergence of regional bourgeois in many parts of the country. In post–Green Revolution India, a new class of rich farmers and intermediate castes grew who did not see the Congress adequately representing their interests.

Programme and Ideology of the Congress Party: Given the socio-economic conditions in which we inherited our country after national liberation, the Congress had to play the role of a movement of social reconstruction in post-colonial India. This provided an opportunity to the people to participate in the political process at the local level, and in turn, the Congress acquired legitimacy as a responsive and responsible regime. It gained the symbolic value of people's trust. Though the spirit of the pre-Independence days was missing, yet, such initiatives helped the party to retain mass support.

The Congress declared itself in favour of a socialistic pattern of development for the Indian society; together with this, the idea of 'democratic socialism' and secularism was stressed. From the beginning, the Congress has been committed to a democratic ideology.[27] The concept of a planned economy was asserted as an economic policy. There was considerable expansion of the public sector, which sometimes proved to be very expensive in their operation. It tried to remove feudalism and took up the task of linguistic reorganization of the States in 1956. The objective of the agrarian reforms was vigorously pursued. Several important sectors were nationalized. The slogan of 'Garibi Hatao' was advocated with the 1971 elections in mind.

Critical Assessment of the Congress: In the later decades, many times the party showed a lack of idealistic visions, as the leaders became more interested in nurturing their own ambitions. Slowly, conflicts originated and gradually it got aggravated between the legislative and organizational wings of the Congress due to personal rivalries and differing interests. In order to enjoy the continuing allegiance of heterogeneous interests, it worked on the principle of negotiation, bargain and many times compromised with its broad objectives. Nehru's failure to provide a remedy to intra-party contradiction led to an erosion of his authority as a leader of the party and the government. Gradually, the Congress went through various splits (1969, 1980, 1994 and 1999). One of these split groups, Congress-I, has projected itself as an inheritor of the Congress party. During the tenure of Mrs Indira Gandhi and Mr Rajiv Gandhi, the Congress displayed authoritarian and monopolistic tendencies, for example, emergency was imposed in 1977 by Mrs Gandhi. The governance became centralized and personalized resulting in the decline and decay of the Party. From 1980s onwards, it became increasingly difficult for the Congress to sustain its mass support.

---

27. Kothari, 'The Congress "System"', p. 46.

It gradually became incapable of providing the leadership accommodating varied interests.[28]

It can be observed that the Congress in its earlier phase used to perform to some degree the work of a national Parliament where clashing viewpoints and concerns need to determine a generally acceptable line of policy.[29] As the oldest political party in India, the Congress has been successful in retaining the goodwill of as many sections of society as it has been feasible. It has harmonized with ease its three basic elements of leadership with national appeal and acceptability, a pan-Indian ideology with recognition and accommodation of local and regional spirit and district-level cadre.[30] Even in a State of decline in the contemporary times, it retains this essential element of its culture. An overall assessment of the Congress party shows that it has attempted to sustain its propensity of preservation of democratic tradition. The Congress has shown great sensitivity on the question of respect for minorities, including political minorities.[31] Several factors have helped the success and survival of the Congress. Due to its heritage and the struggle for the history of Independence, the Congress has always enjoyed tremendous amount of goodwill, respect and support. These factors have also helped the Congress in keeping itself in cohesion. The 2004 Lok Sabha election secured the Congress and its allies sizeable gains at the national level, leading to its victory and the formation of the United Progressive Alliance (UPA) government.

THE CHANGING NATURE OF PARTY POLITICS: IMPORTANT NATIONAL PARTIES AND THE RISE OF NEW FORCES

The nature of political participation has shown considerable changes in the 1990s. With the beginning of coalition politics[32], several changes such as the decline of the Congress, and the rise of the BJP have taken place. A clear shift can be seen from a one-party-dominant system to a multi-party system and minority government in Indian politics. The rise of regionalism has led to a growing demand for greater autonomy by the States in the 1980s, precipitating in the mushrooming of regional political parties. The regional parties have become prominent national actors in coalition formation in the central and

---

28. Zoya Hasan, 'Introduction', in her (ed.), *Parties and Party Politics in India*, p. 11.
29. W. H. Morris Jones, *The Government and Politics in India* (London: Hutchinson University Library, 1964), p. 35.
30. Harish Khare, 'Problems of Survival and Reinvention in Political Parties in South Asia', in Subrata K. Mitra, Mike Enskat and Clemens Spiess (eds.), *Political Parties in South Asia* (Westport, CT: Praeger, 2004), Introduction, p. 32.
31. Kothari, 'The Congress "System"', p. 50.
32. For a detailed discussion on coalition government and politics, please refer to Chapter 17 in this volume.

State governments. The change in the party regime has brought new castes and classes into its folds. These positive changes have augmented the process of democratization in the country.

The democratic process has deepened with the dramatic participatory upsurge among the socially underprivileged in class and caste hierarchy,[33] which have been almost non-existent earlier. This increase in participation and assertion by the marginalized strata of the society indicates a major democratic upsurge[34] that has opened new avenues for the unprivileged. The first remarkable upsurge was in the 1960s when expansion in participatory base took place in order to proceed towards an alternative to hegemony of the Congress party. This downward thrust of mobilization of socially deprived people like Dalits, *adivasi*, Other Backward Castes and all other minorities continues with added vigour in the contemporary times. This symbolizes the second democratic upsurge.[35] However, this democratic wave has reached its saturation as the dominant language and politics of the subaltern has been co-opted by the other parties. The distinctive shift of the 1990s is reflected in terms of three issues—Mandal, Masjid and Market—referring to caste-based reservation, upsurge of Hindu nationalism that led to demolition of Babri Masjid and the liberalization policy, respectively. The results of the 1998 general elections gave the message that the electorate of India had endorsed a two-party or two-national-alliances system to dominate the country's political scene, one led by the Congress and the other led by the Bharatiya Janata Party.

Bharatiya Janata Party

The 1990s saw the rise of the BJP as a ruling party at the national level, which tried to provide Hindu communal orientation to the governance process. Bharatiya Janata Party was founded in 1980; however, its legacy has been traced back to the Bharatiya Jan Sangh (1951) and Rashtriya Swayamsevak Sangh (RSS) (1925). These forces have been known as Hindu right wing that cherished the desire of cultural nationalism under the slogan of 'one country, one nation one culture and rule of law.'

The scene of Indian politics has undergone drastic changes from the 1980s. There has been a continued decay of the Congress party creating a political vacuum that has been filled by the emergence of the BJP as the single largest

---

33. Zoya Hasan, 'Representation and Redistribution: The New Lower Caste Politics of North India,' in Francine R. Frankel, Zoya Hasan, Rajeev Bhargava and Balveer Arora (eds.), *Transforming India: Social and Political Dynamics of Democracy* (New Delhi: Oxford University Press, 2000), p. 147.
34. Yogendra Yadav, 'Understanding the Second Democratic Upsurge', in Frankel et al. (eds.), *Transforming India*, p. 121.
35. For a detailed discussion, refer to ibid.

Table 16.1: Electoral Performance of Major Political Parties in Lok Sabha Elections, 1977–2004.

	Seats Won								
Election Year	1977	1980	1984	1989	1991	1996	1998	1999	2004
Total No. of Seats	542	529	542	529	511	543	543	543	543
INC	154	353	415	197	227	140	141	114	145
BJP	*	*	02	85	119	162	182	182	138
CPI	07	11	06	12	13	12	9	4	10
CPI(M)	22	36	22	33	35	32	32	33	43
JP/JD	298	31	10	143	56	46	6	21	8
BSP	-	-	-	-	-	11	5	14	19

Notes: INC: Indian National Congress; BJP: Bharatiya Janata Party; CPI: Communist Party of India; CPI (M): Communist Party of India (Marxist); JP/JD: Janata Party/ Janata Dal; BSP: Bahujan Samaj Party

** The BJP was a constituent of the Janata Party in these elections.*

Source: Election Commission of India, http://www.eci.gov.in.

party in the recent elections. Earlier, the BJP was considered basically as a part of the opposition bloc. However, the Lok Sabha election of 1998 established its centrality in coalition formation at national and regional level. It marked unprecedented growth in the electoral gains of BJP which swung from two seats in the 8th Lok Sabha in 1984 to 182 seats in the 12th Lok Sabha Elections in 1998 (See Table 16.1). It coveted significant vote share from the Congress and other parties due to a violent backlash by the upper castes against the issue of reservation for OBCs advocated by the Mandal Commission. Now, BJP has been playing a key role in formation of political alliance as a challenge to the Congress or Congress-led alliance at the centre and the states.

The agenda of the BJP is formation of a Hindu nation based on the ideology of Hindutva. This kind of cultural nationalism poses a threat to the democratic and secular credentials of Indian politics. It also highlights the limitations of their commitment to the realization of substantive democracy. Many scholars believe that it will be very difficult for the BJP to implement its agenda of hegemony and Hindutva due to the plural ethos of the Indian society. There has been considerable moderation in ideology and agenda of the party due to the electoral calculations and the pressure of the coalition politics. The BJP sought to accommodate its coalition partners by publishing a national agenda, which omitted the controversial issue of the building of the Ram temple at Ayodhya, the Uniform Civil Code, and Kashmir's special constitutional status as a part of its moderation strategy.[36] The BJP has also broadened its Hindu nationalist agenda. Soon after coming into power in 1998, the BJP by exploding the nuclear bomb asserted its strength and tried to project Hindu nationalism as Indian nationalism. Its policies show apparent support to liberalization, privatization and globalization. It has used the foreign policy, defence policy and issues of internal security to enhance its domestic support base. The BJP has periodically tuned up and subdued its Hindutva rhetoric to come to power and to retain it, displaying cycles of moderation and militancy according to the contingent situation. It wishes to gain support by presenting itself as a centrist party that endorses the common value of the Indian politics. At the same time, it appears problematic for the BJP to transform its fundamental character and beliefs due to its affiliation, proximity and enduring ties with the RSS–VHP network. It is yet to be seen whether BJP will succeed in moulding itself into a liberal framework to provide the national leadership at the same time maintaining cordial relations with Hindu right-wing elements.

The support base of the party is limited to the upper caste and class of the northern Indian States, which make it difficult for the party to provide the national leadership on its own. In non-Hindi speaking states, the BJP mostly remains a marginal player.[37] Therefore, it has been trying to expand its support base by including the Dalits and Muslims in its folds. However, the Congress still enjoys the largest amount of support from the underprivileged sections of the Indian society. In the last three elections, BJP's performance has shown a steady increase in the share of the seats reserved for the Scheduled Tribes. This can be understood by studying the rising communal tensions in the tribal belts of central India, including Gujarat, Maharashtra, Madhya Pradesh, Bihar and Orissa. Three principal obstacles in the BJP's path of further rise are opposition by Muslim voters, division in votes of the backward castes into BJP and the Left Janata parties and the near-total hold of the Scheduled Caste votes by the BSP.

The BJP and the other Hindutva forces harbour a monolithic conception of the State, which is problematic for a multicultural and plural society like India. It is the multicultural nature of the Indian society that is under attack by the proponents of Hindutva.[38] Since no political party can win with majority, all parties are trying to compromise with their agenda and grant concessions to their pre-election allies. The BJP wants to establish itself as an alternative to the Congress. According to the contingencies of the electoral processes, the BJP has been vacillating between extremism and moderation in its agenda and

---

36. Amrita Basu, 'The Transformation of Hindu Nationalism? Towards a Reappraisal', in Frankel et al. (eds.), *Transforming India*, p. 399.
37. In recent years, though, the party has been gaining in strength in the South. It first formed a coalition government with the Janata Dal (Secular) in Karnataka in 2006, and in 2008 won in the Karnataka state elections, thus forming a government in South India without a coalition.
38. Neera Chandhoke, 'Individualism and Group Rights: A View From India', in Granville Austin (ed.), *India's Living Constitution* (New Delhi: Oxford University Press), p. 210.

policy formulation. The defeat of the BJP in the 2004 parliamentary elections has been interpreted as the rejection of communalism and has reinforced faith in secularism among people.

The Communist Party of India

There has been the presence of communist parties in Indian politics from the time of pre-Independence days. They represent Marxist and communist revolutionary tradition in the modern Indian political history.[39] Primarily referred to as reformist political parties, they have functioned by exerting pressure on the ruling parties rather than winning majority to form the government. Left forces represent the radical forces, which aim at the transformation of the society in favour of the weak and the marginalized. The communist parties have associated themselves with the Communist International. There has been a split in the communist forces resulting in two prominent parties the CPI and the CPI (M).

The communist parties have to redefine themselves in terms of their objective and methodology with the changing global context.[40] The remarkable significance of the communist parties has been that they have been very critical of the nefarious ways in which the forces of globalization implicate the lives of the working and poor classes. They have always scrutinized the neo-liberal policies of the government in order to cater to the needs of the impoverished and helpless masses of the country. They are more successful in influencing the policies of the government as coalition partners in the state and at the national level. Their presence is strong in some states like West Bengal, Tripura and Kerala. In contemporary times, there is an urgent need for the communist parties to rejuvenate themselves in the wake of the changing pretext of the society and the world. They need to clearly outline their objectives and methodology in order to reinforce their dominance in the Indian party system.

Regional Political Parties

Apart from the national parties, there are a number of political parties that define themselves with reference to a particular region or ethnic groups. Such parties are Dravida Munnetra Kazhagam (DMK) and All India Anna Dravida Munnetra Kazhagam (AIADMK) in Tamil Nadu, Telegu Desam Party (TDP) in Andhra Pradesh, Asom Gana Parishad (AGP) in Assam, National Conference (NC) in Jammu and Kashmir, Shiromani Akali Dal (SAD) in Punjab, Haryana

---

39. Brass, *The New Cambridge History of India*, p. 64.
40. With the downfall of the Soviet Union, and neoliberal principles and policies becoming the buzz word of the administration and government, communist parties have to contextualize and reinforce the needs and aspirations of poor masses. They should try to monitor the process of liberalization, privatization and globalization in all possible ways.

Vikas Party (HVP) in Haryana, Biju Janata Dal (BJD) in Orissa, Trinamool Congress in West Bengal, etc. Among all such forces, Shiromani Akali Dal, National Conference, Dravida Munnetra Kazhagam, Asom Gana Parishad, Shiv Sena are results of a long-drawn struggle and sustained social movements. DMK is the strongest of all regional parties and was formed in 1949 under C. Annadurai. This party took the shape of a movement that basked in the glory of the Dravidian past inculcating pride in people regarding their language, literature and Tamil culture. It was also an outburst against the social oppression suffered by the non-Brahmins at the hands of Brahmins and Aryan invaders of the north. In 1972, another party, Anna DMK, was formed under the leadership of M. G. Ramachandran. The TDP in Andhra Pradesh has successfully projected itself as an alternate to the Congress dominance since 1980s. It was formed by N. T. Rama Rao in 1982. The TDP has been revered as the upholder of Telugu pride. It secured a great deal in development in its State, yet it put up a poor show in the 2004 elections. In Maharashtra, the Shiv Sena expanded its power and base in the 1980s and gained prominence even at the national level. However, many view it as a parochial Marathi, Hindu communal organization.[41] The Shiv Sena shares many ideologies and beliefs of the BJP.

The Akali Dal was formed in 1920 and was engaged in the issues of sectarian representation and self-determination. After Independence it demanded and acquired Statehood in 1966. In the 1980s, it got involved in militant movement for autonomy and nationhood which in turn splintered the party. In the post-1992 phase, the politics of the party is shaped by the emergence of a sharp and shrill politics of the Hindutva due to the electoral compulsions.[42] The National Conference, one of the oldest regional parties in India, has been central to the politics of Jammu and Kashmir since its formation in 1939. It started participating in power politics since 1947 and has remained the single largest party in the State.

In north India, the Samajwadi Party (SP) represents the Socialist tradition in Uttar Pradesh. It has been greatest beneficiary and carrier of the Mandal upsurge. In its multi-pronged strategy, it seeks to consolidate the caste cleavage by uniting the OBCs and also appealing to the upper caste for votes in the name of development and globalization.[43] The BSP has a strong base among Dalits. SP, under the leadership of Mulayam Singh Yadav, attempted to create a social and political alliance of the SP and the BSP at the State level, which failed to work out after some time. In Bihar, the Rashtriya Janata Dal (RJD) solicits support on caste lines.

---

41. Suhas Palshikar, 'Shiv Sena: A Tiger with Many Faces?' *Economic and Political Weekly*, 39 (14, 15), 3–10 April 2004: 1497.
42. Ashutosh Kumar, 'Electoral Politics in Punjab: Study of Akali Dal', *Economic and Political Weekly*, 39 (14, 15) April 3–10, 2004: 1515.
43. A. K. Verma, 'Samajwadi Party in Uttar Pradesh', *Economic and Political Weekly*, 39 (14, 15), 3–10 April 2004: 1509.

PROBLEMS AND CRISES IN PARTIES AND PARTY SYSTEM IN INDIA

Party politics in most of the developing societies like India is blighted by so many problems and puzzles. Political parties tend to exploit and manipulate the extremely fragmented society based on religion, caste, community and ethnicity to gain dominance and perpetuate themselves in power. Elections and party competitions in view of a politically active caste, tribe, ethnic and religious conflicts, of such societies appears problematic.[44]

There are many problems that face the Indian party system. One of them is the widespread criminalization of politics that has weakened the political culture and democratic foundation of the society. The nexus between criminals and party politics has led to the latter being conditioned by money, muscle and mafia in many parts in the country. The magnitude of criminalization, which has crept into the electoral system, has to a large extent vitiated the value of vote.[45] The party leadership misuses power to satisfy their supporters, generate funds and garner votes, most of the times in undemocratic ways.

There is corporatization of political parties. They generate large funds from the public and private sources; many times adopting corrupt practices of various kinds. The party members survive on such spoils generated by the party. This necessitates the mandatory auditing of accounts of all the parties. The committees on electoral reforms[46] have suggested a compulsory report on the financial status of all parties which should be open and available to public study and inspection. Political parties should make their candidates declare their assets and liabilities at the time of their nomination for election. They should try to limit their expenditure in electoral campaigns and in holding public rallies and demonstrations. This will free the parties from incurring huge expenditures on all sorts of illegitimate or dubious activities adopted to raise enormous amount of money. There is a tendency in political parties to convert its governance into family business. In a way, the Congress displays 'dynastic rule' syndrome, due to the domination of the Nehru-Gandhi leadership.

Many cases of rigging have been reported in the elections in Jammu and Kashmir, the Northeast and in many parts in Bihar. There is a deterioration in the quality of leadership. In comparison to the few outstanding leaders of the past, the present day leadership does not seem to inspire the people.[47] There has been an increase in the authoritarian and undemocratic practices pervading

---

44. Mitra, et al., 'Introduction', p. 9.
45. Manoranjan Mohanty, 'Theorising Indian Democracy', in Rajendra Vora and Suhas Palshikar (eds.), *Indian Democracy: Meaning and Practice* (New Delhi: Sage, 2004), p. 110.
46. Refer to the *Report of the Law Commission of India on Electoral Reforms* submitted to the Government in May 1999, for detailed discussion.
47. M. V. Pylee, *Emerging Trends of Indian Party* (Delhi: Regency Publications, 1998), p.16.

the elections and party politics. Most of the political parties indulge in violence, and display disregard for institutional norms. Besides, they also reflect a lack of coherence, clear vision and well-defined ideology. The growing intra- and inter-party conflicts have eroded the legitimacy and reputation of parties as well as leaders.[48] Rampant illiteracy, lack of education and awareness in ignorant masses and impoverishment in the Indian society enables the opportunist political leaders to misguide and manipulate the masses.

There is increasing politicization of religion manifested in the onslaught of cultural nationalism, which is excessively dismissive of rights of religious minorities.[49] Religious fundamentalism, which is reflected in the programme and policy of communal forces in the party system, can do great harm to the Indian polity. It can destroy the social fabric of the Indian democracy with its advocacy of unified and undifferentiated culture. Parties are seen as oligarchic as the same leaders occupy the same positions for a very long time. Most politicians are busy in personal squabbles and are more concerned in protecting their own interests rather than the public interest. There is a need for ensuring inner party democracy and discipline by all Indian political parties. Coalition alliances in contemporary Indian politics do not have any common objective to bind them together; they are opportunists and seek short-term tactical arrangements rooted in the exchange of mutual benefits and compulsions of power. This leads to the volatility of the system. Also, there should be a check on the process of proliferation and splintering of political parties in order to stabilize the governance process.

However, a remarkable feature of the Indian party system is that in contrast to the situation in many changing societies, non-party actors like the army or militant movements have not taken place in India, but ethnic conflicts and communal violence, which place informal but effective restrictions on the political party, have continued to blight the party landscape.[50] Some scholars sense that there has been a complete breakdown of the party system in India. As a consequence one can observe the shift from political parties to NGOs, civil society groups, social movements and other potential forms of expression of people's representation. Various groups are trying to assert their rights and demands, not through parties, but by other alternatives available. In light of such developments, some scholars have also alluded towards the increasing irrelevance of political parties. They believe that parties are failing to respond successfully to the series of challenges and many of their functions are performed better by less-formally organized social movements, by direct contact between politicians and citizens, through broadcast media or the Internet, or by innovations in direct democracy.[51]

---

48. Hasan, 'Introduction', p. 2.
49. Chandhoke, 'Individualism and Group Rights', p. 217.
50. Mitra, et al., 'Introduction', p. 9.
51. Richard Gunther, Jose Ramon Montero and Juan J. Linz, 'Introduction', in their (ed.), *Political Parties: Old Concepts and New Challenges* (New York: Oxford University Press, 2002), p. 1.

The problems of the party system have to be sincerely taken care of, if the tradition of democracy has to be bolstered in India. Various committees setup for suggesting electoral reforms in the Indian democracy have suggested the exigency for a comprehensive legislation for regulation of functioning of the political parties. Such a legislation can identify the conditions for Constitution, recognition, registration and deregistration of the political parties. Elections must be held to the various levels of the party organs at least once in three years. It has been suggested that political parties should ensure at least 30 per cent reservation for women at every organizational position in the party. All political parties should become more responsive, creative and truly representative. They should rediscover themselves according to the changing time and socio-economic context.

CONCLUSION

In modern democracies, the political parties have to play a very constructive role in creation and promotion of multicultural, pluralist and just societies. It is an achievement of the Indian political system that despite inadequacies and hindrances, it has been successfully functioning as a liberal democracy, unlike its other Asian and African counterparts. India is among the few democracies where the electoral turnout of the lower orders of society is well above that of most privileged sections.[52] However, we have discussed some of the problems pervading the functioning of the Indian party system. The rise of Hindu communalism is undoubtedly one of the counter trends to the democratic process in India. Nevertheless, there are progressive forces of democratization that have taken into their fold all those deprived classes that suffered from historically constituted discrimination and disadvantages. It can be observed that the Indian democracy has been a success, in many ways, due to the successful working of the party system in India.

Suggested Readings

Brass, Paul R. *The New Cambridge History of India: The Politics of India Since Independence*. Cambridge, UK: Cambridge University Press, 1975.

Frankel, Francine R., Zoya Hasan, Rajeev Bhargava and Balveer Arora (eds.). *Transforming India: Social and Political Dynamics of Democracy*. New Delhi: Oxford University Press, 2000.

52. Zoya Hasan (ed.), *Parties and Party Politics in India*, p. 6.

Hasan, Zoya (ed.). *Parties and Party Politics in India*. New Delhi: Oxford University Press, 2002.

Mitra, Subrata K., Mike Enskat and Clemens Spiess (eds.). *Political Parties in South Asia*. Westport, CT: Praeger, 2004.

Questions

1. What are political parties? Describe their significance for any political system.
2. What do you understand by 'one-party-dominant system' or 'Congress system'?
3. Discuss the remarkable changes in the nature of Indian party politics since the last two decades.
4. Enlist significant national and regional parties in Indian party system.
5. Critically analyse various challenges confronting the Indian political parties in the present times.

The Nature of Coalition Politics

Sanjeev Kumar

17

Over the last decade or so, the Indian party system has undergone a paradigm shift. The days of politics as a grand narrative dominated by a single party seems to be over. The general election in 2004 confirmed this trend that first became visible in the Indian political scene in 1989. Unlike every general election until then, the 1989 election yielded a fractured mandate. The formation of the National Front government led by V. P. Singh, with outside support from the BJP and the Left Front, marked the beginning of the phase of enduring coalition politics.

The recurrent splits in the Janata *parivar* and the emergence of identity politics symbolized by Mandir and Mandal in the 1990s further cemented the coalition imperative. The transition towards coalition politics is not a new development. The first experiment in coalition making goes back to 1946 when the Indian National Congress partnered the Muslim League to form the Interim Government in New Delhi. The process, however, failed to make much dent due to their deep-rooted fissures. Later, in the 1960s, following the rise of anti-Congressism, the coalition imperative gained momentum. In 1967, Congress lost power in nine states against a coalition of assorted and regional parties. Following an 18-month (June 1975–January 1977) internal emergency, a coalition of several parties ascended to power at the centre under the banner of the Janata Party (JP).[1] Given the heterogeneous composition of the JP and the fierce ambitions of its three prominent leaders—Morarji Desai, Jagjivan Ram and Bharatiya Kranti Dal (BKD) leader Charan Singh—within two and a half years of its inception, the Janata Party disintegrated and the Congress swept back to power in the general elections held in January 1980.The collapse of the Janata coalition meant that despite a visible change in the texture of the party system, a final social and political realignment to give a definite shape to the Indian

1. The Janata Party drew sustenance from diverse ideological groups. There were those who had been in Congress but had left the party (like Charan Singh, Morarji Desai) at some point the socialists, the right-wing Bharatiya Jana Sangh, and also the CPI(M).

party system was still far away. The moment finally arrived in the 1990s when a large number of state-based regional formations based on caste, linguistic and religious lines emerged on the national scene heralding an era of competitive coalition politics.

It would thus be worthwhile to study the crucial changes that have taken place in the nature of parties and the party system since the late 1980s. Beginning with the appraisal of the Congress system and the growth of regional aspirations, the paper seeks to examine the impact that proliferation of parties has had on the Indian polity. The key question that this chapter seeks to address is whether the process has led to 'fragmentation' or 'federalization', with special reference to the study of the National Front, the United Front, the National Democratic Alliance (NDA) and the United Progressive Alliance (UPA).

The 1990s have witnessed a sea change in the political arena in India. The intensity of electoral competition has increased with the rise in the electoral volatility after the 1989 general **elections**, featuring several hung parliaments and the arrival of coalition politics. This has been accompanied by something of a participatory upsurge. Politics has shifted from the 'all-India' level to the states.[2] The intensification of competitive politics has changed the party systems from being a rivalry between national parties into one between alliances and coalition of national and state parties. In the alliances and coalition arrangements, ideology and policy today generally do not appear as significant as generally construed.[3] The 1989, 1991, 1998, 1999 and 2004 election results are indicative of a transition towards a new region-based, multiparty coalition system. This is a logical development in a federal society with diverse cultural and linguistic regions and is also part of the wider process of democratization since Independence. This transition towards a new party system is an outcome of two interlinked processes: the decline and breakdown of the Congress system in the 1980s and a parallel process of regionalization of politics.

THE DECLINE OF THE CONGRESS SYSTEM

In the 1960s, Rajni Kothari formulated a new conceptual category, the Congress system, to characterize India's party system.[4] It was a bold attempt to theorize the unique party system that India had developed that did not fit the straitjacket of the one-party system or multiparty competition. India's party system, Kothari

2. Yogendra Yadav and Suhas Palshikar, 'Party System and Electoral Politics in the Indian States, 1952–2002: From Hegemony to Convergence', in Peter Ronald de Souza and E. Sridharan (eds.), *India's Political Parties* (New Delhi: Sage Publications, 2006), pp. 73–74.
3. The Left Front, for example, was a partner in the Janata Party coalition government formed in 1971. Further, in 1989, both the Left Front and BJP supported the National Front government led by V. P. Singh from outside.
4. Rajni Kothari, 'The Congress System in India', *Asian Survey*, 4 (12), December 1964.

argued, should be described as a system of one-party dominance, a competitive party system consisting of a party of consensus and a party of pressure. The Congress system formulation shows that in spite of an apparent one-party dominance, inter-party and intra-party competition takes place. The competition often took place within the confines of a consensus because the Congress party occupied the centre and opposition was allowed both within the margins of this centre, inside the Congress party and outside. Apart from the structural features, Kothari's formulation involved an ideological component. The Congress system was a system of legitimacy. The issue was the establishment of democratic authority. This was achieved in India on the basic of historical consensus that was converted by the party system into present consensus. This was possible because the Congress system encompassed all major sections and interests of society. It represented a broad social coalition and Kothari believed that the Congress system combined the efforts to gain legitimacy and the efforts towards social transformation.[5]

The Congress party represented a broad social coalition that encompassed the upper caste and upper-class elite, as well as the poorest and most marginalized sections of the Indian population. The Congress constituency projected itself as the protector of minorities, and as the natural party of members of the Scheduled Castes and Scheduled Tribes. The success of the Congress coalition, it is often argued, was in fact made possible by the cross-cutting cleavages in Indian society that prevented polarization along any one cleavage, whether an ascriptive one such as religion or a secular one such as class. It was this all-encompassing character of the Congress—famously described as an umbrella party—along with its pre-eminent role as the party that had won India Independence, which contributed immeasurably to the supremacy of the Congress in the early years.

The façade of consensus helped the Congress in two respects. In the first place, the Congress system sought to make compromises with upper castes and allowed their domination in the political realm. A consensus about procedural democracy coupled with welfare-oriented developmentalism helped in de-emphasizing the claims of the lower castes. Nehru's plebiscitary leadership also further ensured the dominance of the Congress. As the leading and preponderant political organization, the Congress obtained an absolute majority of seats in parliament in the first four general elections. The political fortunes of the Congress, however, began to decline by the early 1960s. The strain became visible first in the fourth general elections in 1967 when the party lost power in nine states. The elections of 1967 were a kind of watershed because the Congress share of votes declined drastically as compared with 1952, 1957 and 1962. Except in Haryana and Madhya Pradesh (MP), where it gained in votes

5. Yadav and Palshikar, 'Party System and Electoral Politics', pp. 76–80.

and seats, it lost 1.5 per cent to 19 per cent seats in the state where it retained power.[6] The caste-based mobilization, which began in the late 1960s, particularly with the assertion of middle and backward castes in North India, harmed immensely its electoral interests. The defeat of the Congress in 1967 was in fact a defeat of the powers of upper castes by the backwards. The Congress suffered another blow following the split in the party in 1969 which robbed the party of 62 Lok Sabha MPs, and reduced it to a minority in November 1969. The Indira Gandhi government managed to survive with the outside support extended by the Communist Party of India, the Akali Dal, the Muslim League, the DMK and Independents. The twin forces of centralization and de-institutionalization of the Congress party under Indira Gandhi became the major reason for the decline of the party. Under Indira Gandhi, there had been a gradual erosion of inner-party democracy, increasing use of **centralizing** institutional devices and interference in the working of state governments leading to the loss of autonomy and even atrophy of the party organization in the states.

Although the party achieved major victories in the 1980 and 1984 parliamentary elections, this did not restore its structure of dominance that was undermined by its defeat in the 1977 elections by the Janata Party. The Congress no longer draws lower castes and classes in sufficient numbers into its ambit having to contend with the left and left of centre parties that possess greater influence among these groups. The Congress, which once resisted coalitions (articulated in the Panchamarhi declaration of 1988), has shed all delusions that it is an indispensable party of governance, capable of acquiring a popular mandate on its own strength.[7] The key to the Congress success in the 2004 general election clearly lay in the smart alliances that it struck in Andhra Pradesh, Tamil Nadu, Bihar, Jharkhand and Maharashtra.

The Process of Regionalization

The party system since Independence has simultaneously undergone a process of broadening and regionalization, that is, a steady movement away from a single centre towards multiple poles that lie in the states. The emerging region-based, multi-party system as reflected in the result of the 1996 Lok Sabha election is largely an outcome of this process.[8] Some important developments during the 1980s contributed to the quickening of the process of regionalization. There was the rapid increase in politicization and democratic consciousness in the states, the entry of underprivileged groups into the political arena (from 363.5 million

6. For details, see Ajay K. Mehra, 'Introduction' in Ajay K. Mehra, D. D. Khanna and G. W. Kneck (eds.), *Political Parties and Party Systems* (New Delhi: Sage Publications, 2003), pp. 30–31.
7. *Frontline*, 18 June 2004, pp. 4–5.
8. Sudha Pai, *State Politics: New Dimensions* (Delhi: Shipra Publication, 2000), pp. 6–10.

in 1980 to 498.1 million in 1989) due to lowering of the voting age. Regional disparities and political mobilization on the basis of territorial identities generated fresh demands for decentralization and the formation of separate states by non-Congress parties in many states.[9] The abandonment of the Nehruvian consensus in both socialism and secularism in the late 1980s and a growing economic crisis exacerbated the trend.

It was the 1996 Lok Sabha election that formally marked the arrival of the regional political formations on the national scene. Prior to the 1980s, it was only at the state level that regional forces wielded power. The first non-Congress coalition formed in 1977 and even the 1989 National Front coalition were represented largely by the dominant national formations. The 1977 coalition of the Janata government broadly comprised Congress for Democracy (CFD), Bharatiya Lok Dal (Congress U), Jan Sangh and the Socialists, all of whom had an all-India ideological plank, though restricted in their programmatic moblization. The fundamental issue that they were concerned with was the restoration of democratic institutions and protection of civil liberty. The regional issues were pushed into the background in the wake of larger issue of political survival. In 1989, non-Congressism brought many regional parties into the National Front government. These included the Telugu Desam Party (TDP) in Andhra Pradesh, the Congres(S) in Kerala, and the Dravida Munnetra Kazhagam (DMK) in Tamil Nadu. But in the elections, these parties failed to perform well in terms of electoral gains.[10] Despite their disastrous performance, these regional parties became partners in the NF-led government of 1989. Since 1996, regional parties have become indispensable in the formation of the government at the national level. They have been important partners in the coalitions that have come to power since 1996. Besides, the numerical strength of the regional parties has considerably increased, with a sizable vote share being captured by regional parties. In the 1996 Lok Sabha, 137 Members of Parliament (MPs) belonged to the various regional parties. This underscored the centrality of regional parties in national politics. It appeared at that time that most regional parties were gravitating against the Bharatiya Janata Party (BJP). Thus, 95 of the 137 MPs belonging to regional parties were part of the UF coalition. This gave rise to the impression that regional parties were occupying the third space—outside of the Congress and the BJP. Soon, this picture disappeared as the United Front coalition proved to be a short-lived experience although its supporters drew satisfaction from the fact that a large number of parties agreed to block a communal party from coming to power. In 1998, however, the regional forces—at least some of them—quickly switched over to the BJP-led National Democratic Alliance (NDA).

---

9. Demands have been made for the creation of separate states such as Uttarakhand in Uttar Pradesh, Gorkhaland in West Bengal, Khalistan in Punjab, Bodoland in Assam, etc.
10. Except for two seats won by TDP, no regional party could capture a seat. The strength of total members elected from regional parties, however, was 45.

Politics of Coalition (Post-1989): A Critical Overview

By now there is a growing realization that coalition governments are perhaps an inevitable outcome in a multi-cultural and federal polity like India, where the homogenizing effects of political institution may be often insufficient to organize social pluralities into two major parties in electoral and legislation arenas like those in Anglo-American democracies and Australia (excepting Canada since 1993).[11]

India does not neatly fit theories of coalition politics that have developed on the basis of the European experience of parliamentary democracy in mostly unitary states with less ethnic heterogeneity and using proportional representation or mixed electoral systems. First, India's polity is not characterized by a single left–right ideological axis but multiple cross-cutting axes, for example, secular–communal, centrist–regional, autonomist and a variety of caste bloc-based axes, varying state-wise. Second, party identification in India is relatively weak both among politicians and voters and parties tend to be clientelistic, lacking well-defined social bases compared to most Western democracies. Defections and splits that are common in Indian parties are virtually non-existent in most European parties because of well-defined party ideologies policy orientation and relatively stable social constituencies. This is all the more the case in the post-1989 period of considerable electoral volatility with seismic shifts in the formerly stable Congress-dominated party system.

Since the resultant coalition alliances are neither 'ideological' nor have any common objective to cement them, they are merely short-term tactical arrangements established by ambitious politicians that are rooted in the exchange of mutual benefits and compulsions of power. The mobilization of the electorate is done through a strategy of support to regional cum segmental or ethnic issues without giving overriding support either to national or primarily local issues.

The last decade of the 20th century saw a sharp rise in political mobilization on the basis of social cleavages based on ascriptive identities, in particular religion and caste. Casteism, communalism and personality domination have been the main planks around which the fragmentation of political parties has taken place, which has resulted in more caste- and class-based political violence in the society. Political parties have invariably exploited these sentiments to gain electoral support and political mobilization of the voters. There was another significant development after the 1989 elections that affected the party system. The coalition politics gained a new trend: parties tended to lend support to the government from outside without formally joining it, thus ostensibly sharing power without assuming any responsibility. However, the experience of government formation with outside support both at the national and state level has invariably created

11. E. Sridharan, 'Electoral Coalitions in 2004 General Elections: Theory and Practice', *Economic and Political Weekly*, 18 December 2004: pp. 5418–19.

instability in Indian politics. A corollary to these developments has been the emergence of an environment of blackmail within the party alliances, where a minority government or an alliance of parties not only feels insecure to implement its minimum election programme or polices but also faces considerable hindrances in taking hard executive or routine administrative decisions in matters of appointments to the council of ministers or representing a particular interest, constituency or any party's viewpoint in any policy move.

In the six general elections spanning the decade since 1989, India has witnessed coalition government of three important strands—Left-of-centre NF and UF, Right-of-centre NDA, Centrist Congress-led UPA. These coalition governments since 1989 have come in the wake of the end of the dominance of the multi-ethnic, multi-class, multi-regional Congress party precipitated by three major ideological turning points in Indian politics, namely, economic liberalization and globalization, Mandalization of OBC identity politics, and the advent of strong currents of Hindu, Sikh and Islamic revivalism and fundamentalism.

National Front/United Front Coalition Experiment

The National Front experiment, which was a federation of national and regional parties formed under the leadership of the Janata Party in 1988, provides the best example of the fragmentation and re-alignment within the party system along regional lines; it consisted of the JD, TDP, Congress (S), DMK, Asom Gana Parishad (AGP), and other small groupings. The objective of keeping the Congress at bay brought two diametrically opposite political forces: the BJP and the Left under a broad coalition. The NF government lasted barely 11 months in power, from December 1989 to November 1990. Weak coordination and fragmented collective responsibility of the Cabinet marked the end of the National Front coalition.

Following the collapse of the NF government in 1990, the Front went into oblivion and the various constituents, except for some adjustment, fought the 1991 election alone. From September 1995 onwards, efforts were made to revive the front by the TDP, Janata Dal and the ruling Left Front in West Bengal encouraged by the poor performance of the Congress party in the 1994–95 state Assembly elections. By including many regional groupings, an idea of a 'Third Front' was mooted. The opportunity came in 1996 when the JD-led United Front formed the government after the BJP failed to muster a majority in the hung parliament.

The basic constraint of the United Front, however, was its dependence on the Congress support to remain in power. It had to look over it shoulders all the time to ensure that this support was not withdrawn. Ultimately, it collapsed because of the withdrawal of the Congress support. Despite its eclipse as a substantial political force in parliament especially after the 1997 national elections, the Third Front as a model continues to remain viable simply because the political space structured around the opposition to the BJP and the Congress exists. Despite its short tenure at the national level, its achievements cannot be undermined. In fact, it was the acceptance of the Mandal recommendations, under the V. P. Singh-led National Front government that brought about radical changes in India's social fabric.

BJP and National Democratic Alliance

The BJP is a reluctant convert to the strategy of coalition politics. After the failure of the BJP to produce a majority in parliament in 1996, it resorted to the politics of alliance. Prior to 1989, the BJP had never exceeded 10 per cent of the votes. In 1989–91, the BJP contested alone with a communally polarized platform against the backdrop of the Babri Masjid agitation of the late 1980s, the upper-caste backlash against the National Front government decision to implement the Mandal Commission's recommendation for the reservation of government jobs for backward classes. By employing the aggressive strategy of Hindutva, the party witnessed a meteoric rise from just two in 1984 to win 120 seats, becoming the second largest party at the centre. In 1996, the BJP ran into its limits of contesting alone with a community polarizing agenda. Despite being catapulted to its highest ever seat tally of 161, it failed to win parliamentary support from enough other parties to form a coalition government.

Learning from the 1996 debacle, the party in 1998 and 1998 sought a wide range of alliances in its non-stronghold states, in the process shelving temporarily the main community divisible points on its agenda, viz, construction of the Ram temple on the site of demolished Babri Masjid, repeal of Article 370 and promulgation of a common civil code.

The 13th Lok Sabha yielded a decisive mandate to the **political party** of the Hindu Right and its 23 regional allies of varied character and background. The triumph of the BJP-led alliance implied neither a polarization of the votes in its favour nor the emergence of a bipolar national electoral process. There was no swing either towards the BJP (its votes share declined by 1.8 percentage points from 1998) or towards the BJP and its allies (their combined vote share declined by 1.5 per cent from what they won in 12th Lok Sabha). In fact in 1999, the Congress contested 20 fewer seats than in 1998 but improved its vote share by 2.7 percentage points.

Coalition Led by Centrist Congress (UPA)

The end of Congress dominance, and lack of a clear single-party majority since the assassination of Indira Gandhi in 1984, ushered in an era of coalition politics in the context of a fragmented party system. Until as late as December 2003, the party appeared reluctant to concede that the country had entered an era of coalition politics in which a single-party government was ruled out in the foreseeable future. This presents an interesting contrast with the BJP. Like the Congress, the BJP until 1998 saw coalitions as an aberration of sorts and insisted that they were a temporary phenomenon. The polity, the BJP then maintained, was inherently becoming bipolar with the Congress and BJP representing two poles. Subsequently, following the 1998 and 1999 general elections which threw up hung parliaments, the BJP modified its earlier position and accepted that coalitions were here to stay at least for some time. The Congress, on the other hand, continued to staunchly assert that it was capable of governing India on it own. It was only in June 2003 at the Congress party conclave at Shimla that party diluted its position over forming a coalition to oppose the BJP-led NDA. This came close on the heels of the defeat in the state Assembly elections in Rajasthan, Madhya Pradesh and Chattisgarh in early December 2003. Thus, in January 2004, the party started negotiating with secular parties to reach pre-poll alliances.

It reached a seat-sharing arrangement with the DMK and the Pattali Makkal Katchi (PMK) in Tamil Nadu, National Congress Party (NCP) in Maharashtra, Telangana Rashtra Samti (TRS) in Andhra Pradesh. In Bihar and Jharkhand, the Congress party began talks with the Rashtriya Janata Dal (RJD) and Jharkhand Mukti Morcha) (JMM) respectively. In UP, the Congress despite keeping a negotiating process on with both Samajwadi Party (SP) and BSP eventually failed to strike a deal. It was this coalition strategy that struck rich dividends in the election to the 14th Lok Sabha. The National Democratic Alliance (NDA), which was widely expected to obtain the highest number of seats among all formations in the fray, ended up with just 195 as against an impressive tally of 217 seats won by the UPA. The Congress also emerged as the largest party capturing 145 seats as against 138 by the BJP.

CONCLUSION

With the 2004 elections to the 14th Lok Sabha, the Indian polity has entered a phase of fierce competitive politics. The gradual decline of the Congress, the emergence of regional parties as important political players in a number of states, the strengthening of smaller parties (such as the Samata Party, Janata Dal, Samajwadi Party, Rashtriya Janata Dal, and the Bahujan Samaj Party) with their specific group followings and limited areas of influence, mark the changes that are taking place in Indian party politics. The party system is arguably going through a transitional phase in which neither of the two so-called national parties is capable of forming a government on its own.[12] The Congress, which once had this ability, has now lost it, partly through organizational attenuation

12. It is important to remember that the combined vote share of the Congress and the BJP added up to just over 50 per cent in the Lok Sabha elections of 2004.

and partly through the gradual loss of sections of its social base. The BJP has not yet developed such a capacity. Consequently, even as both these parties represent themselves as national forces, they are necessarily dependent on the support of a variety of regional and state-level players that can deliver the seats required to make up a majority. In themselves, they have come to constitute the two poles around which parties may cluster and coalition governments become viable. In the absence of viable forms of electoral mobilization, what we are getting is politics of contingent coalitions.

Given the improbability of either the Congress or the BJP achieving a majority on its own coalition politics have clearly become the order of the day. The coalitions by its very nature involve a sharing of power between its constituents, which make it difficult for any partner to misuse discretionary powers. The texture of the United Front government between 1996 and February 1998 set the trend for the first time that the government at both the state and the centre across the country were formally and overtly very much part of the decision-making process in New Delhi. This has continued since then. What is also significant is that the process which once appeared to have been in a state of flux, uncertainty and change seems to have stabilized now. Basically, the coalitions at the centre have become more federal because they are critically dependent on state-based parties like the TDP, the DMK and AIADMK, the Trinamool Congress, Akali Dal and the BJD. The governments are also becoming more consensual than before.[13] The very nature of coalitions in India allows even a minor coalition partners to play a more decisive role than the leading coalition party as the current political process well indicates.

What does this imply in representational terms? The Congress, for the first few decades after Independence, represented a coalition encompassing a wide range of diversity. The erosion of the Congress is accompanied today by the emergence of a large number of multiple regional/local parties claiming to represent particular sections. Notwithstanding their growing power and influence, it is still the mainstream parties like the Congress and the BJP that appear to have pretensions to being aggregative parties seeking a broad social base. For the rest, the approach of smaller parties is more narrowly focused on the particular social constituency they represent. They are happy to play a prominent role in delivering the vote of their particular social constituency through a coalition with a national party; these parties are generally content with exercising power at the state level rather than becoming national parties. It appears to confirm the hypothesis that, in multi-ethnic societies, national parties are forced

13. Even the formation of the BJP-led coalitions after the general elections of 1998 and 1999 required the shelving of the BJP's controversial Hindutva agenda for most of its pre- and post-election coalition partners to be able to join it in government.

to broad-base their appeal.[14] However, there is an important caveat suggested by the Indian case. The approach of the BJP is clearly not underwritten by the desire to create a social coalition of diverse groups, but rather by the aspiration to homogenize and create a unity (Hindu identity) by submerging diversity.

Suggested Readings

Brass, Paul R. *The Politics of India Since Independence*. Cambridge, UK: Cambridge University Press, 1994.

Hasan, Zoya (ed.). *Parties and Party Politics in India*. New Delhi: Oxford University Press, 2002.

Kothari, Rajni. *Politics in India*. New Delhi: Orient Longman, 1970.

Mishra, Anil and Mahendra Prasad Singh. *Coalition Politics in India: Problems and Prospects*. New Delhi: Manohar, 2004.

Ronald de Souza, Peter and E. Sridharan (eds.), *India's Political Parties*. New Delhi: Sage Publications, 2006.

Questions

1. Discuss the evolution and growth of coalition politics in the post-Independence era.
2. Do you think coalition politics has contributed to the deepening of Indian democracy? Give reasons.
3. Examine the role of regional parties in the present phase of coalition politics?
4. Critically examine the problems and prospects of coalition politics in India?

---

14. See for details, Niraja Gopal Jayal, *Representing India: Ethnic Diversity and the Governance of Public Institutions* (New York: Palgrave Macmillan [UNRISD], 2006), pp. 101–13.

Why Is Secularism Important for India?

18

Neera Chandhoke

INTRODUCTION

The novels of Orhan Pamuk, who won the Nobel Prize for literature in 2006, are fascinating for many reasons: his style of writing, his imagination, and the sheer power of his prose. But for us in India, his novels are riveting, simply because his representations of the moral dilemmas that confront his country, Turkey, are more than familiar to us. For instance, his novel *Snow*, in which Pamuk narrates the debate between religious revivalism and secularism in his country in complex ways, practically mirrors the debates taking place in our country. Was the adoption of secularism as one of the main principles of the Indian polity a wise decision? Can secularism prove effective in India, considering that our society and our people are deeply religious? These are some of the troubled questions that analysts and political theorists ask in India. But then as we read on, we find that the problems the protagonist of *Snow*, Ka, identifies with political Islam in Turkey, are precisely those that democrats in India identify with religious revivalism, whether of the majority or of the minority.

Consider the following passage in the novel. At one point in the conversation, Muhtar, a friend of Ka, says: After my years as a leftist atheist, these people (Muslim conservatives) come as such a great relief. You should meet them. I'm sure you'd warm to them too. Do you really think so? Well, for one thing, all these religious men are modest, gentle, understanding. Unlike Westernized Turks, they don't instinctively despise the common people; they're compassionate and wounded themselves. If they got to know you, they'd like you. There would be no harsh words, replies Muhtar. Pamuk writes about Ka's response thus: 'As Ka knew from the beginning, in this part of the world faith in God was not something achieved by thinking sublime thoughts and stretching one's creative powers to their outer limits; nor was it something one could do alone; above all it meant joining a mosque, becoming part of a community.

Nevertheless, Ka was still disappointed that Muhtar could talk so much about his group without once mentioning God or his own private faith.[1]

What are the questions this passage raises in our minds? First, are leaders who lavishly use religious symbols in politics, themselves religious? Are they using religion for their own ends, that of the pursuit of power? Second, cannot religion be experienced in other ways that are personal; which have to do with the development of our creativity? Must religion only be experienced in the public sphere? Other troubling questions follow: why should political groups who swear by their own religion harm other religious groups? If religion is important for me, is it not as important for those who believe in a different God? Can one group deny other groups the freedom of their religion, just because these groups are in a minority and, therefore, vulnerable? Above all, what is the solution to the problem of violence between religious communities, which has left thousands dead, many injured, which has wreaked sexual violence upon women of the other community, and which has destroyed property, homes, and the workplace? Is there a solution? Perhaps, we can find a possible solution to communalism in the precepts of secularism.

However, this begs the following questions. What does secularism mean? Why is secularism relevant for India? And why is secularism a part of the democratic imagination? These are some of the questions that this chapter will explore.

THE MEANING OF SECULARISM

We can go about exploring the many meanings of secularism in two ways. We could explore secularism as a general concept, or we could look at the way the concept has evolved in India, and see why secularism was adopted as the main organizing principle of the Indian polity. Or we could do both, and see how the concept has evolved in a direction that is unique to India.

The concept of secularism, as it has come to us from the West, simply means that: (*a*) the sphere of politics and that of religion is separated, (*b*) the State will not adopt a religion as the State religion, and (*c*) no one shall be discriminated against on the grounds that he or she belongs to a particular religion. This meaning of secularism has been defined in the US context by President Thomas Jefferson as a **wall of separation** that exists between the State and religion. The First Amendment to the Constitution of the USA has made this clear. The Establishment Clause in the First Amendment prohibits the establishment of a national religion by the Congress, and prohibits preference for one religion over another. In the famous *Board of Education of Kiryas Joel Village School District vs Grumet case*, Justice Souter interpreted the clause to mean that the

1. Orhan Pamuk, *Snow* (New York: Vintage Books, 2005), pp: 60–61.

government should not prefer one religion to another, or religion to irreligion. The second part of the clause, known as the Free Exercise Clause, states that the Congress cannot prohibit the free exercise of religion.

Why did the American Constitution erect this wall of separation between the State and religion? There are two answers to this question. First, many of the European settlers in the USA had fled religious persecution in their own countries. Since some states in Europe had adopted a particular religion, which by that fact became the State religion, members of other religious communities were discriminated against. We see what problems the merger of politics and religion brings in its wake. The State exercises power; and the leaders of religious communities also exercise power. If the State adopts a particular religion, then the State possesses more power than it should: both secular and religious power. But if one institution possesses and exercises too much power, this is always dangerous for individual freedom. More importantly, if a State adopts a particular religion as the State religion, then other religious groups are not only denied the freedom to religion and to their belief systems but they are also oppressed for this reason. The adoption of a State religion, in other words, denies to people who may follow another religion, their beliefs, often through the use of force. It is not surprising that many states in Europe, till the 17th century, were bogged down in religious wars against their own citizens, and against other States who may have adopted another religion. Second, the right to religion is a Fundamental Right. The right to freedom of conscience is one of the important rights that forms a part of the general right to freedom. To deny to individuals this freedom is to deny them freedom in general. This violates the basic principles of democracy, that each human being has rights merely because he or she is human, and that factors such as gender, caste, class, and religion, are simply morally irrelevant when it comes to recognizing individual rights.

Over time, religious wars that the State fought against its own citizens, and against other States in Europe, were controlled through the adoption of the principle of toleration which had been enunciated by the English political theorist John Locke. There was another reason why the religious conflict in Europe could be controlled. The Enlightenment in Europe, the coming of the industrial age, and the development of modern science gave to the people other ways of thinking and believing. Modern science challenged the power of the Church to tell people what to believe and how to believe. Individuals, it came to be argued by many theorists, possessed reason, and reason gives us the power to think and to evaluate various options. To be modern is to have the capacity to question all received wisdom and, in the process, to refashion this wisdom. To be modern is to chart out our own projects in association with others, without the Church or some religious leader telling us what to do and what not to do. Modernity in Europe did not reject religion; nor did the people become irreligious; religion became just another way to help Europeans to understand the world. But there were other ways of understanding the world available to the moderns, ways given by science, by literature, by philosophy, by art, and by the development of social sciences. Religion in effect became a private affair and, in the process, societies became secularized. However, the suspicion that the mix between religion and politics is dangerous for individual freedom, remained. Therefore, the wall-of-separation thesis is important because it separates the secular and the sacred. We can think of secularism as another way of instituting a separation of powers, and checks and balances. Power must be controlled, and the only way to do this is to separate the different forms of power.

THE CASE OF INDIA

In India, however, the project of modernity, which was introduced by the colonial power in the form of modern education and emphasis on science, went in the other direction, that of strengthening the role of religion. By the second decade of the 20th century, violence between religious communities, particularly the Hindus and the Muslims, had become a regular feature of Indian politics. Historians have wondered why people who had lived together for centuries, who shared a common history and traditions, a common language, shared practices, music, and culture, came to be divided in such a murderous fashion. For communal riots kill, maim, and erase all feelings of sharing and belonging. The kinds of atrocities that leaders of one group have subjected another religious group to, are both horrifying and saddening. How can people inflict such harm on fellow beings, on people who belong to the same category of humankind? What motivates them to do so?

Historians give us two explanations to this question. The first explanation suggests that through deliberate policies, the colonial power tried to divide people along the lines of separate religious identities, through what has been called the politics of enumeration or counting of populations. The first census of 1872 divided the Indian people into four categories—aboriginals, Aryans, mixed people, and Muslims. In the 1881 census, the categories of mixed people and aboriginals were merged, the Muslims were treated as a homogeneous category, and Hindus were sub-divided into castes. The 1901 census further sub-divided the Hindu population along caste lines. Such categorization contributed to the making of separate identities because people became aware of the demographic strength; or of the lack of such strength of their own community; that they were in a majority or in a minority, numerically speaking. They also became aware of the strength of the other community. This encouraged the making of a group identity because it gave the leaders a handle they could exploit for political purposes, notably the pursuit of power. If the leaders of the Hindu community were to argue that the country belonged to them because this community was in a majority, leaders of the minority communities began to play on fears of being oppressed by the majority.

Now, no community is homogenous because it is divided on the basis of the rich and the poor, men and women, on the basis of age and language, on the basis of caste, and on the basis of *jati* and *biradri*. Different Hindus worship different gods in the religious pantheon, often in ways that have little in common with each other. But when people are categorized as Hindus or as Muslims, as Sikhs or as Christians, inter-community differences are covered up, and people begin to think of themselves predominantly in religious terms. This was the legacy that the colonial power gave us. The tendency to separatism was further reinforced by the recording of ordinary conflicts, over material issues for instance, as religious conflicts, by British colonial officers. The British believed, or at least claimed that Hindus and Muslims belonged to two separate cultures; and, in time, to two separate nations, even though they had much in common.

We have just begun to understand that colonialism is much more than political domination by another country, or economic exploitation of the labour, the resources, and the markets of one country by another. In the first place, Colonialism in India, as in other parts of the world, involved the colonization of the mind, through the interpretation of our histories, our languages, our traditions, our literatures, and through placing people in discrete categories. Colonized people simply lose control over their own shared histories and traditions, and come to understand themselves and their pasts in the terms coined by the colonial power. This form of soft power is dangerous simply because it is lasting. And this is precisely what happened to religious identities. The categories created by the British government through the politics of ethnic mapping were internalized by the colonized. As a result, individuals and groups began to construct different, even conflicting, identities for themselves. The colonial practice of separate electorates, which was initiated in 1909 through the Morley–Minto Reforms, was designed to further to further consolidate these identities. Even as groups began to mobilize for the reserved seats in the legislatures and local self-government bodies on the basis of religious identity, shared histories and shared languages were driven even more apart and separated into hostile and antagonistic categories.

Second, the Indian people were polarized with the arrival of communal organizations onto the political scene in the form of the Hindu Mahasabha and the Muslim League. If the Muslim League began to speak of the two-nation theory, the Hindu communal organizations began to conceptualize the nation as predominantly Hindu. The slogan of Vinayak Damodar Savarkar (1883–1966), who was the chairman of the Hindu Mahasabha, was Hinduize all politics and militarize Hinduism. This, not surprisingly, alienated the Muslim community, and instilled fear that they were doomed to be dominated by the Hindu majority. The use of overtly Hindu symbols in political rituals helped to strengthen this alienation. Even as religious identities increasingly separated people, the resultant tension led to the partition of the country in 1947. Whatever be the reasons for the division of the country, Partition highlighted the hold of religion in politics. And the problem did not end with the formation of Pakistan; recurrent communal riots have left a trail of death and destruction in their wake.

Looking at the hold of religion on politics and on the collective mind, some scholars have suggested that secularism is an alien concept for India, simply because the Indian society has not been secularized, or that people continue to be religious. T. N. Madan, for instance, writes that from the point of view of a majority of the people, secularism is a vacuous word, a phantom concept, for such people do not know whether it is desirable to privatize religion, and if it is, how this may be done, unless they be Protestant Christians but not if they are Buddhists, Hindus, Muslims or Sikhs. For the secularist minority to stigmatize the majority as primordially oriented and to preach secularism to the latter as the law of human existence is moral arrogance and worse—I say worse since in our times politics takes precedence over ethics—political folly. It is both these—moral arrogance and political folly—because it fails to recognize the immense importance of religion in the lives of the people of South Asia.[2]

T. N. Madan is a respected scholar and we have to take his insights seriously. But at the same time we are also compelled to ask the following question: why did secularism emerge as a viable option in and for Indian politics if religion and politics cannot be separated because the Indian people are deeply religious? The answer to this question is, however, fairly simple; secularism is important for precisely this reason. If people were not religious, we have little use for secularism. Secularism is meant to regulate relations between the State and various religious groups on the principle of equality, on the principle that the State will not discriminate against one religion. This is most important because unless the State is prohibited from discriminating against minority religions, they will be subjected to oppression and denial of their rights to freedom of belief. Further, unless the majority religious group is told that it does not have the right to control the country just because it is in a majority, and unless the minority is assured that it will not be discriminated against even though it is in a minority, the country will be caught up in endless violence. The answer to destructive communal riots is not to abandon secularism, but to deepen secularism. We can only understand this in a historical context.

REVISITING HISTORY

Let us, therefore, go back to our history and see why secularism was adopted in India as the governing principle of the polity. As suggested above, colonial policies, and the activities of communal organizations, had sharpened religious polarization in the country.

---

2. T. N. Madan, 'Secularism in Its Place', in Rajeev Bhargava (ed.), *Secularism and Its Critics* (New Delhi: Oxford University Press, 1997), pp. 297–315, pp. 298–99.

It was in the precise context of politicized religious identities that Mahatma Gandhi tried in the 1920s to bring together various communities to fight a sustained struggle for Independence under the umbrella of the Congress. Seeking to build a cross-community alliance, Gandhiji looked for a principle that could bind together people who subscribed to different faiths; a principle which could weld them into a mass movement. This principle could not be located in one community, in one religion, or in one tradition; it had to stand outside all traditions. More importantly, this principle had to reassure minority groups that they would not be discriminated against, as much as it had to warn the majority that majority rule is not the right path to democracy, which is built upon the twin principles of freedom and equality for all.

Gandhiji found this particular principle in the doctrine of ***sarva dharma sambhava***, which can be read as equality of all religions or that all religions should be treated equally. Given Mahatma Gandhi's belief in religion, *sarva dharma sambhava* was not only a political principle designed to bring people together; it was also a normative principle that recognized the value of religion in people's lives. In a society like India, where people worship different Gods and subscribe to different faiths, it was important to respect each religion, and, thereby, respect the plurality of religious belief. If religion is important to one person, it is equally important to another person. People have a right to religion and culture. To deny one religious group its rights would be undemocratic and unjust. And, to impose a majority religion on the minorities would be equally undemocratic and unjust. But it was democracy and justice, and the rights to freedom and equality that the anti-colonial struggle was fighting for. It was not only fighting for Independence from the British but also struggling to establish justice and democracy in the country. And, the principle of democracy dictated equality of all religions. This was Gandhiji's contribution to the resolution of religious conflict in India.

On the other hand, Pandit Nehru, India's tallest leader and the first Prime Minister of the country, was profoundly uneasy with the kind of political passions that religious identities had the power to evoke. For him, secularism meant something else altogether. A modern Nehru's preferred notion of secularism was that of *dharma nirpekshata* or that the State would not be influenced by religious considerations in enacting a policy. Debates in India have been polarized between those who subscribe to the Nehruvian meaning of secularism as *dharma nirpekshata*, and those who subscribe to the meaning that Gandhiji gave to the concept of *sarva dharma sambhava*. But Pandit Nehru could not continue to believe that the domain of policy making could be separated or abstracted from that of religion, or indeed that religion could be banished from the political and the public sphere, for long. The phenomenon of communal riots throughout the first four decades of the 20th century, particularly the communal violence that accompanied the partition of the country in 1947, proved that religion had become an intrinsic part of political life. To ignore this would have been bad politics because these politics would have been based on bad historical understanding. Pandit Nehru was, reluctantly, forced to come to terms with this. Resultantly, his understanding of secularism came closer to the notion of *sarva dharma sambhava*.

Pandit Nehru made his notion of secularism clear on various occasions. First, secularism did not mean a state where religion as such is discouraged. It means freedom of religion and conscience, including freedom for those who may have no religion.[3] Second, for Nehru the word secular was not opposed to religion. 'It is perhaps not very easy even to find a good word for "secular". Some people think that it means something opposed to religion. That obviously is not correct. What it means is that it is a State which honours all faiths equally and gives them equal opportunities; that, as a State, it does not allow itself to be attached to one faith or religion, which then becomes the State religion'.[4]

In sum, for Nehru, the concept of the secular State carried three meanings: (*a*) freedom of religion or irreligion for all, (*b*) the State will honour all faiths equally and discriminate against none, and (*c*) that the State shall not be attached to one faith or religion which by that act becomes the State religion. In effect, the meaning that secularism acquired in the Indian context, added one more dimension to its general concept: not only did it recognize the freedom of faith and ensured that it would not adopt any single religion, but it also assured *equal* treatment of all faiths.

This understanding has been reinforced in various ways, in the decisions of the judiciary for instance. Former Chief Justice of India P. B. Gajendragadkar interpreted secularism as: (a) the State does not owe loyalty to one religion, (b) it is not irreligious or anti-religious, (c) it gives equal freedom to all religions, and (d) that the religion of the citizen should not interfere in the resolution of socio-economic problems.[5] Jacobsohn, who has carried out a close reading of the various arguments offered by the Supreme Court during the Bommai case in 1994, has isolated the dominant theme in these arguments as 'equal treatment of religions, often referred to in Indian tradition as *sarva dharma sambhava*.... In the same vein, Justice Sawant emphasised that "The State is enjoined to accord equal treatment to all religions and religious sects and denominations". It is a theme that was echoed by Justice Reddy, who literally underlines the point by declaring "*Secularism is...more than a passive attitude of religious tolerance. It is a positive concept of equal treatment of all religions*"'.[6] Accordingly, the judges ruled that the destruction of the Babri Masjid by a mob,

---

3. S. Gopal(ed.), *Jawaharlal Nehru: An Anthology*, (New Delhi: Oxford University Press, 1980), p. 327.
4. Ibid., p. 330.
5. Brenda Crossman and Ratna Kapur, *Secularism's Last Sigh?* (New Delhi: Oxford University Press, 1999), p. 58, note 12.
6. Gary Jeffrey Jacobsohn, *The Wheel of Law: India's Secularism in Comparative Constitutional Context* (New Delhi: Oxford University Press, 2003), pp. 146–47, italics in the original.

which had been encouraged in this task by the state government and BJP party officials, was a clear violation of the equal-treatment principle. Secularism, ruled Justice Sawant, was a part of the basic structure and the soul of the Constitution, and it could not be infringed in any way. For these reasons, the court upheld the dismissal of four state governments ruled by the BJP, and the imposition of President's rule in these states.

Minority Rights

It is worthwhile to note that the leadership of the freedom movement continued to hold fast to its commitment to secularism despite the fact that the country was partitioned ostensibly in the name of religion. Given the polarization of the Indian society, and given the massive massacres and the brutality that marked the partition of India, the leadership could easily have swung in the other direction. But it refused to be swayed by popular passions, and remained bound by its commitment that all religions in a post-Independence India would be treated equally by the State. It was not even considered important that the concept of secularism polity should be spelt out in the Constitution, so firm was the commitment of Pandit Nehru and other leaders, to secularism. The word secular only came to be inserted in the Preamble of the Indian Constitution in 1976.

It is also important to note that in the 1920s the project of fashioning secularism was accompanied by an overlapping project; that minorities had the right to their own culture and religion. This commitment formed part of the Nehru Constitutional Draft of 1928, the Karachi Resolution of 1931, and later documents issued by the Indian National Congress. Admittedly, the commitment to minority rights like the commitment to secularism, initially stemmed from pragmatic considerations. The Congress leaders, who were to draft the Nehru Constitutional Draft, approached the Muslim League to join the project of writing a Constitution for a free India. But the Muslim League was by that time committed to separate electorates, and the Congress rejected this idea. The alternative was to grant the minorities the special right to religion and culture. But in time, minority rights like secularism became a commitment for those Congress leaders who dreamt of a society after Independence, in which all religious communities would be able to live without fear that they were in constant danger of being dominated by the majority. It also recognized that religion and culture are important for individuals, because religion and culture give them the resources, which help them to understand their world, and their own position in the world. For these reasons, individuals have a right to their religion. It was also thought that minorities should have special rights to their religion and culture, because they were, numerically speaking, weak. Majorities are capable of exercising brute power, and vulnerable sections have to be protected against the exercise of this power.

On the surface, the partition of India signified the failure of the secular/minority rights project. The Congress leaders failed to convince the leadership of the Muslim League that the members of the Muslim community would be given equal citizenship rights as well constitutional protection to their own religion in post-Independence India. But in another sense, the secular project can be considered a success. Despite the fact that the Constituent Assembly met in the shadow of the Partition, amidst wide-scale rioting, massacres, and looting of property, and despite the fact that the country had been partitioned in the name of religion, the makers of the Constitution stood firm when it came to secularism and minority rights.

For example, during the course of the deliberations in the Constituent Assembly, Mahavir Tyagi, the Congress representative from the United Provinces, suggested that any consideration of minority rights should be postponed until Pakistan's stand on minorities became clear. To this, Dr Ambedkar was to state resolutely that the

> rights of minorities should be absolute rights. They should not be subject to any considerations as to what another party may like to do to minorities within its jurisdiction. I think that the rights, which are indicated in Clause 18 are rights, which every minority irrespective of any other consideration is entitled to claim.[7]

In the Constituent Assembly, the suggestion that religious minorities should be represented through separate electorates was dropped because Partition was seen as a consequence of the introduction of separate electorates. But the right of minorities to their own culture and the right to run their own religious institutions was granted vide Article 29 but more importantly by Article 30 of the Fundamental Rights chapter. In sum, whereas Article 25 of part three of the Constitution, grants individual rights, Articles 29 and 30 recognize groups as bearers of rights. Today, political theorists have begun to conceptualize minority rights as important parts of the democratic project, simply because minorities are defenceless against majorities, but in India this project was initiated in 1928.

Secularism in India

In sum, the first principle of secularism that was codified in the Constitution carried the assurance that everyone had the freedom to practise their religion via Article 25 of the Fundamental Rights chapter. Now, strictly speaking we do not need to proclaim secularism in order to grant religious freedom. This freedom can emerge from, and form a part of the Fundamental Rights that are assured to every citizen. But a secular State cannot stop at granting the right to religion. The principle of secularism goes further and establishes equality

---

7. *Constituent Assembly Debates*, Official Reports, Vol. 3, *28th April to 2 May 1947* (Delhi: Lok Sabha Secretariat, 1989), pp. 507–508.

between all religious groups. Dr Radhakrishnan, the former president of India, was to phrase this understanding thus:

> We hold that no one religion should be given preferential status, or unique distinction, that no one religion should be accorded special privileges in national life, or international relations for that would be a violation of the basic principles of democracy and contrary to the best interest of religion and government.... No group of citizens shall arrogate to itself rights and privileges which it denies to others. No person shall suffer any form of disability or discrimination because of his religion but all alike should be free to share to the fullest degree in the common life.[8]

Now just as the freedom of religion does not necessarily need secularism to support it, equality of religions can be established via the Fundamental Right of equality vide Article 14. But if we were to stop at this, secularism would be rendered unnecessary. For secularism extends beyond equality and freedom to declare that the State is not aligned to any particular religion. It is this particular commitment that establishes the credentials of a secular State. Or secularism, we can say, promises that the State would neither align itself with any particular religion—especially the majority religion—nor pursue any religious tasks of its own.

The second and the third component of secularism, that is equality of all religions, and the distancing of the State from all religious groups, was specifically meant to assure the minorities that they had a legitimate place in the country, and that they would not be discriminated against. Correspondingly, secularism established that the majority group would not be privileged in any manner. The creed, therefore, discouraged any pretension that the majority religion had any right to stamp the body politic with its ethos. It was necessary to send a clear message to the majority community. For various elements of the Congress were openly seeking to associate the State with the majority religion. This had become more than evident during the rebuilding of the Somnath temple. In order to counteract this particular trend, Nehru in 1951 stated that a secular State is one in which the State protects all religions, but does not favour one at the expense of others and does not itself adopt any religion as the State religion.[9]

Thus, the concept of secularism that emerged in India possesses three substantial components.

- The State will not attach itself to any one religion, which will thereby establish itself as the State religion.
- All citizens are granted the freedom of religious belief.

---

8. S. Radhakrishnan, *Recovery of Faith* (London: George Allen and Unwin, 1956), p. 202.
9. Cited in D. E. Smith, *Nehru and Democracy: The Political Thought of an Asian Democrat* (Calcutta: Orient Longman, 1958), p. 154.

- The State will ensure equality among religious groups by ensuring that one group is not favoured at the expense of the other. Correspondingly, the minorities will not be discriminated against in any way.

In retrospect, it is not surprising that secularism was attractive to the Indian leadership. Secularism had historically emerged in the West as a formula to put an end to the religious wars that had devastated Europe in the 16th century. It was on the principle of secularism that communities that had gone to war over religion, and societies who had tortured the non-believers throughout the period of the Inquisition, could learn to live together. India faced similar problems. The articulation of the principle of secularism: a principle that was strictly outside any particular identity was designed to allow people to live together in civility. This is what contemporary critiques of secularism seem to forget.

The Crisis of Secularism

Nehruvian ideas triumphed for some time, but over time, the commitment of the Congress party to the cause of the minorities was weakened. In the troubled days following Nehru's death, the *Economic and Political Weekly* was to sum up the political mood thus:

> The rudest shocks come from the manner in which the government and the country are allowing themselves to be pushed off the edge of secularism into the abyss of communal reaction; falling back to the frightening atavism of stagnant, dark and medieval ethos of the Hindi speaking areas, the Madhya Desa which had witnessed ages ago the finest blossoming of Indian culture. It spells dark and dank reaction.[10]

These fears were not unfounded, because the later prime ministers of the country belonging to the Congress party were to openly play the Hindu card. In fact, in sharp contrast to Nehru's own position and commitment to the norm, the Congress has been remarkably vacillating when it comes to secularism. At times, individual members of the party have flagrantly violated the secular principle. The Congress has still not been able to establish that its leaders were not involved in the 1984 pogroms against the Sikh community despite ample proof to the contrary. And, recollect that in 1992, the Congress government at the centre remained mute and inactive as the Babri Masjid was razed to the ground. And this is a party that does not uphold the cause of Hinduism like other parties which openly defend the majority religion.

In the 1980s, we were to witness a decisive shift in the discourse on secularism and communalism in the country. This was precisely the moment when the project of Hindutva made its appearance on the political stage in the shape

---

10. 'Government Abdicates', *Economic and Political Weekly*, 5 November 1966: 476.

of a struggle to build a Ram temple on the ground where the Babri Masjid stood. At the very time, India was accepting its integration into the world via globalization, and as it was opening up its borders to the world outside, sections of the society were seeking to turn the country inwards. This turning inward, back to some unspecified Hindu tradition, took the shape of appeals to ideas of a 'strong' nation based on cultural purity and exclusiveness. But the same rhetoric that sought to mobilize the country on the grounds of a 'regenerated' Hinduism served to exclude the minorities from the definition of the nation. After all, if the nation is to be defined by the fact that the majority belong to the Hindu religion, those who do not subscribe to the religion cannot be an equal part of the nation. Aggressive cultural nationalism, is undesirably because it is exclusive, it excludes people who do not belong. On the other hand, minorities have organized themselves under the plank of religious leaders. Both groups have retreated from a common civic space, which at one point of time was painstakingly constructed by the leaders of the freedom struggle.

Secularism and Democracy

Has secularism in India failed because it just does not possess the potential to prevent the recurrence of deadly communal violence? Perhaps, our leaders do not take secularism seriously. The fault is not with secularism, it lies in the violation of secularism. Therefore, instead of attacking the concept, it is important that we, as democratic citizens, strengthen secular practices and restore these practices to their rightful place in collective thinking and practice. This is because secularism is invaluable for any society that is composed of diverse groups, each of which subscribes to different belief systems.

Secularism has been historically designed to regulate relationships between the State and groups who subscribe to different religious persuasions. Towards this end, all groups are promised equality of treatment, and the State is not aligned to any religion. Correspondingly, no person, no matter what religious denomination she or he may belong to, can be denied full citizenship rights on the grounds of her or his religious affiliation. Equally, the right to benefit from the distribution of goods, such as health, education, a fair wage, and equal protection of the law cannot be withheld from any individual on the same ground. The status and the rights of citizenship are simply abstracted from a person's affiliations.

If this is so, and if the basic aim of secularism as it has historically developed in India is to secure equality of all religious denominations, the *concept of secularism* is derived from the principle of democratic equality. In fact, let me suggest that secularism gains meaning and substance only when it refers to the principle of democratic equality. Logically, there is no reason why a society should be committed to secularism, unless it is committed beforehand to the concept of democratic equality. A prior commitment to the principle of equality is a condition for equality of all religious groups. It is a pre-requisite for secularism. In effect, unless a polity subscribes to the principle of equality, there is nothing that compels it to subscribe to secularism, nothing unless democratic equality has been codified as the organizing principle of the polity. Conversely, the principle of secularism is justified by reference to democratic equality. The justification of secularism by referral to the principle of democratic equality carries four distinct advantages.

First, even if a government is not committed to secularism, it cannot but be committed to equality, simply because equality is a constituent feature of the Constitution. This by itself should lead to equality of treatment of all religious groups, which is the first constituent principle of secularism.[11] In effect, what I am suggesting is that even if a particular government dismisses secularism, it is still *bound* by secularism, because it is bound by the Constitution and the Constitution prescribes equality. Further, equality is a part of the Fundamental Rights chapter of the Constitution vide Article 14, and as such it forms a part of the basic structure of the Constitution that cannot be tampered with. This would mean that if a religious group is discriminated against, or if one religious group is given special privileges because it is in a majority, such discrimination constitutes a violation of the Constitution. And violation of the Constitution is punishable, because such an act violates the basic law of the land.

Second, the right to practise one's own religion, which is the second constituent principle of secularism, is a fundamental and indivisible right. Rights by definition are equally granted to each individual. It is important that individuals possess status in a polity, a status that is guaranteed by the recognition of individual rights. But more importantly, each individual has equal rights, and this principle is inviolable. The virtue of rights is not only that they grant status to each individual but also because they grant equal status to every individual. Equality is built into the very structure of rights talk. Therefore, if the individual right to religious belief, which forms an integral part of Article 25 of the Fundamental Rights chapter, is infringed in any manner, the Constitution itself is infringed. And since governments as well as groups in the civil society are bound by the Constitution, an infringement of constitutional rights has to be punished.

Third, the virtue of securing secularism by placing it in the principle of equality is that equality itself guarantees that minorities are protected against majorities. Let me explain this point. Formal equality means that everyone should be treated equally. Therefore, each individual is to have an equal voice in the decisions that a society takes, and each individual decision counts equally. This is basic to the norm of equality. However, it is also true that if opinions clash and the matter is put to vote, inevitably the minority will lose out simply

11. This, of course, implies that religious practices have to fall within the realm of what is democratically permissible.

because the other group has numbers on its side. Therefore, whereas formal equality dictates that every individual has an equal voice in decision-making, the decision itself registers only the opinions of those who are in a majority. The fundamental principle of equality that each individual counts equally in the makings of the decision is thus violated. That is why liberal democrats have always feared the brute force of the majority, for this brute force tends to trample upon the rights of the minorities. After all, we can hardly hold that the right to equality is indispensable because it guards the equal rights of each individual, and then take away those rights because the majority so ordains. The only solution is that majorities cannot be allowed to ride roughshod over the rights of the minorities. And, that the minorities are given special protection against the kind of brute force that majorities tend to exert. This is fundamental to liberal democracy, and that is why liberal democrats control majority opinion by laying down constitutional principles, particularly Fundamental Rights, that trump every rule that is predetermined by the majority. If this is so, then the grant of minority rights vide Article 29 and Article 30 of the Fundamental Rights chapter of the Constitution is perfectly legitimate, simply because it protects minorities against majority opinions that may be violative of individual rights. Minority rights are accordingly not a violation of secularism as equality of all religions; they concretize the principle of equality of all persons irrespective of what a majority believes at a particular point in time.

There is a fourth advantage of locating secularism in the principle of democratic equality. Consider that the principle of democratic equality applies to all persons across the board and there are no exemptions to this rule. Therefore, equality is applicable to both inter-group as well as intra-group relations. Secularism on the other hand cannot be so generalised for one very good reason. It is meant to regulate inter-group relations and not intra-group relations. But it is possible that within the group individual members may be treated unjustly, and in fact deprived of their individual rights. The case of women's rights within religious communities can be cited as one such example.

The case of gender justice has become a politically explosive issue in India. After Independence, the government through a process of social reform gave Hindu women rights through the enactment of the Hindu Code Bill. But minorities were allowed to retain their personal codes. The reasons why the minorities were allowed to do so are complex.[12] But in short, the acceptance that the Muslim and Christian minority could continue to be governed by their personal laws in matters of adoption, marriage, divorce, and inheritance, had to do with the political need to assure the Muslims who remained in the country (and the number of Muslims who opted to remain in the country was far more

---

12. See Niraja Gopal Jayal, *Democracy and the State: Welfare, Secularism and Development in Contemporary India* (New Delhi: Oxford University Press, 1999), Ch. 3.

than the number of those who migrated to Pakistan) that their identities would not be dominated by the majority. Though Article 44 of the Directive Principles of State Policy stated that the government should enact a Uniform Civil Code in due course, the time has still not come for the realization of this particular idea.

Matters came to a head in the mid-1980s with the Shah Bano case. The case at hand was fairly straightforward. Shah Bano, an elderly woman who had been divorced by her husband, appealed to the High Court of Madhya Pradesh that her former husband should pay her maintenance under Section 125 of the Criminal Procedure Code (CrPC). According to this section, the former husband of a divorced woman has to pay her maintenance if she is destitute, and if she possesses no means for her own survival for as long as she lives or until she remarries. The High Court ruled in favour of Shah Bano. However, Shah Bano's husband Ahmed Khan, moved the Supreme Court as an appellant on the ground that he was not obliged to pay his former wife maintenance beyond the traditional three-month period of *iddat* under Section 127 (3) of the CrPC. This section rules that if under the personal law of certain communities, certain sums were payable to women in the form of meher or dower agreed upon at the time of marriage, then this along with maintenance for the period of *iddat* released the husband from further obligation. The Supreme Court in effect had to pronounce on the relation between Section 125, and 127 (3) of the CrPC on the one hand, and the relationship between the CrPC and personal laws on the other.

On 23 April 1985, a Supreme Court Bench under Chief Justice Chandrachud confirmed the judgement of the Madhya Pradesh High Court, and stated that Article 125 of the CrPC overrides all personal laws, and that it is uniformly applicable to all women. The Court thus subordinated not only Section 127, 3(b), of the CrPC to Section 125 but also personal laws to the civil code. The Bench also called upon the Government of India to enact a Uniform Civil Code under Article 44 of the Constitution. Expectedly patriarchal leaders of the Muslim community and in particular the Ulema opposed the judgement on the ground that it constituted a disregard for the personal laws of the Muslim community which are based on the Shariat. The controversy became a major political problem as thousands of Muslims took to the streets to demonstrate against the judgement. Ultimately, Prime Minister Rajeev Gandhi's Congress government, then in power at the centre, in February 1986, introduced a Bill in Parliament, which sought to exempt Muslim women from the protection provided by Article 125 of the CrPC. The Muslim Women (Protection of Rights on Divorce) Bill in essence cancelled the right to maintenance under Section 125 of CrPC. The Bill was passed despite the fact that thousands of women's groups had protested against the passage of the Bill, because it violated the rights of Muslim women.

The Hindu Right accused the Congress of practising pseudo-secularism because the party did not want to interfere in the internal affairs of the minority communities. But secularism cannot handle this issue, simply because it is not equipped to deal with intra-group relations, neither is it meant to do so. Secularism regulates relationships between groups. A better way to approach the issue is to look to democracy and equality. If we grant equality of status to all religious groups and deny it to members of the group, we violate the basic precepts of equality and thereby of the Constitution. We can only overcome this problem by appealing beyond secularism to the principle of equality, from which secularism is derived. If this is so; then the same argument that we apply to the question of inter-group equality, should be capable of proving relevant for intra-group equality. To grant vulnerable groups in society special protection and withhold this protection from the vulnerable sections within the group will be both politically inconsistent as well as morally flawed. The same principle that of equality can thus give us an argument that applies across the board to groups in society and individual members within the group.

CONCLUSION

Finally, why is secularism important and relevant for us? First, taking the violence that has occurred between religious communities on numerous occasions into account; we have to think of ways that will allow Indian people to live in some measure of civility; that will compel people to respect the rights of those who they consider to be different. For, unless we address this mindless spiral of communal violence that threatens our society and our body politic, we will not be able to do anything else—earn our daily bread; enter into social relations based on affection and engagement; or even think of eradicating poverty, homelessness, and disease. This answer cannot but lie in the direction of secularism. Second, secularism is a part of democracy, which grants to citizens equal rights. Third, secularism protects democracy by laying limits on the power of the majority. Fourth, secularism as well as minority rights, protect the equal rights of minorities. Secularism is in essence normative and therefore desirable for a plural society like India.

We have to admit that despite worrying developments, and despite setbacks, secularism has succeeded in institutionalizing a system of checks and balances in the Indian polity in the shape of a free press, human rights, gender, and civil society groups, and an active judiciary. The national press plays a stellar role in exposing communal violence, and civil rights and civil society groups try to see that the perpetrators of violence are brought to court. Six years after the Gujarat carnage, committed human rights activists are trying to bring these agents of violence to the courts, and trying to resurrect FIRs which had been suppressed by the police. Yet, as long as a single Indian citizen is threatened by communal violence, as long as a single woman is subjected to discriminatory patriarchal norms because the democratic project stops short at personal codes, and as long as otherwise sane individuals articulate prejudices against people who are our own, the secular and the democratic project is incomplete.

Let me now wrap up the argument. I have suggested that secularism needs to be urgently strengthened. Secularism has to be cast in a new mode; it has to be located theoretically and practically in the principle of democratic equality. It has to be seen as both a logical outcome of the principle of democratic equality and as legitimized by the principle of democratic equality. This may fetch the following results. Even if a government or group in civil society does not consider itself bound by secularism, it is certainly bound by the principle of equality, which is one of the constitutive features of our Constitution. Respect for Article 14, which prescribes equality, respect for Article 25, which gives the equal right of religious belief to all individuals, and respect for Article 29 and 30, which in the pursuit of equality grants certain protections for minorities rights, may perchance lead to secularism. Locating secularism in the principle of democratic equality has one further advantage; it might ensure that both inter-group as well as intra-group relations are regulated by the norms of equality. We can perhaps serve the cause of secularism by shifting the ground for the debate and by inviting those who deny the principles of secularism, even if they do not deny the rhetoric of secularism, to engage with concepts such as equality, rights, and the Constitution.

Suggested Readings

Bhargava, Rajeev (ed.). *Secularism and Its Critics*. New Delhi: Oxford University Press, 1997.

Crossman, Brenda and Ratna Kapur. *Secularism's Last Sigh?* New Delhi: Oxford University Press, 1999.

Jacobsohn, Gary Jeffrey. *The Wheel of Law: India's Secularism in Comparative Constitutional Context*. New Delhi: Oxford University Press, 2003.

Vanaik, Achin. *Communalism Contested: Religion, Modernity and Secularisation*. Delhi: Vistaar, 1997.

Questions

1. Do you agree with the proposition that secularism is a part of democracy? Give reasons.
2. Why is secularism, in your opinion, appropriate for plural societies?
3. What kinds of practices pose a threat to secularism in India?
4. Write a short story essay on the history of secularism in India.
5. What is the relationship between secularism and minority rights?

Contemporary Debates on Nationalism

Mohinder Singh

19

Rabindranath Tagore, who inspired many leaders of the Indian nationalist movement and who himself actively participated in it, wrote three essays intensely criticizing nationalism during the First World War. In one of these essays titled 'Nationalism in India', Tagore called nationalism a 'menace'.[1] This will appear very surprising to many, particularly to those who consider nation and nationalism to be given and natural condition of human political community. For instance, when this fact is told to students in an undergraduate classroom, they usually react with utter disbelief. How can Tagore criticize nationalism? This is perhaps because the most prevalent view in the popular perception is that although there can be many ways of organizing a nation and living as a nation, nation form is the only available mode of political existence. As a result, nationalism is unquestionably considered a good thing, the legitimacy of which cannot be questioned. The success of the ideology of nationalism has made nationalism ubiquitous because of which it exerts a stronghold over the minds of the people all around the world. Under these circumstances, the knowledge that Tagore, one of the leading lights of the Indian freedom struggle, wrote a powerful critique of nationalism is not easily palatable.

The research in history and social sciences in the last three decades have questioned these assumptions by throwing critical light on the idea and practice of nationalism. There is now a general consensus among scholars that nationalism in India originated in the 19th century and is a historical product of the circumstances created by colonialism.[2] In case of the European nationalism also, it is agreed that nations originated in the modern age, mainly in the 18th and

1. Rabindranath Tagore, 'Nationalism in India', in *Nationalism* (New Delhi: Rupa and Company, 2002), p. 121.
2. Sudipta Kaviraj, 'Crisis of Nation-State in India', in John Dunn (ed.) *Contemporary Crisis of the Nation-State?* (Oxford and Cambridge, UK: Blackwell, 1995), pp. 118–19; Sekhar Bandopadhyay, *From Plassey to Partition: A History of Modern India* (New Delhi: Orient Longman, 2004), p. 184.

19th centuries.[3] In both cases the emphasis is on the nation being a product of the modern age and a specifically modern political concept. In other words, the emphasis is on establishing the historicity of the idea of nation. Confusion usually occurs because this historicity is very different from the histories nations like to give themselves, tracing their origins back to the remote past. To tackle this problem, scholars have suggested that for a better understanding of the phenomenon of nationalism, it is better to stand outside the autobiographies nations give to themselves.[4] These are some of the academic questions relevant for understanding contemporary debates on nationalism in India.

On the political front, many important developments took place in India in the last two decades that have brought the question of meaning and nature of Indian nationalism to the forefront once again. One of the most important events of this period is the rise of communal Hindu nationalism in India. A sustained campaign launched by a group of Hindu right wing political and cultural organizations led to the demolition of the Babri Masjid in Ayodhya in December, 1992. This event challenged the legitimacy of the secular nationalism enshrined in the Constitution and also symbolized a crisis of secular nationalism in India. The contemporary debates on nationalism in India are dominated by an acute awareness of this crisis. Thus, two questions dominate the contemporary debate on nationalism in India. The first is a simple question: what form should Indian nationalism take? The second questions the very legitimacy of the idea of nationalism and asks whether nationalism creates a desirable political community. The question that has always been raised in the discourse on Indian nationalism and which is still asked is this: Is India a nation at all?

As noted earlier, the story of nationalism in India goes back to the 19th century when the anti-colonial freedom struggle began. From its inception, there have been debates on the nature and meaning of Indian nationalism. If a nation is usually defined as a community based on the commonality of culture, language, ethnicity, history and political destiny, then India from the very beginning faced a major problem as it is a land of immense religious, linguistic and cultural diversities. For these reasons, articulating an idea of Indian nation was a very difficult task from the beginning, a task fraught with pitfalls and huge risks as it became clear with the eventual Partition of British Indian territories that gave birth to not one but two nations: India and Pakistan. In order to understand the idea of Indian nationalism, it must be asked who is an Indian and what constitutes the core of the identity that an Indian gives to himself/herself. We will begin our inquiry into the debates on Indian nationalism with this question.

---

3. Benedict Anderson, *Imagined Communities* (London: Verso, 1983).
4. See, for instance, Sudipta Kaviraj, 'The Imaginary Institution of India', in Partha Chatterjee and Gyanendra Pandey (eds.), *Subaltern Studies, Vol. VII* (New Delhi: Oxford University Press, 1992), pp. 1–39.

THE QUESTION: WHO IS AN INDIAN?

One of the ways of understanding the concept of 'nation' is by trying to understand in what ways nations respond to human beings' need to have an identity. Who am I? This question, which human beings confront many times in their lives, can be answered in different ways. We can answer this question by referring to one's language, religion, caste, region, gender, profession, or nationality. The answers to this question refer to one's sense and sources of identity. In other words, there are various sources from which a person can derive his/her identity: religion, gender, region, language, profession, nationality, etc. And many identities can exist in a person at the same time. For example, one person can be a Christian, Malayalam speaking, and an Indian at the same time. There is no need to attach importance to any one of the identities over other. Yet, our different identities become significant in different contexts. For example, when we are abroad, we (i. e. the Indians) usually identify ourselves as Indians. In such contexts our nationality becomes important because most of the foreigners may not know about all the cultural, religious, regional, and linguistic diversity that prevails within India, whereas in India, particularly in the big cities, we are more conscious of our linguistic and regional identity.[5]

In spite of the presence of so many sources of identities, human beings are capable of going beyond all these particular sources and relate to each other as simply human beings with a belief that all human beings are equally dignified. As we mentioned above, a nation is one of the sources of identity of a person. What is the meaning of nation as a source of one's identity? What does it mean when we say that we are Indians? Does it simply mean that we are citizens of a nation-state called India and can legitimately hold an Indian passport. This is certainly true in a very important sense because the Constitution of India guarantees all those people who are born in India and who are naturalized citizens a set of Fundamental Rights along with other rights, and of course a right to hold an Indian passport. But the problem with this answer is that it is tautological, which means that it's like saying: 'an Indian is an Indian, who is a citizen of Indian nation-state.' As we know, the nation-state called India came into existence in 1947. But there certainly existed Indian nationalism before 1947 and this nationalism was based on the claim that there existed a nation called India for which Independence from colonial rule was demanded. Is there then any other, and stronger, sense of defining the sense of being an 'Indian'? All the versions of Indian nationalism claim that there is this stronger sense of being an Indian. The historical and contemporary debates on Indian nationalism are

5. Amartya Sen, *Identity and Violence: The Illusion of Destiny* (London: Allen Lane, 2006), pp. 18–39; for the working of multiple identities in pre-colonial India, see Kaviraj, 'The Imaginary Institution of India'.

centred on what this 'sense' is. We need to go into the historical background of Indian nationalism in order to locate answers to these questions.

HISTORICAL BACKGROUND: COLONIALISM AND THE EMERGENCE OF INDIAN NATIONALISM

A nation is usually defined as a political community with a shared history, culture, and a sense of political goals. By definition, nations are supposed to be culturally homogeneous. Or at least what is claimed on their behalf. The main question then in the Indian context is: if India is a nation, then how do we understand the shared history, culture, and a sense of political destiny of the 'Indians'? There is a broad consensus among historians that the idea of a nation, the sense of national identity, and nationalism in India emerged very recently in history, and they are all products of political and cultural response by the English educated middle-class intelligentsia to the colonial rule.[6] Nationalism emerged as a reaction against and as a challenge to colonialism. Sunil Khilnani in his book, *The Idea of India*, writes:

> [After all,] before the nineteenth century, no residents of the subcontinent would have identified themselves as Indian. There existed intricate, ramified vocabularies of common understanding, which classified people by communities of lineage, locality and sect; but "Indian" would not have figured among its terms.[7]

Let us try to understand the meaning of Khilnani's statement by reading it in the following manner: the residents of the subcontinent before the 19th century could give themselves identities based on religion, locality, caste, lineage, etc. because it was possible for them to do that and there was a need for such identities. But they could not give themselves the *national* identity of being an Indian because there was neither the need for such an identity nor was it possible to do so. If we first elaborate the factors that led to the emergence of the Indian nationalism in the 19th century, we can understand why the need for identifying oneself as an 'Indian' for a resident of the subcontinent were absent.

For an effective struggle to be possible against colonialism it was necessary to have an effective network of communication so that people from different regions of India could establish political links among themselves. There were certain conditions created by the colonial government that made such a unity at the level of the Indian subcontinent possible. The first condition was that the

---

6. Bandopadhyay, *From Plassey to Partition*, pp. 205–18.
7. Sunil Khilnani, *The Idea of India* (New Delhi: Penguin Books, 2004), p. 154.

colonial government established a single unified administration for the whole country for an efficient collection of revenue and for effective governance. It also provided a legal unity by creating a single legal system for the entire British India. The new means of transport and communication such as the railways, post and telegraph, newspapers and magazines also helped in bringing various regions of British India much closer to each other than they had ever been. The introduction of English medium education also led to the emergence of a new middle class—the English educated middle class. The new education system also brought the educated Indians in contact with the modern political theories and ideas of the post-Enlightenment Europe like equality, rule of law, self-determination, liberty and above all the idea of nationalism. Even more significant was the fact that English became the common medium in which the political leaders of different regions like Maharashtra, Bengal, Madras, United Province, and Punjab communicated and in which they articulated their politics.

The importance of the English language for early nationalist politics can be judged from the fact that it was the lingua franca of the Indian National Congress in its early phase.[8] Similarly, the emergence of literary modes of communication like newspapers and magazines both in English and Indian vernaculars played a significant role in spreading the feeling of anti-colonial nationalism across the subcontinent. The vernacular newspapers particularly helped in taking the politics of nationalism beyond the confines of the English educated elites.[9] The resultant anti-colonial movement, the leadership of which was provided by the members of the English educated classes, was launched and carried forward in the name of and on behalf of the Indian nation. The task of imagining India as a nation also fell to the leaders and the thinkers of the nationalist movement. There were many possible ways in which India as a nation could be imagined, elaborated, and defined. And many competing alternatives also appeared in the course of the freedom struggle and after Independence. These alternative perspectives presented different conceptions of nationalism, national history and national culture.[10] One of the chief concerns of the debates on nationalism in India today too revolves around the competing conceptions of national history and national culture.

Nationalism, History, and Culture

The history of a nation is an essential part of the nationalist project since by definition, a nation is understood as a community of people with a shared history. This was no different in the case of Indian nationalism. Thus, the genealogy of the nationalist historiography in India can also be traced back to the

8. Kaviraj, 'The Imaginary Institution of India'; Sumit Sarkar, *Modern India* (Madras: Macmillan India, 1983), pp. 89–92.
9. Sarkar, *Modern India*, p. 96.
10. Kaviraj, 'Crisis of Nation-State in India'.

19th century.[11] It is generally accepted that history writing, both as a modern academic discipline and as a thing of political use is a result of this profound rupture that British colonialism produced in colonized peoples modes of organizing time. Despite having a venerable written culture (with its family genealogies, dynastic chronicles, histories of castes and religious sects, biographies of holy men), Indian ways of narrating the past were discounted by British historians. The colonial historians, instead, wrote their own history of India. Knowledge of India and its past were an essential part of the project of colonial domination. The European historians first began to carry out research into India's past in the late 18th and early 19th centuries. The colonial histories of India during this period mainly took two forms: the liberal and the orientalist histories. The liberals arrogantly deified the modern West and denigrated India's past. The main emphasis in the orientalist scholarship was on discovering greatness and glory of the ancient past of India. The European historians introduced a tripartite division into the study of Indian history.[12] According to this interpretation, after the glorious ancient age there was a period of dark age identified with the Muslim rule until the coming of the British. The main purpose of this strategy was to establish legitimacy of the colonial rule. Europeans historical prejudices against Islam also fed into this image of history.[13]

The Indians started writing the history of the country as a reaction against the foreign, particularly the liberal, interpretation of the Indian past. The basis of this development was the desire to claim a past that was not distorted by such interpretations. But at the same time the methodological assumptions underlying these histories were the same as those of the colonial historiography. It particularly borrowed the basic orientalist notions about India's past. Indian nationalism and the writing of the Indian history developed in close connection and helped the flourishing of each other. The most important feature of the 19th century nationalist history writing is that in this stage of the development of historical and national consciousness the historians [mostly of the Hindu high caste origin] tended to present the coming of the colonial rule as a boon for the country, as an event that liberates the Hindus from the darkness of the Muslim rule. As we can see, already at the formative stage of historical consciousness in India, the sense of self and identity is based on religious community.[14]

The Hindu middle class intelligentsia blamed the corruption in the Hindu society on its long history of subjection to Muslim rule. Thus begins

11. Partha Chatterjee, *The Nation and Its Fragments: Colonial and Postcolonial Histories,* in *The Partha Chatterjee Omnibus* (New Delhi: Oxford University Press, 1999), pp. 76–115; Ranajit Guha, *An Indian Historiography of India: A Nineteenth Century Agenda and Its Implications* (Calcutta: Centre for the Study of Social Sciences, 1988), pp. 1–26.
12. Neeladri Bhattacharya, 'The Problem', *Seminar* 522, special issue on Rewriting History, 2003: pp. 12–13.
13. Chatterjee, *The Nation and Its Fragments*, pp. 102–06.
14. Ibid, pp. 95–115.

the replication of the three-stage schema in the writing of history: beginning (Hindu rule), middle (Muslim rule) and modern (Christian rule) first introduced by the colonial historians of India like James Mill whose *History of British India* was very influential in the formation of early discourse on history in India.[15] As a result of the combined effect of all these factors the construction of prejudices against the Muslims begins. The period of 'Muslim rule' was presented as a time of despotism, misrule and anarchy. The images of the Muslim and Islam are constructed in such a way that the Muslim is always named as the foreigner and aggressor.[16] As we shall see shortly, there is one strand of nationalism that still identifies the history of India with the history of one religion community.

From the beginning of nationalism in India, therefore, there has always existed the problem of inclusion and exclusion of various communities into the entity called nation. The problem can be stated in these terms: if the shared history and shared culture of the nation [and nation by definition must have both] is based on the history and culture of one religious community, then the other religious communities get excluded from the membership of the nation; if on the other hand, all the religious communities are to have equal stake in the nation and its destiny, then the history and culture of the nation have to be discovered in some other, non-religious or secular way. This obviously affected the inter-community relation during the colonial and post–colonial phase. From the late 19th century onwards, there have been various competing political constructs of Indian nationhood.[17] Among these competing versions, there were two major interpretations of Indian nationalism: the first was communal nationalism and the second was secular nationalism. Both these strands of nationalism have played an important role in Indian politics for the last 100 years.

Nation and Religious Communities: Communal and Secular Versions of Nationalism in India

Hindu nationalism in contemporary India is a variant of communal nationalism since it seeks to grant privileges to the Hindu religious community and identifies *national* history and culture with the history and culture understood exclusively from the perspective of the Hindu community. In contemporary India, communal interpretation of nationalism is one of the many ways in which India as a nation is understood. It is particularly important to understand the politics of communal nationalism or communalism as it has led to many tragic consequences for Indian politics and society in the last 100 years including the

---

15. Sumit Sarkar, *Writing Social History* (New Delhi: Oxford University Press, 1997), pp. 1–49; Ranajit Guha, *An Indian Historiography of India: A Nineteenth Century Agenda and Its Implications* (Calcutta: Centre for the Study of Social Sciences, 1988), p. 13.
16. Chatterjee, *The Nation and Its Fragments*, pp. 102–06.
17. Kaviraj, 'Crisis of the Nation-State in India', pp. 118–19.

Partition of the country in 1947, the demolition of the Babri Masjid in December 1992, and countless Hindu-Muslim riots that have taken place during this period. In India, the roots of communal nationalism go back to the 19th century and it is intimately linked with the specific question of nationalism in India. As we have noted above, to link the identity of India as a nation with the identity of a particular religious community was one of the possible ways of imagining the nation. How did this possibility play out in actual politics?

Two versions of communal nationalism were present during the freedom movement: Hindu and Muslim. The anti-colonial nationalism in India gained momentum during the Swadeshi movement against the partition of Bengal in 1905. During this agitation many leaders of the movement, particularly the leaders of the extremist faction of the Indian National Congress, started to make use of Hindu religious festivals and symbols for the political purpose of mobilizing the masses against colonial rulers. The leaders of the swadeshi movement like Bal Gangadhar Tilak and Lala Lajpat Rai also popularized the image of history in which the pre-colonial history of India was presented in such a way that it became a history of conflict of communities and contained a negative representation of the Muslims.[18] The kind of history of India that we discussed in the last section came to be disseminated in the public sphere of political mobilization. This interpretation of the Indian history presented historical figures such as Shivaji and Rana Pratap as the heroes of Hindu resistance to the medieval Muslim tyranny. There were also many incidents of the Hindu-Muslim communal riots during this period of the anti-colonial agitation.

Meanwhile, a new sense of community identity was developing among the educated Muslims from the second half of the 19th century onwards. The English educated intelligentsia among the Muslims became concerned about some things related to the situation of the Muslims in India when they sought to speak on behalf of the Muslims of India. These things were: the colonial census—which was based on religion as a category of enumeration—and told them of the 'minority' status of Muslims in British India compared with the Hindu 'majority'; the Muslims were generally lagging behind the Hindus (particularly the upper castes) in the field of education and government jobs; the nationalism of the Indian National Congress under the leadership of the extremists was alienating the Muslim sections of the population. At the same time, the newly emerging politics of representation, where numbers mattered, was making the educated Muslims acutely aware of the status of Muslim community as 'minority'. This particular concern can be seen in Sir Sayyid Ahmed Khan's speech in the Governor-General's council where he said: The larger community would totally override the interests of the smaller community.[19] It had

18. Bandopadhyay, *From Plassey to Partition*, pp. 250–51, 269–70; Sarkar, *Modern India*, pp. 121–23.
19. Khalid Bin Sayeed, *Pakistan: The Formative Phase 1857–1948* (Karachi: Oxford University Press, 1998), p. 18.

many consequences. On the one hand, the educated Muslim leadership looked towards the British government for safeguarding the interests of the Muslim community. The educated Muslims floated a political party parallel to the Indian National Congress and named it the All Indian Muslim League in December 1906. One of the main demands of the Muslim League was separate electorates for the Muslims. This was recognized when the British government included separate electorate as a provision in the new Indian Council Act of 1909. On the other hand, the Muslim leadership also had to negotiate with the phenomenon of 'Indian' nationalism, which was increasingly becoming popular.

In the face of the identification of India with the identity of the Hindu community, its history and its culture, it was not easy for the Muslim politicians and intellectuals to negotiate with this phenomenon. As it was easier for the leaders of the 'majority' community to create an identity between Indian nationalism and Hindu symbolism, the Muslims found themselves on the margins of the discourse of 'Indian nationalism'. The dilemma faced by the Muslim leaders during this period of Indian politics was expressed by Maulana Muhammad Ali in 1912 in these words: '... the educated Hindu "communal patriot" had turned Hinduism into an effective symbol of mass mobilization and Indian "nationality", but refused to give quarter to the Muslim unless the latter quietly shuffles off his individuality and becomes completely Hinduized.'[20]

The political events that took place in the second decade of the 20th century not only provided an occasion for the unity of the Indian National Congress and the Muslim League in Lucknow in 1916 for a common front against the government, but also led to a rethinking of the relationship between nationalism and religious communities within the Congress camp. The second and third decades of the 20th century also saw the emergence of new and influential political leaders—prominent among whom were Mahatma Gandhi and Jawaharlal Nehru. A decisive shift took place in the thinking of the Indian National Congress on the question of nationalism insofaras the new leadership tried to distance itself from the interpretation of Indian nationalism in terms of Hindu nationalism. The Indian National Congress, from its origins, had tried to present itself as an organization that could represent all groups and communities in India and not merely the majority community of the Hindus. While the supporters of the Hindu nationalism became more and more marginalized within the Indian National Congress, the dominant, Nehruvian faction imagined Indian nationalism as pluralist and secular. We shall discuss the Nehruvian idea of secular nationalism in the next section. By the end of the 1920s three versions of nationalism clearly emerged: Hindu nationalism, Muslim nationalism, and secular nationalism. With the Partition of the subcontinent in 1947 and with the creation of two nation-states of India

---

20. Cited in Sugata Bose and Ayesha Jalal, *Modern South Asia: History, Culture, and Political Economy* (New Delhi: Oxford University Press, 2004), p. 100.

and Pakistan, the Muslim nationalism, articulated by the Muslim League fizzled out in India. The other two versions of nationalism continued in post-Independence India.

HINDU NATIONALISM

In contemporary India, Hindu nationalism is promoted by organizations like Bharatiya Janata Party (BJP), Shiv Sena, Rashtriya Swayamsevak Sangh (RSS), Vishwa Hindu Parishad (VHP) and Bajrang Dal. These organizations promote the idea that India is a Hindu nation and the Hindu community should have a more privileged place in this nation than other religious communities. Hindu nationalism, promoted by these organizations insists on the acceptance of Hinduness or Hindutva as the essence of Indian nationhood.[21] L. K. Advani, the BJP leader and the ex-home minister in the Government of India, said in a TV interview in 1991: 'India is essentially a Hindu country. My party emphasizes that India is *one* nation and not a multi-national state.'[22] At another place he asserted that 'Indian nationalism is rooted in a Hindu ethos.'[23] Similarly, the former chief of the RSS, Rajendra Singh, declared in one of his speeches: 'That is our goal. Our society should be homogeneous. Let India be a Hindu commonwealth.'[24]

Hindu nationalism in India is based on a communal ideology that identifies nationalism with the promotion and protection of the interests of the Hindu religious community. In this process, Hindu nationalism projects other religious communities, particularly Muslims and Christians in a very bad light as it presents them as its principal adversaries. In its extreme version, Hindu nationalism aggressively demands the exclusion of the Muslims from the Indian nation by either an outright denial of citizenship rights to them or by relegating them to the position of second class citizens. In this version of Hindu nationalism, the Muslims are to 'be tolerated at the majorities pleasure as a substitute for full citizenship.'[25] The moderate versions of Hindu nationalism argue in favour of assimilation by the minorities. The proposed assimilation means that the religious minorities in India such as Christians and Muslims must accept the centrality of Hinduism to Indian nationhood.

The most salient components of the Hindu communal ideology of nationalism were developed first by V. D. Savarkar in *Hindutva: Who Is a Hindu?* and by

---

21. Aditya Nigam, *The Insurrection of Little Selves: The Crisis of Secular-Nationalism in India* (New Delhi: Oxford University Press, 2006), p. 68.
22. Cited in Gyanendra Pandey, 'The Civilized and the Barbarian: The "New" Politics of Late Twentieth Century India and the World', in Gyanendra Pandey (ed.), *Hindus and Others: The Question of Identity in India Today* (New Delhi: Viking, 1993), p. 15.
23. Cited in Ashutosh Varshney, *Ethnic Conflict and Civic Life: Hindus and Muslims of India* (New Haven and London: Yale University Press, 2002), p. 71.
24. Yogendra K. Malik and Dhirendra K. Vajpeyi, 'The Rise of Hindu Militancy: India's Secular Democracy at Risk,' *Asian Survey* 29 (3), March 1989: 308–325.
25. Mukul Kesavan, *Secular Common Sense* (New Delhi: Penguin Books India, 2001) pp. 41–47.

Golwalkar in *We, or Our Nation Defined.* In these tracts Savarkar and Golwalkar elaborate a conception of Indian nationalism based on a specific relationship between territory, history, and culture. For Savarkar, only those persons can claim a full membership of the Indian nation who has both his fatherland (*pitribhumi*) and holy land (*punyabhumi*) in the territory of India that he broadly equated with the territory of British India. Savarkar thus defines a Hindu as 'a person who regards this land of Bharatvarsha from the Indus to the Seas as his *pitribhumi* as well as *punyabhumi* that is the cradle land of his religion.'[26] Only Hindus, therefore, can be true patriots, not Indian Muslims or Christians with holy lands in Arabia or Palestine. The edge of the entire argument is clearly directed against them, and not against British colonial rulers who never claimed India to be either their pitribhumi or punyabhumi.[27]

According to these territorial, religious, and genealogical criteria, Hindus, Sikhs, Jains, and Buddhists can be considered the natural members of the Indian nation as all these religions were born here but not Jews, Parsis, Christians, and Muslims for they do not meet the religious criterion of the holy land within the territory. It is in this way the Hindu nationalism builds its theory of the nation by including certain religious communities and by excluding other communities. For the Muslims and Christians, their holy lands are in Arabia or Palestine. Their mythology and godmen, their ideas and heroes did not originate in this land.'[28] In a similar vein, the second chief of the RSS, M. S. S. Golwalkar too defined Indian nationalism in terms of exclusionary religious nationalism based on the primacy of Hinduism. Golwalkar in *We, or Our Nation Defined* argued that 'Muslims living in India should be second class citizens living on Hindu sufferance, with no rights of any kind.'[29] Golwalkar is very clear about his idea of a nation:

> From this standpoint sanctioned by the experience of shrewd old nations, the non-Hindu people in Hindusthan must either adopt the Hindu culture and language, must learn to respect and revere Hindu religion, must entertain no idea but the glorification of the Hindu nation, i.e. they must not only give up their attitude of intolerance and ingratitude towards this land and its age-long traditions, but must also cultivate the positive attitude of love and devotion instead; in one word, they must cease to be foreigners or may stay in the country wholly subordinated to the Hindu nation claiming nothing, deserving no privileges, far less any preferential treatment, not even citizens rights.[30]

---

26. Sumit Sarkar, 'Indian Nationalism and the Politics of Ḥindutva', in David Ludden (ed.), *Making India Hindu: Religion, Community, and Politics of Democracy in India* (New Delhi: Oxford University Press, 1996), p. 274.
27. Ibid., p. 274.
28. Varshney, *Ethnic Conflict and Civic Life*, pp. 65–66.
29. Kesavan, *Secular Common Sense*, p. 100.
30. Ibid., pp. 100–101.

Accordingly, the historiography of Hindu nationalism reduces the complex, multiple and varied histories of the Indian subcontinent to a narrow conflict of religious communities, basically to Hindu–Muslim conflict in the past. In constructing the history of India, the historiography of Hindu nationalism closely follows the tripartite division of Indian history into Ancient, Medieval, and Modern discussed in the previous section. The main motif of the Hindu nationalist historiography is that it ceaselessly paints the picture of Muslims as the main villain of Indian history. According to Gyanendra Pandey, the Hindu communal historiography reduces all of India's past to two propositions. First is the glory of pre-Muslim or Ancient India; and second is the argument that the dark period of Indian history and all the troubles of Indian history start with the coming of the Muslims to the subcontinent.[31] It presents Indian history as a 'history of perpetual Hindu-Muslim conflict, Muslim aggression and Hindu resistance, Good versus Evil, the pure versus the Impure.'[32]

This history stubbornly refuses to recognize any contribution made by the Muslims to India's art, culture, music, literature etc. and it systematically vilifies all the Muslim figures from the history of the Indian subcontinent. Be it Akbar, Aurangzeb, Syed Ahmed Khan, Dara Shikoh, Maulana Azad or any other figure, they are all presented as the incarnations of evil by virtue of their very being the followers of Islam. In this way, no Muslim historical figure, no Muslim cultural or religious symbol finds any place in the conception of Indian culture as conceived by the Hindutva version of nationalism except as negative and impure elements contaminating the pure, inner core of the Indian culture which is of course made of Hindu ethos.[33] The political agendas of contemporary Hindutva movement such as the construction of the Ram temple in Ayodhya at the site of the demolished Babri mosque, repealing of Article 370, and Hinduization of the Indian culture, education, and politics are intimately connected with this image of history. Quite consistent with their narrow communal interpretation of history, the supporters of Hindu nationalism believe that the 'Indian nation can only be reinvigorated when its rightful proprietors, the Hindu majority, resurrect a strong sense of Hindutva (Hinduness).'[34]

Secular Nationalism

As against communal nationalism, secular nationalism in India is born of a desire to construct an identity of Indian nationhood that recognizes the immense diversity that prevailed in India: the diversities of religion, sect, language, caste,

31. Pandey, 'The Civilized and the Barbarian', p. 12.
32. Ibid.
33. Ibid., pp. 12–14.
34. Thomas Blom Hansen, *The Saffron Wave: Democracy and Hindu Nationalism in Modern India* (New Delhi: Oxford University Press, 2004), pp. 4–5.

regions etc. Secular nationalism thus promotes an idea of India that is acceptable to the different sections of the Indian society and in which all can share. Thus, its basic idea is the idea of 'unity in diversity'. From the very beginning of the nationalist politics this idea of the nation constituted by diversity has been present. Mukul Kesavan, for instance, has argued that the Indian National Congress from its very inception understood itself as a 'self-consciously representative assembly of Indians from different parts of India.'[35] From the beginning the Congress leadership sought to bring together diverse sections of the population on a common platform on the agenda of anti-imperialism. In the first phase of the Congress politics, it tried to create a sentiment of unity by highlighting the adverse economic impact of colonialism.[36]

Yet it was only in the 1920s that an influential section of the Congress leadership started to consciously construct theories of secular nationalism. Here it should be clearly noted that the word secular had a special meaning in the Indian historical context. As Sumit Sarkar has argued in his essay on the politics of Hindutva, secular in this context basically meant anti-communal strand of nationalism that based its idea of nationalism on the prior recognition of cultural diversity along with a recognition of the need to have an idea of one common culture.[37] How to discover a common culture in the face of so much diversity? This was a difficult task as it included the discovery of a culture that would be non-sectarian, non-communal and inclusive. Jawaharlal Nehru's *Discovery of India* is usually considered the foundational text of secular nationalism wherein the Indian history is told as a narrative of composite culture and unity in diversity.[38]

In Nehru's *Discovery of India*, pluralism, syncretism, tolerance, peaceful coexistence, and composite culture appear as the main motifs. In this narrative, the heroes of Indian history too are very different figures than those foregrounded in the communal interpretation. They are all syncretistic figures: Ashoka, Kabir, Nanak, Akbar, and Gandhi. They come from different religious communities and tend to promote ideas of peaceful coexistence, unity of mankind, tolerance etc. Nehru also has a very different image, different from the communal version, of how the external interferences affected the Indian civilization. This is the quintessential image of ancient Indian that we get: 'Ancient India, like ancient China, was a world in itself, a culture and a civilization which gave shape to all things. Foreign influences poured in and often influenced that culture and were absorbed. Disruptive tendencies gave rise immediately to an attempt to find a synthesis. Some kind of dream of unity has occupied the mind of India since the dawn of civilization. That unity was not conceived as something imposed from outside, a standardization of beliefs. It was something deeper and within its

35. Kesavan, *Secular Common Sense*, p. 3.
36. Ibid., p. 5.
37. Sarkar, 'Indian Nationalism and the Politics of Hindutva', p. 273.
38. Nigam, *The Insurrection of Little Selves*, p. 70.

fold, the widest tolerance of belief and custom was practiced and every variety was acknowledged and even encouraged.'[39]

The Nehruvian idea of the Indian national identity as based on composite and pluralist cultural traditions was shared by many important leaders within and outside the Congress. Similar interpretations of the Indian history and culture were promoted by influential leaders and activists of the Congress Socialist Party and the Communist Party of India. This group of politicians also sought to relegate the role of religion to the non-political, private sphere. They believed that religion could not play any important role in the political affairs of a modern society.[40] Although Mahatma Gandhi did not promote the separation of religion from politics, he also helped in promoting a pluralist national identity for Indian nationhood.[41] The same concept of pluralist and composite culture was promoted by prominent Muslim leaders not only in the Congress like Abul Kalam Azad but also in the Socialist and Communist parties. Thus, during the last two decades of the freedom movement, mainly under the influence of Gandhi and Nehru, a pluralist identity for the Indian nationhood emerged as a strong contender if not the dominant model. This stream of politicians promoted the struggle for freedom in India as a struggle for a secular republic where all of India's inhabitants were entitled to live, irrespective of religious denomination.[42]

The events such as the partition, the assassination of Mahatma Gandhi by a communal fanatic, and emergence of Nehru as the topmost leader of the Congress and the Prime Minister of the Interim government provided the political background against which the post-Independent Indian State adopted secularism as the principle of State policy. But the idea of secularism that was enshrined in the Constitution and that which was practised was quite different. It was also different from the classical notion of secularism as a wall of separation between religion and State as practised in the USA. Indian secularism was based on a much more modest idea according to which if the State had to deal with religious communities, it would deal with them on the basis of symmetry of treatment between different communities. It was an idea of secularism based on neutrality and equidistance of State with respect to religious communities.[43] The problem of the other important diversity of India, namely, the linguistic

39. Jawaharlal Nehru, *The Discovery of India*, (New Delhi: Jawaharlal Nehru Memorial Fund, 1981), p. 62.
40. Ravinder Kumar, 'The Secular Culture of India', in Rasheeduddin Khan (ed.), *Composite Culture and National Integration* (Shimla and New Delhi: Indian Institute of Advanced Study, in association with Allied Publishers, 1987), p. 371.
41. Ibid., p. 370.
42. Ibid., pp. 367–71.
43. Amartya Sen, 'Secularism and Its Discontents', in Kaushik Basu and Sanjay Subramanyam (eds.), *Unravelling the Nation: Sectarian Conflict and India's Secular Identity* (New Delhi: Penguin Books, 1996), pp. 13–14, and Ashutosh Varshney, *Ethnic Conflict and Civic Life: Hindus and Muslims of India* (New Haven and London: Yale University Press, 2002), pp. 55–64. Also see Blom Hansen, *The Saffron Wave*, p. 11.

diversity, was addressed with the adoption of federalism. Similarly, various other political aspirations of the Indian masses were sought to be accommodated by the instrument of democratic governance with universal franchise.[44]

Indian Nationalism: Critical Perspectives

It should be clear from the discussion above that the secular pluralist version of the Indian nationalism is an inclusive and reconciliatory view in contrast to the exclusive and communal version presented by the Hindu nationalist view. The secular pluralist version seeks to accommodate various religious, ethnic, and linguistic communities in its definition of Indian identity. The image of Indian history foregrounded by this version is also much more inclusive of India's diversity in comparison with the image of history presented by Hindu nationalism emphasizing basically the narrative of Hindu–Muslim conflict in the past. It must also be recognized here that the political vision that inspires the secular-pluralist construction of the Indian identity and the corresponding image of history is morally far superior to the one driving the Hindu nationalist notion of the Indian identity. In the wake of the general escalation of violence against minorities in India that accompanied the rise of Hindutva it should not be difficult to see that the logic of Hindu nationalism like all exclusive nationalisms leads to the imperative of ethnic cleansing. There have been too many such incidents in the recent past to ignore this danger. As we stated in the beginning of this essay, such events indicate a crisis of secular nationalism in India. In the wake of this historical predicament, many scholars have recently argued in favour of a need to go beyond the secular–communal dichotomy in understanding Indian nationalism. Thus, there have appeared many important critiques of Indian nationalism as it has been interpreted so far. Some of them will be outlined briefly in the rest of the essay.

One line of criticism, while defending the need for a secular pluralist framework, Indian polity, has questioned the construction of India's past in both communal and secular historiography. They have argued that none of these historiographies presents the true picture of the relationship between religious communities in India. They argue that both these versions of India's past, secular no less than communal, have been guilty of a selective reading of events from history. In Indian history, it is possible to find incidents of sectarian conflicts between religious groups as well as incidents of syncretism, harmonious relations and mutual influence of different religious cultures. As an example of this approach, Sanjay Subramanyam, in a recent essay on medieval history, has recounted incidents of sectarian conflicts—between Hindus and Muslims, between Shaivaite and Vaishnavaite sects; destruction of temples by Muslim rulers, destruction of temples by Hindu rulers, desecration of

44. Sudipta Kaviraj, 'Crisis of the Nation-State in India', p. 119.

places of worship by both Hindus and Muslims—sometimes for political and material reasons, but sometimes purely for the reasons of religious zeal and fanaticism.[45] It follows from this that any reading of India's past from a nationalist perspective is not possible without gross distortion. Conversely, and more importantly, any derivation of India's national identity from its past history too will remain contested.

There is a second line of criticism, according to which, from its very inception Indian nationalism has always contained an idea of a 'core' in its definition in the sense that some category of people have been understood as more natural and important members than others. To be more specific, Indian nationalism, even in its secular-pluralist versions has always had overtones of majoritarianism and it has been a 'majoritarian nationalism' in a liberal garb.[46] As the first articulation of Indian nationalism historically was done by the members of Hindu intelligentsia, it has always been accompanied by an 'unself-conscious majoritarian conviction that there was no contradiction between 'Hindu' and 'Indian' identities.'[47] Gyanendra Pandey has argued in an essay 'Citizenship and Difference: The Muslim Question in India' that around the time of partition such identification of the Hindu identity with the Indian identity became even more emphatic in political discourse so much so that Hindus were given the status of the 'natural' citizens of India. Pandey writes: 'For the Hindus are not a constituent [of the nation]. They *are* the nation, the 'we' who demand cooperation from the minorities, the 'us' that the Muslims have to learn to live with. Like the land and the trees, the rivers and the mountains, these invisible Hindus are the nation's natural condition, its essence and spirit. Their culture is the nation's culture, their history its history.'[48]

Such majoritarian assumptions of nationalism have been present not merely in the lower and middle level leadership of the Congress but reached the highest levels of the party. Leaders like Valllabhbhai Patel and Madan Mohan Malviya always promoted majoritarian tendencies within the Congress.[49] Such assumptions have been recently shown to be very much present in Nehru's *Discovery of India*, a very important document of secular nationalism in India.[50] Reflecting on the long history of majoritarian tendencies of Indian nationalism G. Balachandran writes: 'Far from being decisively engaged and defeated, majoritarian nationalism in India has been able to preserve itself as a *structural* feature of the

45. Sanjay Subramanyam, 'Before the Leviathan: Sectarian Violence and the State in Pre-Colonial India', in Basu and Subramanyam (eds.), *Unravelling the Nation*, pp. 44–80.
46. G. Balachandran, 'Religion and Nationalism in Modern India', in Basu and Subramanyam (eds.), *Unravelling the Nation*, pp. 108–11.
47. Ibid., p. 89.
48. Gyanendra Pandey, 'Citizenship and Difference: The Muslim Question in India', in Mushirul Hasan and Nariaki Nakazats (eds.), *Unfinished Agenda: Nation Building in South Asia* (New Delhi: Manohar Publishers, 2001), p. 120.
49. Balachandran, 'Religion and Nationalism in Modern India', pp. 108–11.
50. Nigam, *The Insurrection of Little Selves*, pp. 70–76.

system, cloaked in passivity, as long as avenues for rapid employment mobility existed or the unitarian political order was not under any palpable threat, by the rhetoric of building a strong, independent, self-reliant nation, but reappearing, once these avenues ceased or the centralization of power at the centre was challenged, as an attractive alternative to any meaningful attempt to reckon and deal with deep cleavages within Indian society.'[51] The kind of self-assurance with which legal reforms such as Hindu Code Bill were passed in Parliament also exposes the majoritarian assumptions of nationalism in India.

This critique strikes at the very root of Indian nationhood and points out the impossibility of a truly inclusive definition of India as a nation. Recently Pratap Bhanu Mehta has strongly argued that such a quest for finding a clear cut definition of the Indian identity is indeed not possible without marginalizing, or even putting at risk, some sections of Indians. Mehta argues that this happens because of the obsession with benchmarking an essential identity for the Indian nation.[52] This obsession with benchmarking an identity for India or attempt to answer the question Who is an Indian? in the strong cultural sense has been present in both secular and communal versions of Indian nationalism. For Mehta the way out lies in giving up this quest entirely and in looking for ways of acknowledging our differences and in living to learn with these differences in politically acceptable ways. In Mehta's words:

> Politically what India needs is not a new conception of Indian identity, one that emphasizes pluralism and compositeness. Rather, what we need is a social contract over how we may respect and interact with those with whom we disagree about India's identity. We don't need to ask; what do we share? Rather we need to ask: what are the terms on which we relate to those with whom we disagree? The challenge is not to find what we share; the challenge is to find ways of acknowledging difference.[53]

If we recall, in this context, the question we posed in the beginning of this essay Who is an Indian? Mehta is arguing that the very quest for answering this question in the stronger sense is a trap—an identity trap.[54] According to this conception, an Indian is an Indian. No need to ask any further what it means. At the same time, an Indian is also a Hindu, Muslim, Sikh, Christian, Punjabi, Bengali, Manipuri, and many more things.[55]

---

51. Ibid. p. 111.
52. Pratap Bhanu Mehta, 'Secularism and Identity Trap', in Mushirul Hasan (ed.), *Will Secular India Survive?* (New Delhi: Imprint One), pp. 72–81.
53. Ibid. p. 81.
54. Ibid.
55. Pandey, 'Citizenship and Difference', p. 127.

Suggested Readings

Barua, Sanjib. *India Against Itself: Assam and the Politics of Nationality*. New Delhi: Oxford University Press, 2001.

Basu, Kaushik and Sanjay Subramanyam (eds.). *Unravelling the Nation: Sectarian Conflict and India's Secular Identity*. New Delhi: Penguin Books, 1996.

Blom Hansen, Thomas. *The Saffron Wave: Democracy and Hindu Nationalism in Modern India*. New Delhi: Oxford University Press, 2004.

Chatterjee, Partha. *The Nation and Its Fragments: Colonial and Postcolonial Histories*, in *The Partha Chatterjee Omnibus*. New Delhi: Oxford University Press, 1999.

Hasan, Mushirul (ed.). *Will Secular India Survive?* New Delhi: Imprint One, 2004.

Kaviraj, Sudipta. 'The Imaginary Institution of India'. In Partha Chatterjee and Gyanendra Pandey (eds.). *Subaltern Studies: Vol. VII*. New Delhi: Oxford University Press, 1992.

Kesavan, Mukul. *Secular Common Sense*. New Delhi: Penguin Books, 2001.

Khilnani, Sunil. *The Idea of India*. New Delhi: Penguin Books, 2004.

Pandey, Gyanendra (ed.). *Hindus and Others: The Question of Identity in India Today*. New Delhi: Viking, 1993.

Sarkar, Sumit. 'Indian Nationalism and the Politics of Hindutva'. In David Ludden (ed.), *Making India Hindu: Religion, Community, and Politics of Democracy in India*. New Delhi: Oxford University Press, 1996.

Questions

1. Analyse the ongoing debates on the nature of Indian nationalism.
2. Elaborate the ideological tenets on which Indian nationalism was constructed during the nationalist struggle.
3. How do you understand the emergence of Hindu nationalism in contemporary India? Make a distinction between secular Indian nationalism and Hindu nationalism.
4. What are the major challenges to nationalism in India according to you? How, according to you, can these challenges be negotiated?

Dimensions of Indian Federalism

Rajesh Kumar

20

INTRODUCTION

It is not uncommon to hear the states rail against the Centre for paltry financial handouts. For instance, when the Tenth Plan and Eleventh Finance Commission sought to address the issue of poverty, regional disparity and high population growth by enhancing financial allocations to the states in the North, the states in the South murmured amongst themselves that they were being penalized for managing things better. In the current times, one may realize, representatives of political parties run to the President more frequently to protest against the governor's dismissal of governments formed by their parties in the states. They term this as 'undemocratic' and a gross 'constitutional violation'. Well, this is Indian **federalism** at work, exhibiting its dynamism as well as contradictions.

If federalism in India is working in such a way, then there is a reason to be concerned. This is because, it was adopted as a principle and institutional arrangement for governing a large and socio-culturally and territorially diverse country that India is. One may sceptically ask: Why does federalism work in India the way it does? How and why has the present constitutional federal structure come into being? What does it mean in the contemporary times when voices for separatism and secession have gained ground especially in the Naga-inhabited areas in the North East and Jammu and Kashmir? Does the demand for and creation of new territorially reorganized states address and solve the problems of federal arrangement? Or, more bluntly, is federalism worthwhile as a concept in the present context when ethnic resurgence world wide is getting political expression in violent forms?

However, it is significant to note that the arrangement of a polity on federal principles still holds promise for some violence-torn multi-ethnic political communities. Take the case of Sri Lanka where a federation recognizing the rights of self-governance of different ethnic groups is being proposed. This arrangement is being advocated as a solution to end its more than two decade-long conflict between the LTTE demanding for a separate statehood and the government refusing to yield anything more than an 'autonomous' status to Tamil-dominated areas in the north and the east over which the LTTE exercises its de facto jurisdiction.

The institutionalization of federal principles in India should be understood in terms of the peculiar needs of India as a **'post-colonial' society**. Though, democracy and federalism are not synonymous, in case of India, it has been made so by the makers of the **Constitution**, as they thought, this would possibly take care of the socio-cultural diversity of India. However, over the years, the working of federalism has not been true to its promise. Without difficulty it can be understood that there has been something wrong in the way it has worked. The states have been complaining constantly of step motherly treatment and secessionist demands and politics of violence in some areas has seen a remarkable rise. The theoretical desire to fuse democracy and federalism, it seems, has not translated concretely into practice. A mere territorial 'sharing of sovereignty' and 'distribution of resources' has proved to be insufficient. The possible solution, then?

Federalism still is a workable institutional arrangement for pluralistic societies. Federal systems are based upon a compromise between unity and social, ethnic and regional diversity, between the need for an effective central power and also the need for checks or constraints on that power. However, the need is to strengthen the link between democracy and federalism by extending the rights of 'share in sovereignty' to different groups and communities with adequate respect to their history and traditions.

The structurally federal India, in view of these aspects in contemporary times, needs to transform accordingly. This chapter first discusses the theoretical aspects of federalism as an institutional arrangement. It then traces the historical origins of federalism in India. A brief discussion of the provisions of the Constitution which designates India a federation as well as the innovative provisions follows. Subsequently, the chapter discusses the political and fiscal dimensions of Indian federalism along three dimensions: Why the strong centre was preferred, what transformations have taken place in the era of liberalization and globalization and; How has it functioned over the years since Independence. In the end, the chapter concludes that federalism remains the best hope for governing a territorially diverse and pluralistic society like India.

Understanding Federalism: What and Why?

The organization of politics in modern times gives the central position to territorial nation-states. The territorial state governs the citizens through the sovereign exercise of its power. Therefore, governing always has a territorial dimension.[1] In modern times all nation-states are divided on a territorial basis

1. See R. Hague and M. Harrop, *Comparative Government and Politics: An Introduction* (Hampshire, UK: Palgrave Macmillan, 2002), p. 202.

between central and regional, provincial or local institutions. The two most common forms of territorial organization found in today's world are the federal and unitary systems. The federal system, as a concept, offers to provide checks and balances on a territorial basis, keeping some government functions closer to the people and allowing for the representation of ethnic, cultural and regional differences. Therefore, they have been considered to be more suitable institutional arrangement for large and diverse societies. There is also a third form, known as confederation, but it has generally proved to be unsustainable.

A federal system creates two layers of government, with specific function allocated to each. Neither of the two distinct layers of governments is legally subordinate to the other. Legal sovereignty is shared between the federal government and the constituent states. In a federation, the existence and functions of the states are entrenched. This means they can only be modified by amending the Constitution. It is this protected position of the states that distinguishes federations (such as the USA and Canada) from unitary governments (such as the UK and France). Also, in nearly all federations the states have a guaranteed voice in national policy making through an upper chamber of the assembly, in which each state receives representation. Thus, federalism is the principle of sharing sovereignty between central and state (or provincial) governments. It is thus, a part of a broader ideology of pluralism. Pluralism, broadly, can be understood as a belief in, or a commitment to, diversity or multiplicity i.e, existence of many things. It suggests that diversity is healthy and desirable because it promotes liberty, participation and accountability. It also holds that power should be widely and evenly dispersed in society rather than being concentrated in one group or institution. Consequently, it provides a basis for healthy functioning of a democracy.

The terms federation and confederation have been used interchangeably. However, a federation is different from a confederation. In a confederation, unlike federations, the central authority remains the junior partner and is dominated by the component states. It is a looser link between participating countries which retain their separate statehood. In a confederation, the decisions of the central authority apply to the component states, rather than directly to the citizens, and unanimity may be a condition of collective action in such cases.[2] This is the reason why federal systems of government have been more common than confederal systems. Over a third of the world's population is governed by the States that have some kind of a federal structure. These States include the USA, Brazil, Australia, Canada, Switzerland and India.

Although no two federal systems are identical, the central feature of each is a sharing of sovereignty between central and regional, provincial or local institutions. This ensures, at least in theory, that neither level of government can encroach on the powers of the other. As a principle, it ensures realization

---

2. Ibid.

of democratic values such as participation, accountabilility, legitimacy and liberty. As local institutions are closer to the people, they are able to provide citizens more opportunities to participate in the political life of their community. Local sensitivities may be taken care of and, thus, the government can be made accountable and responsive at the same time not only to the overall interests of society, but also to the specific needs of particular groups. Also, the decisions made at the 'local' level can be received as more legitimate. By dispersing government power it is also able to protect the liberty of individuals and the autonomy of institutions by establishing a network of checks and balances.

Unlike some unitary States, federations are necessarily conscious creations, emerging from a deliberate constitutional settlement. The USA, for instance, emerged from a meeting of representatives of 13 American states in Philadelphia in 1787. This convention resulted in the world's first federation, also considered to be the 'model' federation by many. All other federal systems including India have been studied with reference to the USA. Characterizations such as 'quasi-federalism' associated with Indian Federalism is a product of such academic endeavour. Similar conventions, such as the one in the USA, happened in case of Canada and Australia also. So federalism, as we understand today, is usually a compact between separate units pursuing some common interest. But why are federations created?

The creation of a federation is based on certain motives which are more often negative than positive: fear of the consequences of failing to join together must necessarily overcome the natural desire to retain sovereignty. The most common motive, by far, is the ambition to secure the military and economic bonus that accrues to large countries. William Riker emphasizes upon the military factor. Riker took up the project of establishing a general theory of federalism organized around an attempt both to explain the origins and the sustainability of federation as a form of government. In 1964, he produced the seminal volume *Federalism: Origin, Operation, and Significance*, an updated and condensed version of which appeared in the 1975 *Handbook of Political Science*.

Riker dismisses the existing literature on federalism which he considered ideological rather than scientific. Riker characterizes federalism as a rational bargain between prospective national leaders and officials of constituent governments who come together for the purpose of creating a larger territory so as to better facilitate levying of taxes and the raising of armies. The two conditions[3] that Riker claims must always be present before a successful bargain is struck are, first, a desire on the part of those offering the bargain peacefully to expand territory of combining constituent governments into a new political entity in order to meet an external military threat or threat to internal order. Second, for

3. See William Riker, *Federalism: Origin, Operation and Significance* (Boston: Little, Brown, 1964); and William Riker, 'Federalism', in F. I. Greenstein and N. Polsby (eds.), *The Handbook of Political Science*, Vol. 5, *Government Institutions and Processes*, (Reading, MA: Addison Wesley, 1975).

those accepting the bargain some sacrifice of political control is exchanged for the promise of security provided by the new federal government.

Accordingly, Riker explains post-Partition Indian federalism in terms of a need to offset external threats from Pakistan and internal threats from the princely states that historically had controlled large tracts of territory before and during the British colonial period. However, in the case of India, centralizing Indian elites imposed federalism with little reference to provincial interests. Indeed, the boundaries of the new states had, in many instances, little or no historical, cultural, linguistic or ethnic basis. They were, instead, largely the construct of the framers. While security concerns loomed larger in the creation of the Indian State, it is not obvious that they were part of a Rikerian bargain between central and provincial interests that required specifically federal arrangements.

So military motives are not the sole or even the main reason for forming federations. The federal bargain has often been based on economic rather than military reasoning. For instance, the European Union, a federal arrangement, was originally called the European Economic Community, or in popular parlance, 'the common market'.

Threats can also come from within. Hence, federations are useful for bridging ethnic diversity within a society. They are a device for incorporating such differences within a single political community. People who differ by descent, language and culture can nevertheless seek the advantages of membership in a shared enterprise .

Nowadays, military as well as economic factors as the basis of formation of a federation are loosing importance. In the 21st century, there does not seem to be a common threat big enough to require sharing of sovereignty. Forming alliances can serve the purpose. Also, economic gains can be maximised by creating free trade areas, again without compromising political sovereignty. However, ethnic federalism is attracting some attention from countries seeking to maintain the unity of the State in multi-national and pluralistic societies.[4] Its is claimed that such a form of federalism permits diversity within unity and is, thus, an important model for situations of conflicting identities as found in diverse political societies. This holds true for societies such as India and Sri Lanka.

The federal system has become a popular pattern of governance now especially suited for large and diverse countries. The federal principles and arrangements have become so widespread in present times because they not only suit the modern temper, and also federalism, more importantly, is designed to achieve some degree of political integration based on a combination of a self-rule and shared rule.[5]

4. G. Smith, cited by Hague and Harrop, *Comparative Government and Politics*, p. 206.
5. See Daniel J. Elazar, *Exploring Federalism* (Tuscaloosa, AL: University of Alalama Press, 1987), pp. 83–84.

Federalism thus remains a natural and practical arrangement for large and pluralistic nation-states.

INDIAN FEDERALISM: HISTOLOGICAL BACKGROUND

The roots of the Indian Federation can be traced to the British colonial regime. One can say **colonialism** might not have had either the force or time to restructure Indian society entirely according to its own plan and image. Yet that does not mean that it could not have a decisive and irreversible influence on Indian history. What colonialism has changed is probably less the whole structures of the Indian productive life, more the dominating and governing mechanisms and, most emphatically, the *imaginaire*,[6] the way the Indians conceived the social world and its possibilities of organization.

Although the paradoxical idea of a promised but perpetually deferred 'self-government' was part of the ideological discourse of late colonialism, it came to Indian politics in a serious form only after Independence. Earlier, colonial administration, especially in the latter stage of its rule, professed to grant self-government to Indians by prudent degrees, according to their slow acquisition of the rational powers that such intricate operations required. Besides, Indians had to be protected from themselves; from their own primordial loyalties which could tear the society apart if the government devolved to them in unwisely large measure. Slowly, though in stages, democracy certainly came to constitute a central part of the political *imaginaire* of the Indian political **elite**.[7] And, thus, adopting a federal scheme for governance of the newly independent country became a logical step in the realization of democratic values.

Some members of the Constitution-making body did not favour federalism for an independent India. But a majority did support it as a suitable model for a continent-size society with wide regional variations. The objectives Resolution, moved by Pandit Nehru in December 1946 in the Constituent Assembly and endorsed by it in January 1947, envisaged a federal system with a semblance of the classical pattern.

During the British rule, administrative and fiscal centralization was a colonial necessity. At the same time, the difficulty of administering a large country with a number of principalities, different languages, cultures and traditions did force the Central government to devolve some powers to regional units. There were strong arguments for decentralization before Independence too. For example, the Cabinet Mission sent by the imperial government envisaged limited powers for the Union in a three-tiered federal structure.

6. Cornelius Castoriadis, cited by Sudipta Kaviraj, 'Introduction', in his (ed.), *Politics in India* (New Delhi: Oxford University Press, 2002 [1997]), p. 12.
7. Kaviraj, 'Introduction', p. 13.

However, the aftermath of Partition, the Kashmir imbroglio, the secessionist threat by the Naga tribals, and the possible emergence of centrifugal forces changed the perception of the framers. Consequently, both the Indian Union Constitution and the Union Power Committees chaired by Nehru recommended a centralized federal model. B. R. Ambedkar, chairman of the drafting committee, too, did not favour federalism in the beginning and refused to insert the word 'federal'. The drafting committee settled for the term 'Union' instead of 'federation'. The reason for accepting the term 'Union' instead of 'federation' in the draft Constitution as explained by Ambedkar was to 'make it clear that though India was to be a federation, the federation was not the result of an agreement by the states to join in a federation, and that the federation not being the result of an agreement no state has the right secede from it'.[8] He strongly reiterated that this division was only for convenience of administration while the country continued to be one integral whole. The assembly, therefore after much deliberation, produced a new kind of federalism, as Graville Austin puts it, to meet India's peculiar needs.[9]

In some ways, it is possible to view Independence and the adoption in the early years after Independence of a new Constitution as another stage in the evolution of India towards representative government in a process that dates back to the Indian Councils Act of 1861 and continues through the Morley–Minto Reforms of 1909, the Montague–Chelmsford Reforms of 1919, and the Government of India Act of 1935. India got its independence after a long struggle under the British rule. The colonial encounter with the British provided India with multiplicity of heritages and legacies which influenced its post-Independence course in complex ways. The Constitution that was eventually adopted by the Indian Republic closely followed the Government of India Act, 1935, with pronounced 'quasi-federal' features.

The Government of India Act of 1935 is particularly significant for the post-Independence constitutional structure of India as there is a considerable degree of continuity[10] between the Act and the Constitution of India, such as the adoption of a federal system of government with three legislative lists of powers to be exercised exclusively by the Union, exclusively by the states, or concurrently, and a combination of a considerable degree of provincial autonomy with extensive powers left to the centre, including emergency power which made it

---

8. Cited by Jyotirindra Dasgupta, 'India's Federal Design and Multicultural National Construction', in Atul Kohli (ed.), *The Success of India's Democracy* (Cambridge, UK: Cambridge University Press, 2001), p. 50.
9. Granville Austin, *The Indian Constitution: Cornerstone of a Nation* (New Delhi: Oxford University Press, 1966), p. 186.
10. See Paul R. Brass, 'Introduction: Continuities and Discontinuities Between Pre- and Post-Independence India', in his *The Politics of India Since Independence*, 2nd edition (Cambridge, UK: Cambridge University Press, 1990), p. 2.

possible to convert the federal system into a unitary one. Similarly, the Constitution of Independent India is federal, but contains strong unitary features, including a strong central government which retains not only extensive **emergency powers** but the residuary powers of the Unions as well. The states are normally supposed to function autonomously, but the Centre retains the ultimate power to control, even take over the direct administration of states under certain conditions.

The heavy reliance on the 1935 Act was justified on the grounds of 'continuity and harmony'. Naturally, many important features of the Act including a heavy centripetal bias and administrative and judicial arrangements enacted for the limited purpose of colonial administration were formally incorporated into the Constitution. Also, the imperatives of economic development provided a basis for assuming indispensability of centralization of powers in the centre.

The centripetal bias in fiscal matters can be seen mainly in the assignment of and vesting of residuary powers with the Centre. The most important factor that concentrated economic powers with the Union government, however, was entry 22 in the concurrent list—'Economic and Social Planning' and the consequent experiment on social engineering attempted through centralized planning in a mixed economy framework.[11] What is, however, significant is the fact that the development over the years concentrated the financial powers with the Union government.[12]

The Constitutional Structure of the Indian Federation

The British influence, experience with workings of provincial autonomy under the 1935 Act, and the popularity of federalism in the 20th century as a desirable political system for plural societies influenced the framers in favour of federalism.[13]

At the time of India's Independence, the prevalent mood of the country was dominated by a sense of uniform nationalism shaped by the momentum of the freedom movement and the fear generated by the partition of the country about centrifugal potentialities of sub-national identities. Although the framers of the Indian Constitution were far-sighted enough to opt for a federal set-up, they were not entirely uninfluenced by the then national mood. The word 'federal',

11. M. Govinda Rao, 'Fiscal Decentralization in Indian Federalism', paper for the Institute for Social and Economic Change, 2000, p. 6.
12. M. Govinda Rao and Nirvikar Singh have shown in their book *The Political Economy of Federalism in India* (New York: Oxford Univesity Press, 2005) how planned economy and nationalization of banks and financial institutions led to strengthening of already created centralized polity. He studies the present context of economic reforms and liberalization and points out the trends towards greater federalization and decentralization in the recent years.
13. H. M. Rajashekara, 'The Nature of Indian Federalism: A Critique', *Asian Survey*, 37 (3), March 1997: 245.

therefore, is not even mentioned in the Constitution. However the Indian Constitution possesses essential federal features such as:

Dual Polity (Two Layers of Relatively Autonomous Government): The Constitution of India recognizes two layers of government—at the Union and in the states. The territory is divided into twenty-eight states and seven union territories. The Union government governs the entire territory consisting of all the units, and the state governments have their jurisdiction limited only to respective singular units. Both the layers of government possess a range of powers that the other cannot encroach upon. These include a measure of legislative and executive authority and the capacity to raise revenue, thus enjoying a degree of fiscal independence.

Division of Territorial Power and Power of Subjects: The Indian Constitution provides the distribution of the executive, the legislative, and the judicial power between the centre and the states. The Constitution of Indian Republic, like the 1935 Act, provides for the three-fold division of powers. The matters of national importance are placed in the Union list, those of regional importance are placed in the State list and those that would require cooperative solution are placed in the Concurrent list. The residuary powers are assigned to the Union government. The Seventh Schedule to the Constitution specifies the legislative, executive, judicial and fiscal domains of the Union and State governments in terms of Union, State and Concurrent lists. While the state governments have their jurisdiction over the limited unit only, the government at the Union level has jurisdiction over the entire Indian territory.

Written Constitution as a Source of Power: The Constitution of India is supreme and both the Union government and the state governments derive their power from the Constitution, which lays down the responsibilities and powers of each layer of the government. It provides for a formal legal framework within which the relationship between the centre and states is conducted.

This proves that the constitutional position of the states is somewhere in between the status of a parallel and co-equal government, or that of subordinate administrative units as they have been created by the Constitution. The Union Parliament, can reorganize them territorially, but it cannot abolish all of them completely.

The Supremacy of the Constitution: The Constitution is the supreme authority and acts as a source of power for both—the Union and the states.

The Independent Judiciary: The Constitution guarantees the independence of judiciary to resolve the conflicts between different levels of government when the provisions are understood in different ways by the governments. An authoritative interpretation that is binding on the governmental units is provided by the independent judiciary which acts as constitutional arbiter. In determining the respective fields of jurisdiction of each layer, the Supreme Court of India is able to determine how federalism works in India.

But the Indian Constitution is generally described as federal with strong unitary features. It is federal because it provides the duality of state and the national government with well-defined powers subject to the arbitration and authority of an independent judiciary. But the role of governors, centre's emergency powers, financial dependence of the states on the centre, provision of discretionary grants, and long concurrent lists are some of the obvious unitary features. Also, the Constitution provides for a strong central government which retains not only extensive emergency powers but the residuary powers of the Union as well. Though the states are normally supposed to function autonomously, the centre retains the ultimate power to control, even take over the direct administration of states under certain conditions.

The system of sharing of power as encoded in the design, clearly and deliberately, allows for a decisive advantage on the part of the central government. Whether in the matter of Constitutional Amendment or the division of powers or even with respect to the issue of altering the boundaries of the states, the formal advantages of the Centre appear to be formidable.

However, it should be understood that this framework of federalism provided by the founding fathers of the Indian Constitution was an experiment in adapting the federal idea to a large and extremely diverse economic, cultural, social and linguistic society. India's federal design was envisaged as a project to ensure reasonable national agreement across regions and communities to support and develop a durable political order. The new Constitution of 1950 was designed to permit a national political system to reorganize the colonial inheritance of more than 500 units including the provinces, princely states, and also the special territories in the frontier areas.

Political and Fiscal Dimensions (I): Why a Strong Centre ?

The reason why India adopted such a model of federation must be understood in a terms of the context in which the Constitution was framed. India's Constitution was born more in fear and trepidation than in hope and inspiration.[14] Its proceedings began on 9 December 1946 and concluded with the passage of the Constitution of India on 24 January 1950. In the intervening years, India saw final negotiations for the transfer of power which culminated in the country's Independence on 15 August 1947. But the events leading to Independence

14. Paul R. Brass, 'The Strong State and the Fear of Disorder', in F. R. Frankel, Z. Hasan, R. Bhargava and B. Arora (eds.), *Transforming India: Social and Political Dynamics of Democracy* (New Delhi: Oxford University Press, 2000), p. 60.

were associated with communal bloodshed due to the partition of the subcontinent. Negotiations were also taking place under the leadership of Sardar Patel for the integration of the Indian states (i.e. princely states) into the Union of India. These negotiations were fraught with tension that culminated in the use of armed force in three situations, namely, in Junagarh, Hyderabad and most seriously Jammu and Kashmir. Violence associated with these processes claimed a loss of several hundred thousand lives and raised alarming concerns in the minds of the Constitution makers.

Other ominous forces also appeared on the Indian political scene like the militant Hinduism and revolutionary communism. A militant Hindu had assassinated the country's founding father Mahatma Gandhi on 30 January 1948. The act was followed by a ban on the Rashtriya Swayamsevak Sangh (RSS) with which Gandhi's assassin had been previously associated. The issue of integration into the Indian Union exhibited complications in the Telengana region of Hyderabad state due to the communist-led insurrection there which was ultimately suppressed by the Indian Army after its takeover of the state.

As a consequence of the multiplicity of dangerous forces arising out of political movements associated with Muslim separatism, militant Hindu nationalism, Hindu–Muslim communalism, secessionism and revolutionary communism, India's Constitution-makers thought they had good reason to be fearful of disorder and chaos. Extensive communal killings and significant acts of violence made them respond to these threats and dangers by framing a Constitution with numerous provisions designed to deal effectively with the threat of disorder through the creation of a strong, centralized state.

After Independence, the fear of disorder and the desire for a strong central government went together. On this subject, there was virtual uniformity of opinion in the Constituent Assembly even including the critics of the draft Constitution who opposed some clauses that seemed to undermine state autonomy and the Fundamental Rights of the people. There was a palpable feeling of uneasiness over the proposals of the Cabinet plan. In an early speech in the Assembly, before the acceptance of the Partition plan, Dr S. Radhakrishnan, remarked in the context of the Cabinet plan that though 'a strong centre is essential to mould all the peoples [of India] into one united whole' and 'events … in Bihar and Bengal' had demonstrated 'an urgent need for a strong centre', members of the Assembly would have to accept instead the development of 'a multi-national state.'[15]

Under the Cabinet plan, the centre was to be weak, its powers restricted to only three subjects—defence, foreign affairs and communication—and the residuary powers of the Union would lie with the provinces. Once the Cabinet plan was removed from consideration with the acceptance of the division of India, the strength of sentiment in the Assembly for a 'strong Centre' became

15. Cited in ibid., p. 67.

evident. Mahavir Tyagi, a prominent Congressman from Uttar Pradesh, made it clear that he was in favour of recognizing the pre-eminent necessity to maintain the unity and peace of India at all costs. According to him, 'the centre should be strong' because, if it lacked the 'right to interfere' in the governance of the states, 'there will be a tendency towards disintegration', revolt by parties 'wedded to violence', and secession on the part of state governments 'in conjunction with a neighbouring province or a foreign country.'[16] Advocacy of the right of the centre to 'interfere' in the affairs of states was given paramount importance in the Constituent Assembly debates on the powers of the President to proclaim an emergency on the grounds of war or external aggression or internal disturbance. The issue of defining 'internal disturbance' in precise terms or to put a limit (or not) on the powers of the President in such matters dominantly preoccupied the minds of the constitution-makers.

Over and over again the members of the assembly justified the desire for a strong centre in terms of dealing with the threats to the country's unity and integrity. The Union of India was to be permanent and indissoluble and under no circumstances, any further secessionist moves by any groups or units of the Union or any of its peoples was to be tolerated. It is also evident from the constitutional provisions concerning the Fundamental Rights of citizens, as well as the assembly debates that took place concerning them, that the security of the Indian State took precedence over Fundamental Rights. In the debate, the two values were presented as separate issues, requiring a choice between them. Brajeshwar Prasad and Mahavir Tyagi favoured strongly the need to preserve the security of 'an independent state of our own'.[17] Protests of H. V. Kamath, one of the tiny group of two or three members in the entire assembly who consistently expressed their concerns over various aspects of emergency provisions, including the complete abrogation of Fundamental Rights in the event of an emergency, were conveniently ignored.

Nevertheless, there were other underlying reasons behind the desire for a strong centre. There were indeed some positive goals expressed in the Constituent Assembly debates such as that of economic development and even 'social revolution'. The immediate goals of 'the social revolution'—improving the standard of living and increasing industrial and agricultural productivity—provided, another good reason for a strong centre.[18] Although some argued that the welfare of the people was the responsibility of the provincial governments, most of the assembly members believed that the burden rested with the Union government, and that only a national effort could effect the necessary gains.

There was also the food crisis that faced India at Independence. An estimated three million people had perished in Bengal during the famine in 1943,

16. Cited in ibid., p.67.
17. Ibid., p. 68.
18. See Austin, *The Indian Constitution*, p. 191.

precipitated by food shortages and the failure of the British during the War to take adequate measures to cope with them. The framers of the Constitution no doubt felt that stringent measures might have to be taken to deal with the continuing shortage of food and potential price rises, as well as possible urban disorder. The national leaders feared that the provincial governments might not be able to bear the strains under these and other threatening circumstances of the times.

Also, the goals of economic development through centralized planning under the lead of the State were shared by liberals, radicals and conservatives alike. Thus, it was both for the preservation of the newly won Independence and the planned development of the country that the direction of the centre was considered essential. Accordingly, the decision was made that India needed a strong centre and comparatively weak states.

Political and Fiscal Dimensions (II): Indian Federalism in the New Contexts of Coalition Politics, Economic Reforms and Globalization

The process of evolution of Indian federalism has been influenced, inter alia, by political development, including rise of regional identities, end of one-party dominant era, and judicial interpretations of the Constitution.[19] As discussed in earlier sections, three quarters of a century of thought and struggle over defining the Indian nation, over freeing the country from foreign occupation, and over the desirable shape of the social and economic order in a future independent India had provided the nationalist leadership at Independence with a set of ideas and goals that helped to structure their responses to the problems of governing the newly independent country. At the top of their goals, the sine qua non for everything else was an abiding faith in and determination to preserve the national unity and integrity of the country against all potential internal and external threats to it at all costs. The partition of the country only strengthened their resolve.

Two strict rules have been followed since Independence[20] in dealing with dissident domestic ethnic, religious, linguistic, and cultural group demands. First, no secessionist movement will be entertained and that any group which takes up a secessionist stand will, while it is weak, be ignored and treated as illegitimate, but should it develop significant strength, be smashed, with the help of the armed forces if necessary. All secessionist demands in post-Independence India that acquired any significant strength have been treated in

19. Balraj Puri, 'The Evolution of Indian Federalism: Strengths and Weaknesses', in L. C. Jain (ed.), *Decentralisation and Local Governance: Essays for George Mathew* (New Delhi: Orient Longman), p. 91.
20. See Brass, 'Introduction', pp. 6–7.

this way, especially in the northeastern part of the country and lately in Punjab and Kashmir. Second, there has been a prohibition against concession of demands for any form of political recognition of a religious community. Religious minorities were free to preserve their own law and practice their religion as they see fit, but not to demand either a separate state for their community even within the Indian Union or separate electorates or any form of proportional representation in government bodies. Any such demand would not be considered legitimate.

Also shifts have occurred in the major thrust of centre–state conflicts and contradictions since Independence.[21] The considerations of interest are major political tensions within the ruling party at the centre and tension between it and a wide variety of opposition parties, which offer more or less plausible alternative centres of power in different regions (and also at the centre, in form of coalition partners) are clearly reflected in the unfolding of the centre–state tensions in any given period.

A parallel trend has been displayed by economic tensions. Contradiction between the rising urban and rural working classes and the ruling classes and the subsequent fragmentation and emasculation of the working class organizations due to the shift in logic of development can be noticed.

Cultural and linguistic differences have contributed to the political idiom specific to centre–state relations right from Independence. While political and economic conflicts develop centre–state conflict dimensions of their own, conflicts involving linguistic and cultural (and even communal) dimensions have tended to assume significance under certain circumstances. Language and culture are emphasized (especially in the regions lying outside the Hindi-speaking heartland of India, embracing Uttar Pradesh, Bihar, Madhya Pradesh and Rajasthan) as features unique to the different 'nationalities' comprising India. Demands for an equitable distribution of political power and privileged access for the weaker regions to economic resources are often couched in the language of demands for greater autonomy for the different states as well as for a more generous investment of the central plan resources in regions far away from the 'heartland.'

The change in the nature of conflicts and their resolution has clearly followed the pattern of political development in India. Predominance of the Congress party at both the centre and state level during the early years of the post-Independence period provided for a unique mechanism for resolution of such conflicts. However, the Congress dominance began to wane when the party became less democratic and more centralized in later years. The period of the Congress decline saw a related phenomenon of the increase in strength of

21. T. V. Sathyamurthy, 'Impact of Centre–State Relations on Indian Politics: An Interpretative Reckoning 1947–1987', in Partha Chatterjee (ed.), *State and Politics in India* (New Delhi: Oxford University Press, 1997), pp. 232–36.

regional or state parties who came to capture power in the states. Their demand for more autonomy as well as for evolving proper mechanism for implementation of federal features grew. Even as the political system demanded more federalism, the Congress responded with less. But a transformation of the party system in the recent times coupled with emergence of coalition politics as a norm at both the centre and states levels have rewritten the federal equation in cotemporary times.

The relationship between India's parliamentary federalism and coalition politics is in some ways *sui generis*.[22] The distinction between national and state parties is not on the basis of the arena in which they compete. Most of them compete in both assembly and parliamentary elections. Since the states in India differ vastly in terms of population and size, they play for different stakes in Parliament. With their increasing importance at the national level, they have been able to minimize the manoeuvrability and discretion of the centrist parties. This has resulted in the reconfiguration of the federal relationship in India.

A new shift has occurred in the economic domain also. The path of development which India undertook in the initial years of the post-Independence period has undergone a change now with India undertaking to reform its economy through liberalization. Economic reforms and the phenomenon of globalization has necessitated examination of India's federal system, especially when all the layers of federations now simultaneously interact with foreign governments and corporations in the global economy. Contemporary India is characterized by transition from a planned to market economy, redefinition of the role of the state' and emphasis on decentralization.

The traditionally prevailing system has been of constitutional demarcation of fiscal power of generation of resources. But adoption of centralized planning in a mixed economy framework for social engineering in accordance with entry 22 in the concurrent list—'Economic and Social Planning'—concentrated economic powers with the centre. Development over the years such as the creation of the Planning Commission, nationalization of major financial institutions including banking and insurance consolidated the financial position of the centre and enhanced their political control over the states by aggravating the financial dependence of the states over the centre.

The economic reform in India which began slowly in the 1980s accelerated its pace at the beginning of the 1990s under the pressure of an external crisis. The most visible component of reforms so far, has been the relaxation of various internal and external controls on private economic activity, the scrapping of the 'licence–permit quota raj' and integration of India's economy with the rest of

22. See Balveer Arora, 'Negotiating Differences: Federal Coalitions and National Cohesion', in Frankel, et al. (eds.), *Transforming India*, p. 179.

the world. Mainly two groups of reform can be identified.[23] The first involves redrawing of state-market boundaries, including changes in ownership and regulations, financial sector reforms, assignment of regulatory powers, infrastructure reform and development, and privatization. The second is concerned with the reconfiguration of federal institutions themselves such as tax reforms, reform of centre–state fiscal transfer mechanisms and local government reforms.

These reforms have restricted the role of the State machinery as a 'facilitator' or merely a 'regulator.' Developmental planning in India is now no more a command economy model which called for a massive intervention of the State. With the restructuring of the State–market relationship which saw an increased role for the private players, a loosening of control by the centre over states is easy to detect. Whereas, in the period just after Independence, strong faith in centralised planning led to the concentration of the economic and political power in the centre, a move towards decentralization and shift to accommodate greater say of private players and the corporates in the planning process has yielded more space for states and, thus, enhanced their manoeuvrability. States now have more freedom to raise resources for their socio-economic development from the market—domestic as well as global. This has redefined the nature of political control of the centre over the states. These reforms have re-defined centre–state relations.

Political and Fiscal Dimensions (III): An Assessment of Working of Federalism in India

The complex and culturally heterogeneous democracy such as India tried to manage its diversity through federal institutional arrangements. But the demands of groups in the Indian society for greater power, resources and autonomy have been growing. Some of those demands have been successfully accommodated by politicians, parties and governments through creative 'management' of the centre–state relations.[24] The centre–state relations have tended strongly to remain 'manageable' because—first, powerful group demands remain mainly a product of intra-state conflict and seldom take the form of states' demands which impinge mainly on the centre and which if frustrated—might generate secessionist sentiments. Nonetheless, in some cases, things have gone spectacularly wrong and violent separatist movements have developed with implications for the democratic process underlying the centre–state relations.

23. Nirvikar Singh and T. N. Srinivasan, 'Indian Federalism, Economic Reform and Globalisation', Working Paper No. 150, Centre for Research on Economic Development and Policy Reform, Stanford University, pp. 2–5. M. Govinda Rao has sought inclusion of the Panchayati Raj Institutions as the third level of federation. See Rao, 'Fiscal Decentralization in Indian Federalism'.
24. James Manor, 'Centre–State Relations', in Kohli (ed.), *The Success of India's Democracy*, p. 79.

Second, secessionism requires a sort of state-wide solidarity. The social and cultural complexities and heterogeneity within most states are so formidable that they hinder any development of such solidarity.

Third, preoccupations of the Indian citizens from one to another of the many identities (such as caste, religion, regional, linguistic, communal or sectarian) which they have available to them shift with great fluidity. This tendency reduces the severity and longevity of most conflicts within most states and prevents tension and conflicts from building up along a single fault line in society.

Finally, the capacity of the political institutions (both formal and informal) to respond and accommodate successfully various demands (reflective of states' politics of bargaining) remain intact despite suffering decay in recent years. It prevents escalation of conflicts into any major crisis.

During the first 20 years or so after Independence in 1947, the society in most of India was sufficiently self-regulating and posed few serious problems for political institutions—formal or informal. The Congress party's cluster of regional political 'machines' possessed the substance and the reach to manage most of the social tension that arose.

Since the late 1960s, things have become more difficult on both the socio-cultural and political fronts. On the one hand, interest groups have crystallized identities along language, culture and religion. With the growing awareness of their political concerns, these groups have pressed harder for resources, power and respect and have exhibited growing impatience with mere tokenism. On the other hand, political decay has afflicted most formal and informal political institutions mainly due to the attempts by politicians to erode the substance and autonomy of institutions in the interest of personal rule, creating a crisis in 'management' techniques and sowing the seeds of frustration among organized interests. The result has been the production of far more strife of a destructive sort.

India has seen escalation of ethnic discontent into violence, armed struggle and demands for separation. What has made 'management' of these violent conflicts difficult, is the considerable degree of overlap between expression of demands and politics in violent mode with **identity** issues.[25] Secessionist demands in states such as Punjab, Mizoram, Jammu and Kashmir and Manipur can be expressly interpreted in terms of ethnic/religious identity. Today, Punjab and Mizoram are post-conflict societies but until the late 1980s these two states were wracked by tremendous violence and demands for secession. The other two states—Jammu and Kashmir, and Manipur—continue to be torn apart by the same phenomenon. It should be noted that the erstwhile militants in Punjab and today's militants in the Kashmir valley are caught in a fight in the cause of a religion that differs from the dominant religion in India which is Hinduism. The Mizo community is Christian. Radical sections of the Metei community in

---

25. Neera Chandhoke, 'A State of One's Own': Secessionism and Federalism in India', Working Paper No. 80, Crisis States Research Centre, London School of Economics, p. 1.

Manipur increasingly reject Hinduism and opt for their traditional Sanamali religion. Looking at the violent pattern of politics in such areas leads one to question the performance of democratic and federal institutions in this part of the country.

The conflicts have occurred when the ability of political institutions to contain the demands is incapacitated by the misuse of public office for private gain. This leads to misgovernance, on the one hand, and to lack of confidence in the capacity of institutions to govern according to rules, on the other. These are the processes which breed such expected results. However, the other important cause for such instances is violation of democratic and federal principles and dissociation of democratic value from federal principles. If democracy rests on the normative principles of participation and accountability, federalism best serves to realize them. When the federal principle is violated through infringement on regional autonomy by the centre, the democratic principles of participation and accountability are also violated. The violations of the federal/democratic principles when combined with politicization of **ethnicity** lead to conflicts, which become intractable.[26]

But politics of violence and secessionism has inflicted incalculable harm in the form of dislocations, homelessness, violations of human rights and loss of lives. The fragmentation of demands reflect democratization of society. The challenge cannot be responded merely by territorial distribution of resources and power. Principles of democracy and federation, in its truest sense, would demand extension of rights, opportunities and resources to diverse groups and communities as well.

CONCLUSION

Federalism, historically, has been a natural and practical choice for large countries such as India. By studying the constitutional structure we can conclude without difficulty that India is a federation. Both the centre and the states derive their authority from the Constitution. However, it is interesting to note that the Indian constitution itself contains explicit provisions which make the centre so powerful even under normal circumstances as to make India appear more like a unitary political system. It is clearly manifested in the political and fiscal dimensions of Indian federalism.

But the dynamics of Indian federalism cannot be understood only through its structure. The regionalization of politics, the loss of authority of central

26. Ibid., p. 8. In such cases, identities are politicized, and harnessed to projects of violent resistance/secessionism due to violation of political agreements, decay of institutions and non-realisation of popular expectations due to denial of opportunity for participation and lack of accountability.

government institutions, the rise of separatist movements in Punjab and Kashmir, the growing pattern of politics of violence and demands for sovereignty in the North East, especially in Naga-inhabited areas, and the erosion of cultural unity that is being undermined by religious and caste identities, have exposed the limitation of the structural approach. Preoccupation with legal formalism, it was felt, at the cost of ignoring social and cultural basis of state has yielded myopic understanding of the nature of the Indian federalism.[27] The concept of federalism is composed of three determinants: federalism as a socio-cultural theory of pluralism, federalism as a political principle involving a diffusion of power, and federalism as an administrative arrangement based on distribution of power and jurisdiction. Federalism also encompasses four ideological principles: composite nationalism, participatory democracy, secularism, and social justice. In short, the study of federalism, must focus not only on the reconstruction of centre–state relations, regionalism and reorganization but also on issues of socio-cultural pluralism and accommodation. Thus, federalism must build and sustain not only the unity of the polity but also promote the plurality of the society.

Federalism, in the Indian context, remains a potent concept despite failing in some cases to keep its promise of providing a democratic institutional mechanism for its diverse society. Despite its shortcomings, it remains the best hope for governing a territorially diverse and pluralistic society like India. Its ability to make the centre strong as well as sustain itself in view of the growing demands for regional and group autonomy gives it a unique flexibility, and hence, is its strength. The only requirement in the present time is to ensure sharing of resources and opportunities with different ethnic and cultural groups and communities as well to reconcile democratic polity with increasing democratization of society. In short, federal India needs only to contemporize itself.

Suggested Readings

Austin, Granville. *The Indian Constitution: Cornerstone of a Nation*. New Delhi: Oxford University Press, 1966.

Brass, Paul R. *The Politics of India Since Independence*, 2nd edition. Cambridge, UK: Cambridge University Press, 1990.

Chatterjee, Partha (ed.), *State and Politics in India*. New Delhi: Oxford University Press, 2000.

Frankel, F. R., Z. Hasan, R. Bhargava and B. Arora (eds.), *Transforming India: Social and Political Dynamics of Democracy*, New Delhi: Oxford University Press, 2000.

27. See Rasheeduddin Khan (ed.), *Rethinking Indian Federalism* (Shimla: Inter-University Centre for Humanities and Social Sciences, 1997).

Hague, R. and M. Harrop, *Comparative Government and Politics: An Introduction* (Hampshire, UK: Palgrave Macmillan, 2001).

Jain, L. C. (ed.). *Decentralisation and Local Governance: Essays for George Mathew*. New Delhi: Orient Longman, 2005.

Kaviraj, Sudipta (ed.). *Politics in India*. Delhi: Oxford University Press, 2002[1997].

Kohli, Atul (ed.). *The Success of India's Democracy*. Cambridge: Cambridge University Press, 2001.

Questions

1. Why is federalism important for India?
2. Does it hold significance in view of growing demands of secessionism? What alternatives would you suggest?
3. Do you agree that India needs to have unique unitary features?
4. Is it correct to say that India is federal in structure but unitary in spirit?
5. What future, in your view, does federalism have in a polity like India?

Democratic Decentralization and Panchayati Raj

21

Moitree Bhattacharya (Mukhopadhyay)

Democratic decentralization provides an opportunity to resolve the problems inherent in the working of our system. It is an opportunity that can easily be lost unless implemented properly. The concept of democratic decentralization has dominated the development discourses over the last two and a half decades. It became a popular policy in many Asian, African and Latin American countries since the 1960s. The idea behind democratic decentralization is that people will become the end as well as the means of development. Democratic decentralization rejects the idea of a highly centralized State and replaces it with the concept of distribution of power to people at large. In this process, the government represents a variety of people, responds to a variety of interests, and distributes power and resources in an effective manner. People occupy the centre-stage of the development process. Like many other countries, India too has adopted the policy of democratic decentralization. **Panchayats** were considered its key institutions. At the beginning, it started as a part of the administrative reforms to enable rural development projects to be implemented well in the remote areas. Later, the same panchayats were sought to be utilized as institutions of self-government in rural areas when the idea of people's participation through Panchayati Raj Institutions (PRIs) gained popularity.

The chapter reviews democratic decentralization in India with the objective of exploring key issues like people's involvement in issues of governance, accountability of the government to the people, reaching the fruits of development to the people and also bridging the gaps in fulfilment of these objectives, that is, failures in the course of implementation. On the whole, it demonstrates that although some of the expectations have been fulfilled, many have not been met, thus, the results have been mixed. The project of democratic decentralization through local governments has neither been fully realized nor completely unrealized. Despite various achievements, there are several areas that need to be addressed.

THEORETICAL PERSPECTIVE

Decentralization is the transfer of planning, decision-making or administrative authority from the central government to its field organizations, local administrative units, and semi-autonomous parastatal organizations.[1] It brings administration closer to the people. But mere administrative decentralization means delegation of functions along with some financial powers in order to implement the policies that central authorities cannot undertake. What makes administrative decentralization more meaningful is when it is combined with political decentralization. Political decentralization gives the decentralized units not only the authority to implement policies but also to take decisions themselves. Democratic decentralization is different from fiscal decentralization (in which case funds are not only transferred to the local bodies, but the power of raising funds is also given to these bodies although they are not necessarily elected bodies) as well as mere administrative decentralization (which envisages deconcentration and transfer of administrative power and functions from higher to lower levels). Democratic decentralization combines both administrative and fiscal decentralization as well as something more. It envisages devolution of decision-making powers along with funds to elected bodies at local levels which enjoy some degree of autonomy. The Indian model of decentralization, which began in the 1990s, was intended to conform to democratic decentralization.

Decentralization ensures wider participation. Wider, because people at lower levels get the opportunity to participate as a result of decentralization. Being away from the top layer, it enhances proximity towards the base, that is, the people. It is this participatory aspect that lends the prefix democratic to the term decentralization. Participation, however, cannot be absolute. First of all, it is naive to think that each and every person in a village or any rural area can sit together and decide every matter. It amounts to direct democracy, which is unrealistic in today's world. Second, it is a common illusion that the poor people want to participate in deciding community affairs leaving behind their bread-earning activities. Thus, to make decentralization really democratic there is a need to make profound socio-economic changes. Third, it is wrong to think that higher authorities are willing to promote decentralization. On the contrary, the higher authorities, be they elected representatives at higher forum, or bureaucrats, are reluctant to make room for popular governance.[2] Participation of the people, therefore, has its own limitations. We cannot achieve it; we can at best approximate to the goal.[3]

---

1. G. S. Cheema and D. A. Rondinelli (eds.), *Decentralisation and Development: Policy Implementation in Developing Countries* (New Delhi: Sage, 1983), p. 18.
2. Moitree Bhattacharya, *Panchayati Raj in West Bengal: Democratic Decentralisation or Democratic Centralism* (New Delhi: Manak, 1992), p. 7.
3. Ibid., p. 8.

Although participation has its own limits, it is not desirable to confine people's participation to exercising electoral choice after every five years. Democratic decentralization at least increases the scope for active participation of the people in local institutions of government. It gives the people at the local level an opportunity to influence decisions that affect their lives. It widens the democratic base of the country. It is considered better in terms of economy in time and cost. If decisions are taken at the local levels, planning and implementation take place locally, obviously the cost of development works come down. It makes decisions more sensitive towards local needs. The common saying is that the wearer knows where the shoe pinches. The local people know their needs better than those coming from outside. Instead of central officers, if the local people take decisions, they are likely to be sensitive to local requirements. It makes the government more accountable to the people. At the local level, the elected representatives and the people know each other due to their physical proximity. It, therefore, becomes difficult for them to ignore their voters.

The absence of people's participation in governance and effective accountability mechanisms are important loopholes in the Indian system. It could not improve its service delivery system in spite of the fact that it is the world's largest and highly competitive electoral democracy. Mere democracy, in the limited sense of electoral competition, cannot improve services. As a result, India's achievement in economic and human development terms remains quite low. Of course, less democracy is not a solution either. There must be accountability within democracy. The twin objectives of participation and accountability can be obtained through democratic decentralization.

Being such a huge and highly populated country, India felt the need for introducing democratic decentralization as a way to make democracy more sustainable. Reform was initiated from the top, not as a result of demands made from below. The panchayats, which are the key institutions in India for bringing about democratic decentralization, were enforced upon us by administrative regulation, governmental legislation and political interference.

HISTORICAL DEVELOPMENT

Panchayati Raj Institutions (PRIs) are not new in India. They have existed in India since time immemorial. The age-old village society used to have a sort of a village council which was popularly known as a panchayat. Such panchayats were barely representative of the whole village but they were the last word in the internal matters of the village. They also assessed what should be the tax contribution of each villager and negotiated the village's collective tax with the king's representative.[4] They collected tax from villagers and transferred a part

4. A. L. Basham, *The Wonder That Was India* (Calcutta: Rupa, 1991), pp. 105–08, section on Village Administration.

of it to the king's representative. In all other ways, they were independent of the king.

The British period witnessed the destruction of these village bodies. The tentacles of the British administration could reach even the remotest areas due to the growth of communication. There used to be a British representative, tax collector, in every district to administer development works and collect taxes from that area. The village bodies lost their autonomy. The villagers increasingly became dependent on State administration for even the minutest needs. Administration became the domain of imperial bureaucracy, law and order came under the British police and justice delivery no longer remained in the hands of the nyaya panchayats. Statutes like the Indian Penal Code and Criminal Procedure Code were created by the British to replace traditional and customary laws. Collectorates and courts usurped the powers of village panchayats. The rigid structure of the rule of law replaced flexible customary laws. However, after some years, the British understood the need for Indianization of services, and decentralized administration.[5] Accordingly, District Boards and Union Boards were created under provincial governments. But these were aimed at channelizing the British government's authority down to the village level. The spontaneous, autonomous village panchayats never came up again. The imperial bureaucracy upheld the cause of colonial masters and thwarted any attempt to develop autonomous panchayats.

When the British left and the Draft Constitution was being prepared, debates arose as to which form of government India should follow to establish democracy in the country. The Westminster model was not considered ideal by many. They wanted to strive for something more participative and democratic. They suggested alternative forms of government to achieve the ideal. One of the most scathing critics of the western democratic model was Mahatma Gandhi. He thought that *swaraj* would be an absurdity if we surrendered to the judgement of the majority. The weakest should have the same opportunity as the strongest. He felt democracy could not be successful unless power was shared by all. And this was possible only in a decentralized structure of a self-sufficient village republic which, on the whole, was a self-regulated system where no representation was required. But Ambedkar and his supporters felt that only a strong, centralized State could deliver the goods and developmental services to the downtrodden.[6] They rejected the idea that parliamentary democracy leads to the concentration of powers in a few hands.

---

5. Reference may be made to the Indian Council's Acts 1861, 1892 and 1909, Lord Mayo's Resolution, 1870, Lord Ripon Resolution, 1882, the 1909 report of Royal Commission on Decentralisation under the chairmanship of Hobhouse, and the Montague–Chelmsford Reform of 1919.
6. Rajendra Vora and S. Palshikar (eds.), *Indian Democracy: Meanings and Practices* (New Delhi: Sage, 2004), pp. 12–14.

After all the debates that took place, we finally adopted the parliamentary form of government in the post-Independence period. Centralized control was compatible with development theories that emerged at that time. Development was to concentrate in a few centres and trickle down to the whole economy. It was hoped that in this process disparities would reduce and the fruits of development would reach the majority. To bring development to rural areas under the leadership of the central government, a community development programme was initiated in 1952. But India in the mid-1950s was still to reach the take-off stage[7] and it was understood that government officers at the block and district levels would not be able to deliver, in the absence of the local people's participation. Policy framers realized that only panchayat institutions could provide a new leadership in the rural areas to bring about faster development.

A committee was formed under the chairmanship of Balwantrai Mehta to study the possibility of establishing Panchayati Raj Institutions in India. The recommendations of the Balwantrai Mehta Committee led to the formation of the PRIs all over the country.[8] While distributing powers between Union and states, the Constitution referred to panchayats as a subject under the jurisdiction of the states but did not elaborate further. A passing reference to panchayats was made in Article 40 (Directive Principles of State Policy) which stated that, the State shall take steps to organize village panchayats and endow them with such powers and authority as may be necessary to enable them to function as units of self-government.

After the Balwantrai Mehta Committee gave its recommendations, panchayats were formed in most of the states but they were not very successful at the beginning. The panchayati raj system initiated at that time faced several problems. The absence of regular elections; supersession of panchayats for many years; non-participation of various marginalized sections in PRIs like women, Dalits and tribals; lack of funds; deliberate attempts made by bureaucracy to thwart the functioning of panchayats; and a lack of political will were some of the reasons which made panchayats unviable. They also suffered from a lack of resources. At the village level, the panchayats used to be hijacked by the social and economic elites and vested interests. The local bureaucracy resisted the devolution of powers to panchayats. Traditional rivalry in village societies was also a cause for concern. Panchayats even lacked a uniform structure. While in some states there were three-tier panchayats, some had two, some even had a four-tier structure, giving rise to a lot of confusion and structural inconsistencies. Therefore, several high-level committees were set up from time to time to study the ways in which they could be made more viable. These were the Balwantrai Mehta Committee 1957, Ashok Mehta Committee 1978, G. V. K. Rao Committee 1985, L. M. Singhvi Committee 1987, and Thungon Committee 1988.

---

7. The notion of 'take off' has been taken from W. W. Rostow, *The Stages of Economic Growth—A Non-Communist Manifesto* (Cambridge, UK: Cambridge University Press).
8. Rajasthan was the first state to introduce PRIs after this.

The Ashok Mehta Committee report recommended a two-tier system removing the block-level bodies. It also recommended direct party-based elections to these bodies. Many state governments, however, rejected these proposals. Subsequently, two other committees were set up to make further recommendations. These were the Rao and Singhvi committees. The Thungon Committee, for the first time, recommended the need for constitutional recognition for strengthening the PRI system. Accordingly, the 64th Amendment Bill was drafted, placed before Parliament in 1989. The Bill was passed in the Lok Sabha but could not be passed in the Rajya Sabha. However, it opened the subject for countrywide deliberations and discussions. On the basis of the overall consensus arrived from these discussions, the 73rd Amendment was drafted and could easily be passed.

The Constitution (73rd Amendment) Act, 1992, which came into force in April 1993 introduced Part 9 (Articles 243–243O) and Eleventh Schedule (29 subjects on which PRIs would work) to the Constitution of India. The state laws on panchayats were also amended in conformity with the 73rd Amendment. It was binding on the states to pass the conformity acts within one year of the commencement of the 73rd Amendment Act.

Basic Features of the 73rd Amendment

Rigid Structure. It provided for a three-tier structure in the village, intermediary, and district level. It further said that intermediary panchayat may not be constituted in a state with a population not exceeding 20 lakhs. This uniform pattern of PRIs was necessary to reduce the structural confusion that existed in the pre-amendment period (Article 243B).

Continuity. The Amendment made it clear that PRIs shall be constituted for a fixed period of five years from the date of its first meeting. In case a panchayat is dissolved and a new election takes place, the newly elected panchayat shall work for the remaining period and not for the full five years. An election shall take place before expiry of six months from the date of dissolution. (Article 243E). All this was necessary to provide a continuity to the panchayats and to reduce the possibilities of long-term supersessions of elected panchayats on political grounds.

Representativeness. Seats were mandatorily reserved for the SC/ST population and women in all the tiers of panchayats by the Amendment Act. Article 243D provided for reservation of seats for SC/ST in every panchayat on the basis of their proportion to the total population of that panchayat, and such seats may be allotted by rotation to different constituencies in the panchayat. Not less than one-third of the total seats in the panchayat and those reserved for SC/ST shall be reserved for women and such seats may be allotted by rotation to different constituencies in a panchayat. This was an enabling provision that gave an opportunity to the hitherto marginalized sections to get represented in panchayats.

The article further stated that reservation of seats for SC/ST shall cease to have an effect on expiration of period specified in Article 334. Sub-clause 6 stated that the state legislatures can reserve seats for backward class of citizens in panchayats and nothing shall prevent them from doing that.

Political space to the marginalized was further widened vide clause (1) of Article 244. Parliament extended the 73rd Amendment to the scheduled areas by legislating the Panchayats (Extension to the Scheduled Areas) Act, 1996 (PESA). PESA is supposed to apply to scheduled areas located in eight states—Andhra Pradesh, Madhya Pradesh, Rajasthan, Gujarat, Maharashtra, Bihar, Orissa, and Himachal Pradesh.

Accountability. The provision of the gram sabha attempts to bring about accountability of the elected representatives at local levels. Article 243A provided that a gram sabha may exercise such powers and functions at the village level as the legislature of a state may provide by law. Article 243 defined gram sabha as a body consisting of persons registered in the electoral rolls relating to a village comprised within the area of panchayat at the village level. Gram sabha is the only forum where all citizens can participate, discuss, deliberate, criticize, reject, approve proposals made by panchayats, especially gram panchayats; act as a watchdog, provide transparency to panchayat activities and build up accountability at grassroots level. They have been endowed with powers to identify beneficiaries for various poverty-alleviation programmes, propose and approve annual plans of gram panchayats too.

Constitution of the State Election Commission. The governors of states have been empowered by Article 243O of our Constitution to appoint a State Election Commission. Elections to panchayats are to be held under supervision of this body. This was necessary to bring the panchayats out of the clutches of state bureaucracy and state governmental machinery.

Constitution of the State Finance Commission. The governors of states are also empowered to constitute the State Finance Commission (Article 243L) to review the financial position of panchayats and to make recommendations to the governor on financial matters like division of funds and finances between states and PRIs, grants-in-aid to PRIs. Without a strong financial base PRIs cannot function as viable units.

Constitution of District Planning Committee. Under Article 243 ZD of the Constitution, district planning committees (DPCs) are to be set up in every state except Meghalaya, Mizoram, J&K, Nagaland, and the National Capital Territory of Delhi, at the district level to consolidate the plans prepared by panchayats and municipalities in the district and to prepare a draft plan for the district as a whole. The state legislature is to make a law regarding composition of the DPCs and the manner in which seats are to be filled.

The 11th Schedule. The Amendment provided for the special list of 29 subjects which would be devolved to PRIs by the state government. This list was provided so that the powers and functions are actually devolved to local levels, and by performing those functions the panchayats maintain their viability and do not become defunct as it used to become earlier. Some of the subjects included in the list are drinking water, rural electrification, village markets and fairs, roads, culverts, fisheries, animal husbandry, village industry, etc.

But legislations with such enabling provisions become meaningful when implemented with care and interest. This legislation sought to strengthen local governments, improve delivery of public services in rural areas, instil in villagers a sense of empowerment, enhance communication between the government and citizens, increase governmental accountability and improve management of development works and fiscal management. Could PRIs achieve all these goals as envisaged? The actual progress of democratic decentralization has been uneven across states. While some states have fared well, others have not.

Initiatives Taken and Gaps to Be Addressed: The Post-1993 Period

The panchayats in the post–73rd Amendment period have, more or less, a uniform structure. They have been able to institutionalize and create strong panchayats. However, although structural impediments could be removed procedural anomalies still remain. Elections are being held, more or less, regularly. Most of the states passed their Conformity Acts within one year as directed, and started making preparations for elections, although with some exceptions. Today, more than 21 lakh representatives stand elected to three tiers of panchayats. Of these, more than 40 per cent are women, 16 per cent belong to SCs and 11 per cent to STs, making India the largest democratic country with the widest possible democratic base.[9]

With reservation, women, SCs and STs have become a part of Panchayati Raj Institutions. Without this, panchayats would continue to remain in the hands of the rural elites as they were earlier. In spite of this, there are some

---

9. According to *Annual Report 2005–2006* of Ministry of Panchayati Raj, Government of India, there are total 2,34,676 village panchayats in India to which there are 20,73,715 elected representatives; 6,097 intermediate panchayats to which there are 1,10,070 elected representatives; and 537 district panchayats to which there are 11,825 elected representatives (see page 8 of the report).

provisions which are creating practical difficulties and need to be reconsidered. With reservation many who are coming to power are first-timers and lack experience. Even many of the chairpersons are first-timers and bureaucracy usurps the power and functions of these novice persons and exercises indirect control over them.[10] The concept of rotation prescribed by the Act in respect of reserved seats has posed certain problems. It was said that seats shall be allotted by rotation to different constituencies in a panchayat at the end of every five years. If this policy is followed, no such candidate will have the opportunity to be re-elected to that seat the second time as it is highly unlikely that these persons will be allowed to contest from the same seat once the reservation is removed. If we take it for granted that most of the reserved candidates are first-timers and do not have much experience, then the chances are that many of these first-timers will also be last-timers and, by the time they gather experience, it is time for them to leave office. However, it may be argued here that even if he or she is not re-elected, the exposure and experience will not only empower them but also enhance their awareness levels. A woman or a lower-caste person who gets elected for at least one term is no longer the same ignorant person as earlier. S/he is bound to be more aware, confident and likely to be more involved in all collective matters.

One of the concerns of the 73rd Amendment was how to involve the common people into the political system, give them decision-making powers by providing centrality to gram sabhas. Several suggestions were made to revitalize the gram sabhas. The year 1999–2000 was declared the Year of Gram Sabha by the Government of India to popularize the idea among the people. But in reality, it has been found in many cases, that gram sabhas, which were supposed to be the pivot of panchayati raj in the new dispensation, have not been given due importance. First, gram sabhas usually constitute one big village or two to three villages together making the gathering very large. Participation in such large gatherings cannot be meaningful. Very often, villagers are reluctant to express their needs and priorities in front of so many people. So it is only those in the leadership category who speak while others remain mere spectators. It is being recommended that there is a need to reduce the size of gram sabhas. West Bengal, for example, constituted smaller unit, called gram sansads or ward sabhas to fulfil this purpose. If their size is reduced, it will not only make the gram sabhas a well-knit body but it will also make it easier for the villagers to attend such meetings. Now they have to travel long distances to attend them which acts as a deterrent and many do not want to participate. Hence, ward sabhas should be formed everywhere. Second, gram sabhas do not meet often. According to our Constitution, it should meet at least twice a year. Unfortunately the

10. P. D. Kaushik, 'Panchayati Raj Movement in India: Retrospective and Present Status', in Bibek Debroy and P. D. Kaushik (eds.), *Emerging Rural Development Through Panchayats* (New Delhi: Academic Foundation, 2005).

minimum is being interpreted as the maximum and most of the sabhas are meeting only twice. If they do not meet more often, it will not be possible for them to make any meaningful contribution in deciding the affairs of the village.

Devolution of funds and functionaries is one of the pre-conditions of successful decentralization. The decentralized units must have autonomy in exercising their functions. For this, they must have adequate funds as well as functionaries. Otherwise, their dependence on state governments and the bureaucracy will continue. But in reality, the absence of adequate finance from above and the absence of mobilization from below has made the PRIs constitutionally mandated structures without the required fuel. Economic backwardness of masses made local fund mobilization very difficult. Many of the states in India have devolved as many as 29 subjects to the PRIs, some of them devolved lesser than that but most of the PRIs do not have adequate funds and functionaries for functional devolution. There should be a clear understanding that local bodies are institutions of self-government and not mere delivery agencies.

Another problem is the lack of coordination and harmonious understanding among the three tiers of PRIs regarding which function will be undertaken by which strata of PRI. There is a need to do activity mapping as was discussed at the First Round Table Conference in Kolkata. It was said that there is a need to attribute each of the 29 subjects to the appropriate level of panchayat keeping in mind the principle of subsidiarity. It was agreed in the First Round Table that activity mapping should be undertaken for this purpose, by all states and this work should be over by the end of 2004–05.[11] A total of seven round table conferences were held in 2004 to deliberate on the blueprint for future action and sought the cooperation of state governments in implementing the 73rd Amendment in letter and spirit.

Regarding devolution of functionaries, it is often alleged that PRIs do not have adequate functionaries. The problem is specially faced by gram panchayats who have only one secretary and one job assistant at their disposal. With such a lot of responsibility, they need more functionaries. Regarding funds, efforts are on to make PRIs more independent by raising resources of their own, like raising tax from village markets, on fairs, house building tax, and vehicular tax. States have constituted their respective state finance commissions to advise them on issues of distribution of taxes, and other ways by which panchayats can be made financially more viable.

The 73rd Amendment not only visualized administration of development works by PRIs it also wanted to initiate planning from below. The states were directed by the 73rd Amendment to set up their District Planning Committees DPCs and go for decentralized planning. The DPCs were entrusted with the task of making composite plans for the districts. However, what is unfortunate

---

11. Ministry of Panchayati Raj, *Annual Report 2005–2006*, (New Delhi: Government of India, 2006), p. 12.

is that many states are still reluctant to set up DPCs in their own states, thereby thwarting the idea of planning from below. States like Andhra Pradesh, Gujarat, Haryana, Punjab, Tripura, Uttar Pradesh, Uttaranchal, Maharashtra and Jharkhand, are yet to form DPCs of their own states.[12] What is interesting is that they are evading their constitutional responsibility without being punished. Some of the states which have constituted DPCs have either ministers or any government official as their chairperson. Others, going by the spirit of the Constitution, have constituted the DPC in such a way that it is being chaired by an elected chairperson of the zilla parishad. There is a need to develop political will in order to implement these things properly. Experience from the field level reveals that grassroots planning is yet to be taken seriously by the states. It may be noted here that the People's Plan model of Kerala, launched in 1996 with the aim of empowering local bodies and local people, got widescale appreciation and is worth replicating in other states incorporating some modifications, if necessary. At a review meeting chaired by Prime Minister in June 2005, it was decided that the Planning Commission and Ministry of Panchayati Raj would work together and prepare the 11th Five-Year Plan based on district plans.

Another area of concern is the rise of parallel bodies in many states which are transgressing the authority of PRIs as mandated by the Constitution. It creates duality in functions, and responsibility. Some view it as an opportunity to ensure development of villages through involvement of alternative bodies while others think that the duality it creates leads to distracted efforts and wasteful expenditure. What is creating great concern in some quarters is that these bodies are usurping the role of democratically elected and constitutionally created PRIs. In Haryana, the gram vikas samitis, in Andhra Pradesh the janmabhoomi scheme, in Uttar Pradesh the users' groups, are some of the examples of parallel bodies that were running in different states along with the PRIs. The most common parallel body is the District Rural Development Agency (DRDAs). They came into existence in the early 1980s and got funds directly from central government programmes. After 1993, when elected panchayats came to be set up, the DRDAs continued to exist as parallel bodies and continued to receive funds from the Central government. Setting up such parallel bodies goes directly against the letter and spirit of the 73rd Amendment. It undermines panchayats empowered under law to undertake several functions.

Capacity building, a popular term today, needs to be applied to panchayat members and villagers. It includes complete awareness of the whole panchayati raj system, proper training in panchayat activities, education of rural development schemes, fiscal prudence, attitudinal changes, etc. Without all this, they would not be able to make the best use of the Constitutional Amendment. At present, training and capacity-building initiatives are not adequate. Emphasis

12. Ibid., p. 40.

should be given to neo-literates, women and weaker sections. Databases to pool all national-, state- and district-level resources should be created and updated from time to time. States are already undertaking e-governance for panchayats. If implemented well, it is going to have a positive impact on the delivery of services by panchayats. It may also enable information sharing which is otherwise very limited. There should be greater accessibility to official records for public accountability. There cannot be any significant impact of democratic decentralization when voters and elected representatives at local level are so poorly informed.

The PESA was passed in 1996 and is applicable to Fifth Schedule areas only. Under PESA, the gram sabha is empowered to approve the plans, programmes, and projects for social and economic development, identify beneficiaries under poverty alleviation and other programmes, certify utilization of funds by the gram panchayat, protect common property resources and be consulted prior to land acquisition.

CONCLUSION

Decentralization has its own possibilities. Although PRIs in India have multifarious problems, we need to remove the impediments in its path and make it successful instead of rejecting it. There are enormous regional variations of the manner in which states design and implement decentralization in India. There is a lot to learn and unlearn from Indian states and any comparative study of Indian states and their PRIs can be very helpful. A proper evaluation of the working of PRIs in different states may enable us to correct ourselves wherever necessary and to proceed ahead with confidence.

Panchayati Raj in India has gone a long way despite its shortcomings. It still faces problems arising out of paucity of funds, lack of involvement of people in planning, continuing weakness of gram sabhas and administrative interference. But despite these problems it is evident that there has been an unprecedented widening of the democratic base of our country due to PRIs. Thousands of men and women have occupied the seats of power, something that was unthinkable earlier. It empowered the women, Dalits, tribals, and others who earlier remained absolutely marginalized. They have the power to alter development priorities today. This enables them to address their own needs and priorities and bring about development. This, in itself, is no mean achievement and raises hopes from the panchayat system. The PRIs have also inculcated the idea of collective decision making, and commitment towards community interests. This culture of collective approach should permeate the minds of the people. It is only then that they will take interest in panchayat activities and aspire to make it successful.

In the age of globalization, decentralization of governance is all the more important for these marginalized sections. The regulatory role of the State is being discouraged in order to facilitate economic integration. The losers in this process are the poor masses who need to empower themselves, use the decentralized governance process as a protective shield to fight against wrongs done towards them and take care of their lives themselves.

In assessing the achievements of India in this sphere it is necessary to distinguish between democratic ideals, democratic institutions and democratic practice.[13] India has inherited democratic ideals ever since the freedom movement. In terms of democratic institutions, India did reasonably well. The main limitation of the Indian democracy relates to democratic practice. The performance of democratic institutions is contingent on a wide range of social conditions, from educational levels and political traditions to the nature of social inequalities.[14] Achieving local democracy is an important component of a successful democracy. Local democracy increases public accountability, contributes to social equity, and is potentially a stepping stone towards democratic participation. It also helps in better management of the local public services. Higher level governments may establish fair price shops, health centres, and schools in villages. But who will ensure that teachers and doctors actually come in time and deliver services as desired? Only an informed and active village community can exercise restraint upon persistent dereliction of duty. The idea of social audit has, therefore, gained grounds. In fact, no amount of financial auditing by auditors coming from outside can improve the system as much as social auditing itself. But the importance of local democracy cannot be confined to these instrumental roles only. Participation has an intrinsic value, too. Being able to be a part of some decision making is something people have reasons to value and for that all efforts should be made to strengthen our local institutions.

Suggested Readings

Bardhan, Pranab. 'Decentralization of Governance and Development.' *Journal of Economic Perspective* 16 (4), 2002: 185–205.

Bhattacharya, Moitree. *Panchayati Raj in West Bengal*. Delhi: Manak, 2002, esp. the Introduction.

Chakrabarty, Sukhamoy. *Development Planning: The Indian Experience*. New Delhi: Oxford University Press, 1987.

Debroy, Bibek and P. D. Kaushik (eds.). *Emerging Rural Development Through Panchayats*. New Delhi: Academic Foundation, 2005, esp. Ch. 5.

---

13. Jean Drèze and Amartya Sen (eds.), *India: Development and Participation* (New Delhi: Oxford University Press, 2002), p. 347.
14. Ibid., p. 350.

Drèze, Jean and Amartya Sen (eds.). *India: Development and Participation*. New Delhi: Oxford University Press, 2002, Ch. 10.

Jayal, Neerja Gopal, Amit Prakash and Pradeep K. Sharma (eds.). 'Introduction' in their *Local Governance in India: Decentralization and Beyond*. New Delhi: Oxford University Press, 2006.

Ministry of Panchayati Raj, Government of India. *The State of the Panchayats: A Mid-Term Review and Appraisal*. New Delhi: Government of India, 2006.

UNDP. *Decentralisation in India: Challenges and Opportunities*. New Delhi: Human Development Resource Centre, UNDP, 2004.

Questions

1. PRIs in India are facing multifarious problems. Explain them.
2. Discuss the basic features of the 73rd Amendment.
3. What are the problems that first-generation panchayats faced in India? Do you think that the post-73rd Amendment period was an improvement over it?

The Changing Nature of Public Administration

22

Suranjita Ray

INTRODUCTION

Public administration is both a profession as well as a discipline. As a profession it is as old as civilization itself. But it emerged as a discipline only after Woodrow Wilson first systematically conceptualized it in 1887. As a great protagonist of the managerial approach to public administration, Woodrow Wilson was the first to shift the focus from exclusive discussion on the nature of the State and the purpose of government to 'government in action'. He believed that 'if administration had an effective role in a democracy then its practice must be constantly improved by studying its problems in one's country as well as learnt by carefully examining the ways and means by which foreign governments conduct their own public business'.[1] Thus, he emphasized the importance of comparative administration. Ever since then the study of the discipline has been focusing on revising the meaning, nature and scope of public administration keeping in mind the practice of administration. The perspectives, views, theories and approaches to understand public administration have, therefore, been developed empirically.

Public administration has been defined and redefined in terms of its meaning and scope in specific contexts with the change in time and space. It has evolved and grown over the years and in the process of its evolution the gap between public administration in practice and its study as a discipline has been reduced. In the context of India, the planners were conscious of the need for a different administrative system to implement the planned objectives of development. Thus, many committees were appointed by the government to suggest changes in the administrative system. It was because of the concern for reforms in administration that public administration emerged as

1. S. R. Maheshwari, *Administrative Thinkers* (New Delhi: Macmillan India Limited, 1998), p. 73.

an academic discipline aimed at providing an intellectual background for suggestions to improve public administration in practice.[2] Therefore, it is important to analyse the historical growth of the discipline of public administration to capture the growing complexity of government activities. Public administration is the government's central instrument to deal with the problems of society. The indeterminate boundaries of public administration and the expansion of governmental programmes to address the problems have resulted in the broadening of the concept of public administration.[3] In addition, the government in transition often reinforces a new paradigm. It is the new paradigm which calls for reinventing public administration both as a discipline as well as in practice. Therefore, a comprehensive understanding of public administration requires engaging in the continuing process of socio-economic transformations and political developments, which shape the character of public administration.[4]

In recent years, public administration has acquired new characteristics in the context of **liberalization** in the decade of the 1990s, which saw the advent of a new corporate millennium. This resulted in the movement towards a new era of corporate forms and processes which affected the existing forms of governance.[5] Important structural as well as ideological changes have contributed to the changing character of public administration. Though the diversified and complex character of the structural and ideological changes raises several important issues, questions and debates, this chapter confines itself to looking at the changing character of public administration and corporate governance, particularly in the context of India, without going into the ideological debates.

It is significant to conceptualize the evolution of public administration, which reflects its changing characteristics worldwide. Though there are several approaches to conceptualize its evolution one can broadly divide the process of evolution into two dominant phases based on significant characteristics as the traditional/classical or Weberian and the non-classical/behavioural

---

2. Kuldeep Mathur, 'Administrative Reforms in India: Policy Prescriptions and Outcomes', in Bidyut Chakravarty and Mohit Bhattacharya (eds.) *Administrative Change and Innovation: A Reader* (New Delhi: Oxford University Press, 2005), p. 279.
3. Because public administration has so greatly broadened its role and borrowed from many disciplines some writers believe that it suffers from identity crisis. Also see A. Felix Nigro and G. Lloyd Nigro, *Modern Public Administration*, 6th edition (New York: Harper and Row, 1984).
4. Dwight Waldo cautions us against the dangers of defining public administration as he stated that 'The immediate effect of all one sentence or one paragraph definition of public administration is mental paralysis rather than enlightenment and stimulation.' See Mohit Bhatacharya, *New Horizons of Public Administration* (New Delhi: Jawahar Publishers and Distributors, 2003), p. 6.
5. R. B. Jain, *Public Administration in India: 21st Century Challenges for Good Governance* (New Delhi: Deep and Deep Publications, 2001), p. 30.

or non-Weberian model of administration.[6] While the first phase belongs to the pre–Second World War period, which focused on formal structures of administration, the later phase in the post–Second World War era shifted its focus to informal and behavioural factors.

THE EVOLUTION OF PUBLIC ADMINISTRATION AS A DISCIPLINE

Since the approaches to understand the discipline developed empirically one can understand the characteristics of public administration in specific social and historical contexts dominated by different schools of thought. A systematic study of the discipline first began with the publication of the famous essay of Woodrow Wilson, 'The Study of Administration', published in the *Political Science Quarterly* in 1887. He referred to public administration as a science, which was an intrinsic part of the orderly, organized and efficient world of business.[7] It was separate from politics and was confined to the execution of policies.

The justification for politics–administration dichotomy laid the foundation for identifying objective principles and specific functions of administration. Frank Goodnow—an advocate of juridical approach—in his book, *Politics and Administration,* stated that politics had to do with formulation of policies or expressions of the states' will while administration was concerned with the execution of these policies.[8] Public administration was defined in a narrower sense which was apolitical in nature. In the 1920s, it began picking up academic legitimacy when Leonard D. White's book, *Introduction to the Study of Public Administration*, in 1926 reflected the general characteristics of administration as non-partisan. Public administration was stated to be a 'value-free' science and the administration in practice would aim at economy and efficiency. It was a scientific enquiry based on facts, which kept the social, psychological and behavioural factors out of its study. W. F. Willoughby's 1927 book, *Principles of Public Administration* reinforced the scientific principles of administration, which could be applied successfully in any administrative setting. The notion of purposive State with a proactive administration was also developed by Fredrick W. Taylor in 1911 in his work, *Principles of Scientific Management*. He believed that the State is a

6. Frederickson stated that public administration is rich with theories and perspectives and there is probably no need for there to be one single agreed upon theory. In fact, those who manage the affairs of government are engaged in highly varied and differing activities and no single theory or concept could possibly hope to comprehend all these activities. Also see Nigro and Nigro, *Modern Public Administration*, p. 16.
7. R. K. Sapru, *Administrative Theories and Management Thought* (New Delhi: Prentice-Hall of India, 2006), p. 31.
8. Nicholas Henry, *Public Administration and Public Affairs* (New Delhi: Prentice-Hall of India, 2007), p. 28.

scientifically guided enterprise dedicated to ensure the wellbeing of the people.[9] The focus of the mechanical approach was on formal, structural, technical, and managerial factors to enhance efficiency in the administrative system.

A structural approach to study public administration based on seven principles, which was coined as 'POSDCORB' (Planning, Organizing, Staffing, Directing, Coordinating, Reporting, and Budgeting) by Luther Gullick and Lyndall Urwick in their 1937 essays in *The Science of Administration*. 'It could be studied as a technical question, irrespective of the purpose of the enterprise, the personnel comprising it or any constitutional, political or social theory underlying its creation'.[10] Thus, the study of public administration repeatedly focused on a centralized model of administration as a requisite for efficient and effective functioning of democracy.

Mary Parker Follett was amongst the foremost administrative thinkers who discussed new characteristics of administration. As a protagonist of the behavioural approach, she stated that 'purposive administration should be participatory and democratic and suggested a location specific administration capable of controlling the situation only through unity of views'.[11] It is, therefore, important to understand the theories and approaches that defined the essential characteristics of administration. In fact, no discourse on administration is complete without referring to Max Weber's views on bureaucracy, which was central to public administration.

Max Weber in his ideal theory of bureaucracy refers to the class character of society. He believed that capitalism and bureaucracy mutually reinforce each other. He defined bureaucracy in terms of its structural and behavioural characteristics. Unlike many scholars, he applied the concept of bureaucracy to all forms of large organizations, such as the civil service, political parties, universities and industrial enterprises, and asserted that both public and private administration were becoming more and more bureaucratized. He advocated a kind of organization which is impersonal, where authority is exercised by administrators only by virtue of the office they hold. It should be based on defined hierarchy of authority, written rules and regulations, division of labour and political neutrality. He argued that bureaucracy based on such principles has advantages of certainty, neutrality, precision and predictability.

Weber's ideal theory of bureaucracy became the reference point to justify an administrative structure based on hierarchical and centralized authority. All the classical thinkers defended public administration that was Weberian in nature. Even the British in colonial India practised an administrative system based on the Weberian principles of an ideal form of organization. The adminstrative system was hierarchical, bureacratized and centralized and was isolated

9. Ibid.
10. Ibid., p. 30.
11. Maheshwari, *Administrative Thinkers*, p. 142.

from the people. Weber's interpretation that bureaucratic behaviour was predictable was proved wrong in practice. Several scholars from the behavioural school challenged the focus on non-behavioural characteristics of bureaucracy by Weber, which was based on certain universal principles to be applied irrespective of socio-economic circumstances.

It was Elton Mayo from the human relations school and Herbert Simon from the behavioural school who focused on socio-psychological dimensions of human action as an important determinant of administrative behaviour in an organization.[12] The mainstream public administration as separate from politics was challenged by Chester I. Barnard's work, *The Functions of the Executive*, in 1938. Fritz Morstein Marx, in his edited book *Elements of Public Administration* in 1946, questioned the assumption that politics and administration could be dichotomized. In 1950, the dichotomy died with the declaration that 'A theory of public administration means in our times a theory of politics also'.[13] As a consequence, the nature of public administration was fundamentally altered and instead of a science based on facts, the focus was on social psychology, administrative behaviour and democratic values.

The public choice approach is another landmark in the evolution of public administration. As a critique of the hegemony of bureaucracy, Vincent Ostrom conceptualized democratic administration as being based on two underlying assumptions: (*a*) individuals act rationally with adequate information and ordered preferences and (*b*) individuals are utility maximizers.[14] Thus, a theory of public organizations to serve consumer's interest and preferences was constructed. This approach challenged the hegemonic position of the State as well as bureaucracy and emphasised the role of non-State agencies such as the private sectors, which are citizen-friendly and can cater to the interests of the consumers. The critical theorists also believe that public interest and bureaucratic interests are at loggerheads and concentrating power in the hands of bureaucracy alienates it from the public.[15] This view suggests that democratization of management and a customer-driven government will enable to build a relationship with the citizens who are customers and should be offered choices.

Thus, the evolutionary process illustrates the shifting boundaries of the discipline in response to constant changes in society. While in the past, public administration was claimed to be a neutral and value-free science, 'the New Public Administration postulates that public officials should drop the façade of neutrality and use their discretion in administering social and other programmes

12. Elton Mayo and his colleagues through the Hawthorne experiments rejected the formal institutionalization and mechanistic study of structure and principles of organisation. Herbert Simon considered decision-making as the heart of public administration and therefore it was important to understand the behavioural factors in the processes of decision-making.
13. Henry, *Public Administration and Public Affairs*, p. 30.
14. Bhattacharya, *New Horizons of Public Administration*, p. 22.
15. Ibid.

to protect and advance the interests of the less privileged groups in society'.[16] Osborne and Gaebler's *Reinventing Government* in 1992 was a landmark in building new public administration as his ideas influenced scholars to redefine the functions of the government as an 'entrepreneurial government'. Public management would be improved through performance, measurement and evaluation, reducing budgets, downsizing the government, selective privatization of public enterprises and contracting out in selective areas.[17] The traditional organizational principles of the classical theory based on centralization became irrelevant and the post-Weberian public administration has been people-oriented as distinguished from structure-oriented. The rigid structural characteristics were rejected and instead adaptability, flexibility, initiative and participation by the people at the grassroots were encouraged. The focus on debureaucratization, democratization and decentralization of administrative processes in the interest of social equity and humane delivery of public services became important in development administration.[18]

Thus, in the post–Second World War period, public administration was more than structures, management techniques and principles as it became result-oriented, goal-oriented, client-oriented and change-oriented. It was important to emphasise the political character of public administration. Thus, public administration was to adjust itself to the continuous process of popular criticism, attitudes and needs.[19] It is not merely governance but also a process in which administration is meaningfully articulated. While in the past, the internal dynamics of the domestic needs influenced the characteristics of public administration, today, international factors also play a vital role. It is, therefore, important to capture the changing characteristics of public administration.

In the 1980s and early 1990s in the globalizing era, there was a need for governments to reinvent themselves less in terms of power and hierarchy and more in terms of partnerships and collaboration. The hegemonic role of the State was challenged due to the economic reforms based on neo-liberal ideologies. The government was no longer the sole provider of goods and services. The focus shifted to market mechanisms, which promoted competition between diverse providers of goods and services. This shift is called new public management (NPM), which focuses on the entrepreneurial government. Today it is a catalytic

---

16. H. George Frederickson stated that 'A public administration which fails to work for changes which try to redress the deprivation of minorities will likely be eventually used to repress those minorities.' H. George Frederickson, 'Organization Theory and New Public Administration', in Frank Marini (ed.), *Toward a New Public Administration: The Minnowbrook Perspective* (New Delhi: Scranton, PA: Chandler, 1971).
17. Also see Bidyut Chakravarty and Mohit Bhattacharya (eds.), *Public Administration: A Reader* (New Delhi: Oxford University Press, 2003), p. 24.
18. Also see Nigro and Nigro, *Model Public Administration*, p. 14.
19. Paul Appleby pointed out that administration must orient itself to the general political situation of the time. Also see Mathur, 'Administrative Reforms in India', p. 282.

government, which is catalysing all sectors—public, private and voluntary—to compete in order to maximize the level of performance and minimize the cost. It is a participatory management and community-owned government, in which consumers are reconceptualized as active customers and not as passive recipients of policies. Today, public administration should empower citizens. The focus is on outputs, performance appraisal and efficiency outcomes rather than inputs and processes.[20] Decentralization and strengthening of local governments is critical to ensure greater accountability. Unlike the past where 'accountability was basically an internal organizational affair to bring congruence between top-down policy and bottom line implementation, accountability under New Public Management has undergone radical change'.[21] Citizens are customers and State and public administration accountability is ascertained through various external agencies, including the Citizen's Charter.[22]

The philosophy of good governance has redefined public administration beyond the monopoly of a formal government where multiple actors play a vital role in governance:

> In this definitional shift we are moving away from government towards governance or configurations of laws, policies, organizations, institutions, cooperative arrangements, and agreements that control citizens and deliver public benefits. It was crucial to strengthen democracy by focusing on greater participation, transparency, openness, flexibility, rule of law, human rights, delivery of high quality services which citizens' value, rigorous performance measurements of individuals and organizations.[23]

Thus, in the recent years, public administration has been given the task to manage the complex art of governance that is being reinvented both structurally as well as ideologically to provide space for civil society organizations.

Today, the traditional State system has lost its relevance and instead the corporate State has become important with the shift in the paradigm. The State-centred theories of bureaucracy, its organizations, structures and functions have been challenged and the network-based organizations drawn on the neo-liberal values and market economy play a critical role in the era of a globalizing world. The State no longer continues to be the only actor in welfare and development activities. Rather, the role of a corporate State is to engage in facilitating

---

20. Also see Bhattacharya, *New Horizons of Public Administration*, p. 22.
21. Ibid.
22. Under the Charter, citizens have been brought at the centre of all government activities and aim at demanding from the government and all service organisations accountability, transparency, quality and choice of services provided to the people. See Bidyut Chakravarty, *Reinventing Public Administration: The Indian Experience* (New Delhi: Orient Longman, 2007), pp. 260–62.
23. Ibid.

the latter activities, which are the domain of non-State actors. The distinction between public as well as private does not appear to be as critical as it was in the past in conceptualizing public administration. Instead, it is the public–private partnership that characterizes public administration in the recent years.[24]

Changing Characteristics of Public Administration in India

Some of the major landmarks in the evolution of public administration in India illustrate how the changing needs of the society and the role of the State influence characteristics of the administrative system. One can divide the phases of its evolution as pre-Independence and post-Independence period to identify the distinct characteristics of public administration in the changed context.

In British India, there was a structurally monolithic hierarchical administrative structure with line of command running from the Viceroy and Governor-General to the village.[25] The purpose of administration was to protect the interest of the British and it was confined to maintenance of law and order and revenue collection. However, several Acts were passed to change the structures of administration for efficiency in administering India as a colony. The Regulating Act, 1773 was a major milestone in the history of India's public administration, as it was the outcome of concern of the rulers in England about the governed in India.[26] The Governor-General-in-Council was required to consult the council and was accountable to the British Parliament. But the administrative distortions in India could not be addressed and as the latter lacked control over the company, it led to a constitutional crisis. In response to this, the Pitts India Act of 1784 was enacted and structural mechanisms were adopted to make the system of governance different from that in the past. It was now the crown that controlled the territories under the company. One of the most significant legislative interventions in India's public administration was the Charter Act, 1833, which marked the culmination of the process of centralized administration by establishing the authority of the crown over public administration in India.[27] The nature of public administration was radically altered by the Government of India Act of 1858, which transferred the government's territories and revenues from the company to the crown. Unlike in the past the Indian Councils Act, 1861 introduced non-official members in administration. As a political strategy, the 1909 Act introduced a separate electorate and public administration continued to remain partisan in nature. The Government of India Act, 1919 was a critical step, which empowered governors to exercise control over transferred

24. The approach paper to the 11th plan also focuses on public–private partnership as an important strategy for development. For details, see *Towards Faster and More Inclusive Growth: An Approach to the 11th Five Year Plan* (New Delhi: Government of India, 2006), p. 29.
25. Jain, *Public Administration in India*, p. 4.
26. Chakravarty, *Reinventing Public Administration*, p. 153.
27. Ibid, p. 157.

subjects in the provinces. The Government of India Act, 1935 redefined the public in public administration as provincial autonomy enabled the Indian ministers to be directly involved in administration though under the restriction of colonialism.[28] Public administration in the colonial administrative culture was based on the Weberian characteristics of a centralized hierarchical structure and rigidity of rules and regulations.

In the post-Independence period this model of a centralized, status quoist administrative structure was inadequate to meet the new challenges of economic development and social change. The transition from a colonial system of government to a parliamentary democracy with federal structures and commitment to welfare State compelled the planners to bring about reforms in public administration.[29] Though the framework of the British bureaucracy was accepted because of its structural utility, the adoption of the socialistic pattern of society called for a **committed bureaucracy**. Thus, it had to undergo structural, functional and ideological reforms. The democratic administration of independent India went beyond parochial interests and was ideologically different from that of the British.

Since administration is not a mechanical device but one that is intertwined with the environment in which it is based and from which it draws its sustenance as well, administrative reforms are entry points to trace the evolution of public administration as a process located in specific socio-economic circumstances. Administration is purpose driven and is constantly engaged with negotiations with the changing nature of the State. Therefore, in spite of accepting the framework of the British bureaucracy, the founding fathers sought to radically alter its nature by locating its functioning within a system of democratic governance. Its functions were to serve the interest of the indigenous population and were thus geared to the task of development—it focused on results rather than procedures. The First Five-Year Plan pointed out that economic planning was not merely development of resources in a narrow, technical sense, but development of human faculties as well as building institutional frameworks to meet the needs and aspirations of the people. Thus, it admitted that the administrative agenda changed from maintenance of law and order and revenue collection to 'the development of human and material resources and the elimination of poverty and want'.[30] The strategy of planned economic growth adopted in the five-year plans to tackle the problems of poverty required **democratic decentralization**. The Gandhian model of rural development based on decentralization was

---

28. Ibid.
29. The debates in the Constituent Assembly are important to understand the nature of public administration in India. The report of the Secretariat Reorganisation Committee commented on the unresponsive nature of the administration, which was incapable of handling the new challenges in the aftermath of British withdrawal.
30. Planning Commission, *First Five-Year Plan* (New Delhi: Government of India, 1956), p. 126, also see Mohit Bhattacharya, *Social Theory: Development Administration and Development Ethics* (New Delhi: Jawahar Publishers and Distributors, 2006), pp. 40–41.

adopted to increase people's participation. The three-tier Panchayati Raj system and urban local bodies were conceived as institutions to accelerate participatory development.[31] However, the Community Development Programme remained a bureaucratic activity and did not involve people's participation until 1992 when the 73rd and 74th Amendments brought about significant changes to strengthen the financial and administrative capacity of the local bodies by providing for regular elections and vesting them with adequate financial resources and powers. It restructured rural administration by bringing peripheral sections into decision-making.[32]

Several suggestions for reorganizing and improving the administrative machinery to secure integrity, efficiency, economy, public cooperation, ensuring speed implementation of plans, effectiveness and accountability, training to avoid nepotism and patronage, establishment of vigilance, focus on poverty alleviation and people's participation in development were emphasized in the five-year plans.[33] In 1966, the Administrative Reforms Commission (ARC) played a vital role in bringing about administrative changes in India keeping in mind the goals of a socialist pattern of society. It recommended that a close relation between civil service and politics should be arrested.[34] Thus, public administration

---

31. The B. R. Mehta Committee's recommendations marked beginning of people participation and the process of democratic decentralization. The Ashok Mehta Committee Report proposed structural and organizational changes in 1977 to revitalize the Panchayati Raj System. Also see Chakravarty, *Reinventing Public Administration*, p. 233.
32. Refer to Chapter 21 in this volume.
33. During 1952–66, policies of administrative reform were influenced by disciplinary understanding of public administration in United States as well as several suggestions by scholars and experts on public administration. See Mathur, 'Administrative Reforms in India', p. 282. The report of A. D. Gorwala in 1951 suggested steps to ensure efficiency and discipline in the civil service. It emphasized that coordination between the politics and administration was important for efficiency and smooth functioning of public administration. It influenced the five-year plans as well as the Administrative Reforms Commission to bring efficiency in achieving socio-economic goals and to be responsive to people. See Chakravarty *Reinventing Public Administration*, p. 275. In 1953, Paul Appleby was invited by the Government of India to report on Indian administration. He suggested structural changes in the basic principles and concept of the administrative system, which was feudalistic and inadequate with a long colonial history. La Palombara Stated that 'Public Administration steeped in the tradition of the Indian Civil Service may be less useful as developmental administrators than those who are not so rigidly tied to the notion s of bureaucratic status, hierarchy and impartiality'. J. la Palombara (ed.), *Bureaucracy and Political Development* (Princeton, NJ: Princeton University Press, 1963), p. 1. The Santhanam Committee in 1964 also recommended the creation of central vigilance commission as a permanent administrative wing to keep watch on civil servants. See Jain, *Public Administration in India*, pp. 21–24; also Chakravarty, *Reinventing Public Administration*, pp. 225–26 and 227.
34. The Committee made a total of 581 recommendations. Also see Maheshwari, *Administration Thinkers*. The most significant recommendations of ARC were the appointment of Lok Pal and Lokayukta at the centre as well as in the States, introduction of the concept of performance budgeting and the need for depoliticization of services, also see Chakravarty, *Reinventing Public Administration*, pp. 231–32.

was not merely an instrument of rule based on control and authority but also an instrument of development based on democratic decentralization. The focus on participatory development from the Sixth Five-Year Plan onwards emphasised the role of non-State actors and non-government organizations as new actors in development activities. It is significant to analyse the important role of the non-State actors in the process of development.

Traditionally, public administration has basically been an inward looking discipline concerned with the management of the country's domestic public affairs. But, in the recent years it has responded to the processes of globalization and their impact on domestic administrative management. The search has been to reinvent the discipline in the context of a newly emerging world order. Therefore, recent changes in Indian administration owe a great deal to the new economic policy in the 1990s, which has attempted to dismantle the centralized administration by making it a part of a network involved in public affairs. Administration was to become representative and responsive in character by involving rural people in the planning and implementation of development programmes. De-bureaucratizing public administration has legitimized civil society organizations, which play a vital role in reinventing the government. Civil society has emerged as a third sector along with the State and market and is critical to governance. 'It contributes to the consolidation of the decentralized bottom-up people-centric grassroots governance'.[35] It mediates between the citizen and the State by articulating the citizen's interest to the government. In the early 1990s, the importance of NGOs as closer to the ground realities was recognized and they were viewed as promoters of peoples participation. The action plan in 1994 of the Planning Commission to bring about a collaborative relationship between the voluntary organizations and the government emphasized on two important roles of the NGOs: (i) delivering services and implementation of government programmes and (ii) mobilization and organization of the marginalized sections with the view to empowering them.[36] The mushrooming growth of NGOs and their increasing role in policy making, implementation and evaluation at all levels during the last few decades needs to be viewed in the context of the neo-liberal ideology. Thus, participatory democracy focused on increased decentralization and greater role of civil society organizations, community based organizations, social action groups, non-governmental organizations, citizen-friendly bureaucracy and market.

The Fifth Pay Commission of 1997 emphasized the vital issues of governance in India. It articulated the changed role of the government in response to global inputs. Besides the new pay structure for civil services, it has made recommendations of a far-reaching nature, affecting the size, efficiency, morale and motivation, training and recruitment and general operation procedures. The

---

35. Chakravarty, *Reinventing Public Administration*. p. 321.
36. Planning Commission, Government of India, 1995, pp. 4–5.

commission recommended downsizing the government through dismantling of excessive controls, the corporatization of activities, debureaucratization and economy in government operation through privatization of activities and contracting out services that were performed by the government. It suggested transparency, openness, flexibility, citizen-friendly bureaucracy and right to information. The residual role of the State should be confined to core activities as a developer of infrastructure, as an investor in social services and as a promoter and implementer of poverty alleviation schemes.[37]

The 1998 action plan, which evolved from the conference of chief ministers for an effective and responsive government seeks to make administration accountable and citizen-friendly, ensure transparency and right to information and take measures to cleanse and motivate the civil services.[38] 'The Government of India has directed ministries/departments and other agencies with public interface to formulate the Citizen's Charter and to lay down time limits and standards for services, avenues of grievance redressal, and put in place monitoring systems and independent scrutiny to ensure implementation of the charters. Though the charter is not proposed to be made justifiable, it would carry a moral commitment of the government and would provide a framework under which public services can be evaluated'.[39] The Citizen's Charter as well as the Right to Information Act has significant influence in the latest efforts undertaken by the government to make public administration citizen-friendly, open, transparent, sensitive and accountable. Administrative changes are inevitable because public administration engages in negotiation with the changing priorities of society. It reinvents itself to accommodate the dominant values from which its legitimacy is drawn. Administrative reform does not take place in a vacuum and responds effecively to the social and political needs of the governed. Thus, it is a continuous process and should be studied in a historical perspective.[40]

While in the past, under the State patronage system in India the traditional hierarchical centralized structured bureaucracy had a critical role to play in the development of the country and its people, today this role has been altered. The need to de-bureaucratize and democratize the administration process by focusing on structures based on decentralization, delegation, increasing

37. R. B. Jain, 'Striving for Governance: Fifty Years of India's Administrative Development', in his *Public Administration in India Public Administration*, p. 34.
38. Ibid, p. 32, also see Chakravarty and Bhattacharya (ed.), *Public Administration*, pp. 349–58, and Chakravarty, *Reinventing Public Administration*, pp. 258–59.
39. Mathur, 'Administration Reforms in India', p. 350.
40. Hoshiar Singh (ed.), *Administrative Reforms in India and the Agenda for the Future in Expanding Horizons of Public Administration* (Jaipur: Aalekh Publishers, 2005), pp. 109–10. Administrative reforms can be divided into several phases. The first phase is from 1947–64, which is a period of institutional building, the second phase is from 1965–76, which is a period of comprehensive reforms and era of ARC, the third phase is from 1977–90, which is a period of new ideas and reforms, and the fourth phase is from 1990 onwards, which has responded to the neo-liberal ideology and international economic changes.

people's participation, transparency, openness, cooperation, coordination and accountability has been prioritized. The ideological pressures of globalization and neo-liberalism have compelled the downsizing of the functions of public administration. Therefore, the State should confine itself to only those functions which cannot be performed by the market and the development sectors. It plays only a techno-managerial role in development. 'Government through public administration is being treated as just one form of governance. The concept of governance opens up possibilities of government through non-bureaucratic agencies, other than formal government'.[41] Thus, it is important to understand the changing characteristics and spatial nature of public administration.

The democratic upsurges in a pluralist society of India based on class, caste, gender and ethnicity along with globalization and its ideological package of structural adjustment radically altered the administrative structures and the values on which it was based. The structural adjustment programme, World Bank, IMF, WTO and IT revolution led to a free flow of funds as well as collaboration, partnership, corporatization and networking. This shift in the paradigm called for a new administrative role of the State based on the two-pronged strategy of making way simultaneously for NGOs and the market forces, which is more complex and challenging than the past. The State has to interact with multiple partners/actors from diverse regions, cultures, occupations and interests in the processes of planning, negotiating and decision-making. The need for the Indian State to roll back and regulate and support the private community is a difficult task. The contemporary enabling and regulating role of public administration calls for a networking capacity to function in association with many agencies and organizations both at the national and international levels. Unlike the traditional public administration, this agenda raises the possibility of conflicting pressures for the administration. It might not always represent the publicness of public administration.[42]

41. Chakravarty and Bhattacharya, *Public Administration*, p. 25.
42. Ali Farazmand has pointed out several challenges that public administration faces today. He states that 'the increasing dominance of the corporate sector, government's role in the allocation of resources and equitable distribution of wealth, the stabilisation of economy and economic growth has been overruled by the globalising corporate elites'. As a result, the public sphere and public participation have shrunk and public administration should resist shrinking this realm of public services by engaging citizens in the administration of public affairs and by playing a proactive role in managing societal resources. Therefore, nothing less than the future legitimacy of public administration is at stake. Second, the challenge is the shift from civil administration to non-civil administration. Now, the balanced administrative State has been replaced by the corporate-coercive State and thus public administration is being transformed from administrating public affairs to administrating the public itself, 'for social control and facilitation of capital accumulation'. Public administration with a social conscience, he argues, should resist this change. Third challenge of privatization promotes greater opportunities for corruption. Public administration he contends must resist the market-based concepts of treating the citizens as customers and degrading them to market commodities quoted in Mohit Bhattacharya, *New Horizons of Public Administration*, pp. 445–46.

Suggested Readings

Bhattacharya, Mohit, *New Horizons of Public Administration*. New Delhi: Jawahar Publishers and Distributors, 2003.

———. *Restructuring Public Administration: Essays in Rehabilitation*. New Delhi: Jawahar Publishers and Distributors, 2006.

Chakravarty, Bidyut, *Reinventing Public Administration: The Indian Experience*. New Delhi: Orient Longman, 2007.

Chakravarty, Bidyut and Mohit Bhattacharya (eds.). *Public Administration: A Reader*. Oxford University Press, 2003.

———. *Administrative Change and Innovation: A Reader*. New Delhi: Oxford University Press, 2005.

Henry, Nicholas. *Public Administration and Public Affairs*. New Delhi: Prentice-Hall of India, 2007.

Maheswari, S. R., *Administrative Thinkers*. New Delhi: Macmillan India Limited, 2007.

Questions

1. What do you understand by public administration? Discuss the evolution and growth of the discipline.
2. Over the years, the characteristics of public administration have changed in the context of India. Discuss with examples.
3. Examine the model of rural development based on decentralization and increasing people's participation in the recent years.
4. Critically analyse the increasing role of non-State actors in the process of development in, the context of a globalizing world.

India in the Global Strategic Environment

Satyajit Mohanty

23

The end of the **Cold War** resulted in a major transformation of the global security and strategic environment. It marked the end of superpower confrontation based on the principles of nuclear deterrence, containment and balance of power. The fall of the Berlin Wall established the preponderance of American power.[1] It also resulted in the broadening and transformation of the security agenda and rise of political and economic regionalism. The global financial and environmental crisis attract as much attention, if not more, as military and defence-related issues marking a shift in the security paradigm from 'military alone' to 'military plus'.[2]

The combined impact of the above changes has led to an ascendancy of neo-liberal values like cooperative security, economic interdependence and democratization.[3] While the significance of military security is not denied, the post–Cold War international system, assigns a great value to soft power. The soft power resources of a country rests primarily on its culture (in places where it is attractive

1. Charles Krauthammer, 'The Unipolar Moment', *Foreign Affairs,* 70, 1990–91: 23–33; and Joseph S. Nye, *Bound to Lead: The Changing Nature of American Power* (New York: Basic Books, 1990).
2. Barry Buzan, 'Rethinking Security After the Cold War', *Cooperation and Conflict,* 32 (1), March 1997: 5–28; and Barry Buzan and Ole Wæver, *Regions and Powers: The Structure of International Security* (Cambridge, UK: Cambridge University Press, 2003).
3. The realist tradition in international relations argues that State capabilities measured primarily in terms of military power determine State behaviour. For realists, cooperation in the international system is not possible as relative gains affect the balance of power. The liberal tradition gives importance to State preferences, rather than State capabilities. Liberalism believes that nation-states are concerned first and foremost with their absolute gains rather than relative gains to other nation-states. Liberalism also holds that interaction between States is not limited to the political (high politics), but also economic (low politics) whether through commercial firms, organizations or individuals. Thus, instead of an anarchic international system, there are plenty of opportunities for cooperation amongst State and non-State actors. See James E. Dougherty and Robert L. Pfaltzgraff, *Contending Theories of International Relations: A Comprehensive Survey* (New York: Longman Publishing Group, 2000).

to others), its political values (when it lives up to them at home and abroad), and its foreign policies (when they are seen as legitimate and having moral authority.[4]

A nation's ranking in the global pecking order is measured by how successfully it has been able to dovetail its hard and soft power resources into its grand strategy.[5] The focus of this chapter will be to assess how India is augmenting its hard power resources to enhance its security, on the one hand, and how it is using its foreign policies to bolster its status in the international system, on the other.

INDIA: HARD POWER RESOURCES AND IMMEDIATE SECURITY CONCERNS

Nations apportion a premium to territorial and military security because the history of war and violence, far from ending, has taken newer forms. India's security, as understood in the traditional sense of the term, rests on the twin pillars of nuclear and conventional deterrence.

NUCLEAR INDIA

Nuclear weapons are supposed to be a currency of hard power—the military equivalent of the dollar in the international financial system. Although India could have gone nuclear in the 1960s, the Gandhi–Nehru moral framework of governance instead ensured that India strives for universal **disarmament**.[6]

The post–Cold War era resulted in perpetuation of the iniquitous global nuclear system through the indefinite extension of the Nuclear Non-Proliferation Treaty (NPT).[7] The Comprehensive Test Ban Treaty (CTBT) sought to ban all nuclear explosions, but left a window open for the recognized nuclear powers to continue with sub-critical tests.[8]

---

4. Joseph S. Nye, *Soft Power: The Means to Success in World Politics* (New York: Public Affairs, 2003), p. 11.
5. Grand strategy refers to the collection of military, economic and political means and ends with which a State attempts to achieve security, prosperity and power in both war and peace. See Baldev Raj Nayar and T. V. Paul, *India in the World Order: Searching for Major-Power Status* (Cambridge, UK: Cambridge University Press, 2003), p. 61.
6. Homi J. Bhabha claimed in a conversation in February 1965 that India could go nuclear within eighteen months. See Stephen P. Cohen, *India: Emerging Power* (New Delhi: Oxford University Press, 2001), p. 147.
7. Article IX (3) of the Nuclear Non-Proliferation Treaty, 1968 states that for the purposes of this Treaty, a nuclear-weapon State is one which has manufactured and exploded a nuclear weapon or other nuclear explosive device prior to 1 January, 1967.'
8. In a sub-critical test no critical mass is formed and no self-sustaining nuclear chain reaction can occur. This technically does not qualify to be called a nuclear explosion, which is prohibited under Article 1 of the CTBT. Between 1997 and August 2006, the United States has conducted 23 such tests maintaining that such tests are within the ambit of the CTBT and are fully consistent with the nuclear moratorium it has maintained since 1992. http://www.abc.net.au/news/newsitems/200608/s1728616.htm (last accessed on 16 May 2008).

Disillusioned, India crossed the nuclear *'lakshman rekha'* in 1998 and has since continued its clean track record of being a responsible nuclear weapon state—a fact that has got a stamp of approval with the Indo-US Nuclear Cooperation Act, 2006 (Hyde Amendment). France, Germany and China have also evinced interest to establish civilian nuclear cooperation with India.

The anti-nuclear voice has maintained that India's going nuclear acted as a trip wire for Pakistan to cross the nuclear rubicon. Pakistan also effectively blunted India's conventional weapons superiority by resorting to nuclear blackmail during the 1999 Kargil conflict.[9] However, Kenneth Waltz forcefully argues that the limited nature of conflict both during the Kargil war and in the aftermath of the December 2001 terrorist attacks on the Indian Parliament show that 'the presence of nuclear weapons prevented escalation from major skirmish to full-scale war. This contrasts starkly with the bloody 1965 war, in which both parties were armed only with conventional weapons'.[10] As nuclear weapons limit escalation, they may tempt countries to fight small wars—a phenomenon identified as the strategic stability/tactical instability paradox.[11] Prominent Indian strategic thinkers like K. Subrahmanyan also believe that nuclear India can seek strategic parity with China, deter outside powers from interfering in South Asia, and stabilize the regional military situation, allowing India's larger economy and cultural superiority to prevail in the broader competition between India and Pakistan.[12]

India's nuclear doctrine is 'based on the principle of a **minimum credible deterrent** and no-first-use as opposed to doctrines or postures of launch-on-warning'.[13] Deterrence requires India to maintain sufficient, survivable and operationally prepared nuclear forces with a robust command and control system. While not specifying 'how much is too much', 'sufficiency' factors in the capability to survive surprise first strike attacks with adequate retaliatory capabilities for a punishing strike which would be unacceptable to the aggressor. The *Bulletin of Atomic Scientists* has made a guesstimate that India has a stockpile of approximately 40–50 assembled nuclear warheads.[14]

---

9. Praful Bidwai and Achin Vanaik, *South Asia on a Short Fuse: Nuclear Politics and the Future of Global Disarmament* (New Delhi: Oxford University Press, 1999); Kanti Bajpai, 'The Fallacy of an Indian Deterrent', in Amitabh Mattoo (ed.), *India's Nuclear Deterrent: Pokhran II and Beyond* (New Delhi: Har-Anand Publishers, 1999).
10. Scott D. Sagan and Kenneth N. Waltz, *The Spread of Nuclear Weapons: A Debate Renewed* (New York: W. W. Norton & Co., 2003), pp. 115–22.
11. Ibid., p. 122.
12. Cohen, *India: Emerging Power*, no. 6, p. 167.
13. For the full report, refer to Ministry of Defence, Government of India website http://mod.nic.in/reports/welcome.html, p. 12 (last accessed on 16 May 2008).
14. http://www.thebulletin.org/article_nn.php?art_ofn=so05norris

India's Missile Programme

India's Integrated Guided Missile Development Programme (IGMDP), launched in 1983, comprises five core systems, namely, the Agni range of intermediate ballistic missiles (IRBMs), Prithvi short-range ballistic missiles, the Trishul surface-to-air missiles, the Akash medium-range missiles, and the Nag anti-tank guided missiles. India is also developing Sagarika, a 300-km submarine-launched nuclear capable cruise missile, and the BrahMos range of supersonic missiles.[15] India also has plans to add to its deterrence arsenal the Surya range of intercontinental ballistic missiles (ICBMs) within the next decade. Our 'minimal deterrent' based on a triad of land-, air-, and sea-based nuclear forces will rely heavily on the strike capabilities of these ballistic and cruise missiles.

In November 2006, India successfully conducted the Prithvi Air Defence Exercise (PADE) and became the fourth nation to acquire a missile defence system.[16] India and the US Defence Policy Group have also decided to step up cooperation in Missile Defence to make it more robust.[17]

India's Conventional Defence and Border Management

The conventional wing of India's defence forces is expected to manage an array of internal security threats, protect India's land and maritime borders and participate in regionally or globally coordinated efforts for conflict management such as ensuring safety of global supply chain or contributing to in the United Nations peacekeeping operations. India maintains the third largest military force and the largest paramilitary force in the world. The defence allocation was raised by 7 per cent from $18 billion in 2005–06 to $20 billion in 2006–07. But at 2.3 per cent of its GDP, India's defence spending as a proportion of GDP is much lower than that of China or Pakistan. Power projection through military means and translation of economic gains into defence spin-offs have never been India's strategic goal.

India has 14,880 kilometres of land borders, whose management becomes difficult due to inhospitable terrain and extreme climatic conditions. India shares over 3,000 kms of land border with both Pakistan and China. India's border situation remains fluid particularly due to the easy flow of terrorists, insurgents, illegal migrants and smugglers, often aided and abetted from across the borders. Four of the seven north-eastern states of India share a 1,643 kilometre-long land border with Myanmar. Prospects of peace and economic prosperity in the North East is intricately linked to the stability across both sides of the

---

15. For details refer to Ministry of Defence Annual Report, no. 13. pp. 88–90.
16. 'Prithvi Missile Interception Test a Success', *Indian Express*, 28 November, 2006.
17. Refer to the 23 May 2002, India–US Defense Policy Group Joint Statement issued at Washington, DC. http://meaindia.nic.in/declarestatement/2002/05/23js1.htm (last accessed on 16 May 2008).

Indo-Myanmar border.[18] The task force on border management, which submitted its report in 2000, has reported that about 1.5 crore Bangladeshi nationals have illegally entered India and altered the demographic profile in states like Assam. The Indo-Nepal border has traditionally been an open border and this has helped Maoists to establish a contiguous red corridor from south India right into the heart of Nepal. However, the participation of Maoists in the newly elected democratic government in Nepal has raised hopes of a peaceful frontier with India. The military operations conducted by the Royal Bhutanese Army in 2003–04 against Indian insurgent groups was a milestone in our joint response to terrorist activities.

India also has a long coastline of 5,422 kilometres. The 1,197 islands account for 2,094 kilometres of additional coastline. Certain Myanmarese islands like the Coco Islands, where China has reportedly established radar and communication signalling equipment, are very close to the Andaman Islands. We have a dispute with Pakistan over Sir Creek Island and a joint survey has been accepted by both countries to arrive at an amicable solution. Security threats also arise from plans by terrorist groups to use the sea route to infiltrate and induct arms and ammunition into India and occupy uninhabited islands for attacking coastal areas and vital oil installations.[19]

To manage India's land and maritime borders, a number of proactive measures, such as increasing the number of border outposts and fencing and floodlighting the borders, have been undertaken. Unmanned arial vehicles (UAVs), advanced land nagivation systems (ALNS) and global positioning systems (GPS), night vision devices and thermal imagers have already been provided to the Border Security Force (BSF), Indo-Tibetan Border Police (ITBP) and Coast Guard. The Border Area Development Programme (BADP) was started in the Seventh Five-Year Plan to fill up critical gaps in the social and physical infrastructure so as to negate the attractiveness of anti-State violence as a means of protest. A proposal to build 600 kilometres of road along the borders at a cost of Rs 9 billion will also facilitate accessibility of our forces to the border areas.[20]

Defence Modernization and Defence Diplomacy

Strategic defence dialogue and joint military exercises with countries like France, Israel, Russia and the USA have been a key feature of our current diplomatic strategy. Indian armed forces are being exposed to the Revolution in Military Affairs (RMA) to prepare for future information network-centric wars

18. For a general overview of border issues and management, see Sanjai Singh, 'Management of Western Land Borders of India', *World Focus*, 320, August 2006, pp. 3–12, and Anil Kamboj, 'Border Management: Bangladesh, Nepal and Bhutan', *World Focus* 320, August 2006: 22–29.
19. http://www.dnaindia.com/report.asp?NewsID=1065520 (last accessed on 16 May 2008).
20. Bhartendu Kumar Singh, 'China Comes Closer', *Peace and Conflict*, 9 (6), June 2006: 20–21.

in the digitalized battlefield of tomorrow. An estimated $17 billion spent in 2004 on arms imports, and scheduled imports of P-75 submarine from France and the Hawk Advance Jet Trainer (AJT) from the UK, indicate increased defence cooperation with European countries other than Russia. The induction of T-90 and T-72 tanks, armoured recovery vehicles (ARVs) and infantry combat vehicles will provide firepower to the Indian army.

China is shaping the maritime battlefield in the Indian Ocean by strengthening the naval wing of PLA.[21] For maintaining primacy at sea and ensuring maritime security and safety of the sea lanes of communication (SLOCs), the Indian Navy is in the process of augmenting its force by adding aircraft carriers, destroyers, frigates, submarines and offshore patrol vessels. Six French-designed Scorpene submarines and one aircraft carrier are being built in India. The Indian Navy has institutionalized bilateral exercises with the USA, Russia, France, Germany, and Singapore, and joint patrols with Indonesia and Thailand. Our navy was part of the multinational tsunami disaster mitigation force and has escorted American cargo ships safely in the Indian Ocean.

The induction/planned induction of force multipliers like flight refuelling aircraft (FRA), multi-role combat aircraft (MCRA), air-borne warning and control system (AWACS), fighter Su-30 and MiG aircraft coupled with credible strategic lift capabilities is meant to prepare our air force to face the asymmetric nature of modern warfare. Joint exercises like the 'Garuda-II' with the French Air Force and 'Cope India-2005' with the US Air Force provide inter-operability options to the Indian Air Force.[22]

Thus, India's strategy, true to its emerging power status, is to augment its hard power resources so that it can secure and stabilize its borders and tackle and take on greater sub-systemic challenges affecting Asian security.

POST–COLD WAR DIRECTIONAL CHANGES IN INDIAN FOREIGN POLICY

The period from Independence till the end of the cold war can be labelled as the ideological value-laden era in Indian foreign policy. India, after a long history of anti-colonial struggle, found it incongruous to align itself as a junior player with either of the superpowers. To underline its presence, India decided to tread the path of non-alignment and assume the leadership role in raising moral issues on behalf of the newly independent Afro-Asian countries. Such a strategy

---

21. Chief of Naval Staff, Admiral Suresh Mehta, speaking on the occasion of Navy Day on 4th December 2006. http://www.moneycontrol.com/india/news/currentaffairs/navydaysinoindianrivalry/sinoindianrivalryoverindianoceanoutopen/market/stocks/article/254225 (last accessed on 19 May 2008).
22. For an overview of India's defence modernization, refer to the *Annual Defence Report 2004–05*, 13.

suited us as we could not have competed for a place at the top on the basis of our hard power resources. Thus, during this period *moralpolitik* and non-alignment became focal points around which Indian foreign policy revolved. India was at the forefront of raising the '3D' issues of development, disarmament and decolonization at various multilateral and bilateral fora.

The end of the Cold War made non-alignment, the cornerstone of Indian foreign policy, passé. The collapse of the USSR with whom India shared a very close relationship and economic crisis and the unstable governments resulted in an uneasy transition in Indian foreign policy in the early 1990s.

By the mid-1990s, Indian foreign policy submitted itself to a process of adaptive learning to boost its status and influence in the global pecking order. Our foreign policy has shifted from an overemphasis on idealism during the Cold War era to pragmatic realism in the post-Cold War era, its proactive 'catch-all' diplomacy fanning in an omni-directional manner to establish tangible economic and security partnerships with major regions and countries of the world. While India felt the need to reach out to countries beyond its immediate neighbourhood, the world also took cognizance of India's growing economic, political and military might and its potential for positive contribution to the international system. Within this overarching scheme, the focus nonetheless remains on forging economic and strategic partnerships with the major powers in the system, pursuing a proactive diplomacy in Asia and securing South Asia. India's big emerging market, 9 per cent GDP growth rate and growing export basket have also contributed in building mutually synergetic relationships with other countries and trade blocs across the globe. As a result, the economic and energy security components have become as strong as the strategic, security and defence components of our diplomacy. As C. Raja Mohan puts it,

> If a single image catches India's strategic style in the past, it was that of a porcupine—vegetarian, slow-footed and prickly. The famous defensiveness of the porcupine became the hallmark of India's approach to the world. India was a reactive power; when the world impinged on it, India used to put up its sharp quills to ward off the threats. The quills symbolized the principles of fairness, justice and equality as defence against what India saw an unacceptable demand from the international system. India, it was widely believed at home and abroad, would not seek opportunities or be opportunistic in pursuit of its national interests. In the domain of the foreign policy the decade of the 1990s, however saw a sea-change in India's foreign policy. It was as if the porcupine became a tiger.[23]

23. C. Raja Mohan, *Crossing the Rubicon: The Shaping of India's New Foreign Policy* (New Delhi: Penguin Books, 2003), pp. 260–63.

INDIA AND THE UNITED STATES: MOVING TOWARDS A NATURAL PARTNERSHIP

If we were to identify the single great transformation in Indian foreign policy in the last decade it is India's changed relationships with the USA. We have moved from estranged to engaged democracies with a mutually beneficial strategic partnership.[24] Post 9/11, the USA's revised strategy towards a liberal democratic India was not to contain but to engage and 'help India become a major world power in the 21st Century'.[25] The highpoint of our relationships has been the de-hyphenation of the Indo-US relations from US–Pakistan relations and intensified defence and security engagement. The Indo-US civilian nuclear cooperation deal has been the icing on the cake.

In June 2005, India and the USA entered into a 10-year defence partnership agreement, which involves arms trade, technology transfer and even co-production of military equipment.[26] In the same year, both India and the USA reiterated their support for a global democracy initiative and for the United Nations Democracy Fund. The first phase of the 2004 Next Steps in Strategic Partnership (NSSP) agreement has been implemented with the USA lifting sanctions against India's space programmes. Greater Indo-American cooperation in tackling terrorism through Indian participation in the Container Security Initiative (CSI) and bilateral intelligence sharing is in the offing.

The Hyde Amendment is a *quid pro quo* arrangement that will allow India access to all aspects of a complete nuclear fuel cycle in return for India's assurances of separating its civilian reactors from the military ones. The joint statement of 18 July 2005 and, subsequently, the separation plan of 2 March 2006 requires India to place the civilian nuclear facilities under the full scope International Atomic Energy safeguards, but only when all nuclear restrictions have been withdrawn. For its part, the USA had to change the US Atomic Energy Act of 1954 to facilitate such cooperation and approach the Nuclear Suppliers' Group (NSG) to enable international civilian nuclear cooperation between India and the international community.

This deal will be the first step in increasing our reliance on nuclear energy. Nuclear energy accounts for a paltry 3 per cent of our energy needs as against 79 per cent for France, 60 per cent for Belgium, 31 per cent for Japan and 20 per cent for the USA. High import bills due to the rising prices of crude have made energy security one of the foremost issues of Indian foreign policy. By 2030,

---

24. See Dennis Kux, *India and the United States: Estranged Democracies, 1941–1991* (Washington: National Defense University Press, 1992).
25. US Department of State, 'Background Briefing by Administration Officials on US–South Asia Relations', 25 March 2005, available at www.state.gov/r/pa/prs/2005/43853.htm
26. Baldev Raj Nayar, 'India Rising, but Uphill Road Ahead', *Asian Survey*, 46 (1), January/February 2006.

India will be the third largest energy consumer in the world and, thus, greater reliance on nuclear energy is necessary to keep our economy growing.[27]

Both countries have decided to increase bilateral trade from $27 billion in 2005 to $40 billion by 2007–08 and measures like the establishment of the Indo-US Trade Policy Forum (TPF) and the High Technology Cooperation Group (HTCG) to remove tariff and non-tariff barriers to trade will serve this end.

Although we recognize that good relations with the USA are in our national interest, this does not mean compromising with the independent nature of India's foreign policy or the integrity of our strategic programmes.[28] While India supported the USA in voting against Iran in IAEA on the nuclear issue, it has made it clear that the US intervention in Iraq has been a mistake and, hence, did not send troops to Iraq. India has refused to accept an annual audit of India's fissile material stock or a moratorium on the production of fissile material.

INDIA'S RELATIONS WITH MAJOR NON-ASIAN POWERS

India's policy has been one of 'association maximization' to secure wider international support. India sought to take off its relationship with the Russia Federation from where it had left off with the USSR. Although Russia mooted the idea of a 'strategic triangle' with India and China in the mid-1990s, Russia's current President Vladimir Putin has made it clear that Russia did not visualize a Moscow–Beijing–New Delhi axis to evolve into a political or military bloc, least it be perceived as one directed against the USA. In 2000, India and Russia signed a Declaration on Strategic Partnership and followed it up with the 2002 New Delhi declaration to deepen and diversify cooperation in areas like energy security, information technology and fight against international terrorism. Stability in Afghanistan and the Central Asian Republics (CARs) also remains an immediate internal security concern to both India and Russia.

Russia is the largest source of Indian weapons and it has agreed to extend its defence knowhow to help India acquire the advanced technology vehicles (ATV), multi-role transport aircraft and fifth generation unique interceptor fighters. Both countries are keen to arrest the decline in bilateral trade, which has slipped from $950 million in 2000 to $650 million in 2005, by exploring the feasibility of a Comprehensive Economic Cooperation Agreement (CECA). Prospects for energy cooperation remain bright as India's ONGC Videsh Limited (OVL) and Russian firms have cooperated in the Sakhalin-1 project. OVL is interested to buy Russian firms and exploit oil and gas in areas like Siberia.

---

27. Abhishek Singhvi, '1, 2, 3, and Go', *Hindustan Times*, 20 December 2006.
28. Manmohan Singh replying to a discussion on the Indo–US civilian nuclear issue on 17 August 2006. *Strategic Digest*, 36 (9): 1151–59.

On global concerns related to democracy, human rights, terrorism and environment, both India and the European Union have a common approach. Recognizing India's growing power and economic importance, the 2004 Indo-EU Summit upgraded bilateral relationship to that of a 'strategic partnership'. India had already entered into a 'strategic partnership' with Germany in 2001. India's bid for a permanent membership in the Security Council has the support of France, Britain, Germany, Luxembourg and Romania. One of the significant outcomes of Indo-EU political relations has been EU's balanced position that the Kashmir dispute be resolved through political dialogue—a position acceptable to India. India and the EU have been cooperating in the International Thermonuclear Experimental Reactor (ITER) Project and the Indo-US nuclear deal might enhance civilian nuclear cooperation between India and the EU.

However, till date the thrust remains trade and economic relations. The EU accounts for more than 20 per cent of India's exports and 16 per cent of our imports and our target is to achieve the $50 billion trade in the next couple of years. The EU is also one of the most important sources of investment in India, although we get only one-sixth of European investments going to China. Some of the most contentious trade issues like restricted market access to Indian agro and marine products, textiles, chemicals and pharmaceuticals due to the Technical and Sanitary and Phyto-Sanitary (SPS) barriers need to be addressed. Indian products have also not been accorded preferential market access under the generalized system of preferences (GSP) scheme.

Earnest efforts to facilitate trade have been undertaken by signing the Bilateral Investment Protection Agreement (BIPA) and the Double Taxation Avoidance Agreement (DTAA) with a majority of the European countries like France, the Czech Republic and Serbia-Montenegro. India and the EU have formed a Joint Task Force (JTF) to negotiate a Comprehensive Economic Cooperation and Partnership Agreement. India and many European countries like Denmark, and Sweden have signed joint agreements in the fields of biotechnology and information technology.

India is also improving its relationships with countries in Latin America and Oceania. The recently formed India, Brazil and South Africa (IBSA) forum has already shown spark by reaching agreements in the field of shipping and finance and the aim is to double trilateral trade and investments by the turn of the decade. India is engaged in Regional Trading Arrangement (RTA) negotiations with South African Customs Union (SACU) in which South Africa is the major economy and Mercosur, in which Brazil and Argentina are the major economies. Indian goods have a very low penetration in Latin America and the Mercosur RTA along with the Preferential Trading Agreement (PTA) with Chile will increase India's visibility in Latin America. A proposed RTA encompassing SACU, India and Mercosur (SIM) is also being contemplated at the highest levels. Argentina, Brazil and India (ABI) have formulated a common position on a host of global trade issues notable being the common position on the Non-Agricultural Market Access (NAMA) negotiations at the Doha Round of Trade Negotiations. In 2005, India and Venezuela inked an oil-for-knowledge deal, where long-term supply of oil would be available to India at a discount if prices rose above $50 per barrel in exchange for knowledge transfer, investments in medicines and the IT sector.

Nearly half of India's coking coal requirements come from Australia but India, like China, is more interested in getting access to Australian uranium. While China has access to this, India has so far been denied it, as it is not a signatory to the NPT.

India's African diplomacy fits into a classical emerging power diplomacy framework. India has stepped up its aid to and economic diplomacy with African nations to ensure its economic and energy security and obtain political support on critical issues like permanent Security Council membership. India has extended economic support for the New Partnership for African Development (NPAED) and signed an MoU with eight east African states for assistance in critical sectors like information technology, education, healthcare, transportation, tourism and agriculture under the Techno-Economic Approach for Africa–India Movement or TEAM 9 initiative. The pan-African e-initiative involves the creation of a distance education network and telemedicine facilities. India is also in the process of providing preferential market access to LDCs through the Duty Free Quota Free (DFQF) Scheme. The influence of Indian diaspora in Africa is also gradually increasing and Indian presence in the R&D projects, educational sector, construction industry, tourism and health sectors has led to capacity building in various African countries like Ghana and Nigeria. India has reached out to oil and gas-rich African nations like Nigeria and Angola for oil and gas exploration ventures.

In a nutshell, Indian foreign policy has broken itself free from the shackles of idealism and forged mutually symbiotic political and economic relationships with countries across the globe.

India in the Asian Security System

India's Asia policy has three parallel but mutually interdependent tracks. First, as part of our 'Look East policy, India seeks to establish close ties with the Association of Southeast Asian Nations (ASEAN) and maintain cordial relations with other East Asian nations such as China, South Korea and Japan. Second, India's 'Look West' policy strives to forge geo-strategic ties with countries like Saudi Arabia and Iran and ensure energy security. Finally, securing South Asia and engaging and maintaining cordial ties with our neighbours has been the prime goal of India's neighbourhood policy.

India's Look East policy, launched in 1991, should aim at specific gains by, say, 2010. Such an engagement needs to take place at four different levels. India needs to engage China politically and economically at the most proximate level and extend non-reciprocal support to Cambodia, Laos, Myanmar and Vietnam (CLMV) in line with something contemplated in the Gujral doctrine for South Asian LDCs. At the next level, it should intensify economic engagement with the original ASEAN-5 countries of Malaysia, Indonesia, Thailand, the Philippines and Singapore and explore options of defence diplomacy, democratic alliance and trade and investment options with Japan and South Korea at the final level.

While some Asian countries have tried to project India as a counter to the growing Chinese influence, India has dispelled notions of both Asian giants being strategic competitors. Smilarly, China has propounded the doctrine of 'peaceful rise' to show that it is in the mutual economic interests to cooperate and intensify the regional economic integration process. The visit of Premier Li Peng to India in 1991 and President R. Venkataraman to China in 1992 led to the decline of mutual hostilities, establishment of a joint working group to resolve the boundary issue and resumption of border trade. India reiterated that Tibet is an autonomous region of China. The visit of President Jiang Zemin to India in 1996 marked a breakthrough as both countries decided not to use force against each other, reduce troops and armaments across the border and not to cross the Line of Control. However, India is still worried about Chinese claims on Arunachal Pradesh from certain Chinese quarters and increased PLA accessibility and activity along the Indo-Tibetan border.

The year 2006 was designated as the 'Sino-India Friendship Year' and in the 21 November 2006 joint statement issued during the visit of the Chinese President Hu Jintao to India, both countries reiterated that the tempo built up in the earlier Declaration on Principles for Relations and Comprehensive Cooperation in 2003 and in the April 2005 Joint Statement on Strategic and Cooperative Partnership for Peace and Prosperity should be sustained. A 'ten-pronged strategy', which included a plan for comprehensive development of bilateral relations and an endeavour to raise the volume of bilateral trade to $40 billion by 2010 was also chalked out. The Nathu-La Pass was opened up for trade and both countries are exploring the feasibility of an FTA in the near future. India has welcomed China's observer status in South Asian Association for Regional Cooperation (SAARC) and China has supported India's observer status in Shanghai Cooperation Organisation (SCO). Both countries have taken interest in a proposed Asian energy grid and have agreed to share information while bidding for oil and gas contracts and, if possible, undertake joint bids to ensure energy security.

India has extended multi-sectoral economic and technical assistance for capacity building of the CLMV countries in a bid to enhance its soft power and has already committed itself to non-reciprocal tariff preferences under the proposed Indo-ASEAN FTA. India's interests particularly lie in stabilizing the border with Myanmar and in having access to Myanmarese oil and natural gas. President A. P. J. Abdul Kalam visited Myanmar in March 2006 and entered into an MoU on cooperation in the petroleum sector. However, Myanmar has declined gas supply to India while having agreed to supply 6.5 trillion cubic feet of gas to

China. The Myanmar–Bangladesh–India gas pipeline has also not kick started due to security concerns and differences with Bangladesh over transit fees.

The original Association of Southeast Asian Nations (ASEAN) nations visualize India not only as a nation with tremendous economic opportunities but also as a country which could provide strategic stability over land and sea and counter terrorism, sea piracy and drug trafficking. On the economic front, at the Twelfth ASEAN summit meeting in January 2007, as China and ASEAN signed an agreement to open up key services sectors, India and ASEAN finally settled their differences over the negative list so that the FTA could be finalized quickly. The Indo-Singapore Comprehensive Economic Cooperation Agreement (CECA) and the Early Harvest Scheme (EHS) of Indo-Thailand FTA have already been put in place. Singapore has emerged as India's third largest investor and trade with Thailand has doubled since operationalisation of the EHS. Indo-ASEAN trade had grown by about 30 per cent in 2005 and was set to surpass the target of $30 billion by 2007. A swathe of economic cooperation agreements like the Bay of Bengal Initiative for Multi-Sectoral Technical and Economic Cooperation (BIMSTEC) FTA, deepened Asia–Pacific Trade Agreement (APTA) coupled with gradual opening up of services and investment sectors and open skies policy will definitely intensify Indo–ASEAN relations and possibly lead to the creation of a Pan-Asian Free Trade Agreement (PAFTA)—a goal laid down by India in the 2005 East Asian summit meeting.

India, Japan and South Korea, with fairly long democratic traditions, can put in place a 'democratic troika' to act as a model for other Asian countries. India and Japan are 'determined to make up for the lost decade in bilateral relations'[29] and go beyond the mono-dimensional economic component and cooperate to formulate joint naval exercises, disaster management etc. In 2005, both countries reiterated their commitment to the global partnership agreement of 2000 and announced an eight-fold initiative to boost bilateral cooperation. India and Japan began engaging in regular comprehensive security dialogues and the Japanese Prime Minister Shinzo Abe called for a strategic dialogue between the USA, India, and Australia.

India has started Comprehensive Economic Partnership Agreement negotiations with both Japan and South Korea. India can act as a hub for South Korean and Japanese investments and be a part of their regional production networks (RPNs). Although Japan is one of India's largest trading partners, India accounts for less than 1 per cent of Japan's total trade, whereas, China accounted for about 20 per cent of Japan's trade in 2004. The quantum of Japanese investments in India is still minscule when compared with their investments in ASEAN although we are the largest recipient of Japanese Official Development Assistance (ODA). Future cooperation in nanotechnology, health sector, bio-technology and energy security will boost India's relations with Northeast Asian democracies.

29. Jerry Pinto, 'Japan and India: Making Up for the Lost Decade', *Economic and Political Weekly*, 24 June 2006, p. 2519.

After strengthening India's Look East policy, India looks forward to provide stability to its hitherto see-saw Look West policy. The Gulf accounts for more than 70 per cent of India's oil imports and has a strong 3.7 billion Indian presence that remit around $8 billion per annum. India and Israel opened Embassies in each other's country in 1992 and the later is one of the major suppliers of defence equipment like Phalcon Advanced Air Warning System and Barak-II Air Defence Missiles to India. India has helped Kuwait's reconstruction, held military exercise with Oman and signed the Indo-Gulf Cooperation Council Framework Agreement on Economic Cooperation to explore the possibility of an FTA. India and Saudi Arabia signed an anti-terrorism pact to fight money laundering, drug menace and arms smuggling and entered into a strategic energy partnership to channel Saudi investments into Indian energy infrastructure and further Indian participation in Saudi oil ventures. India hopes that strain in the US–Iran relationship over Iran's nuclear policy will not affect Indo-Iranian relations.

Last, but not the least, India seeks to follow a good neighbourhood policy. Emergency and political instability in Bangladesh, nascent and fragile democracy in Nepal, decades of civil insurgency in Sri Lanka, the drug-torn economy of Afghanistan and terrorism, fundamentalism and dictatorship in Pakistan affect India's growth. India's main foreign policy dilemma over the past 50 years has been to resolve its bilateral disputes with Pakistan. Both nuclear powers have fought four wars over Kashmir in the past. Our relations go through good, bad and ugly phases of the roller coaster ride. However, since 2004, overall relations have been less tense. Under the 'Composite dialogue' process we have agreed to discuss the Kashmir, Siachen and Sir Creek issue and undertake confidence-building measures through establishment of rail and road links, troop reduction at the borders, prior notification of any ballistic missiles tests, exchange of lists of nuclear installations and facilities covered under the Agreement on Prohibition of Attacks on nuclear installations. Visa restrictions have been eased to allow movement of goods and people across the Line of Control and Track-II dialogue mechanisms are firmly in place.

However, several contentious issues apart from Kashmir remain to be resolved. The cross-border support and abatement of terrorism has been strongly condemned by India and, despite evidence, Pakistan denies any involvement in terror attacks like the Mumbai blasts. India has also rejected Pakistan's proposals for demilitarization of Kashmir, joint control and self-governance stating that these are internal issues of the country. The World Bank brokered Indus Water Treaty of 1960, a model of Indo-Pakistan cooperation for distribution of six river waters, is under strain. Islamabad has already knocked on the doors of World Bank to arbitrate the issue of India's construction of Baglihar dam on Chenab river, while India has shared technical details with Pakistan to negate claims that it is violating the Indus Water Treaty. India has also protested against the proposed construction of the Bhasha Dam on Indus in Pakistan Occupied Kashmir while Pakistan, in turn, has raised the issue of construction of Wullar Barrage on Jhelum by India.

Although South Asian Free Trade Area (SAFTA) became operational, Pakistan has refused to confer India with the Most Favoured Nation status even though studies have shown conclusively that Pakistan will stand to benefit from it. A strong SAFTA will promote interdependence and reduce the proclivity for disputes. Another area of Indo-Pakistan cooperation is the Iran–Pakistan–India Gas Pipeline project and both India and Pakistan hope that their anti-Iran vote in IAEA will not derail the project. Only through mutual cooperation and political will can both countries resolve these disputes and devote more time energy and resources for socio-economic development.

India has traditionally shared warm and cordial political, economic and cultural ties with Bhutan and Maldives. Relations with Nepal have been strained in the past when Nepal tried to use the China card to leverage concessions from India and contemplated allowing China and Pakistan to open consulates on the sensitive Indo-Nepal border. Infiltrations from both sides of the border, treatment to Indians in Nepal and vice versa, issues related to trade and transit have hamstrung efforts to strengthen bilateral relations. However, bilateral relations are poised to takeoff with restoration of democracy which has been supported by India with about Rs 1,000 crore economic assistance for Nepalese reconstruction.

A poverty-stricken Bangladesh has been the hotbed of Islamic fundamentalism, and anti-India propaganda and a safe haven for Indian insurgent groups like ULFA. The recent Mumbai terror attacks had a Bangladesh link. Thus, India needs to bolster its economic and political influence in Bangladesh to promote mutual cooperation. Politically, India has had a strained relationship with Bangladesh due to differences over drawing of water from Ganga and Teesta rivers, border skirmishes and differences over border fencing, dispute over sovereignty of New Moore island, illegal immigrants etc. A host of summit level and joint working group meetings have led to a mutual appreciation of such problems. On the economic front, India and Bangladesh entered into a Revised Trade Agreement in 2006 to reduce the latter's trade deficit. India has extended significant concessions under the Asia-Pacific Trading Agreement (APTA) to Bangladesh and, under SAFTA, India brought its tariffs down to nil for LDCs starting 1 January 2008, thereby providing major market for Bangladeshi products.

Indo-Sri Lankan relations in the field of trade and investment have increased dramatically. India signed its first FTA with Sri Lanka and both sides will soon enter into a Comprehensive Economic Partnership Agreement. While Sri Lanka is keen on a defence agreement with India to end the country's long-standing ethnic conflict, India has followed a 'hands-off' policy on the issue stating that the dispute be resolved internally. Although India has resumed non-lethal military aid to Sri Lanka after Pakistan pitched in to supply military equipment, it has refused to join Norway, Japan and the EU to broker a peace deal between the LTTE and Sri Lankan government.

Afghanistan's entry into SAARC, which India supported, will firmly establish it as a South Asian country. India signed a Preferential Trading Agreement with Afghanistan in 2005 and facilitated Afghan reconstruction through bilateral aid and assistance package amounting to about $550 million. Afghanistan is key to India's energy security due to its borders with both Central and West Asia. India is keen on getting gas from Turkmenistan via Afghanistan and Pakistan. However, strained Afghanistan–Pakistan relations in the post-Taliban period and an upswing in Indo-Afghanistan relations have made Pakistan wary about India's influence in the region. Bilateral relationships still have to overcome significant obstacles to be dubbed as a diplomatic success. China is increasing its influence in South Asia through measures like construction of the Gwadar port in Pakistan, bidding for oil and gas in Bangladesh, providing military assistance to Nepal and India needs to and establish friendly ties with all its South Asian neighbours to emerge as a great power. It is rare in history for a regional power to emerge without securing its own backyard.

CONCLUSION

India has augmented its hard power resources, propped its global diplomatic presence with an 8–9 per cent GDP growth rate per annum and enhanced its soft power with a vibrant multicultural democracy, long civilization and contribution to the philosophical and scientific body of knowledge.

However, not all that is associated with India's growth story is rosy. The huge population growth, skewed regional development, growing unemployment, struggles for resources and basic civic amenities and stark class differences emerging alongside the already existing ethno-religious and linguistic inequalities put enormous pressure on the distributional capacities of the State. India also appears to be facing a siege within as a plethora of internal security crises, ranging from ultra-Left Maoist violence to secessionist movements, which threaten to dismantle the composite socio-cultural fabric of India.

As part of South Asia, India still has to devote most of its diplomatic and security resources in managing the traditional and non-traditional threats arising from within the region. The demands of regional great power nomenclature have not been met successfully as India's ambiguity and diplomatic silence on many of the burning regional issues points at the ineluctable tension between the ideal and pragmatic strands in Indian foreign policy. We have not been able to prove our crisis prevention capabilities in South Asia and it remains a matter of conjecture whether our diplomacy can contribute positively in resolving the Iranian or North Korean nuclear crisis. Our limited leverage and influence to resolve these matters only indicates that our power ascendancy has relied heavily on the economic dimension of power.

Thus, from the above balance sheet, we can say that India is a middle power on the rise. At present, India cannot be called a great power and it does not appear that India will emerge as one in the next decade or so. Great powers have tremendous military, political and economic strength and are endowed with soft power which bestows them with system-shaping capabilities. On the contrary, middle powers are those

> '... special category of states that lack the system-shaping capabilities of the great powers, but whose size, resources and role, nonetheless, precludes them from being ignored by the great powers. The middle powers score fairly high in the major indices of hard and soft power to have a generalized influence in the international system and in the regional affairs in particular.'[30]

Rapid economic growth is likely to increase India's hard and soft power resources, but, at this point, we do not rank high on the various indices of power resources that are possessed by the United States, Europe and Japan. As the Cold War alliance and counter alliance system fades into history, it can be expected that middle powers like India having an economic prowess and soft power will stand to exert greater influence in the regional state of affairs.

Suggested Readings

Cohen, Stephen P. *India: Emerging Power*. New Delhi: Oxford University Press, 2001.

Mohan, C. Raja. *Crossing the Rubicon: The Shaping of India's New Foreign Policy*. New Delhi: Penguin Books, 2003.

Nayar, Baldev Raj and T. V. Paul. *India in the World Order: Searching For Major-Power Status*. Cambridge, UK: Cambridge University Press, 2003.

Questions

1. Write an essay on the ideological tenets of foreign policy of Independent India.
2. Elaborate the changes taking place in global strategic environment in the post-cold war era. Analyse the changes in India's foreign policy in this wake.
3. Write an essay on the Indian foreign policy in a world dominated by the United States of America.
4. Do you agree with the view that in the contemporary global environment, foreign policy is influenced by economic factors? Give arguments.

---

30. Varun Sahni, 'From Security in Asia to Asian Security', *International Studies*, 41 (3), 2004.

Glossary

Absolute Poverty: Subsistence below minimum, socially acceptable living conditions, usually established based on nutritional requirements and other essential goods.

Basic Needs: A term used by the International Labor Organization to describe the basic goods and services (food, shelter, clothing, sanitation, education, etc.) necessary for a minimum standard of living.

Balance of Payment: A statement of the transactions of a country with foreign countries and international institutions.

Bureaucratic Rationality: The term was coined by Max Weber. It signifies that the authority of bureaucracy is based on rational rules and procedures, and not on any tradition or charisma. In other words, it means institutionalization of the official machinery, in which rules and procedures based on rationality are the guiding principles of the decision-making process. In turn, people abide by these decisions because they follow set rules and procedures.

Capital Goods Industries: Industries that produce materials basic to production process, such as steel, machines and chemicals.

Caste: Society in India is divided into a number of social groupings, membership of which is determined by birth. The relationship between these groups is hierarchical, discriminatory and exclusive. Originally a feature of Hindu society, caste is now a part of other religious groups such as Muslims, Sikhs and Christians as well. It has often been used for political mobilization and making demands upon the State.

Centralization: It means the concentration of political powers or government authority at the national level, a tendency that goes against the federal division of power between the centre and the states. It is also considered to be a problem for democracy. De-centralization became one of the major political values that led to induction of local governance institutions—the Panchayati Raj—in the Indian constitutional scheme.

Character of Economic Growth: The distributive implications of the process of economic growth. In other words, how that economic growth is achieved and who benefits.

Civil Society: A notional space between the state and the family where people engage in political activities. It is the domain where competition and struggle for political power play themselves out. The power dynamics in the state is but a reflection and codification of the power dynamics in civil society. Lately, the term civil society has often been used to describe non-governmental organizations in particular and associational life of the people in general.

Class: Generally used to categorize people in a society on the basis of economic position, the term was made popular as a conceptual category by Marxist thinkers. Marxism broadly perceived that societies are divided into two classes: One class owns all the resources necessary for production, while the other owns nothing and survives by selling its labour. The class of an individual is therefore based on the fact if she owns the resources for production or not.

Class-based Mobilization: Mobilization that is sought by appealing to the economic condition of the people and emphasizing class as the primary identity. See also **Class**.

Coalition Politics: Grouping of rival political actors brought together either through the perception of a common threat or for realizing the goals they cannot achieve by working separately. With the decline of the Congress and its dominance over party politics, Indian politics is now dominated by the formation of coalition governments both at the central as well as at the state level. The United Progressive Alliance and National Democratic Alliance are the examples of coalition political formation.

Cold War: It refers to the half-century-long military and ideological rivalry and tension between the US-led liberal democratic bloc and the USSR-led socialist bloc. The two groups dominated and defined world politics in the second half of the 20th century, never engaged each other militarily, but nevertheless brought the world to the brink of complete annihilation with the threat of a nuclear war. The Cold War came to an end with the decline of USSR and the socialist bloc.

Colonialism: It refers to the historical practice of establishing direct political control over a foreign territory. British rule in India and other parts of Asia and Africa in the last three centuries is an example of the practice of colonialism. Colonialism was generally aimed at exploitation of colonized territories as captive reservoirs of natural resources and as captive markets.

Commercial Loans: These are raised for short periods with the market rate of interest from foreign institutions and banks.

Committed Bureaucracy: As opposed to the notion of neutral bureaucracy that envisages the neutrality of bureaucracy from the ideology of the government of the day, committed bureaucracy means that the bureaucracy should adhere to the ideology of the government. The term was made popular in the late 1960s by Prime Minister Indira Gandhi, who criticized bureaucratic neutrality and called for a bureaucracy that shared her political ideology and helped her implement it.

Constitution: It is a document that codifies the institutional and procedural organization of a State. Often drafted by a constituent assembly, it often consists of a set of rights, powers and procedures that regulate the relationship between public authorities in any State, and between the public authorities and individual citizens. For example it is the Indian constitution that lays down the rules for creation of institutions such as parliament, the seat of the president and the supreme court and divides and defines their authorities. It also has a set of Fundamental Rights that is available to the people. Constitutions are generally typified as rigid or flexible, depending on the strictness of rules of amendment.

Currency Devaluation: A deliberate downward adjustment in the official exchange rate established by a government against another currency.

Current Account: A part of balance of payment consisting of visible trade (goods) and invisible trade (services).

Current Account Balance: The difference between the nation's total exports of goods, services, and transfers and its total imports of them. Current account balance calculations exclude transactions in financial assets and liabilities.

Dalit: The term 'Dalit' literally means 'ground down' or 'broken down to pieces'. It was first used by B. R. Ambedkar in 1928 in his newspaper *Bahishkrit Bharat*. Dalits occupy the lowest rank in the Hindu caste system and are called 'avarna' that is, those who are outside the 'varna' system. The term generally refers to exploited and oppressed social groups but is more particularly used for members of Scheduled Castes. The other terms used are 'untouchables', 'depressed classes', and 'Harijan' (children of God).

Democratic Decentralization: This is a process whereby power and resources are delegated to the local authority to ensure accountability and enable participation.

De-ritualization: De-ritualization refers to the breakdown or loss of ritualized activities that occur in daily life within a society. It often happens with changing economic or social status of a caste or community.

Devaluation: This is a reduction in the external value of the domestic currency made by the government.

Developmentalist State: This refers to the State with development as its most important concern. The term is used to describe some post-colonial states, which sought to transform people's economic lives through controlled economy and centralized planning. The post-Independence (but pre-liberalization) Indian State is one such example.

Disarmament: It refers to the movement for abolition of arms, particularly nuclear arms, in the wake of the arms race that began between the two dominant blocks during the Cold War. India, as a part of non-aligned movement, favoured such an initiative.

Drain of Wealth: The term refers to economic exploitation of colonies by the colonizers under colonial rule. Dadabhai Naoroji was the first to use this concept to denote the transfer of wealth from colonies like India to colonial powers like Britain. He adopted two crude methods to prove his case. One was to give extensive quotations from his observations of Bristish administrators in India to show how the drain had impoverished the country. The other was to make a rough calculation of the actual extent of the drain. By taking the total value of exports and imports of India from 1835 to 1872, he concluded that Britain had drained out £500 million for its own benefit.

E-commerce: commerce conducted over the Internet, most often via the World Wide Web. E-commerce can apply to purchases made through the Web or to business-to-business activities such as inventory transfers. A customer can order items from a vendor's Web site, paying with a credit card (the customer enters account information via the computer) or with a previously established 'cyber cash' account. The transaction information is transmitted (usually by modem) to a financial institution for payment clearance and to the vendor for order fulfillment. Personal and account information is kept confidential through the use of 'secured transactions' that use encryption technology

E-governance: It means utilizing the Internet and the World Wide Web for delivering government information and services to citizens. It has become a buzzword in post-liberalization India, with the belief that information technologies can be used to make government practices more accessible, transparent and responsive.

Economic Growth: The steady process by which the productive capacity of the economy is increased over time to bring about rising levels of national output and income.

Egalitarianism: This holds that if people are unequally situated in a given social order then they should be treated differently. Therefore, it reconsiders that procedural fairness needs to be supplemented by measures to ensure that those who are adversely situated in the socio-economic order, can also enjoy equal opportunities in society.

Elasticity of Employment: It is a measure of the percentage point change in employment within a given sector associated with a 1 percentage point change in value added in the sector.

Election: The procedure for authoritatively aggregating political preferences of the mass electorate. It is a process in which people participate to choose their representatives as well as to accept or reject political agendas. It is one of the most important markers for democracy. Presence or absence of democracy has often been associated very closely with regular elections.

Elite: An elite is a small group of people that are at the top of some sphere of social life, or has leadership of society as a whole. Every political system, according to elitist theory, whatever its official ideology, is in fact ruled by a political elite or elites.

Emergency Powers: They are special powers granted to a government or executive agency which allow normal legislative procedures and/or judicial remedies to be by-passed or suspended. In a democratic set up such emergency powers are strictly controlled by the legislature and are permitted only for the duration of the emergency. These powers may be used during wartime or a national security or domestic crises.

Endogamy: Endogamy signifies the practice of marrying within a specific social group, classes, or ethnicities. Herein, despite the fact that most of the people are inclined to marry members of their own social group, there are some groups that practice endogamy quite rigidly in simulation with their moral values, traditions or religious beliefs. The caste system of India itself is based on an order of (mostly) endogamous groups. Consequently, endogamy also encourages group affiliation and bonding, by encouraging group solidarity and ensuring greater control over group resources.

Ethnic Mobilization: As opposed to class mobilization, ethnic mobilization privileges and appeals to various ascribed identities such as caste, religion, region, and tribe. See **Class**; **Class Mobilization**.

Ethnicity: It refers to a sometimes rather complex combination of racial, cultural and historical characteristics by which societies are occasionally divided into separate, and probably hostile, political families. Ethnicity becomes politically significant when one of all these identities, or a combination of some sort, is privileged to mobilize people and to make political demands.

Export Pessimism: This was the prevalent notion during the 1950s and 1960s. It states that a nation that is primarily exporting the primary commodities cannot gain from participation in the international trade.

Federalism: It refers to legal and political structures that distribute power territorially within a State. The word federalism has been derived from the Latin *foedus,* which means 'pact' or covenant. The term originally indicated a loose alliance or union of States for limited purposes, usually military or commercial. It is now used to describe such a form of government, in which power is constitutionally divided between different authorities in such a way that each exercise responsibility for a particular set of functions and maintains its own institutions to discharge those functions.

Financial Institution: An institution that uses its funds chiefly to purchase financial assets (loans, securities), as opposed to tangible property.

Fiscal Policy: It is concerned with the revenue and expenditure of the government. This policy has an important bearing on macroeconomic variables.

Food Security: The condition when all people, at all times, have physical and economic access to sufficient, safe, and nutritious food to meet their dietary needs and food preferences for an active and healthy life.

Foreign Exchange Reserves: These comprise foreign currency assets and gold holdings of the Reserve Bank of India and special drawing rights of the International Monetary Fund.

Gender Gap: Any statistical gap between the measured characteristics of men and women in areas such as educational attainment, wage rates, or labour force participation.

Globalization: The increasing integration of national economies into expanding international markets.

Head Count Ratio: It is a method through which the percentage of population living below the poverty line is calculated.

Identity: It is the awareness of an individual about themselves. In social sciences, identity is used to denote the way an individual relates with a social or a political group. In political science, it is used as synonymous with ethnic and other types of ascribed identities. In India, it has emerged as an important conceptual category after preponderance of caste and community based mobilizations since the 1980s.

Import Substitution Strategy: This is a strategy of producing domestically the commodities that are imported in the country. The basic rationale of the policy has been to provide the protection to domestic industry to help them grow.

Income Gap: The gap between the incomes accruing to the bottom (poor) and the top (rich) sectors of a population. The wider the gap, the greater the inequality in the income distribution.

Income Inequality: The existence of disproportionate distribution of total national income among households, whereby the share going to rich persons in a country is far greater than that going to poorer persons.

Income Per Capita: Total gross national product of a country divided by total population.

Inflation: The persistent rise in the general level of prices.

Integrated Child Development Programme: In 1975, the Government of India launched the Integrated Child Development Programme, which aims to provide a package of services to ensure the all-round development of the child, such as early child care, schooling, health and nutrition, and clean drinking water.

Jajmani System: This system constituted a significant component of the socio-economic institution at the religious and at the economic plane of the pre-industrial self-subsistent Indian village economy. A *jajman* was one who employed a Brahmin for the performance of any solemn or religious ceremony. Religiously, it was an institutional arrangement that made the Brahman dependent for subsistence on the jajmans who comprised his clients. On the economic plane, this was marked by the exchange of products and services between the followers of various occupations within the framework of jajmani institution.

Judicial Review: The power possessed by the high courts and the supreme court to review and pronounce on the constitutional validity of legislative acts and its implementation.

Labour-intensive Industries: Industries that need relatively more labour value as input per unit of output than other factors of production.

Liberal Theory: The theory based on the basic liberal principle that considers individual freedom and rights as the most important. It believes in the minimum intervention of the State in the affairs of an individual.

Liberalization: It refers to the process of loosening of State restrictions from private and foreign participation in economic process of the country. The post-Independence Indian State strictly controlled private and foreign participation in most of the areas of economy. However, they have been encouraged since 1991 through a series of changes in the policy regime.

Macro Economy: This term refers to the whole economic system or the aggregate of the functioning of individual economic units.

Macroeconomic Crisis: Price level, inflation, balance of payment, interest rate, fiscal deficit, unemployment, and GDP growth rate are some of the prime indicators of macroeconomic health of a nation. When these indicators turn severely unfavourable, this is termed as a macroeconomic crisis. See **Macro Economy**.

Malnutrition: A condition resulting from the interaction of inadequate diet and infection. It is reflected in poor infant growth and an excess of morbidity and mortality in adults and children alike.

Market Failure: A situation where a market, left to itself, does not allocate resources efficiently.

Media: Systems specially designed to disseminate news and information to a large audience. The term is used interchangeably with mass media. The media have existed in some form for centuries, but technological advancements such as invention of printing press, radio, television and, now, the Internet have enhanced their speed, reach and power.

Millennium Development Goals (MDGs): Eight goals to be achieved by 2015 that respond to the world's main development challenges. The MDGs are drawn from the actions and targets contained in the Millennium Declaration that was adopted by 189 nations and signed by 147 heads of state and governments during the UN Millennium Summit in September 2000.

Minimum Credible Deterrent: It refers to notion according to which nuclear weapons become necessary for a country when it has a clear nuclear threat. In such a situation, having nuclear weapons becomes inevitable in order to deter and neutralize the threat. India, for example, while developing its nuclear weapon system, argued that it had such a threat from China. Pakistan, in turn, used the same argument against India when it developed its own nuclear weapons.

Nation: A nation is a political community that has one or more identities that unite people. It is a group of people bound together by a common language, religion, history and traditions or a combination of these, who regard themselves as a natural political community with a desire to establish or maintain statehood. The most popular academic understanding of the term is the one suggested by Benedict Anderson in his *Imagined Communities*. He refers to the nation as an 'imagined community'. When a nation identifies substantially with a State, the political entity of a nation-state is formed.

Nationalism: It is an ideology that seeks to establish a relationship between individuals on the basis of a common membership of a territory, language, history or ethnicity. In the process is constructed a political unit called the nation. In the colonial context, a national movement has the objective of forging links among members of a colonized country in order to seek freedom from the colonial power and to constitute an independent nation. Nationalism normally has two variants: civic, as in the case of France, and cultural, as in the case of Germany.

One-Party-Dominant System: The term refers to an overwhelming dominance of one political party over others; that is, even though the number of parties may be many, one party dominates the others.

Organic Solidarity: Emile Durkheim saw 'modern' society as a place where the individual is rationally (Weber would say bureaucratically), rather than morally or socially, tied to the community as is the case with mechanical solidarity (in 'primitive' societies).

Panchayat: Panchayats are traditional village councils that discuss and decide issues related to the village. Traditional panchayats were not representative in nature. Panchayats also refers to caste panchayats that are exclusive to a particular caste, as opposed to a village panchayat that included the entire village community. After the introduction of the 73rd Constitutional Amendment, the village panchayats are democratically elected and are vested with powers of local governance.

Parliamentary System: This is a form a government in which, within the constitutional framework, the parliament as the citizens' representative is supreme, as opposed to the presidential system in which the executive is supreme.

Political Economy: It refers to economic analysis of political phenomena. It implies offering an account of socio-economic forces, and analysing economic relationships between individuals or groups, in terms of their implications for politics (such as the role of the government).

Political Party: A group of people organized to gain formal representation or win government power; a party usually displays some measure of ideological cohesion.

Post-colonial Society: The term is used to refer to societies that were under colonial rule. For example, India is a post-colonial society because it was under the colonial rule of Britain before 1947. Post-colonialism, as a theory, seeks to interrogate the colonial encounter and analyses the effects of colonialism on post-colonial period politics, society, economy and culture.

Poverty Line: An income measure established by costing a minimum basket of essential goods for basic human survival, using income, consumption or expenditure data of households.

Procedural Justice: This is associated with the idea of fairness in processes that resolve disputes and allocate resources. In a narrow sense, it is used to morally evaluate the processes by which decisions are made, in terms of fairness.

Public Interest Litigation: According to this practice that began in the 1980s, in India, any citizen or a group of citizens can ask the court to intervene in a matter or issue of public interest.

Rayatwari System: The rayatwari system was a direct arrangement of revenue sharing between the 'rayat', or cultivator, and the State. In this system, the ownership right was given to the cultivators, and so this system was less exploitative as compared to the zamindari system. The rayatwari system was prevalent in relatively less fertile areas than the zamindari, which was prevalent in highly fertile areas. See **Zamindari System**.

Representation: The concept of representation predates democracy, but it has increasingly come to be attached to democracy, as in the phrase 'representative democracy'. Since in a large and complex society people cannot directly participate in the decision-making process, they choose representatives to do so. Representatives, therefore, are elected by, and accountable to, their constituency.

Republic: This refers to a State or country that is not led by a hereditary monarch, but in which at least part of its people forms the government. A State is a republic when its affairs are commonly run by the people who make up the population.

Sanskritization: Sanskritization, as explained by M. N. Srinivas, is a process by which 'a low Hindu caste, or tribal or other group, changes its customs, ritual ideology, and way of life in the direction of a high and frequently "twice-born" caste. Generally such changes are followed by a claim to a higher position in the caste hierarchy than that traditionally conceded to the claimant class by the local community...'

Sarva Dharma Sambhava: The phrase coined by Gandhi, which means that all religions are equal.

Self-respect Movement: The movement that started by Periyar in South India in the early part of 20th century. The objective of the movement was to challenge Brahminical domination.

Social Capital: As against the Marxian notion of capital as 'money [that] begets more money with the help of external labour', Pierre Bourdieu explains social capital as 'embodied' capital, which cannot be passed down like pocket money, salary or alms but can be acquired from one's parents, families, surroundings, culture, etc. Everyone invariably has some social capital, owing to where one is born and where one grows, but the one that most often is most coveted by the society is that of a particular kind of culture, the possession which is to have 'cultural capital'. The expressions like 'A is cultured' denote, not that B to Z people are uncultured, but that A's etiquette, knowledge, successes, etc. are part of a culture(s) that appears most desirable in a given society.

Social Indicators: Non-economic measures of development, such as life expectancy at birth, infant mortality rate, literacy rate, and physicians per 100,000 population.

Social Justice: Social justice stands for revision of social order and a redistribution of rights. It includes remedial actions towards the unprivileged sections of society who have been historically deprived of material resources.

Symbolic Violence: Social actors, especially children, who do not see themselves as part of the culture that has the most legitimacy in society, and find their own familiar cultures completely absent from their textbooks and from the mores of the 'successful', they assert themselves in various ways. Abuse, graffiti, brash living, imitation and ridicule of the authorities are some of the ways in which it is seen to be expressed; statistically, however, 'drop-outs' are the strongest indicator of symbolic violence.

Tightening of Monetary Policy: When a monetary policy is used to control and reduce the growth of monetary supply, this is called tightening of the monetary policy.

Trade Deficit: The excess of exports over imports.

Trickle-down Theory of Development: The notion that development is purely an economic phenomenon in which rapid gains from the overall growth of gross national product and income per capita would automatically bring benefits to the masses in the form of jobs and other economic opportunities.

Unemployment Rate: The ratio of unemployment to the labour force of a country.

Underdevelopment: An economic situation in which there are persistent low levels of living along with absolute poverty, low income per capita, low rates of economic growth, low consumption levels, poor health services, high death rates, high birthrates, dependence on foreign economies, and limited freedom to choose among activities that satisfy human wants.

Undernutrition: A form of malnutrition due to a deficiency of calories and vitamins and minerals and interacting with acute infection.

Varna: The four-fold division within the traditional Hindu society that divided it on the basis of occupation.

Wall of Separation: Thomas Jefferson had emphasized that religion and politics should be separated as if by a wall. This is the traditional Western notion of secularism, as a 'Separation of church and State'.

Well-being: When human beings have access to basic preconditions of living a good life such as food, health, nutrition, education, employment, and shelter, when they are able to participate in the political processes of their society, and when they can exercise Fundamental Rights, we say that a society provides well being to its citizens.

Zamindari System: Introduced under the Permanent Settlement in 1793, under the zamindari system, the government granted ownership rights to zamindars that were subject to the payment of a fixed sum of revenue. In the pre-colonial era, zamindars were like administrators, but the British government turned them into revenue collectors and land-owners. This system was highly exploitative. There were many intermediaries between zamindars and the actual tillers of the land. See **Rayatwari System**.

About the Editors and the Contributors

NEERA CHANDHOKE is Professor at the Department of Political Science, and Director of the Developing Countries Research Centre at theUniversity of Delhi from where she also received her MA (1968) and her PhD (1984). Her main teaching and research interests are political theory, comparative politics, and the politics of developing societies with special focus on India. She has authored *The Conceits of Civil Society* (2003, New Delhi: Oxford University Press); *Beyond Secularism: The Rights of Religious Minorities* (1999, New Delhi, Oxford University Press); and *State and Civil Society: Explorations in Political Theory*, 1995 (Delhi, Sage), and has edited *Mapping Histories* (2000, Delhi: Tulika); *Grass-Roots Politics and Social Transformation* (1999, Delhi: University of Delhi Press); *Understanding the Post-Colonial World* (1995, published under the auspices of Nehru Memorial Museum and Library, New Delhi). Professor Chandhoke regularly contributes articles to national and international journals and to Indian newspapers on contemporary themes.

PRAVEEN PRIYADARSHI is doing his PhD in development studies from the London School of Economics and Political Science (LSE). He is also a research associate with the Crisis States Research Centre, LSE. He is presently on leave from teaching political science at Zakir Husain College (Evening), University of Delhi. His interests are in the history of political institutions in India and their relation with development processes. He has published papers in journals such as *Economic and Political Weekly* and *Social Science Research Journal*.

THE CONTRIBUTORS

WASUDHA BHATT is a doctoral fellow at the University of Texas-Austin and a trainee at the Population Research Center.

MOITREE BHATTACHARYA (MUKHOPADHYAY) teaches political science at Daulat Ram College, University of Delhi.

SWAHA DAS teaches political science at Indraprastha College, University of Delhi.

NEHA KHANNA is a postgraduate in the fields of history and education. She is currently involved in research on the health issues of Black, minority and ethnic groups in London.

RAJESH KUMAR teaches political science at the Delhi College of Arts and Commerce, University of Delhi. He is also an affiliated fellow with the Developing Countries Research Centre, University of Delhi.

SANJEEV KUMAR teaches political science at Zakir Husain College, University of Delhi. He is also a research fellow with the Centre for the Study of Developing Societies, Delhi.

PUSHPA KUMARI teaches political science at Miranda House, University of Delhi. She is also a fellow with the Developing Countries Research Centre, University of Delhi.

N. R. LEVIN is a research scholar at the Department of History, University of Delhi.

SUJIT MAHAPATRA is a research scholar at the Department of English, University of Delhi. He is also associated with the Developing Countries Research Centre, University of Delhi and Bakul Foundation, Bhubaneshwar.

BINDU MENON teaches journalism at Lady Sri Ram College, University of Delhi.

SATYAJIT MOHANTY is with the Indian Revenue Service. The views expressed in his chapter are, however, personal.

HARI NAIR is an independent scholar working on the philosophy of law.

SATYAJIT PUHAN studied economics and obtained an MPhil degree from Jawaharlal Nehru University, New Delhi. He is currently based in Orissa and is associated with the Bakul Foundation, an initiative for volunteerism and social change.

KUMAR RAHUL teaches political science in Ramjas College, University of Delhi.

SURANJITA RAY teaches political science in Daulat Ram College, University of Delhi. She is also a fellow with the Developing Countries Research Centre, University of Delhi.

MOHINDER SINGH is a fellow at the Indian Institute of Advanced Studies, Shimla. He is presently on leave from teaching political science at Ramjas College, University of Delhi.

RAVI NANDAN SINGH teaches sociology at Hindu College, University of Delhi.

SAMIR KUMAR SINGH teaches economics at Kirori Mal College, University of Delhi. He is also associated with the Developing Countries Research Centre, University of Delhi.

AMBUJA KUMAR TRIPATHY teaches political science in Sri Ram College of Commerce University of Delhi. He is also associated with the Developing Countries Research Centre, University of Delhi.

SILKY TYAGI is a research scholar at the Department of Political Science, University of Delhi. She is also associated with the Developing Countries Research Centre, University of Delhi.

Index